THEORY OF FICTION: HENRY JAMES

OTHER BOOKS BY JAMES E. MILLER, JR.

A Critical Guide to Leaves of Grass (1957)
Start with the Sun: Studies in the Whitman Tradition, with Karl Shapiro
and Bernice Slote (1960)
Walt Whitman (1962)
Reader's Guide to Herman Melville (1962)
F. Scott Fitzgerald: His Art and Technique (1964)
J. D. Salinger (1965)
Quests Surd and Absurd: Essays in American Literature (1967)
Word, Self, Reality: The Rhetoric of Imagination (1972)

(Books edited)
Walt Whitman: Complete Poetry and Selected Prose (1959)
Myth and Method: Modern Theories of Fiction (1960)
The Dimensions of Poetry, with Bernice Slote (1962)
The Dimensions of the Short Story, with Bernice Slote (1964)
Whitman's "Song of Myself": Origin, Growth, Meaning (1964)
Literature of the United States (rev. ed.), with Walter Blair, Theodore
Hornberger, and Randall Stewart (1966)
The Dimensions of Literature, with Bernice Slote (1967)
The Arts and the Public, with Paul D. Herring (1967)
Man in Literature: Comparative Studies in Translation, with Robert O'Neal
and Helen M. McDonnell (1970)

Theory of Fiction:
HENRY JAMES

EDITED WITH AN INTRODUCTION BY

James E. Miller, Jr.

UNIVERSITY OF NEBRASKA PRESS
LINCOLN

Publishers on the Plains

UNP

Copyright © 1972 by the University of Nebraska Press
All rights reserved
International Standard Book Number 0–8032–0799–9
Library of Congress Catalog Card Number 78–147168

Manufactured in the United States of America

Contents

America and a *grasping* imagination (1871) · 46; Turgénieff's themes are all Russian (1874) · 47; making do with small things (1875) · 47; art blooms only where the soil is deep (1879) · 48; solitary workers vs. groups (1879) · 48; the absent things in American life (1879) · 49; it takes an old civilization (1880) · 50; an American . . . *must* deal . . . with Europe (1881) · 51; the life of his time . . . reflected in his novels (1883) · 52; a big Anglo-Saxon total (1888) · 52; the Western imagination (1898) · 53; "business" plays a part in the United States (1898) · 53; the acute sense of "Europe" . . . of the American mind (1898) · 55; the American case and character (1912) · 58; the old conditions of contrast and color (1913) · 60

impressions never lost (1881) · 62; to catch and keep something of life (1881) · 63; the great thing is to be saturated (1888) · 63; impressions personal and unique (reality or illusion) (1888) · 63; the courage of one's perceptions (1888) · 65; the novelist is a particular *window* (1890) · 65; experience conditioned, infinitely, in this personal way (1891) · 66; *imitation* of observation (1903) · 67; the only way to know is to have lived (1913) · 68

V. DEFINITIONS AND DISCRIMINATIONS · 92

Part A: Novel, Poem, Play

Part B: Picture, Anecdote, Short Story, Nouvelle

Part C: Allegory, the Extraordinary, Romance, Fairy Tale, Ghost Story

VI. SUBJECTS: THE WHOLE HUMAN CONSCIOUSNESS · 115

Part A: Subjects: Given, Important, Free

IX. Rendering: Execution • 168

Part A: Art

Part B: Presence of the Author

Part C: Picture, Preparation, Scene, Drama

Part D: Foreshortening; Time-Sequence; Dialogue

X. Characters • 195

Part A: The Dominance of Characters

Preface

This book started out as a conventional volume of James's critical essays. But it soon became clear that what was needed—what, astonishingly, had never been done for James—was a collection of selections and excerpts that presented in comprehensive and definitive fashion James's theory of fiction. This is all the more astonishing when it is realized that James is probably the greatest fictional theorist ever to have written. The problem has been that he scattered his theory throughout a voluminous body of work, including his stories about writers, his critical and speculative essays, his *Notebooks*, Prefaces, and letters.

This volume opens with James's famous essay, "The Art of Fiction" (1884), and closes with a brief prophetic piece, "The Future of the Novel" (1899). In between, in a systematic arrangement designed to give order and coherence to James's fictional theory, are brought together a collection of perceptions and insights drawn from the entire body of James's work, and ranging in date from 1865, when he was twenty-two years old, to 1915, the year before his death. The resulting book makes the most comprehensive, exhaustive, and innovative volume of fictional theory ever published. In many ways it represents the consummation of James's contribution to letters. It carries not only its own authority in its inherent brilliance, but also the authority of James's own performance in his great body of fiction.

In spite of a few shifts and redirections, James remained remarkably consistent in his views from the beginning to the end of his career. Reversals are much less frequent than simply a growth or development in complexity with an accompanying complication of language and elaboration of figurative explanation. James spoke out, often more than once, on some of the most difficult and subtle problems of fictional theory. He always spoke with assurance and authority, and the keen sense of his own deep involvement as a novelist.

The period from 1865 to 1915 represents a transitional period in our literature, from the Victorian era to the Modern. James was a great transitional figure in both the theory and practice of his fiction. In many ways he was the climax of one period, carrying some of its tendencies to the ultimate in experimentation, and at the same time he was the forerunner, model, and source for the Modern period, pointing the way to the remarkable innovations in fictional technique of the twentieth century. Most of the technical experimentation of the 1920s and beyond, by such major figures as James Joyce,

Virginia Woolf, Ernest Hemingway, and William Faulkner, can be found in embryo in James, in both practice and theory. His influence was felt not only where he was respected, but even by those who denied him. Moreover, his fictional theory has a continuing relevance for today. Over and over again his theoretical speculation appears to speak directly to specific problems or questions that readers, critics, or novelists continue to explore and debate in current conferences and publications.

For those who feel that a theory of fiction must be a set of rules, this note of disclaimer should be added at the outset. James never believed in rules, and, indeed, said over and over again that the only thing a novel can rightfully be expected to be in advance is *interesting*. Otherwise, it has a perfect and absolute freedom to be what the novelist wishes to make it. In "The Future of the Novel" James said: "It [the novel] can do simply everything, and that is its strength and its life. Its plasticity, its elasticity are infinite; there is no color, no extension it may not take from the nature of its subject or the temper of its craftsman."

A Note on the Collection of Items for This Book

I found many passages throughout James's work clearly theoretical or general statements and thus indisputable candidates for inclusion. But of course I found many other passages that were comments on specific works or writers, or on James's own stories and novels—all with theoretical implications. I have stressed theory throughout, but have often included particular judgments or applications because of the theory implicitly present. Selection has been a necessity, but I am confident that I have collected James's major statements, along with many miscellaneous comments, that present the totality of his theoretical views. Of all his works—fiction, essays, *Notebooks*, letters, and Prefaces—his Prefaces not surprisingly proved the richest source for theory. I was astonished to discover that frequently over half a preface was devoted to theoretical speculation. In poring over all the materials repeatedly, I developed some notions about the writers that called forth James's most intensive efforts. The two writers that James admired most inspired the two most resonant essays: "Ivan Turgénieff" (1874) and "The Lesson of Balzac" (1905). Among the British, George Eliot and Robert Louis Stevenson called forth James's most inspired critical efforts; his 1888 essay "Robert Louis Stevenson" is particularly valuable. And among the Americans, Nathaniel Hawthorne and William Dean Howells were recurrent subjects of immense interest for James; the 1879 book *Hawthorne* reveals as much of James as it does of Hawthorne.

An essay called "The New Novel," published in 1914, demonstrated James's continuing interest, to his last years, in experimentation and innovation in the novel, and provided a perceptive examination of, among others,

Joseph Conrad, John Galsworthy, H. G. Wells, Arnold Bennett, Hugh Walpole, Compton Mackenzie, and D. H. Lawrence; moreover, it is rich in
implications for matters of fictional theory. In addition to "The Art of
Fiction" and "The Future of the Novel," one other essay has been included
in its entirety in this volume. "Criticism" (1891) appears in Chapter XVI
("Readers and Critics") under a new title that indicates its theoretical thrust:
"perception at the pitch of passion."

A Note on the Form of the Book

The Introduction is meant to stimulate thought as well as demonstrate the
use of the book. Its presentation of an outline of James's theory is not meant
to be either definitive or exhaustive, but provocative. The titles devised for
the excerpts from James's various works use his own language as much and as
closely as possible. Sources and dates of the excerpts are given to expedite
location. Each title used is listed in the Bibliography, together with the
various appearances in print of the item so that the reader may consult a
source available to him. Because items have usually been published in several
places, page references are not given for excerpts. An index has been compiled
mainly as a guide to critical terms used by James. His critical vocabulary has
been the source of much confusion; perhaps the index will help to establish
definitions for these terms.

A Note on Locating Items

James's reputation as a fictional theorist has suffered largely because of the
inaccessibility of his comments—scattered as they are through many books
and journals, many pieces uncollected and many books out of print. For this
reason I have, in this book, emphasized accessibility by supplying abundant
entries and guides. The book has a detailed table of contents of the more than
two hundred and fifty items included. Each item is identified as precisely as
possible as to content with the title supplied by James's own language. For
those who may want to find out what passages I have taken from particular
James pieces, the Bibliography locates, immediately after title entry and
date, each item reprinted by chapter, part, and item designation. In addition,
there is the index, which emphasizes James's critical terms. It is hoped that
the book, so organized, will finally give James's complex theory of fiction
the currency it deserves.

A Note on the Texts and Editing

The texts reprinted here are those listed for the first appearance of each
item in Part II of the Bibliography. I have not attempted to impose consis-

tency in spelling, punctuation, or printing style, thus, the reader will note variant spellings of proper names and variant treatment of titles of books and articles. Since nearly all the items in Chapters II through XVI have been excerpted from books, essays, letters, etc., I have dispensed with the use of suspension points at the beginning and end of items to indicate that they are excerpts. When an ellipsis occurs at the end of an item, it was a feature of the original punctuation. I have used ellipses only when matter is omitted from the body of an item. In most cases I have supplied the titles of items from James's own language, as discussed above.

THEORY OF FICTION: HENRY JAMES

Introduction

A THEORY OF FICTION IN OUTLINE: HENRY JAMES

Although James has long been acknowledged as one of the greatest of literary theorists, no one has yet brought together, in compressed form, an overall view of his basic concepts. Percy Lubbock's *The Craft of Fiction* (1921) remains a popular book, but it distorts James a bit by overstressing point of view (an important but not totally transcendent element in James's theory). Richard P. Blackmur's 1934 "Introduction" to the collected 1907-09 Prefaces, misleadingly entitled *The Art of the Novel*, suffers from capricious organization and a fatal imitation of the late James style. Books like Morris Roberts's *Henry James's Criticism* (1929) and Harold McCarthy's *The Creative Process* (1958), though they have contributed to understanding, have not succeeded in clarifying or solidifying James's position as a great fictional theorist.

The outline of James's theory presented in this brief scope is based on a reading and interpretation of all James's available work, including his reviews and critical essays, his *Notebooks*, his Prefaces, his fiction about writers and artists, and his letters. The material is voluminous, and ranges in date from 1865 to 1915, a half-century during which James was privileged to change his mind, especially as the times moved through radical literary changes from the romantic through the realistic to the naturalistic and up to the edge of the explosive experimental movements of the 1920s. James was an imposing transitional figure, spanning the Victorian and the Modernist worlds, assessing the old, encouraging the new, and finally contributing definitively to the revolutionary innovations of the twentieth century—innovations which he shaped but did not live to see. During all this turbulent period, James shifted a bit, particularly from the assertiveness of the early reviews, but he remained remarkably stable in his theoretical views. A chronological survey of his concepts reveals not so much a succession of sharp twists and turns as a broadening and deepening, a gradual realization of the infinite complexity of both life and its multi-varied fictional images.

James's most famous essay on fictional theory, "*The Art of Fiction*," appeared in 1884 and stands at the midpoint of his productive life. It may serve as a base from which to start and to which to return in this outline of his theory. It comes at a time of the maturity of his thought on fictional art, and deserves the wide attention it gets. But it should be remembered

1

that it was a rebuttal to Walter Besant's conventional and simplistic "*Art of Fiction*," and as a result is silent or extremely brief on many aspects of the subject. It does not, for example, have much to say about the role of the imagination in the artistic process, and it is completely silent on the subject of point of view—both matters that are central to James's total theory.

I. The Writer

Contrary to the suggestion of some James critics, who place emphasis at the outset on James's concern for the work of fiction in and of itself, there are some preliminary considerations important to James's theory. They concern the writer, his relationship to his culture, his use of experience, and his need for an imagination for the mystical transmutation of experience into fiction.

1. *The Writer and His Culture*. At the base of James's entire theory of fiction stands his vision of the crucial interdependence of the writer and his culture. This view was, no doubt, shaped in large part by James's own experience as a writer in finding his subjects not in his native land but most frequently abroad, where he simply moved some of his compatriots. Out of this experience grew James's conviction that cultures differed radically in what they offered for the consumption of the writer's imagination. Some cultures, like the European he favored, offered more, offered a denser social structure and a more complex civilization, with its intricate layers of history and custom. Others, like the American, offered less: a thinness that could discourage if not defeat the novelist. This is not to say that James felt America was hopeless as a subject. On the contrary he marvelled at the achievements of Hawthorne and Howells in the face of the immense handicaps they faced. Although this line of thought runs all through James's work, it comes out perhaps most dramatically in *Hawthorne* (1879), where he made his famous list of the "absent things in American life," and where he supported his view that "art blooms only where the soil is deep." But it comes out too in the several essays on two of James's favorite writers, Balzac and Turgénieff, who, James felt, had certain advantages in coming to terms imaginatively with cultures as variegated, socially complex, and historically complicated as France and Russia.

But James saw a writer's culture as more than simply the source for his material. It provided both the environment in which he might flourish or wither and the critical reaction to his work which might encourage or dismay and defeat him. The prevailing attitude toward fiction did, James felt, make a difference. If the general interest was intent upon hunting and football, on getting and spending, the art of fiction could fade and die. As James stated in "The Future of the Novel" (1899): "The future of fiction is intimately bound up with the future of the society that produces and consumes it."

2. *The Writer and His Experience*. James's stress on a writer's culture makes it natural that he would likewise stress his experience, so intimately bound up with his cultural environment. James said, in "The Art of Fiction," that in the most general sense, a novel was "a personal, a direct impression of life." The words are chosen with care and charged with meaning. Probably one of the two most important words in James's critical vocabulary was *impressions;* the other was *consciousness.* The connection between the two is obvious—the consciousness is the storehouse of one's impressions. To understand the importance of these elements, it is necessary to glimpse James's view of reality. Life, he said in the Prefaces, was all "inclusion and confusion," a "thick jungle," an endless and multitudinous stream. Experience was, in the last analysis, simply a gathering of impressions from whatever encounters offered, and storing them in the consciousness where they might be examined, sifted, and sorted, and thus used or re-used for creating an idea, a concept, a view of the world. Gathered and stored impressions thus became, when arranged and ordered, a window giving bounds, outline, and shape to one's view of experience and life.

One of James's favorite metaphors was the million-windowed "house of fiction," with an individual (and, indeed, self-built) window for each novelist. There was, James felt, no single reality, but only the flux and flow of life. Each novelist discovered and reported his own "reality" through *his* window. A good summary of James's concept appears in his 1891 review, "Mr. Kipling's Early Stories": after asserting that Kipling had "an identity as marked as a window-frame," James said: "It is the blessing of the art he practices that it is made up of experience conditioned, infinitely, in this personal way— the sum of the feeling of life as reproduced by innumerable natures; natures that feel through all their differences, testify through their diversities. These differences, which make the identity, are of the individual; they form the channel by which life flows through him, and how much he is able to give us of life—in other words, how much he appeals to us—depends on whether they form it solidly."

It may be seen, then, that when James spoke of the novel as "a personal, a direct impression of life," each of the qualifying words, *personal* and *direct*, carried important meaning: both were crucial to authenticity. Life was the source of art, direct and first-hand impressions made up the materials, and the personal and individual consciousness shaped them into a unique image and a form that constituted their value. (James felt the impression-created consciousness was the source of a person's individuality and constituted his hold, if he was to have one, on immortality, as he revealed in "Is There a Life After Death?" [1910]).

In the gathering of impressions there can be no planning and no end. The novelist snatches what he can, or what his net of consciousness can hold, from whatever is "floated" into his mind "by the current of life." Over and over again James described in his *Notebooks* and Prefaces the "germs" from which his novels grew. The germs ranged from random anecdotes to occasional encounters with characters, from the vivid impression of a particular house or city to a reported speech or an observed action that sounded reverberations in the deeper levels of consciousness. These germs or "seeds" found their way to settle among all the stored impressions, some related but most not, where germination might ultimately be expected—a germination which involved innumerable and entangled impressions of life, fragments of experience, deliberate observations and stray perceptions, but all in a state of strange fermentation which would produce something entirely new.

3. *The Writer and His Imagination.* However important the word *impressions* was for James's critical vocabulary, the word *imagination*, though perhaps not so visible, was just as vital. Transcending both was that repository of the individual's individuality, the *consciousness*, the storehouse of impressions. But of course, consciousness served as something more than a mere storehouse: it was a kind of alchemist's melting pot which turned ordinary ingredients (impressions of life) into things strange and new, rich alloys worth much more than their original contents. Over and over again James spoke of the "crucible of the imagination," and in his Preface to *The Lesson of the Master*, he gave one of his most brilliant metaphoric descriptions of the mysterious process of the imagination, beginning with this image: "We can surely account for nothing in the novelist's work that hasn't passed through the crucible of his imagination, hasn't, in that perpetually simmering cauldron his intellectual *pot-au-feu*, been reduced to savoury fusion. We here figure the morsel, of course, not as boiled to nothing, but as exposed, in return for the taste it gives out, to a new and richer saturation. In this state it is in due course picked out and served, and a meagre esteem will await, a poor importance attend it, if it doesn't speak most of its late genial medium, the good, the wonderful company it has, as I hint, aesthetically kept. It has entered, in fine, into new relations, it emerges for new ones. Its final savour has been constituted, but its prime identity destroyed—which is what was to be demonstrated. Thus it has become a different and, thanks to a rare alchemy, a better thing."

James called this process of the imagination "almost mystical," and felt that, though it could be generally understood, it could not be fully explained. And indeed, the process was so far outside the willed control of the writer that the imagination seemed to have a will and life of its own. In his Preface to *What Maisie Knew*, James described the suddenness and unexpectedness of what he called the "experience of the suddenly-determined *absolute* of perception": "The whole cluster of items forming the image is on these occasions born at once; the parts are not pieced together, they conspire and interdepend; but what it really comes to, no doubt, is that at a simple touch an old latent and dormant impression, a buried germ, implanted by experience and then forgotten, flashes to the surface as a fish, with a single 'squirm,' rises to the baited hook, and there meets instantly the vivifying ray." This initial perception may be supplemented in the process of execution by a kind of surrender. Note the language James used to describe the method of the artist in "The Middle Years" (1893): "He dived once more into his story and was drawn down, as by a siren's hand, to where, in the dim underworld of fiction, the great glazed tank of art, strange silent subjects float. He recognized his motive and surrendered to his talent." Over and over again James suggested the artist's exploitation of his unconscious, an exploitation that required the act of surrender—the kind of surrender to "the luminous paradise of art," that James courted repeatedly, almost like a muse, in the privacy of his *Notebooks*.

It may well be that this conception of the mysteriously operating imagination, on both conscious and unconscious levels, was what separated James from the other realists of his time. Whereas they tended to locate the criteria for realism in an apprehendable reality in experience or life itself, James tended to locate the criteria inside the author or artist, and in what the crucible of the imagination did to or for the materials gathered from experience and life. Far from believing that there was a single reality to apprehend, James believed that each novelist, in his individual perspective, by the garnering of impressions that in combination were his and his alone, and through the mystifying processes of his unique crucible of imagination, actually created a reality that was impossible of duplication by any other writer. It was, surely, something of this sort that James meant when he wrote in 1915 to H. G Wells: "It is art that *makes* life, makes interest, makes importance . . . and I know of no substitute whatever for the force and beauty of its process."

II. PRELIMINARY CONCEPTS

James developed, throughout the body of his work, some notions about the various forms and modes of literature. He never systematized these notions, but when they are brought together they provide a fairly comprehensive view of literary structures. He also developed some impressive ideas about the nature of fictional subjects—ideas which appear now both astonishingly astute and liberal.

4. Definitions and Discriminations. Basic to all of James's views of the various forms was his definition of fiction as "a personal, a direct impression of life." This definition remained constant throughout James, though he occasionally shifted his emphasis and renewed his vocabulary. In his 1883 essay "Alphonse Daudet" he said: "The main object of a novel is to represent life. . . . the success of a work of art, to my mind, may be measured by the degree to which it produces a certain illusion; that illusion makes it appear to us for the time that we have lived another life—that we have had a miraculous enlargement of experience." James realized that there was vagueness in his statement that the object of the novel was "to represent life." But it was precisely the imprecision he believed necessary to encompass all possibilities; after all, he added, "may not people differ infinitely as to what constitutes life—what constitutes representation."

There is something of a clarification of his views in his 1889 letter to the Deerfield Summer School for those attending a class on the novel: "Oh, do something from your point of view. . . . Any point of view is interesting that is a direct impression of life. You each have an impression colored by your individual conditions; make that into a picture, a picture framed by your own personal wisdom, your glimpse of the American world. The field is vast for freedom, for study, for observation, for satire, for truth."

James felt that there were detectable differences among the forms of fiction —short story, nouvelle, novel—that made different demands on the writer. The short story, which he found in some ways the most difficult in its confinements, he compared to a "hard, shining sonnet." He divided short stories into two types: the anecdote, which is constructed on "something that has oddly happened to someone"; and the picture, which aims "at those richly summarised and foreshortened effects" and in which "parts hang together even as the interweavings of a tapestry." Some ideas, James believed, were by their nature "anecdotal" and thereby suitable for short stories, while others were "developmental," and suitable for the longer form of the nouvelle or novel. In the nouvelle, James said, "the main merit and sign is the effort to do the complicated thing with a strong brevity and lucidity—to arrive, on behalf of the multiplicity, at a certain science of control."

For a realist, James devoted an inordinate amount of space in his theoretical digressions and asides to non-realistic forms. It is, of course, important to remember that James himself wrote some of the most provocative ghost stories of our literature. The point to make here, however, is that James's theory of fiction was broad enough in its scope to include romance, fairy tale, and ghost story. In his 1888 essay on Robert Louis Stevenson, James defended the non-realistic forms by declaiming the absolute freedom of the novel: "The breath of the novelist's being is his liberty, and the incomparable virtue of the form he uses is that it lends itself to views innumerable and diverse, to every variety of illustration." James felt that any novelist who left the "extraordinary" out "of his account" was "liable to awkward confrontations" with the reality which even the daily newspapers carried: "The next report of the next divorce case (to give an instance) shall offer us a picture of astounding combinations of circumstance and behaviour, and the annals of any energetic race are rich in curious anecdote and startling example."

5. *Subjects: The Whole Human Consciousness.* James stated repeatedly, in "The Art of Fiction" and elsewhere, that the novelist's subject must be granted him, and that the only area for critical comment was the *treatment* of the subject. But he also said repeatedly that subjects were important, and if he could have his way he would have novelists choose only the richest. But the question that hovered over many of James's comments was whether the choice was ever free. As he put it in the Preface to *Lady Barbarina:* "One never chooses one's general range of vision—the experience from which ideas and themes and suggestions spring: this proves ever what it has had to be, this is one with the very turn one's life has taken."

James believed that subjects must be free in two senses. In the first sense, he felt that the writer should have absolute freedom to treat any subject he chose (or which chose him). He said in "The Future of the Novel" that the form took in "the whole human consciousness": "It can do simply everything, and that is its strength and its life. Its plasticity, its elasticity are infinite; there is no color, no extension it may not take from the nature of its subject or the temper of its craftsman." But in addition to this freedom was another—the freedom that the author in turn must grant his subject while he is in the midst of treating and shaping it. This, indeed, turns out to be "The Lesson of Balzac" (1905): "It comes back, in fine, to that respect for the liberty of the subject which I should be willing to name as *the* great sign of the painter of the first order. Such a witness to the human comedy fairly holds his breath for fear of arresting or diverting that natural license; the witness who begins to breathe so uneasily in presence of it that his respiration not only warns off the little prowling or playing creature he is supposed to be studying, but drowns, for our ears, the ingenuous sounds of the animal, as well as the general, truthful hum of the human scene at large—this demonstrator has no sufficient warrant for his task." In short, subjects live their own lives, and for the author to impose his abstractions—ideas, morals, philosophy—on them is to violate their freedom and to silence that "truthful hum of the human scene at large."

In line with his belief in freedom of subject, James welcomed the extension of the novel to areas of experience before excluded or only sketchily treated. For example, in his 1888 essay "Guy de Maupassant," he noted that the French treat "of that vast, dim section of society which, lying between those luxurious walks on whose behalf there are easy presuppositions and that darkness of misery which, in addition to being picturesque, brings philanthropy also to the writer's aid, constitutes really, in extent and expressiveness, the substance of any nation." In England, he added, "where the fashion of fiction still sets mainly to the country house . . . that thick twilight of mediocrity of condition has been little explored. May it yield triumphs in the years to come!" Such passages, devoted not only to the middle class but also the lower "darkness of misery," show that James's own fiction, limited largely to the upper middle or upper class, did not mark the limits of his interest but rather the boundaries of his experience—his "general range of vision" which was beyond his deliberate choice.

6. *Sex: An Immense Omission.* James's insistence on the freedom of subject extended, as he again and again insisted throughout his criticism, to that great and vital area forbidden of treatment in English and American fiction —sex. For one who has by his enemies frequently been pictured as faint-hearted and squeamish on the subject, James indulged repeatedly in bold discussions of sex and the novel, explored the French freedoms in this area, and bemoaned the chains that bound the Anglo-American. Throughout James's discussions, reasoned as they are, there runs an undercurrent of indignation at the hypocrisy and immaturity of the taboos imposed. In "The Art of Fiction," he pointed his finger at the strange gap resulting between life and fiction—between "that which people know and that which they agree to admit that they know." And in "The Future of the Novel" he prophesied that one day, the very innocents (youths, women) the taboos were said to protect would rise and smash the window—an image whose violence suggests the depth of James's feeling.

Moreover, his prophecy has in some sense come true. The window has been smashed and the frame itself destroyed. James may seem, for this reason, somewhat out of date. But on the contrary, his advice appears valid because he understood that the freedom—or license—could not substitute for art itself. Today's writers who attempt to let sex substitute for talent might heed James's words from his 1904 essay on Gabriele D'Annunzio: "That sexual passion from which he extracts such admirable detached pictures insists on remaining for him [D'Annunzio] *only* the act of a moment, beginning and ending in itself and disowning any representative character. From the moment it depends on itself alone for its beauty it endangers extremely its distinction, so precarious at the best. For what it represents, precisely is it poetically interesting; it finds its extension and consummation only in the rest of life. Shut out from the rest of life, shut out from all fruition and assimilation, it has no more dignity than—to use a homely image—the boots and shoes that we see, in the corridors of promiscuous hotels, standing, often in double pairs, at the doors of rooms. Detached and unassociated these clusters of objects present, however obtruded, no importance. What the participants do with their agitation, in short, or even what it does with them, *that* is the stuff of poetry, and it is never really interesting save when something finely contributive in themselves makes it so."

III. The Work in its Elements

Although James frequently insisted that form and substance were inseparable, and that the parts of a work could not be disentangled, in actual critical practice he talked about the elements of a work as though they could be isolated. Indeed, some of his most perceptive theoretical insights relate to such elements as "plot," "rendering," "character," and "setting."

7. *Plots, Actions, Centers*. From the beginning to the end of his career, James rebelled against the conventional notions of plot in fiction. He was particularly incensed by the demand, echoed by Walter Besant, that fictions live by their "stories," and that above all there must be "adventures." In refuting Besant in "The Art of Fiction," James stretched the meaning of "actions" to include the most subtle and psychological. What is an incident, after all? "It is an incident for a woman to stand up with her hand resting on a table and look out at you in a certain way. . . . When a young man makes up his mind that he has not faith enough after all to enter the church as he intended, that is an incident. . . . It sounds almost puerile to say that some incidents are intrinsically much more important than others." What James was doing, of course, was pushing the action from the outside to the inside, removing it from the realm of the physical and depositing it in the realm of the psychological. He said: "A psychological reason is, to my imagination, an object adorably pictorial; to catch the tint of its complexion—I feel as if that idea might inspire one to Titianesque efforts." This remarkable image—painting the mind, depicting visually the airy nothingness of psychological drama—compresses in small space the immense contribution James made to the novel in pointing the direction away from external action and toward internal action—or reaction, counteraction, and inaction.

If James was in rebellion against simplistic notions about the necessities of adventures in fiction, he was also in rebellion against discursive and diffusive fictions that were presented as social histories or as "slices of life." As early as 1873, in his review of George Eliot's *Middlemarch*, James concluded: "It sets a limit, we think, to the development of the old-fashioned English novel. Its diffuseness, on which we have touched, makes it too copious a dose of pure fiction. If we write novels so, how shall we write History? But it is nevertheless a contribution of the first importance to the rich imaginative department of our literature." Even as a young man, and in confrontation with one of the most difficult cases to come to terms with (because of its sheer genius), James established his ground for inquiring of a novel's "centre." And just as he found *Middlemarch*, even at the moment of its appearance, "old-fashioned," he distinctly saw himself as moving in the direction of the new and innovative: he could not find or locate that center in a conventional plot or external action.

In a curious 1912 essay called "The Novel in 'The Ring and the Book,'" James raised in essence the same question he had earlier raised with *Middlemarch*—but by then his touch had become more sure and his language less tentative. His principles had long since been worked out with care: "The question of the whereabouts of the unity of a group of data subject to be wrought together into a thing of art, the question in other words of the point at which the various implications of interest, no matter how many, *most* converge and interfuse, becomes always, by my sense of the affair, quite the first to be answered; for according to the answer shapes and fills itself the very vessel of that beauty—the beauty, exactly, *of* interest, of maximum interest, which is the ultimate extract of any collocation of facts, any picture of life, and the finest aspect of any artistic work." In response to his own dictum, James found the center of *The Ring and the Book*, not in a "plot," not in a picture or slice of life, but in the "embracing consciousness" of one of the principal characters (Caponsacchi) whose psychological sensitivity and drama would clearly evoke controlling interest.

Over and over again in his earlier Prefaces (1907–09), James had analyzed the centers and actions of his own novels not in relation to the external events but in terms of a character's consciousness. In the Preface to *Roderick Hudson:* "The centre of interest throughout 'Roderick' is in Rowland Mallet's consciousness." In the Preface to *What Maisie Knew:* "The action of the drama is simply the girl's 'subjective' adventure—that of her quite definitely winged intelligence; just as the catastrophe, just as the solution, depends on her winged wit." In the Preface to *The Portrait of a Lady:*" 'Place the centre of the subject in the young woman's own consciousness,' I said to myself, 'and you get as interesting and as beautiful a difficulty as you could wish. Stick to *that*—for the centre; put the heaviest weight into *that* scale, which will be so largely the scale of her relation to herself.'" These are sufficient instances to suggest the dominance of the "drama of consciousness" in James's work.

That James saw this psychological drama (action or inaction) as in some sense in competition with conventional plot is demonstrated in his own analysis of *The Portrait of a Lady*. In the Preface he points, as the best thing in the book, to Isabel Archer's "meditative vigil" (a little past the middle, in which she sits up alone deep into the night and finally comes to an awareness of the hidden relationship between her husband and her "friend" Madame Merle). James carefully indicates the absolute absence of any action: "It all goes on without her being approached by another person and without her leaving her chair." But in spite of this stasis, this "meditative vigil," says James, "throws the action further forward than twenty 'incidents' might have done. It was designed to have all the vivacity of incident and all the economy of picture. She [Isabel] sits up, by her dying fire, far into the night, under the spell of recognitions on which she finds the last sharpness suddenly wait. It is a representation simply of her motionlessly *seeing*, and an attempt withal to make the mere still lucidity of her act as 'interesting' as the surprise of a caravan or the identification of a pirate." The sense of initiation and discovery here leads us to believe that this magnificent scene in James's 1881 novel and this brilliant insight in James's 1908 Preface represent the conscious beginning of the practice and theory of the modern psychological novel, a crystallization of tendencies that came before, and a foreshadowing of extravagant experiments that were to follow, leading ultimately to the interior monologue and the stream of consciousness as they emerged full-blown in the 1920s after James's death.

8. *Rendering: Execution.* After the finding of a subject, after deciding on an action external or internal, after determining to present a drama whether of piratical events or of meditative consciousness, the writer confronts the immensities and complexities of rendering or of execution. James put the matter this way in his Preface to *The Ambassadors:* "Art deals with what we see, it must first contribute full-handed that ingredient; it plucks its material, otherwise expressed, in the garden of life—which material elsewhere grown is stale and uneatable. But it has no sooner done this than it has to take account of a *process.* . . . The process, that of the expression, the literal squeezing-out, of value is another affair—with which the happy luck of mere finding has little to do. . . . The subject is found, and if the problem is then transferred to the ground of what to do with it the field opens out for any amount of doing."

James's *Notebooks*, Prefaces, and critical essays are filled with commentaries on or explorations of the "doing." And one of the first questions that arises in the doing is the absence or presence of the author. Because James, on a number of occasions, scolded Trollope for constantly telling his readers in asides that he was only "making believe," it has been widely assumed that James believed the author should disappear from his work. On the contrary, James's presence in the form of the first-person singular is felt throughout his own work, and he contended that as a matter of fact an author could not escape his work because he left his stamp everywhere. In his 1888 essay on Guy de Maupassant, James asserted: "M. de Maupassant is remarkably objective and impersonal, but he would go too far if he were to entertain the belief that he has kept himself out of his books." In "The Lesson of Balzac" (1905), James elaborated on his concept of the nature of an author's presence in his work—"the projected light of the individual strong temperament in fiction."

This light, said James, "more or less unconsciously suffuses [a writer's] picture. I say unconsciously because I speak here of an effect of atmosphere largely, if not wholly, distinct from the effect sought on behalf of the special subject to be treated; something that proceeds from the contemplative mind itself, the very complexion of the mirror in which the material is reflected.

This is of the nature of the man himself—an emanation of his spirit, temper, history; it springs from his very presence, his spiritual presence, in his work, and is, in so far, not a matter of calculation and artistry. All a matter of his own, in a word, for each seer of visions, the particular tone of the medium in which each vision, each clustered group of persons and places and objects, is bathed."

Although the author's "spiritual presence" was always distinctive though largely unconscious, his "rendering" of his subject was a matter of acute consciousness. As James said in "The Art of Fiction," "To 'render' the simplest surface, to produce the most momentary illusion, is a very complicated business." Just how complicated James frequently revealed in his Prefaces. There were the difficult choices, in the rendering of particular events, between picture and drama (Preface to *Wings of the Dove*: "Picture, at almost any turn, is jealous of drama, and drama [though on the whole with greater patience, I think] suspicious of picture"). In his passion for drama, James produced one work, *The Awkward Age*, in which there was little or no "going behind," and in which the chapters in their devotion to scene and dialogue were like the acts of a play. But he gradually evolved a rhythmical alternation between picture and scene, the one preparing for the other—a balanced combination that reached a kind of perfection in *The Ambassadors*.

James borrowed from painting the term "to foreshorten" (as also "to render") to indicate that infinitely complex task of evoking a sense of reality. In painting, to foreshorten is to create illusion through perspective. James's most explicit description of literary foreshortening appears in his Preface to *Roderick Hudson*: "To give the image and the sense of certain things while still keeping them subordinate to his [the writer's] plan, keeping them in relation to matters more immediate and apparent, to give all the sense, in a word, without all the substance or all the surface, and so to summarise and foreshorten, so to make values both rich and sharp, that the mere procession of items and profiles is not only, for the occasion, superseded, but is, for essential quality, almost 'compromised'—such a case of delicacy proposes itself at every turn to the painter of life who wishes both to treat his chosen subject and to confine his necessary picture. . . . This eternal time-question is accordingly, for the novelist, always there and always formidable; always insisting on the *effect* of the great lapse and passage, of the 'dark backward and abysm,' by the terms of truth, and on the effect of compression, of composition and form, by the terms of literary arrangement." Thus both space and time are for the writer a challenge of perspective; and picture, scene, and dialogue will all be determined by the total strategy of foreshortening—"the art of figuring synthetically, a compactness into which the imagination may cut thick, as into the rich density of a wedding-cake."

9. Characters. Throughout James's criticism, extraordinary attention is given to the characters created by novelists. Two of James's favorite writers, Balzac and Turgénieff, were singled out for praise precisely because of their "portraiture of people." In his 1883 essay on Anthony Trollope, James revealed his rationale for the dominance of "character" in fiction: "If he [Trollope] had taken sides on the droll, bemuddled opposition between novels of character and novels of plot, I can imagine him to have said . . . that he preferred the former class, inasmuch as character in itself is plot, while plot is by no means character. It is more safe indeed to believe that his great good sense would have prevented him from taking an idle controversy seriously. Character, in any sense in which we can get at it, is action, and action is plot, and any plot which hangs together, even if it pretend to interest us only in the fashion of a Chinese puzzle, plays upon our emotion, our suspense, by means of personal references. We care what happens to people only in proportion as we know what people are." Such a view was perhaps inevitable for a writer who found his "centres" most frequently in dramas of consciousness in individual characters.

James frequently found the "germs" for his fictions in characters, and he believed his favorites Turgénieff and Balzac did too. And though the novelist might well start with an actual person, the process of art transfigured him beyond recognition. James observed in *Hawthorne* (1879): "From the moment the imagination takes a hand in the game, the inevitable tendency is to divergence, to following what may be called new scents. The original gives hints, but the writer does what he likes with them, and imports new elements into the picture." The creation of characters was, for James, infinitely complex —like any "rendering." The humorous novelist, like Dickens, might end up with "bundles of eccentricities." The allegorical novelist, like Hawthorne, might end up with "representatives." But a consummate novelist like Balzac most frequently ended up with breathing characters: "In reading him over, in opening him almost anywhere today, what immediately strikes us is the part assigned by him, in any picture, to the *conditions* of the creatures with whom he is concerned. Contrasted with him other prose painters of life scarce seem to see the conditions at all." Portrayal of the *conditions* was, in effect, "evocation of the medium . . . distillation of the natural and social air." Characters, said James, "are interesting, in fact, as subjects of fate, the figures round whom a situation closes, in proportion as, sharing their existence, we feel where fate comes in and just how it gets at them. In the void they are not interesting—and Balzac, like nature herself, abhorred a vacuum."

James once (1899) wrote to Mrs. Humphry Ward concerning her characters: "*Specify*, localize." Many passages in his *Notebooks* and Prefaces indicate that he struggled with such matters himself. He wrote out long lists of names in his *Notebooks* in search of the right specific name. And he reminded himself of the structural balance of contrasting a perceptive with a dense character (as in *The Spoils of Poynton*); or of the delicate complexities of adopting a heroine who is sick (as in *The Wings of the Dove*). And he gave much attention to the peripheral figures, attempting to bring them to life, but trying, also, to avoid overtreatment, a congenital weakness. Perhaps the most novel of James's inventions in this area was the concept of the *ficelle*—the minor character who belonged more to the treatment than to the subject of a novel. The challenge of the *ficelle* was to make him appear "important and essential"—this without letting him inadvertently push on to stage center.

10. *Setting*. When James said in "The Art of Fiction" that "to 'render' the simplest surface . . . is a very complicated business," he suggested the difficulties or complexities the novelist faces in "doing" place—cities, towns, houses, rooms, streets, balconies, galleries, businesses, etc. In his own writing James gave close attention to setting, debating with himself the weaknesses and strengths of a particular setting for a particular character or event—Northampton, Massachusetts, for the opening of *Roderick Hudson*, for example, or Paris for the main action of *The Ambassadors*. Throughout his career, James found Balzac a kind of touchstone in the evocation of place. In his 1875 essay "Honoré de Balzac," James stressed Balzac's "overmastering sense of the present world," especially as evidenced in the "background" or "mise-en-scène" of his novels: "This part of his story had with Balzac an importance—his rendering of it a solidity—which it had never enjoyed before, and which the most vigorous talents in the school of which Balzac was founder have never been able to restore to it. The place in which an event occurred was in his view of equal moment with the event itself; it was part of the action; it was not a thing to take or to leave, or to be vaguely and gracefully indicated; it imposed itself; it had a part to play; it needed to be made as definite as anything else. There is accordingly a very much greater amount of description in Balzac than in any other writer, and the description is mainly of towns, houses and rooms."

In contrast with Balzac, Zola was the epitome of superficiality in the rendering of place. In "Emile Zola" (1903), James described Zola as "stating in one breath that his knowledge of Italy consisted of a few days spent at Genoa," but "was ready to declare in the next that he had planned, on a scale, a picture of Rome." James added: "It showed how he had marched from subject to subject and had 'got up' each in turn—showing also how consummately he had reduced getting-up to an artifice." With deep undercurrents of annoyance, James mused: "But was the adored Rome . . . to be his on such terms, the Rome he was already giving away before possessing an inch of it? One thought of one's own frequentations, saturations—a history of long years, and of how the effect of them had somehow been but to make the subject too august. Was *he* to find it easy through a visit of a month or two with 'introductions' and a Baedeker?" The subsequent appearance of Zola's

Rome, James said, bore out his reservations and fears: "The presumptuous volume, without sweetness, without antecedents, superficial and violent, has the minimum instead of the maximum of *value*: so that it betrayed or 'gave away' just in this degree the state of mind on the author's part responsible for its inflated hollowness."

James's strictures on Zola are especially interesting in the light of his own wide-ranging choice of setting for his voluminous works—New York, Boston, Washington, Rome, Florence, Venice, Paris, London, Liverpool, and many more. But James did, in some sense, earn the right to render these places through his prolonged experience in and of them. Although James would never, like Zola, go to a place foreign to his experience simply to "do" it, he was certainly committed to revisitations and reexplorations in quest of additional precious impressions. In anticipation of giving London a dominant role in *The Princess Casamassima*, James (as he says in the Preface) returned to immerse himself in it: "I recall pulling no wires, knocking at no closed doors, applying for no 'authentic' information; but I recall also on the other hand the practice of never missing an opportunity to add a drop, however small, to the bucket of my impressions or to renew my sense of being able to dip into it. To haunt the great city and by this habit to penetrate it, imaginatively, in as many places as possible—*that* was to be informed, *that* was to pull wires, *that* was to open doors, *that* positively was to groan at times under the weight of one's accumulations."   Perhaps the difference between Zola and James in approach to place was that Zola gathered information through his books, while James gathered impressions through his penetrating imagination: the one method kept to the surface, the other led to the depths beneath.

IV. The Work in its Unity

James had many important things to say about certain elements or aspects of fiction that contribute decisively to the overall unity of individual works. Indeed some of his most important contributions to fictional theory were in the realm of point of view, form, and style.

11. Point of View. Perhaps the most significant single contribution James made to the theory of fiction was to call attention to the transcendent importance of point of view. If it is a mistake to cite "point of view" as the totality of James's theory (as Percy Lubbock tends to do in *The Craft of Fiction*), so it is also misleading to relegate point of view to a list of fictional techniques which it is nice for novelists to know about. It is not the totality of the theory, but it is central and vital. James probably developed his notions about point of view as he developed his concept of the drama of consciousness. He noted frequently in his criticism that action by itself and characters by themselves,

in vacuums so to speak, failed to arouse interest. Only when the action
involves people who live and breathe, and only when the people feel and
respond to their situations or contexts of action—only then does interest
begin to grow. The matrix of character and action is consciousness. Thus
consciousness becomes the key to fictional interest, and feelings, meditations,
inner responses, flow of thought surge to the fore as major material for
representation.

In the Preface to *The Princess Casamassima*, James presented the case for
deliberate consideration by the writer in handling point of view: "In the
immediate field of life, for action, for application, for getting through a job,
nothing may so much matter perhaps as the descent of a suspended weight
on this, that or the other spot, with all its subjective concomitants quite
secondary and irrelevant. But the affair of the painter is not the immediate,
it is the reflected field of life, the realm not of application, but of *appreciation*
—a truth that makes our measure of effect altogether different. My report of
people's experience—my report as a 'story teller'—is essentially my appreciation of it, and there is no 'interest' for me in what my hero, my heroine or
any one else does save through that admirable process. As soon as I begin
to appreciate simplification is imperilled: the sharply distinguished parts of
any adventure, any case of endurance and performance, melt together as an
appeal. I then see their 'doing,' that of the persons just mentioned, as,
immensely their feeling, their feeling as their doing; since I can have none
of the conveyed sense and taste of their situation without becoming intimate
with them."

The distinctions James makes are subtle ones, but crucial for his conception
of point of view. For life itself, the important terms are *immediacy* and
application: for art, these become *reflection* and *appreciation*. We are involved
in the action of life, and must act and apply; we are interested in the action of
fiction (if we are), and appreciate it most intensely in its reflection on the
feelings and thoughts of characters. James says: "I confess I never see the
leading interest of any human hazard but in a consciousness (on the part of the
moved and moving creature) subject to fine intensification and wide enlargement. It is as mirrored in that consciousness that the gross fools, the headlong
fools, the fatal fools play their part for us—they have much less to show us in
themselves. . . . This means, exactly, that the person capable of feeling in the
given case more than another of what is to be felt for it, and so serving in the
highest degree to *record* it dramatically and objectively, is the only sort of
person on whom we can count not to betray, to cheapen, or, as we say, give
away, the value and beauty of the thing. By so much as the affair matters *for*
some such individual, by so much do we get the best there is of it, and by so
much as it falls within the scope of a denser and duller, a more vulgar and
more shallow capacity, do we get a picture dim and meagre."

In the midst of this rationale (still from the Preface to *The Princess*

Casamassima) for the careful allowance for point of view, with the use of a sensitive reflector or mirror, James turns to the question of the great novelists of the past and their concern for point of view: "The great chroniclers have clearly always been aware of this; they have at least always either placed a mind of some sort—in the sense of a reflecting and colouring medium—in possession of the general adventure (when the latter has not been purely epic, as with Scott, say, as with old Dumas and with Zola); or else paid signally, as to the interest created, for their failure to do so. We may note moreover in passing that this failure is in almost no case intentional or part of a plan, but has sprung from their limited curiosity, their short conception of the particular sensibility projected."

Throughout his *Notebooks* and Prefaces, James discussed again and again the point of view of his individual works, first in a search for the precisely right point of view, and finally in an evaluation of successes and failures. The only rule to apply was no rule: the subject itself, its action and characters, would determine the best, the most fruitful, point of view. The problem only was to find it. In James's three great novels of his "major phase," he hit upon a variety of solutions. In *The Wings of the Dove* he used a series of successive reflectors; in *The Ambassadors* he reveled in the economy, unity, and intensity achieved through the use of a single "centre"; in *The Golden Bowl* he found the material most amenable to the use of "two registers," one in each half of the novel. Although it cannot be said that point of view constituted the whole of James's theory, it may well be asserted that point of view is pivotal, and without some concept of it the elements of James's theory could not hang together.

12. *Form and Structure.* In "The Art of Fiction," James described the relation of idea to form as that which existed between needle and thread: "I never heard of a guild of tailors who recommended the use of the thread without the needle, or the needle without the thread." The ultimate meaning of this metaphor is that there is never art without form—good or bad. And in this sense form is everything—whether it is called execution, treatment, technique —which is done to the unrefined lump of life, the patch of actual experience, to turn it into the finished work of art, product of the imagination.

James's concept of form can best be comprehended in the light of his high praise for Flaubert and his strictures on Dostoevski and Tolstoy, using in each case the criterion of form. In "Gustave Flaubert" (1902), James said: "*Madame Bovary* has a perfection that not only stamps it, but makes it stand almost alone; it holds itself with such a supreme unapproachable assurance as both excites and defies judgment. For it deals not in the least, as to unapproachability, with things exalted or refined; it only confers on its sufficiently vulgar elements of exhibition a final unsurpassable form. The form is in *itself* as interesting, as active, as much of the essence of the subject as the idea, and yet so close is its fit and so inseparable its life that we catch it at no moment on any errand of its own." In a 1912 letter to Hugh Walpole, James wrote: "Strenuous selection and comparison are . . . the very essence of art, and . . . Form *is* substance to that degree that there is absolutely no substance without it. Form alone takes, and holds and preserves, substance—saves it from the welter of helpless verbiage that we swim in as in a sea of tasteless tepid pudding, and that makes one ashamed of an art capable of such degradations. Tolstoi and D[ostoevski] are fluid puddings, though not tasteless, because the amount of their own minds and souls in solution in the broth gives it savour and flavour, thanks to the strong, rank quality of their genius and their experience. But there are all sorts of things to be said of them, and in particular that we see how great a vice is their lack of composition, their defiance of economy and architecture, directly they are emulated and imitated; then, as subjects of emulation, models, they quite give themselves away. There is nothing so deplorable as a work of art with a *leak* in its interest; and there is no such leak of interest as through commonness of form. Its opposite, the *found* (because the sought-for) form is the absolute citadel and tabernacle of interest."

The "found form," as opposed to the imposed or manufactured form, was the ideal James sought for throughout his own work. He felt that of all his novels, *The Ambassadors* and *The Portrait of a Lady* were his highest achievements in " 'architectural' competence," proportion, and roundness. And they were shaped by the very nature of their own materials, not by a preconceived shape into which they were molded. James presented his creed of form in his Preface to *The Tragic Muse:* "A picture without composition slights its most precious chance for beauty, and is moreover not composed at all unless the painter knows *how* that principle of health and safety, working as an absolutely premeditated art, has prevailed. There may in its absence be life, incontestably, as 'The Newcomes' has life, as 'Les Trois Mousquetaires,' as Tolstoi's 'Peace and War,' have it; but what do such large loose baggy monsters, with their queer elements of the accidental and the arbitrary, artistically *mean?* We have heard it maintained, we will remember, that such things are 'superior to art'; but we understand least of all what *that* may mean, and we look in vain for the artist, the divine explanatory genius, who will come to our aid and tell us. There is life and life, and as waste is only life sacrificed and thereby prevented from 'counting,' I delight in a deep-breathing economy and an organic form."

For James the "found form" was the organic form, and had nothing to do with the "accidental and the arbitrary," but everything to do with the nature of the materials themselves, and what they suggested or dictated—as, indeed, in the case of the point of view also. Looseness of form was simply wasteful of materials—so many elements were not made to "count" in the totality. Tightness of form meant simply the most economical use of materials—making everything "count" to the utmost. Thus for James, a "deep-breathing economy" and "organic form" were in essence synonymous: one achieved the other. And thus *economy*, one of James's favorite compositional terms, had no reference to size or length but full relevance to architecture and shape.

13. Style. James's concern for style manifested itself in his earliest reviews. He was fond of attacking pretentious and unnatural styles in the popular books of the day. In an 1865 review of Harriet Elizabeth Prescott's *Azarian: An Episode*, he said: "If the dictionary were a palette of colors, and a goose-quill a brush, Miss Prescott would be a very clever painter. But as words possess a certain inherent dignity, value, and independence, language being rather the stamped and authorized coinage which expresses the value of thought than the brute metal out of which forms are moulded, her pictures are invariably incoherent and meaningless." He complained of Swinburne's style (in "Swinburne's Essays," 1875): "It is always listening to itself—always turning its head over its shoulders to see its train flowing behind it."

James spends several pages in his essay on Robert Louis Stevenson (1888) praising Stevenson's style, and thereby revealing much of his basic conception of the role of language in literature: "Mr. Stevenson delights in a style, and his own has nothing accidental or diffident; it is eminently conscious of its responsibilities, and meets them with a kind of gallantry—as if language were a pretty woman, and a person who proposes to handle it had of necessity to be something of a Don Juan." In a passage that seems to refer as much to James himself as to Stevenson, James points out that the writer who is also an artist is "thrown on the defensive," and such a writer must not appear to be too artistic: "This queer superstition has so successfully imposed itself, that the mere fact of having been indifferent to such a danger constitutes in itself an originality. How few they are in number and how soon we could name them, the writers of English prose, at the present moment, the quality of whose prose is personal, expressive, renewed at each attempt!" *Personal, expressive, renewed:* these terms perhaps characterize the Jamesian ideal of style better than any other. But above all the style must never become an end in itself. Stevenson, James says, "regards an expressive style only, after all, as a means. . . . Much as he cares for his phrase, he cares more for life, and for a certain transcendently lovable part of it. He feels, as it seems to us, and that is not given to every one. . . . He does not feel everything equally, by any manner of means; but his feelings are always his reasons. He regards them, whatever they may be, as sufficiently honourable, does not disguise them in other names or colours, and looks at whatever he meets in the brilliant candle-light that they shed."

One important principle that was sounded over and over again, especially in James's later criticism, was the absolute fusion of style and substance. In his 1907 essay "The Tempest" he gives one of the best statements of this principle: "He [Shakespeare] points for us as no one else the relation of style to meaning and of manner to motive; a matter on which, right and left, we hear such rank ineptitudes uttered. Unless it be true that these things, on either hand, are inseparable; unless it be true that the phrase, the cluster and order of terms, *is* the object and the sense, in as close a compression as that of body and soul, so that any consideration of them as distinct, from the moment style is an active, applied force, becomes a gross stupidity: unless we recognize this reality the author of *The Tempest* has no lesson for us. It is by his expression of it exactly as the expression stands that the particular thing is created, created as interesting, as beautiful, as strange, droll or terrible—as related, in short, to our understanding or our sensibility; in consequence of which we reduce it to naught when we begin to talk of either of its presented parts as matters by themselves."

This principle of the inseparability of style and meaning sheds some light on James's own last works, both fiction and criticism, written in the intricate, flowing, parenthetical, convoluted style that has caused some readers to charge deliberate obfuscation—as though James were consciously obscuring his meaning. If we take James seriously in equating style with meaning, we must then assume that the meanings of his later works are enfolded in those intricacies of style. The meanings, like the style, are infinitely complex—just as James believed that life itself, and the smallest of experiences, were infinitely complex. The complex style is the only instrument for penetration of the complex nature of reality.

Some time in the late 1890s James began to dictate his work to a stenographer at a typewriter. He was able to walk as he dictated—and the language flowed without cease. Some critics have assumed that the dictation encouraged him to be verbose, garrulous, pointlessly complicated. It is more likely, however, that James found more and more that his vision of experience required a style that flowed deep from within, from the depths of the conscious near that crowded storehouse of life's accumulation of impressions, from the levels near the teeming unconscious itself. Here was where he found his own style *personal, expressive, renewed.*

Such a style suggests a flow, a release, and even a letting go, but it does not indicate loss of control. James was, as we have seen, the most conscious of artists in setting about deliberately finding subjects, developing them, and releasing from them their organic form to return to them again. In this involved process, James was willing (as he says in the Preface to *The American*) to resort to the "deep well of unconscious cerebration," in the hopes that what he dropped there might "eventually emerge from that reservoir . . . with a firm iridescent surface and a notable increase of weight." With his style flowing from near the resources of that same reservoir, James must have believed that some of the same values of iridescence and density would flow with it. The style represented a release, all right, but within the structure already elaborately worked out and erected in James's fully conscious mind. Whatever the final truth of the style and form of James's last period, it is the James of this "major phase" that is most closely allied to the great twentieth-century innovations in the novel of such writers as James Joyce, Virginia Woolf, and William Faulkner. As a great transitional figure, James through his style and form moved the novel forward from the Victorian to the Modern period to help create the climate of experimentation that made such modern writers as Joyce, Woolf, and Faulkner possible.

V. Meaning and Impact

With all his concern for rendering, for execution, for the "doing" of fiction, James's ultimate concern was for something more—for what he variously termed the "morality," the "philosophy," the "meaning," the "theme." Although James groped about for the right language in which to describe this extra dimension in fiction, he never doubted its existence or its overriding importance. And he had some fairly comprehensive notions about the appropriate strategies of readers and critics in apprehending, and responding to, fiction. James never found his ideal reader or critic, but he left some cogent suggestions for those who would try.

14. Morality and Philosophy; Meaning and Theme. One of the most interesting aspects of "The Art of Fiction" is the vigor with which James, at the end of the essay, attacked Besant's contention that a novel must have a "conscious moral purpose." James said: "To what degree a purpose in a work of art is a source of corruption I shall not attempt to inquire; the one that seems to me least dangerous is the purpose of making a perfect work." Although many readers have concluded that James dismissed morality out-of-hand, his enduring faith was that the very perfection of a work of art would assume a pervasive and *unconscious* morality. James went on to say that there was one point at which "the moral sense and the artistic sense" of a work "lie very near together; that is in the light of a very obvious truth that the deepest quality of a work of art will always be the quality of the mind of the producer. In proportion as the intelligence is fine will the novel, the picture, the statue partake of the substance of beauty and truth. To be constituted of such elements is, to my vision, to have purpose enough. No good novel will ever proceed from a superficial mind."

Thus, though James rejected *conscious* and *purpose* from Besant's "conscious moral purpose," he did not reject the moral dimension. Indeed, he devised a kind of revision that might read, "unconscious moral quality"—something that derives from the depth of the artist's mind and the perfection —as art—of his work. In his 1876 essay on Charles Baudelaire, James put the matter this way: "The whole thinking man is one, and . . . to count out the moral element in one's appreciation of an artistic total is exactly as sane as it would be (if the total were a poem) to eliminate all the words in three syllables." James observed that the "advocates of 'art for art' " often talk of morality as though it were a "physic": "They allude to its being put into and kept out of a work of art, put into and kept out of one's appreciation of the same as if it were a coloured fluid kept in a big-labelled bottle in some mysterious intellectual closet. It is in reality simply a part of the essential richness of inspiration—it has nothing to do with the artistic process and it has everything to do with the artistic effect. The more a work of art feels it at its source, the richer it is; the less it feels it, the poorer it is."

In "Ivan Turgénieff" (1874) James presented a specific—and brilliant—example of a work of art with the morality not lying on its surface but deeply felt at its source, *The Memoirs of a Sportsman:* "For never, surely, was a work with a polemic bearing more consistently low in tone, as painters say. The author treats us to such a scanty dose of flagrant horrors that the moral of the book is obvious only to attentive readers. No single episode pleads conclusively against the 'peculiar institution' of Russia; the lesson is in the cumulative testimony of a multitude of fine touches—in an after-sense of sadness that sets wise readers thinking. It would be difficult to name a work that contains better instruction for those heated spirits who are fond of taking sides on the question of 'art for art.' It offers a capital example of moral meaning giving a sense to form, and form giving relief to moral meaning."

In another passage in this same 1874 Turgénieff essay, James spoke of a writer's "vision" in the totality of his work: "The great question as to a poet or a novelist is, How does he feel about life? what, in the last analysis, is his philosophy? When vigorous writers have reached maturity we are at liberty to look in their works for some expression of a total view of the world they have been so actively observing. This is the most interesting thing their works offer us. Details are interesting in proportion as they contribute to make it clear." The remarkable thing about this passage is the resemblance it bears to "The Figure in the Carpet" (1896), in which the novelist Hugh Vereker tells the critic: "There's an idea in my work without which I wouldn't have given a straw for the whole job. It's the finest fullest intention of the lot. . . . It stretches, this little trick of mine, from book to book, and everything else, comparatively, plays on the surface of it. The order, the form, the texture of my books will perhaps someday constitute for the initiated a complete representation of it. So it's naturally the thing for the critic to look for." This concern for a totality of meaning persisted in James to the end. In his 1914 essay "The New Novel," writing of Compton Mackenzie's *Sinister Street,* he said: "We ask ourselves what *Sinister Street* may mean as a whole in spite of our sense of being brushed from the first by a hundred subordinate purposes, the succession and alternation of which seem to make after a fashion a plan, and which, though full of occasional design, yet fail to gather themselves for application or to converge to an idea.''

Probably James's most brilliant statement on morality and fiction appeared in the famous "house of fiction" passage in his Preface to *The Portrait of a Lady*, in which he again insisted on "the perfect dependence of the 'moral' sense of a work of art on the amount of felt life concerned in producing it": "The question comes back thus, obviously, to the kind and the degree of the artist's prime sensibility, which is the soil out of which his subject springs. The quality and capacity of that soil, its ability to 'grow' with due freshness and straightness any vision of life, represents, strongly or weakly, the projected morality.'' The morality *is* the vision, not a container into which the vision is placed. James added: "One is far from contending that this enveloping air of the artist's humanity—which gives the last touch to the worth of a work— is not a widely and wondrously varying element.'' In other words the morality— the "enveloping air of the artist's humanity"—is not rigidly fixed and monolithic, but richly flexible and various, as with sensibility and vision themselves. Indeed: "The house of fiction has in short not one window, but a million—a number of possible windows not to be reckoned, rather. . . . These apertures, of dissimilar shape and size, hang so, all together over the human scene that we might have expected of them a greater sameness of report than we find. . . . But they have this mark of their own that at each of them stands a figure with a pair of eyes, or at least with a field glass, which forms, again and again, for observation, a unique instrument, insuring to the person making use of it an impression distinct from any other. . . . The spreading field, the human scene, is the 'choice of subject;' the pierced aperture, either broad or balconied or slit-like and low-browed, is the 'literary form;' but they are, singly or together, as nothing without the posted presence of the watcher—without, in other words, the consciousness of the artist. Tell me what the artist is, and I will tell you of what he has *been* conscious. Thereby I shall express to you at once his boundless freedom and his 'moral' reference.'' Consciousness thus becomes not only the storehouse of impressions but the repository of that "prime sensibility" which contains the moral sense, vision, or imagination. The artist's vision, limited by his own consciousness or sensibility, *is* his "projected morality.''

15. *Readers and Critics*. Although James made, in his own novels, inordinate demands on the reader, at the same time he insisted on the principle that the critic could not obligate anyone to *like* something—even an excellent work of art—that he did not or could not like. In short, James had a deep understanding of the psychology of the reader, and an aesthetic that did not require violation of it. James once (in "London Notes," July, 1897) described himself in the role of reader in a way that most readers instinctively understand: "The great thing to say for them [novelists] is surely that at any given

moment they offer us [readers] another world, another consciousness, an experience that, as effective as the dentist's ether, muffles the ache of the actual and, by helping us to an interval, tides us over and makes us face, in the return to the inevitable, a combination that may at least have changed. What we get of course, in proportion as the picture lives, is simply another actual—the actual of other people; and I no more than any one else pretend to say *why* that should be a relief, a relief as great, I mean, as it practically proves. We meet in this question, I think, the eternal mystery—the mystery that sends us back simply to the queer constitution of man and that is not in the least lighted by the plea of 'romance,' the argument that relief depends wholly upon the quantity, as it were, of fable. It depends, to my sense, on the quantity of nothing but art—in which the material, fable or fact or whatever it be, falls so into solution, is so reduced and transmuted, that I absolutely am acquainted with no receipt whatever for computing its proportion and amount."

In such a fashion James leads us to believe that he is mounting a defense of the commonplace idea of "reading to escape," only to subvert the element of romance by substituting art. But in the process he offers a view of the basic motive for reading literature—to enter that other world, that other consciousness, that other experience which will give us a temporary relief, and which, "in the return," will "make us face . . . a combination that may at least have changed." The "combination" must surely be a combination of our own experience plus that of the fictional world, two "actuals," each illuminating in some fashion the other so as to change the old by addition of the new. Mere "escape" could never achieve such serious ends. James felt that the reader who invested the close "attention of perusal" had the right to expect the greatest returns. He said in the Preface to *The Wings of the Dove:* "The enjoyment of a work of art, the acceptance of an irresistible illusion, constituting, to my sense, our highest experience of 'luxury,' the luxury is not greatest, by my consequent measure, when the work asks for as little attention as possible. It is greatest, it is delightfully, divinely great, when we feel the surface, like the thick ice of the skater's pond, bear without cracking the strongest pressure we throw on it."

Although somewhat indulgent in his demands on readers, James was much more severe in his requirements of critics. He insisted, first and foremost, that the critic make no "*à priori* . . . rule for a literary production but that it shall have genuine life." This meant that the critic must avoid allegiances outside literature that determined perspective and judgment. In his 1872 review of "Taine's English Literature," James noted Taine's tribute "to the great service rendered by Sainte-Beuve to the new criticism," and asserted of Sainte-Beuve: "In purpose the least doctrinal of critics, it was by his very horror of dogmas, moulds, and formulas, that he so effectively contributed to the science of literary interpretation." It was Sainte-Beuve's great virtue that "he never pretended to have devised a method which should be a key to truth." In comparing the approaches of Taine and Sainte-Beuve in the critical quest for "truth," James provided admirable figures for the dogmatic critic in contrast with the uncommitted inquirer: "The truth for M. Taine lies stored up, as one may say, in great lumps and blocks, to be released and detached by a few hammer-blows; while for Sainte-Beuve it was a diffused and imponderable essence, as vague as the carbon in the air which nourishes vegetation, and, like it, to be disengaged by patient chemistry."

In his early criticism, especially in his reviews, James sounded the moral note frequently, exploring a dimension that lay not beyond art or outside it, but deep within it. For example, in his 1875 essay "Swinburne's Essays," he noted the "absence of the moral sense" in Swinburne, and then added: "By this we do not mean that Mr. Swinburne is not didactic, nor edifying, nor devoted to pleading the cause of virtue. We mean simply that his moral plummet does not sink at all, and that when he pretends to drop it he is simply dabbling in the relatively very shallow pool of the picturesque. A sense of the picturesque so refined as Mr. Swinburne's will take one a great way, but it will by no means, in dealing with things whose great value is in what they tell us of human character, take one all the way. One breaks down with it (if one treats it as one's sole support) sooner or later in aesthetics; one breaks down with it very soon indeed in psychology." This view of the "moral sense" (or its absence) in a critic is compatible—though the terms shift—with James's later view in his Preface to *The Portrait of a Lady* that there is a "perfect dependence of the 'moral' sense of a work of art on the amount of felt life concerned in producing it."

Although James's insistence on a criticism without dogmas and doctrines endured throughout his career, his call for morality faded to the background. In his essay entirely devoted to criticism ("Criticism," 1891), he did not find need to mention the word. He described the critic as offering himself "as a general touchstone": "To lend himself, to project himself and steep himself, to feel and feel till he understands and to understand so well that he can say, to have perception at the pitch of passion and expression as embracing as the air, to be infinitely curious and incorrigibly patient, and yet plastic and inflammable and determinable, stooping to conquer and serving to direct— these are fine chances for an active mind, chances to add the idea of independent beauty to the conception of success. Just in proportion as he is sentient and restless, just in proportion as he reacts and reciprocates and penetrates, is the critic a valuable instrument; for in literature assuredly criticism *is* the critic, just as art is the artist; it being assuredly the artist who invented art and the critic who invented criticism, and not the other way round." What is no doubt involved here, in some measure, in this emphasis on understanding rooted in feelings ("perception at the pitch of passion") is something akin to that "prime sensibility" described in the Preface to *The Portrait of a Lady* as the source for the "projected morality" of the artist. James's principles did not change so much as his vocabulary, and his understanding of human complexity broadened and deepened.

In his Preface to *The Lesson of the Master*, James said that his story, "The Figure in the Carpet," had its origins in his observation of the "marked collective mistrust of anything like close or analytic appreciation—appreciation, to *be* appreciation, implying of course some such rudimentary zeal; and this though that fine process be the Beautiful Gate itself of enjoyment." There was, he noted, an "odd numbness of the general sensibility, which seemed ever to condemn it, in presence of a work of art, to a view scarce of half the intentions embodied, and moreover but to the scantest measure of these . . . ." Those of us who have passed through the era of the New Criticism may recognize some of its cherished principles in embryo in these lines, especially in the suggestions for close and analytical reading. But James phrases his principles as to place emphasis on *appreciation, zeal, enjoyment*—words not very prominent in the New Criticism. James's term, "analytical appreciation" (in contrast with the popular term "critical analysis"), indicates a crucial difference that goes back to feelings, the artist's "prime sensibility" as the "soil" for his "projected morality." These were all factors that did not figure in the forefront of New Critical thinking (which, for example, numbered among its dogmas something called the "affective fallacy"). Indeed, if James in some measure bears to us the truth in these matters, it is possible that he can help us to understand the causes for the passing of the New Criticism. And it might be that he can point some directions for future exploration, not only in his principles of criticism, but also through the implications of his comprehensive and provocative theory of fiction.

But above all, readers, critics, and novelists might do well to heed James's proclamation of freedom for fiction in "The Future of the Novel" (1899). The novel, he wrote, "has the extraordinary advantage—a piece of luck scarcely credible—that, while capable of giving an impression of the highest perfection and the rarest finish, it moves in a luxurious independence of rules and restrictions. Think as we may, there is nothing we can mention as a consideration outside itself with which it must square, nothing we can name as one of its peculiar obligations or interdictions." Such freedom *from* rules and regulations and freedom *for* experimentation and creation should prove exhilarating for both writers and their audience. James would advise both to be bold in what they try. The novel, he said, in a final warning we should all heed, "has so clear a field that if it perishes this will surely be by its fault— by its superficiality, in other words, or its timidity."

JAMES E. MILLER, JR.

University of Chicago

Chapter I

"THE ART OF FICTION"

"*The Art of Fiction*" *has made its way to become perhaps the most popular and surely the most influential brief statement of fictional theory ever made. It is a curious fate for an essay that was designed originally as a rebuttal. Walter Besant delivered his lecture, "The Art of Fiction," at the Royal Institution in London on April 25, 1884, and later published the lecture as a pamphlet. James published his* "reply," *adopting the same title, in* Longman's Magazine *in September, 1884. In paragraph 6, James presents enough of a summary of Besant's points as to enable his essay to stand by itself, and he adds:* "I should find it difficult to dissent from any one of these recommendations. At the same time, I should find it difficult positively to assent to them." *This, of course, is James's gentle way of launching an elaborate refutation of Besant's simplistic and frequently banal principles—a refutation that has itself become a set of fictional principles that have contributed to the shaping of modern fiction.*

But because these remarks were aimed at Besant's lecture, and are therefore silent on many aspects of fiction; and because they are brief and sometimes cryptic; and because they were written in 1884, about a third of a century before James's death—for all these reasons, it is valuable and even sometimes necessary to place them in the context of the entire range of James's views on the art of fiction. This book has been designed to make it simple for the reader to do just that. Amplifications provided in this larger context show that many assumptions and interpretations have, in fact, been wrong, or distortions of James's fundamental meaning.

Introductions to succeeding chapters make clear many of the connections between statements in "The Art of Fiction" *and other James statements that appeared before and after. But it might be valuable here to provide a list of references to suggest directions for exploration:*

> *Par. 1 & 2: on the writer and his culture, Chapter II*
> *on critical discussion, Chapter XVI*
> *Par. 3: on the nature of the novel, Chapter III, IV, V*
> *on authorial asides, Chapter IX*
> *Par. 4: on the nature of fiction as serious art, Chapter XV*
> *on the nature of readers, Chapter XVI*

These are perhaps enough suggestions to indicate the many interconnections and interrelationships weaving through the chapters of this book. But it is important to remember that, though "The Art of Fiction" is remarkably comprehensive for its length, it is silent, or virtually so, on many of the elements or subjects that were extremely important to James. For example, there is no reference to point of view or to style, and little is made of form or of setting. Other subjects are slighted or treated cryptically. This volume as a whole is designed to present the totality of James's views of the art of fiction—thus in a sense filling out, amplifying, and completing the task he merely began in his 1884 essay.

THE ART OF FICTION
(1884)

1. I should not have affixed so comprehensive a title to these few remarks, necessarily wanting in any completeness upon a subject the full consideration of which would carry us far, did I not seem to discover a pretext for my temerity in the interesting pamphlet lately published under this name by Mr. Walter Besant. Mr. Besant's lecture at the Royal Institution—the original form of his pamphlet—appears to indicate that many persons are interested

in the art of fiction, and are not indifferent to such remarks, as those who practice it may attempt to make about it. I am therefore anxious not to lose the benefit of this favorable association, and to edge in a few words under cover of the attention which Mr. Besant is sure to have excited. There is something very encouraging in his having put into form certain of his ideas on the mystery of story-telling.

2. It is a proof of life and curiosity—curiosity on the part of the brotherhood of novelists as well as on the part of their readers. Only a short time ago it might have been supposed that the English novel was not what the French call *discutable*. It had no air of having a theory, a conviction, a consciousness of itself behind it—of being the expression of an artistic faith, the result of choice and comparison. I do not say it was necessarily the worse for that: it would take much more courage than I possess to intimate that the form of the novel as Dickens and Thackeray (for instance) saw it had any taint of incompleteness. It was, however, *naïf* (if I may help myself out with another French word); and evidently if it be destined to suffer in any way for having lost its *naïveté* it has now an idea of making sure of the corresponding advantages. During the period I have alluded to there was a comfortable, good-humored feeling abroad that a novel is a novel, as a pudding is a pudding, and that our only business with it could be to swallow it. But within a year or two, for some reason or other, there have been signs of returning animation—the era of discussion would appear to have been to a certain extent opened. Art lives upon discussion, upon experiment, upon curiosity, upon variety of attempt, upon the exchange of views and the comparison of standpoints; and there is a presumption that those times when no one has anything particular to say about it, and has no reason to give for practice or preference, though they may be times of honor, are not times of development—are times, possibly even, a little of dullness. The successful application of any art is a delightful spectacle, but the theory too is interesting; and though there is a great deal of the latter without the former I suspect there has never been a genuine success that has not had a latent core of conviction. Discussion, suggestion, formulation, these things are fertilizing when they are frank and sincere. Mr. Besant has set an excellent example in saying what he thinks, for his part, about the way in which fiction should be written, as well as about the way in which it should be published; for his view of the "art," carried on into an appendix, covers that too. Other laborers in the same field will doubtless take up the argument, they will give it the light of their experience, and the effect will surely be to make our interest in the novel a little more what it had for some time threatened to fail to be—a serious, active, inquiring interest, under protection of which this delightful study may, in moments of confidence, venture to say a little more what it thinks of itself.

3. It must take itself seriously for the public to take it so. The old supersti-

tion about fiction being "wicked" has doubtless died out in England; but the spirit of it lingers in a certain oblique regard directed toward any story which does not more or less admit that it is only a joke. Even the most jocular novel feels in some degree the weight of the proscription that was formerly directed against literary levity: the jocularity does not always succeed in passing for orthodoxy. It is still expected, though perhaps people are ashamed to say it, that a production which is after all only a "make-believe" (for what else is a "story"?) shall be in some degree apologetic—shall renounce the pretension of attemping really to represent life. This, of course, any sensible, wide-awake story declines to do, for it quickly perceives that the tolerance granted to it on such a condition is only an attempt to stifle it disguised in the form of generosity. The old evangelical hostility to the novel, which was as explicit as it was narrow, and which regarded it as little less favorable to our immortal part than a stage play, was in reality far less insulting. The only reason for the existence of a novel is that it does attempt to represent life. When it relinquishes this attempt, the same attempt that we see on the canvas of the painter, it will have arrived at a very strange pass. It is not expected of the picture that it will make itself humble in order to be forgiven; and the analogy between the art of the painter and the art of the novelist is, so far as I am able to see, complete. Their inspiration is the same, their process (allowing for the different quality of the vehicle) is the same, their success is the same. They may learn from each other, they may explain and sustain each other. Their cause is the same, and the honor of one is the honor of another. The Mahometans think a picture an unholy thing, but it is a long time since any Christian did, and it is therefore the more odd that in the Christian mind the traces (dissimulated though they may be) of a suspicion of the sister art should linger to this day. The only effectual way to lay it to rest is to emphasize the analogy to which I just alluded—to insist on the fact that as the picture is reality, so the novel is history. That is the only general description (which does it justice) that we may give of the novel. But history also is allowed to represent life; it is not, any more than painting, expected to apologize. The subject-matter of fiction is stored up likewise in documents and records, and if it will not give itself away, as they say in California, it must speak with assurance, with the tone of the historian. Certain accomplished novelists have a habit of giving themselves away which must often bring tears to the eyes of people who take their fiction seriously. I was lately struck, in reading over many pages of Anthony Trollope, with his want of discretion in this particular. In a digression, a parenthesis or an aside, he concedes to the reader that he and this trusting friend are only "making believe." He admits that the events he narrates have not really happened, and that he can give his narrative any turn the reader may like best. Such a betrayal of a sacred office seems to me, I confess, a terrible crime; it is what I mean by the attitude of apology, and it shocks me every whit as much in Trollope as it would have shocked me in Gibbon or Macaulay. It implies that the novelist is less occupied in looking for the truth (the truth, of course I mean, that he assumes, the premises that we grant him, whatever they may be) than the historian, and in doing so it deprives him at a stroke of all his standing room. To represent and illustrate the past, the actions of men, is the task of either writer, and the only difference that I can see is, in proportion as he succeeds, to the honor of the novelist, consisting as it does in his having more difficulty in collecting his evidence, which is so far from being purely literary. It seems to me to give him a great character, the fact that he has at once so much in common with the philosopher and the painter; this double analogy is a magnificent heritage.

4. It is of all this evidently that Mr. Besant is full when he insists upon the fact that fiction is one of the *fine* arts, deserving in its turn of all the honors and emoluments that have hitherto been reserved for the successful profession of music, poetry, painting, architecture. It is impossible to insist too much on so important a truth, and the place that Mr. Besant demands for the work of the novelist may be represented, a trifle less abstractly, by saying that he demands not only that it shall be reputed artistic, but that it shall be reputed very artistic indeed. It is excellent that he should have struck this note, for his doing so indicates that there was need of it, that his proposition may be to many people a novelty. One rubs one's eyes at the thought; but the rest of Mr. Besant's essay confirms the revelation. I suspect in truth that it would be possible to confirm it still further, and that one would not be far wrong in saying that in addition to the people to whom it has never occurred that a novel ought to be artistic, there are a great many others who, if this principle were urged upon them, would be filled with an indefinable mistrust. They would find it difficult to explain their repugnance, but it would operate strongly to put them on their guard. "Art," in our Protestant communities, where so many things have got so strangely twisted about, is supposed in certain circles to have some vaguely injurious effect upon those who make it an important consideration, who let it weigh in the balance. It is assumed to be opposed in some mysterious manner to morality, to amusement, to instruction. When it is embodied in the work of the painter (the sculptor is another affair!) you know what it is: it stands there before you, in the honesty of pink and green and a gilt frame; you can see the worst of it at a glance, and you can be on your guard. But when it is introduced into literature it becomes more insidious—there is danger of its hurting you before you know it. Literature should be either instructive or amusing, and there is in many minds an impression that these artistic preoccupations, the search for form, contribute to neither end, interfere indeed with both. They are too frivolous to be edifying, and too serious to be diverting; and they are moreover priggish and paradoxical and superfluous. That, I think, represents the manner in which the latent thought of many people who read

novels as an exercise in skipping would explain itself if it were to become articulate. They would argue, of course, that a novel ought to be "good," but they would interpret this term in a fashion of their own, which indeed would vary considerably from one critic to another. One would say that being good means representing virtuous and aspiring characters, placed in prominent positions; another would say that it depends on a "happy ending," on a distribution at the last of prizes, pensions, husbands, wives, babies, millions, appended paragraphs, and cheerful remarks. Another still would say that it means being full of incident and movement, so that we shall wish to jump ahead, to see who was the mysterious stranger, and if the stolen will was ever found, and shall not be distracted from this pleasure by any tiresome analysis or "description." But they would all agree that the "artistic" idea would spoil some of their fun. One would hold it accountable for all the description, another would see it revealed in the absence of sympathy. Its hostility to a happy ending would be evident, and it might even in some cases render any ending at all impossible. The "ending" of a novel is, for many persons, like that of a good dinner, a course of dessert and ices, and the artist in fiction is regarded as a sort of meddlesome doctor who forbids agreeable aftertastes. It is therefore true that this conception of Mr. Besant's of the novel as a superior form encounters not only a negative but a positive indifference. It matters little that as a work of art it should really be as little or as much of its essence to supply happy endings, sympathetic characters, and an objective tone, as if it were a work of mechanics: the association of ideas, however incongruous, might easily be too much for it if an eloquent voice were not sometimes raised to call attention to the fact that it is at once as free and as serious a branch of literature as any other.

5. Certainly this might sometimes be doubted in presence of the enormous number of works of fiction that appeal to the credulity of our generation, for it might easily seem that there could be no great character in a commodity so quickly and easily produced. It must be admitted that good novels are much compromised by bad ones, and that the field at large suffers discredit from overcrowding. I think, however, that this injury is only superficial, and that the superabundance of written fiction proves nothing against the principle itself. It has been vulgarized, like all other kinds of literature, like everything else today, and it has proved more than some kinds accessible to vulgarization. But there is as much difference as there ever was between a good novel and a bad one: the bad is swept with all the daubed canvases and spoiled marble into some unvisited limbo, or infinite rubbish-yard beneath the back-windows of the world, and the good subsists and emits its light and stimulates our desire for perfection. As I shall take the liberty of making but a single criticism of Mr. Besant, whose tone is so full of the love of his art, I may as well have done with it at once. He seems to me to mistake in attempting to say so definitely beforehand what sort of an affair the good

novel will be. To indicate the danger of such an error as that has been the purpose of these few pages; to suggest that certain traditions on the subject, applied *a priori*, have already had much to answer for, and that the good health of an art which undertakes so immediately to reproduce life must demand that it be perfectly free. It lives upon exercise, and the very meaning of exercise is freedom. The only obligation to which in advance we may hold a novel, without incurring the accusation of being arbitrary, is that it be interesting. That general responsibility rests upon it, but it is the only one I can think of. The ways in which it is at liberty to accomplish this result (of interesting us) strike me as innumerable, and such as can only suffer from being marked out or fenced in by prescription. They are as various as the temperament of man, and they are successful in proportion as they reveal a particular mind, different from others. A novel is in its broadest definition a personal, a direct impression of life: that, to begin with, constitutes its value, which is greater or less according to the intensity of the impression. But there will be no intensity at all, and therefore no value, unless there is freedom to feel and say. The tracing of a line to be followed, of a tone to be taken, of a form to be filled out, is a limitation of that freedom and a suppression of the very thing that we are most curious about. The form, it seems to me, is to be appreciated after the fact: then the author's choice has been made, his standard has been indicated; then we can follow lines and directions and compare tones and resemblances. Then in a word we can enjoy one of the most charming of pleasures, we can estimate quality, we can apply the test of execution. The execution belongs to the author alone; it is what is most personal to him, and we measure him by that. The advantage, the luxury, as well as the torment and responsibility of the novelist, is that there is no limit to what he may attempt as an executant—no limit to his possible experiments, efforts, discoveries, successes. Here it is especially that he works, step by step, like his brother of the brush, of whom we may always say that he has painted his picture in a manner best known to himself. His manner is his secret, not necessarily a jealous one. He cannot disclose it as a general thing if he would; he would be at a loss to teach it to others. I say this with a due recollection of having insisted on the community of method of the artist who paints a picture and the artist who writes a novel. The painter *is* able to teach the rudiments of his practice, and it is possible, from the study of good work (granted the aptitude), both to learn how to paint and to learn how to write. Yet it remains true, without injury to the *rapprochement*, that the literary artist would be obliged to say to his pupil much more than the other, "Ah, well, you must do it as you can!" It is a question of degree, a matter of delicacy. If there are exact sciences, there are also exact arts, and the grammar of painting is so much more definite that it makes the difference.

6. I ought to add, however, that if Mr. Besant says at the beginning of his essay that the "laws of fiction may be laid down and taught with as

much precision and exactness as the laws of harmony, perspective, and proportion," he mitigates what might appear to be an extravagance by applying his remark to "general" laws, and by expressing most of these rules in a manner with which it would certainly be unaccommodating to disagree. That the novelist must write from his experience, that his "characters must be real and such as might be met with in actual life"; that "a young lady brought up in a quiet country village should avoid descriptions of garrison life," and "a writer whose friends and personal experiences belong to the lower middle-class should carefully avoid introducing his characters into society"; that one should enter one's notes in a common-place book; that one's figures should be clear in outline; that making them clear by some trick of speech or of carriage is a bad method, and "describing them at length" is a worse one; that English Fiction should have a "conscious moral purpose"; that "it is almost impossible to estimate too highly the value of careful workmanship—that is, of style"; that "the most important point of all is the story," that "the story is everything": these are principles with most of which it is surely impossible not to sympathize. That remark about the lower middle-class writer and his knowing his place is perhaps rather chilling; but for the rest I should find it difficult to dissent from any one of these recommendations. At the same time, I should find it difficult positively to assent to them, with the exception, perhaps, of the injunction as to entering one's notes in a common-place book. They scarcely seem to me to have the quality that Mr. Besant attributes to the rules of the novelist—the "precision and exactness" of "the laws of harmony, perspective, and proportion." They are suggestive, they are even inspiring, but they are not exact, though they are doubtless as much so as the case admits of: which is a proof of that liberty of interpretation for which I just contended. For the value of these different injunctions—so beautiful and so vague—is wholly in the meaning one attaches to them. The characters, the situation, which strike one as real will be those that touch and interest one most, but the measure of reality is very difficult to fix. The reality of Don Quixote or of Mr. Micawber is a very delicate shade; it is a reality so colored by the author's vision that, vivid as it may be, one would hesitate to propose it as a model: one would expose one's self to some very embarrassing questions on the part of a pupil. It goes without saying that you will not write a good novel unless you possess the sense of reality; but it will be difficult to give you a recipe for calling that sense into being. Humanity is immense, and reality has a myriad forms; the most one can affirm is that some of the flowers of fiction have the odor of it, and others have not; as for telling you in advance how your nosegay should be composed, that is another affair. It is equally excellent and inconclusive to say that one must write from experience; to our supposititious aspirant such a declaration might savor of mockery. What kind of experience is intended, and where does it begin and end? Experience is never limited, and it is never complete; it is an immense sensibility, a kind of huge spider-web of the finest silken threads suspended in the chamber of consciousness, and catching every air-borne particle in its tissue. It is the very atmosphere of the mind; and when the mind is imaginative—much more when it happens to be that of a man of genius—it takes to itself the faintest hints of life, it converts the very pulses of the air into revelations. The young lady living in a village has only to be a damsel upon whom nothing is lost to make it quite unfair (as it seems to me) to declare to her that she shall have nothing to say about the military. Greater miracles have been seen than that, imagination assisting, she should speak the truth about some of these gentlemen. I remember an English novelist, a woman of genius, telling me that she was much commended for the impression she had managed to give in one of her tales of the nature and way of life of the French Protestant youth. She had been asked where she learned so much about this recondite being, she had been congratulated on her peculiar opportunities. These opportunities consisted in her having once, in Paris, as she ascended a staircase, passed an open door where, in the household of a *pasteur*, some of the young Protestants were seated at table round a finished meal. The glimpse made a picture; it lasted only a moment, but that moment was experience. She had got her direct personal impression, and she turned out her type. She knew what youth was, and what Protestantism; she also had the advantage of having seen what it was to be French, so that she converted these ideas into a concrete image and produced a reality. Above all, however, she was blessed with the faculty which when you give it an inch it takes an ell, and which for the artist is a much greater source of strength than any accident of residence or of place in the social scale. The power to guess the unseen from the seen, to trace the implication of things, to judge the whole piece by the pattern, the condition of feeling life in general so completely that you are well on your way to knowing any particular corner of it—this cluster of gifts may almost be said to constitute experience, and they occur in country and in town, and in the most differing stages of education. If experience consists of impressions, it may be said that impressions *are* experience, just as (have we not seen it?) they are the very air we breathe. Therefore, if I should certainly say to a novice, "Write from experience and experience only," I should feel that this was rather a tantalizing monition if I were not careful immediately to add, "Try to be one of the people on whom nothing is lost!"

7. I am far from intending by this to minimize the importance of exactness —of truth of detail. One can speak best from one's own taste, and I may therefore venture to say that the air of reality (solidity of specification) seems to me to be the supreme virtue of a novel—the merit on which all its other merits (including that conscious moral purpose of which Mr. Besant speaks) helplessly and submissively depend. If it be not there they are all as nothing, and if these be there, they owe their effect to the success with which the author

has produced the illusion of life. The cultivation of this success, the study of this exquisite process, form, to my taste, the beginning and the end of the art of the novelist. They are his inspiration, his despair, his reward, his torment, his delight. It is here in very truth that he competes with life; it is here that he competes with his brother the painter in *his* attempt to render the look of things, the look that conveys their meaning, to catch the color, the relief, the expression, the surface, the substance of the human spectacle. It is in regard to this that Mr. Besant is well inspired when he bids him take notes. He cannot possibly take too many, he cannot possibly take enough. All life solicits him, and to "render" the simplest surface, to produce the most momentary illusion, is a very complicated business. His case would be easier, and the rule would be more exact, if Mr. Besant had been able to tell him what notes to take. But this, I fear, he can never learn in any manual; it is the business of his life. He has to take a great many in order to select a few, he has to work them up as he can, and even the guides and philosophers who might have most to say to him must leave him alone when it comes to the application of precepts, as we leave the painter in communion with his palette. That his characters "must be clear in outline," as Mr. Besant says —he feels that down to his boots; but how he shall make them so is a secret between his good angel and himself. It would be absurdly simple if he could be taught that a great deal of "description" would make them so, or that on the contrary the absence of description and the cultivation of dialogue, or the absence of dialogue and the multiplication of "incident," would rescue him from his difficulties. Nothing, for instance, is more possible than that he be of a turn of mind for which this odd, literal opposition of description and dialogue, incident and description, has little meaning and light. People often talk of these things as if they had a kind of internecine distinctness, instead of melting into each other at every breath, and being intimately associated parts of one general effort of expression. I cannot imagine composition existing in a series of blocks, nor conceive, in any novel worth discussing at all, of a passage of description that is not in its intention narrative, a passage of dialogue that is not in its intention descriptive, a touch of truth of any sort that does not partake of the nature of incident, or an incident that derives its interest from any other source than the general and only source of the success of a work of art—that of being illustrative. A novel is a living thing, all one and continuous, like any other organism, and in proportion as it lives will it be found, I think, that in each of the parts there is sonething of each of the other parts. The critic who over the close texture of a finished work shall pretend to trace a geography of items will mark some frontiers as artificial, I fear, as any that have been known to history. There is an old-fashioned distinction between the novel of character and the novel of incident which must have cost many a smile to the intending fabulist who was keen about his work. It appears to me as little to the point

as the equally celebrated distinction between the novel and the romance—
to answer as little to any reality. There are bad novels and good novels, as
there are bad pictures and good pictures; but that is the only distinction in
which I see any meaning, and I can as little imagine speaking of a novel of
character as I can imagine speaking of a picture of character. When one says
picture one says of character, when one says novel one says of incident, and
the terms may be transposed at will. What is character but the determination
of incident? What is incident but the illustration of character? What is either
a picture or a novel that is *not* of character? What else do we seek in it and
find in it? It is an incident for a woman to stand up with her hand resting on
a table and look out at you in a certain way; or if it be not an incident I think
it will be hard to say what it is. At the same time it is an expression of
character. If you say you don't see it (character in *that—allons donc!*), this
is exactly what the artist who has reasons of his own for thinking he *does*
see it undertakes to show you. When a young man makes up his mind that
he has not faith enough after all to enter the church as he intended, that is an
incident, though you may not hurry to the end of the chapter to see whether
perhaps he doesn't change once more. I do not say that these are extraordinary
or startling incidents. I do not pretend to estimate the degree of interest
proceeding from them, for this will depend upon the skill of the painter. It
sounds almost puerile to say that some incidents are intrinsically much more
important than others, and I need not take this precaution after having pro-
fessed my sympathy for the major ones in remarking that the only classi-
fication of the novel that I can understand is into that which has life and that
which has it not.

8. The novel and the romance, the novel of incident and that of character—
these clumsy separations appear to me to have been made by critics and readers
for their own convenience, and to help them out of some of their occasional
queer predicaments, but to have little reality or interest for the producer,
from whose point of view it is of course that we are attempting to consider
the art of fiction. The case is the same with another shadowy category which
Mr. Besant apparently is disposed to set up—that of the "modern English
novel"; unless indeed it be that in this matter he has fallen into an accidental
confusion of standpoints. It is not quite clear whether he intends the remarks
in which he alludes to it to be didactic or historical. It is as difficult to suppose a person intending to write a modern English as to suppose him
writing an ancient English novel : that is a label which begs the question.
One writes the novel, one paints the picture, of one's language and of one's
time, and calling it modern English will not, alas! make the difficult task
any easier. No more, unfortunately, will calling this or that work of one's
fellow-artist a romance—unless it be, of course, simply for the pleasantness
of the thing, as for instance when Hawthorne gave this heading to his story
of *Blithedale*. The French, who have brought the theory of fiction to

remarkable completeness, have but one name for the novel, and have not attempted smaller things in it, that I can see, for that. I can think of no obligation to which the "romancer" would not be held equally with the novelist; the standard of execution is equally high for each. Of course it is of execution that we are talking—that being the only point of a novel that is open to contention. This is perhaps too often lost sight of, only to produce interminable confusions and cross-purposes. We must grant the artist his subject, his idea, his *donnée:* our criticism is applied only to what he makes of it. Naturally I do not mean that we are bound to like it or find it interesting: in case we do not our course is perfectly simple—to let it alone. We may believe that of a certain idea even the most sincere novelist can make nothing at all, and the event may perfectly justify our belief; but the failure will have been a failure to execute, and it is in the execution that the fatal weakness is recorded. If we pretend to respect the artist at all, we must allow him his freedom of choice, in the face, in particular cases, of innumerable presumptions that the choice will not fructify. Art derives a considerable part of its beneficial exercise from flying in the face of presumptions, and some of the most interesting experiments of which it is capable are hidden in the bosom of common things. Gustave Flaubert has written a story [*Un Coeur Simple*] about the devotion of a servant-girl to a parrot, and the production, highly finished as it is, cannot on the whole be called a success. We are perfectly free to find it flat, but I think it might have been interesting; and I, for my part, am extremely glad he should have written it; it is a contribution to our knowledge of what can be done—or what cannot. Ivan Turgenev has written a tale about a deaf and dumb serf and a lap-dog [*Mumu*], and the thing is touching, loving, a little masterpiece. He struck the note of life where Gustave Flaubert missed it—he flew in the face of a presumption and achieved a victory.

9. Nothing, of course, will ever take the place of the good old fashion of "liking" a work of art or not liking it: the most improved criticism will not abolish that primitive, that ultimate test. I mention this to guard myself from the accusation of intimating that the idea, the subject, of a novel or a picture, does not matter. It matters, to my sense, in the highest degree, and if I might put up a prayer it would be that artists should select none but the richest. Some, as I have already hastened to admit, are much more remunerative than others, and it would be a world happily arranged in which persons intending to treat them should be exempt from confusions and mistakes. This fortunate condition will arrive only, I fear, on the same day that critics become purged from error. Meanwhile, I repeat, we do not judge the artist with fairness unless we say to him,

"Oh, I grant you your starting-point, because if I did not I should seem to prescribe to you, and heaven forbid I should take that responsibility. If I pretend to tell you what you must not take, you will call upon me to tell you then what you must take; in which case I shall be prettily caught. Moreover, it isn't till I have accepted your data that I can begin to measure you. I have the standard, the pitch; I have no right to tamper with your flute and then criticize your music. Of course I may not care for your idea at all; I may think it silly, or stale, or unclean; in which case I wash my hands of you altogether. I may content myself with believing that you will not have succeeded in being interesting, but I shall, of course, not attempt to demonstrate it, and you will be as indifferent to me as I am to you. I needn't remind you that there are all sorts of tastes: who can know it better? Some people, for excellent reasons, don't like to read about carpenters; others, for reasons even better, don't like to read about courtesans. Many object to Americans. Others (I believe they are mainly editors and publishers) won't look at Italians. Some readers don't like quiet subjects; other don't like bustling ones. Some enjoy a complete illusion, others the consciousness of large concessions. They choose their novels accordingly, and if they don't care about your idea they won't, *a fortiori*, care about your treatment."

10. So that it comes back very quickly, as I have said, to the liking: in spite of M. Zola, who reasons less powerfully than he represents, and who will not reconcile himself to this absoluteness of taste, thinking that there are certain things that people ought to like, and that they can be made to like. I am quite at a loss to imagine anything (at any rate in this matter of fiction) that people *ought* to like or to dislike. Selection will be sure to take care of itself, for it has a constant motive behind it. That motive is simply experience. As people feel life, so they will feel the art that is most closely related to it. This closeness of relation is what we should never forget in talking of the effort of the novel. Many people speak of it as a factitious, artificial form, a product of ingenuity, the business of which is to alter and arrange the things that surround us, to translate them into conventional, traditional moulds. This, however, is a view of the matter which carries us but a very short way, condemns the art to an eternal repetition of a few familiar *clichés*, cuts short its development, and leads us straight up to a dead wall. Catching the very note and trick, the strange irregular rhythm of life, that is the attempt whose strenuous force keeps Fiction upon her feet. In proportion as in what she offers us we see life *without* rearrangement do we feel that we are touching the truth; in proportion as we see it *with* rearrangement do we feel that we are being put off with a substitute, a compromise and convention. It is not uncommon to hear an extraordinary assurance of remark in regard to this matter of rearranging, which is often spoken of as if it were the last word of art. Mr. Besant seems to me in danger of falling into the great error with his rather unguarded talk about "selection." Art is essentially selection, but it is a selection whose main care is to be typical, to be inclusive. For many people art means rose-colored window-panes, and selection means picking a

bouquet for Mrs. Grundy. They will tell you glibly that artistic considerations have nothing to do with the disagreeable, with the ugly; they will rattle off shallow commonplaces about the province of art and the limits of art till you are moved to some wonder in return as to the province and the limits of ignorance. It appears to me that no one can ever have made a seriously artistic attempt without becoming conscious of an immense increase—a kind of revelation—of freedom. One perceives in that case—by the light of a heavenly ray—that the province of art is all life, all feeling, all observation, all vision. As Mr. Besant so justly intimates, it is all experience. That is a sufficient answer to those who maintain that it must not touch the sad things of life, who stick into its divine unconscious bosom little prohibitory inscriptions on the end of sticks, such as we see in public gardens—"It is forbidden to walk on the grass; it is forbidden to touch the flowers; it is not allowed to introduce dogs or to remain after dark; it is requested to keep to the right." The young aspirant in the line of fiction whom we continue to imagine will do nothing without taste, for in that case his freedom would be of little use to him; but the first advantage of his taste will be to reveal to him the absurdity of the little sticks and tickets. If he have taste, I must add, of course he will have ingenuity, and my disrespectful reference to that quality just now was not meant to imply that it is useless in fiction. But it is only a secondary aid; the first is a capacity for receiving straight impressions.

11. Mr. Besant has some remarks on the question of "the story" which I shall not attempt to criticize, though they seem to me to contain a singular ambiguity, because I do not think I understand them. I cannot see what is meant by talking as if there were a part of a novel which is the story and part of it which for mystical reasons is not—unless indeed the distinction be made in a sense in which it is difficult to suppose that any one should attempt to convey anything. "The story," if it represents anything, represents the subject, the idea, the *donnée* of the novel; and there is surely no "school"— Mr. Besant speaks of a school—which urges that a novel should be all treatment and no subject. There must assuredly be something to treat; every school is intimately conscious of that. This sense of the story being the idea, the starting-point, of the novel, is the only one that I see in which it can be spoken of as something different from its organic whole; and since in proportion as the work is successful the idea permeates and penetrates it, informs and animates it, so that every word and every punctuation-point contribute directly to the expression, in that proportion do we lose our sense of the story being a blade which may be drawn more or less out of its sheath. The story and the novel, the idea and the form, are the needle and thread, and I never heard of a guild of tailors who recommended the use of the thread without the needle, or the needle without the thread. Mr. Besant is not the only critic who may be observed to have spoken as if there were certain things in life which constitute stories, and certain others which do not. I find the same odd

implication in an entertaining article in the *Pall Mall Gazette*, devoted, as it happens, to Mr. Besant's lecture. "The story is the thing!" says this graceful writer, as if with a tone of opposition to some other idea. I should think it was, as every painter who, as the time for "sending in" his picture looms in the distance, finds himself still in quest of a subject—as every belated artist not fixed about his theme will heartily agree. There are some subjects which speak to us and others which do not, but he would be a clever man who should undertake to give a rule—an *index expurgatorius*—by which the story and the no-story should be known apart. It is impossible (to me at least) to imagine any such rule which shall not be altogether arbitrary. The writer in the *Pall Mall* opposes the delightful (as I suppose) novel of *Margot la Balafrée* to certain tales in which "Bostonian nymphs" appear to have "rejected English dukes for psychological reasons" [see Henry James's own *An International Episode* (1879)]. I am not acquainted with the romance just designated, and can scarcely forgive the *Pall Mall* critic for not mentioning the name of the author, but the title appears to refer to a lady who may have received a scar in some heroic adventure. I am inconsolable at not being acquainted with this episode, but am utterly at a loss to see why it is a story when the rejection (or acceptance) of a duke is not, and why a reason, psychological or other, is not a subject when a cicatrix is. They are all particles of the multitudinous life with which the novel deals, and surely no dogma which pretends to make it lawful to touch the one and unlawful to touch the other will stand for a moment on its feet. It is the special picture that must stand or fall, according as it seem to possess truth or to lack it. Mr. Besant does not, to my sense, light up the subject by intimating that a story must, under penalty of not being a story, consist of "adventures." Why of adventures more than of green spectacles? He mentions a category of impossible things, and among them he places "fiction without adventure." Why without adventure, more than without matrimony, or celibacy, or parturition, or cholera, or hydropathy, or Jansenism? This seems to me to bring the novel back to the hapless little *rôle* of being an artificial, ingenious thing—bring it down from its large, free character of an immense and exquisite correspondence with life. And what *is* adventure, when it comes to that, and by what sign is the listening pupil to recognize it? It is an adventure—an immense one—for me to write this little article; and for a Bostonian nymph to reject an English duke is an adventure only less stirring, I should say, than for an English duke to be rejected by a Bostonian nymph. I see dramas within dramas in that, and innumerable points of view. A psychological reason is, to my imagination, an object adorably pictorial; to catch the tint of its complexion—I feel as if that idea might inspire one to Titianesque efforts. There are few things more exciting to me, in short, than a psychological reason, and yet, I protest, the novel seems to me the most magnificent form of art. I have just been reading, at the same time, the delightful story of *Treasure Island*, by Mr. Robert Louis Stevenson and, in a manner less consecutive, the last tale from M. Edmond de Goncourt, which is entitled *Chérie*. One of these works treats of murders, mysteries, islands of dreadful renown, hairbreadth escapes, miraculous coincidences and buried doubloons. The other treats of a little French girl who lived in a fine house in Paris, and died of wounded sensibility because no one would marry her. I call *Treasure Island* delightful, because it appears to me to have succeeded wonderfully in what it attempts; and I venture to bestow no epithet upon *Chérie*, which strikes me as having failed deplorably in what it attempts—that is in tracing the development of the moral consciousness of a child. But one of these productions strikes me as exactly as much of a novel as the other, and as having a "story" quite as much. The moral consciousness of a child is as much a part of life as the islands of the Spanish Main, and the one sort of geography seems to me to have those "surprises" of which Mr. Besant speaks quite as much as the other. For myself (since it comes back in the last resort, as I say, to the preference of the individual), the picture of the child's experience has the advantage that I can at successive steps (an immense luxury, near to the "sensual pleasure" of which Mr. Besant's critic in the *Pall Mall* speaks) say Yes or No, as it may be, to what the artist puts before me. I have been a child in fact, but I have been on a quest for a buried treasure only in supposition, and it is a simple accident that with M. de Goncourt I should have for the most part to say No. With George Eliot, when she painted that country with a far other intelligence, I always said Yes.

12. The most interesting part of Mr. Besant's lecture is unfortunately the briefest passage—his very cursory allusion to the "conscious moral purpose" of the novel. Here again it is not very clear whether he be recording a fact or laying down a principle; it is a great pity that in the latter case he should not have developed his idea. This branch of the subject is of immense importance, and Mr. Besant's few words point to considerations of the widest reach, not to be lightly disposed of. He will have treated the art of fiction but superficially who is not prepared to go every inch of the way that these considerations will carry him. It is for this reason that at the beginning of these remarks I was careful to notify the reader that my reflections on so large a theme have no pretension to be exhaustive. Like Mr. Besant, I have left the question of the morality of the novel till the last, and at the last I find I have used up my space. It is a question surrounded with difficulties, as witness the very first that meets us, in the form of a definite question, on the threshold. Vagueness, in such a discussion, is fatal, and what is the meaning of your morality and your conscious moral purpose? Will you not define your terms and explain how (a novel being a picture) a picture can be either moral or immoral? You wish to paint a moral picture or carve a moral statue: will you not tell us how you would set about it? We are discussing the Art of Fiction; questions of art are questions (in the widest sense) of execution;

questions of morality are quite another affair, and will you not let us see how it is that you find it so easy to mix them up? These things are so clear to Mr. Besant that he has deduced from them a law which he sees embodied in English Fiction, and which is "a truly admirable thing and a great cause for congratulation." It is a great cause for congratulation indeed when such thorny problems become as smooth as silk. I may add that in so far as Mr. Besant perceives that in point of fact English Fiction has addressed itself preponderantly to these delicate questions he will appear to many people to have made a vain discovery. They will have been positively struck, on the contrary, with the moral timidity of the usual English novelist; with his (or with her) aversion to face the difficulties with which on every side the treatment of reality bristles. He is apt to be extremely shy (whereas the picture that Mr. Besant draws is a picture of boldness), and the sign of his work, for the most part, is a cautious silence on certain subjects. In the English novel (by which of course I mean the American as well), more than in any other, there is a traditional difference between that which people know and that which they agree to admit that they know, that which they see and that which they speak of, that which they feel to be a part of life and that which they allow to enter into literature. There is the great difference, in short, between what they talk of in conversation and what they talk of in print. The essence of moral energy is to survey the whole field, and I should directly reverse Mr. Besant's remark and say not that the English novel has a purpose, but that it has a diffidence. To what degree a purpose in a work of art is a source of corruption I shall not attempt to inquire; the one that seems to me least dangerous is the purpose of making a perfect work. As for our novel, I may say lastly on this score that as we find it in England today it strikes me as addressed in a large degree to "young people," and that this in itself constitutes a presumption that it will be rather shy. There are certain things which it is generally agreed not to discuss, not even to mention, before young people. That is very well, but the absence of discussion is not a symptom of the moral passion. The purpose of the English novel—"a truly admirable thing, and a great cause for congratulation"—strikes me therefore as rather negative.

13. There is one point at which the moral sense and the artistic sense lie very near together; that is in the light of the very obvious truth that the deepest quality of a work of art will always be the quality of the mind of the producer. In proportion as that intelligence is fine will the novel, the picture, the statue partake of the substance of beauty and truth. To be constituted of such elements is, to my vision, to have purpose enough. No good novel will ever proceed from a superficial mind; that seems to me an axiom which, for the artist in fiction, will cover all needful moral ground: If the youthful aspirant take it to heart it will illuminate for him many of the mysteries of "purpose." There are many other useful things that might be said to him,

superficial

but I have come to the end of my article, and can only touch them as I pass. The critic in the *Pall Mall Gazette*, whom I have already quoted, draws attention to the danger, in speaking of the art of fiction, of generalizing. The danger that he has in mind is rather, I imagine, that of particularizing, for there are some comprehensive remarks which, in addition to those embodied in Mr. Besant's suggestive lecture, might without fear of misleading him be addressed to the ingenuous student. I should remind him first of the magnificence of the form that is open to him, which offers to sight so few restrictions and such innumerable opportunities. The other arts, in comparison, appear confined and hampered; the various conditions under which they are exercised are so rigid and definite. But the only condition that I can think of attaching to the composition of the novel is, as I have already said, that it be sincere. This freedom is a splendid privilege, and the first lesson of the young novelist is to learn to be worthy of it.

14. "Enjoy it as it deserves," I should say to him; "take possession of it, explore it to its utmost extent, publish it, rejoice in it. All life belongs to you, and do not listen either to those who would shut you up into corners of it and tell you that it is only here and there that art inhabits, or to those who would persuade you that this heavenly messenger wings her way outside of life altogether, breathing a superfine air, and turning away her head from the truth of things. There is no impression of life, no manner of seeing it and feeling it, to which the plan of the novelist may not offer a place; you have only to remember that talents so dissimilar as those of Alexandre Dumas and Jane Austen, Charles Dickens and Gustave Flaubert have worked in this field with equal glory. Do not think too much about optimism and pessimism; try and catch the color of life itself. In France today we see a prodigious effort (that of Emile Zola, to whose solid and serious work no explorer of the capacity of the novel can allude without respect), we see an extraordinary effort vitiated by a spirit of pessimism on a narrow basis. M. Zola is magnificent, but he strikes an English reader as ignorant; he has an air of working in the dark; if he had as much light as energy, his results would be of the highest value. As for the aberrations of a shallow optimism, the ground (of English fiction especially) is strewn with their brittle particles as with broken glass. If you must indulge in conclusions, let them have the taste of a wide knowledge. Remember that your first duty is to be as complete as possible—to make as perfect a work. Be generous and delicate and pursue the prize."

Chapter II

THE WRITER AND HIS CULTURE

Throughout his career as a writer and critic, Henry James saw an intimate connection between an author and his culture. He wrote in 1899 in "The Future of the Novel": "The future of fiction is intimately bound up with the future of the society that produces and consumes it. In a society with a great and diffused literary sense the talent at play can only be a less negligible thing than in a society with a literary sense barely discernible. . . . A community addicted to reflection and fond of ideas will try experiments with the 'story' that will be left untried in a community mainly devoted to traveling and shooting, to pushing trade and playing football."

But aside from a society's overt literary sense, James found a close relationship between the nature and condition of a society and the fiction it produced. He wrote in 1888 ("Pierre Loti"): "An achievement in art or letters grows more interesting when we begin to perceive its connections" (see Chapter XVI, "Readers and Critics"). Again and again in his critical essays, James explored these connections, speculating on cause and effect. The most interesting case was his own, and his use of the American scene and society in his fiction. Throughout his career, James maintained that America presented a special problem to the imaginative writer in that its culture was thin, immature, simple, or monotonously uniform—in contrast with the cultural density and complexity of Europe, especially as it presented itself at an earlier period to the imaginative genius of a Balzac.

In making such a complaint James was joining a distinguished line of American writers, including James Fenimore Cooper and Nathaniel Hawthorne, who bemoaned the hard lot of the American novelist in search of material on what they took to be barren grounds. Whereas Cooper and Hawthorne delved deep into the mythic American past, James more frequently than not simply carried his Americans abroad. (It is of interest to note that a mid-twentieth century writer like Wright Morris, in A Bill of Rites, A Bill of Wrongs, A Bill of Goods *[1968], would come to grieve the loss of that very same "barren" material—raw material of the American frontier culture—as it has come to be replaced by the arid wastes of a contemporary homogenized culture of universal conformity. The irony revealed is that one age's barrenness is another's riches.)*

Just as a culture can impose or withhold subjects by providing or with-

45

holding the possibilities of certain kinds of experience, so too it may determine the boundaries of representation beyond which a writer dare not go. One area of experience—sex—was tabooed in the English and American novel, whereas it was acceptable in the French (see Chapter VII, "Sex: An Immense Omission").

The nature of a society's criticism made, James thought, a major difference to its literature. A superficial or heavy-handed criticism could not only harm, but could actually kill. He said in "Criticism" (1891; see Chapter XVI, "Readers and Critics"): "Literature lives essentially, in the sacred depths of its being, upon example, upon perfection wrought, . . . like other sensitive organisms, it is highly susceptible of demoralization, and . . . nothing is better calculated than irresponsible pedagogy to make it close its ears and lips. To be puerile and untutored about it is to deprive it of air and light, and the consequence of its keeping bad company is that it loses all heart."

James saw the work of fiction, from its conception to its end, as intimately bound to the culture out of which it developed and in which it discovered its fate. James's keen interest in national cultures was manifested not only in all his fictional work and criticism, but also in his travel pieces, and came to the fore in his influential volume of cultural analysis, The American Scene *(1907). All of these works taken together present a comprehensive view of James's complex concept of culture.*

1. *America and the grasping imagination*

(*Letters*, 1871, to Charles Eliot Norton)

Howells edits, and observes and produces—the latter in his own particular line with more and more perfection. His recent sketches in the *Atlantic*, collected into a volume, belong, I think, by the wonderous cunning of their manner, to very good literature. He seems to have resolved himself, however, [into] one who can write solely of what his fleshly eyes have seen; and for this reason I wish he were "located" where they would rest upon richer and fairer things than this immediate landscape. Looking about for myself, I conclude that the face of nature and civilization in this our country is to a certain point a very sufficient literary field. But it will yield its secrets only to a really *grasping* imagination. This I think Howells lacks. (Of course *I* don't!) To write well and worthily of American things one need even more than elsewhere to be a *master*. But unfortunately one is less! . . . I myself have been scribbling some little tales which in the course of time you will have a chance to read. To write a series of good little tales I deem ample work for a life-time. I dream that my life-time shall have done it. It's at least a relief to have arranged one's life-time. . . .

2. *Turgénieff's themes are all Russian*

("Ivan Turgénieff," 1874)

M. Turgénieff's themes are all Russian; here and there the scene of a tale is laid in another country, but the actors are genuine Muscovites. It is the Russian type of human nature that he depicts; this perplexes, fascinates, inspires him. His works savour strongly of his native soil, like those of all great novelists, and give one who has read them all a strange sense of having had a prolonged experience of Russia. We seem to have travelled there in dreams, to have dwelt there in another state of being. M. Turgénieff gives us a peculiar sense of being out of harmony with his native land—of his having what one may call a poet's quarrel with it. He loves the old, and he is unable to see where the new is drifting. American readers will peculiarly appreciate this state of mind; if they had a native novelist of a large pattern, it would probably be, in a degree, his own. Our author *feels* the Russian character intensely, and cherishes, in fancy, all its old manifestations—the unemancipated peasants, the ignorant, absolute, half-barbarous proprietors, the quaint provincial society, the local types and customs of every kind. But Russian society, like our own, is in process of formation, the Russian character is in solution, in a sea of change, and the modified, modernized Russian, with his old limitations and his new pretensions, is not, to an imagination fond of caressing the old, fixed contours, an especially grateful phenomenon. A satirist at all points, as we shall have occasion to say, M. Turgénieff is particularly unsparing of the new intellectual fashions prevailing among his countrymen. The express purpose of one of his novels, "Fathers and Sons," is to contrast them with the old; and in most of his recent works, notably "Smoke," they have been embodied in various grotesque figures.

3. *making do with small things*

("Howells's A Foregone Conclusion," 1875)

We have always thought Mr. Howells's, in spite of his Italian affiliations, a most characteristically American talent; or rather not in spite of them, but in a manner on account of them, for he takes Italy as no Italian surely ever took it—as your enterprising Yankee alone is at pains to take it. American literature is immature, but it has, in prose and verse alike, a savor of its own, and we have often thought that this might be a theme for various interesting reflections. If we undertook to make a few, we should find Mr. Howells a capital text. He reminds us how much our native-grown imaginative effort is a matter of details, of fine shades, of pale colors, a making of small things do great service. Civilization with us is monotonous, and in the way of contrasts, of salient points, of chiaroscuro, we have to take what we can get. We have to look for these things in fields where a less devoted glance would see little more than an arid blank, and, at the last, we manage to find them. All this refines and sharpens our perceptions, makes us in a literary way, on our own scale, very delicate and stimulates greatly our sense of proportion and form.

4. *art blooms only where the soil is deep*

(*Hawthorne*, 1879)

Hawthorne, on the one side, is so subtle and slender and unpretending, and the American world, on the other, is so vast and various and substantial, that it might seem to the author of *The Scarlet Letter* and the *Mosses from an Old Manse*, that we render him a poor service in contrasting his proportions with those of a great civilisation. But our author must accept the awkward as well as the graceful side of his fame; for he has the advantage of pointing a valuable moral. This moral is that the flower of art blooms only where the soil is deep, that it takes a great deal of history to produce a little literature, that it needs a complex social machinery to set a writer in motion. American civilisation has hitherto had other things to do than to produce flowers, and before giving birth to writers it has wisely occupied itself with providing something for them to write about. Three or four beautiful talents of trans-Atlantic growth are the sum of what the world usually recognises, and in this modest nosegay the genius of Hawthorne is admitted to have the rarest and sweetest fragrance.

5. *solitary workers vs. groups*

(*Hawthorne*, 1879)

The best things come, as a general thing, from the talents that are members of a group; every man works better when he has companions working in the same line, and yielding the stimulus of suggestion, comparison, emulation. Great things, of course, have been done by solitary workers; but they have usually been done with double the pains they would have cost if they had been produced in more genial circumstances. The solitary worker loses the profit of example and discussion; he is apt to make awkward experiments; he is in the nature of the case more or less of an empiric. The empiric may, as I say, be treated by the world as an expert; but the drawbacks and discom-

forts of empiricism remain to him, and are in fact increased by the suspicion
that is mingled with his gratitude, of a want in the public taste of a sense
of the proportions of things. Poor Hawthorne, beginning to write subtle
short tales at Salem, was empirical enough; he was one of, at most, some
dozen Americans who had taken up literature as a profession. The profession
in the United States is still very young, and of diminutive stature; but in the
year 1830 its head could hardly have been seen above-ground. It strikes the
observer of to-day that Hawthorne showed great courage in entering a field
in which the honours and emoluments were so scanty as the profits of authorship must have been at that time.

6. the absent things in American life

(Hawthorne, 1879)

It takes so many things, as Hawthorne must have felt later in life, when he
made the acquaintance of the denser, richer, warmer European spectacle—
it takes such an accumulation of history and custom, such a complexity of
manners and types, to form a fund of suggestion for a novelist. If Hawthorne
had been a young Englishman, or a young Frenchman of the same degree
of genius, the same cast of mind, the same habits, his consciousness of the
world around him would have been a very different affair; however obscure,
however reserved, his own personal life, his sense of the life of his fellow-
mortals would have been almost infinitely more various. The negative side
of the spectacle on which Hawthorne looked out, in his contemplative
saunterings and reveries, might, indeed, with a little ingenuity, be made
almost ludicrous; one might enumerate the items of high civilisation, as
it exists in other countries, which are absent from the texture of American
life, until it should become a wonder to know what was left. No State, in
the European sense of the word, and indeed barely a specific national name.
No sovereign, no court, no personal loyalty, no aristocracy, no church, no
clergy, no army, no diplomatic service, no country gentlemen, no palaces,
no castles, nor manors, nor old countryhouses, nor parsonages, nor thatched
cottages, nor ivied ruins; no cathedrals, nor abbeys, nor little Norman
churches; no great Universities nor public schools—no Oxford, nor Eton,
nor Harrow; no literature, no novels, no museums, no pictures, no political
society, no sporting class—no Epsom nor Ascot! Some such list as that might
be drawn up of the absent things in American life—especially in the American life of forty years ago, the effect of which, upon an English or a French
imagination, would probably, as a general thing, be appalling. The natural
remark, in the almost lurid light of such an indictment, would be that if

these things are left out, everything is left out. The American knows that a good deal remains; what it is that remains—that is his secret, his joke, as one may say. It would be cruel, in this terrible denudation, to deny him the consolation of his natural gift, that "American humour" of which of late years we have heard so much.

7. it takes an old civilization

(*Letters*, 1880, to W. D. Howells)

Your review of my book [*Hawthorne*] is very handsome and friendly and commands my liveliest gratitude. Of course your graceful strictures seem to yourself more valid that they do to me. The little book was a tolerably deliberate and meditated performance, and I should be prepared to do battle for most of the convictions expressed. It is quite true I use the word provincial too many times—I hated myself for't, even while I did it (just as I overdo the epithet "dusky.") But I don't at all agree with you in thinking that "if it is not provincial for an Englishman to be English, a Frenchman French, etc. so it is not provincial for an American to be American." So it is not provincial for a Russian, an Australian, a Portuguese, a Dane, a Laplander to savour of their respective countries: that would be where the argument would land you. I think it is extremely provincial for a Russian to be very Russian, a Portuguese very Portuguese; for the simple reason that certain national types are essentially and intrinsically provincial. I sympathize even less with your protest against the idea that it takes an old civilization to set a novelist in motion—a proposition that seems to me so true as to be a truism. It is on manners, customs, usages, habits, forms, upon all these things matured and established, that a novelist lives—they are the very stuff his work is made of; and in saying that in the absence of those "dreary and worn-out paraphernalia" which I enumerate as being wanting in American society, "we have simply the whole of human life left," you beg (to my sense) the question. I should say we had just so much less of it as these same "paraphernalia" represent, and I think they represent an enormous quantity of it. I shall feel refuted only when we have produced (setting the present high company —yourself and me—for obvious reasons apart) a gentleman who strikes me as a novelist—as belonging to the company of Balzac and Thackeray. Of course, in the absence of this godsend, it is but a harmless amusement that we should reason about it, and maintain that if right were right he should already be here. I will freely admit that such a genius will get on *only* by agreeing with your view of the case—to do something great he must feel as you feel about it. But then I doubt whether such a genius—a man of the faculty of

Balzac and Thackeray—*could* agree with you! When he does I will lie flat on my stomach and do him homage—in the very centre of the contributor's club, or on the threshold of the magazine, or in any public place you may appoint!

8. an American . . . must deal . . . with Europe

(*Notebooks*, 1881)

Here I am back in America, for instance, after six years of absence, and likely while here to see and learn a great deal that ought not to become mere waste material. Here I am, *da vero*, and here I am likely to be for the next five months. I am glad I have come—it was a wise thing to do. I needed to see again *les miens*, to revive my relations with them, and my sense of the consequences that these relations entail. Such relations, such consequences, are a part of one's life, and the best life, the most complete, is the one that takes full account of such things. One can only do this by seeing one's people from time to time, by being with them, by entering into their lives. Apart from this I hold it was not necessary I should come to this country. I am 37 [actually 38] years old, I have made my choice, and God knows that I have now no time to waste. My choice is the old world—my choice, my need, my life. There is no need for me today to argue about this; it is an inestimable blessing to me, and a rare good fortune, that the problem was settled long ago, and that I have now nothing to do but to act on the settlement.— My impressions here are exactly what I expected they would be, and I scarcely see the place, and feel the manners, the race, the tone of things, now that I am on the spot, more vividly than I did while I was still in Europe. My work lies there—and with this vast new world, *je n'ai que faire*. One can't do both—one must choose. No European writer is called upon to assume that terrible burden, and it seems hard that I should be. The burden is necessarily greater for an American—for he *must* deal, more or less, even if only by implication, with Europe; whereas no European is obliged to deal in the least with America. No one dreams of calling him less complete for not doing so. (I speak of course of people who do the sort of work that I do; not of economists, of social science people.) The painter of manners who neglects America is not thereby incomplete as yet; but a hundred years hence —fifty years hence perhaps—he will doubtless be accounted so. My impressions of America, however, I shall, after all, not write here. I don't need to write them (at least not *à propos* of Boston): I know too well that they are. In many ways they are extremely pleasant; but, Heaven forgive me! I feel as if my time were terribly wasted here!

9. the life of his time . . . reflected in his novels

("Anthony Trollope," 1883)

Trollope did not write for posterity; he wrote for the day, the moment; but these are just the writers whom posterity is apt to put into its pocket. So much of the life of his time is reflected in his novels that we must believe a part of the record will be saved; and the best parts of them are so sound and true and genial, that readers with an eye to that sort of entertainment will always be sure, in a certain proportion, to turn to them. Trollope will remain one of the most trustworthy, though not one of the most eloquent, of the writers who have helped the heart of man to know itself. The heart of man does not always desire this knowledge; it prefers sometimes to look at history in another way—to look at the manifestations, without troubling about the motives. There are two kinds of taste in the appreciation of imaginative literature: the taste for emotions of surprise, and the taste for emotions of recognition. It is the latter that Trollope gratifies, and he gratifies it the more that the medium of his own mind, through which we see what he shows us, gives a confident direction to our sympathy. His natural rightness and purity are so real that the good things he projects must be real. A race is fortunate when it has a good deal of the sort of imagination—of imaginative feeling—that had fallen to the share of Anthony Trollope; and in this possession our English race is not poor.

10. a big Anglo-Saxon total

(Letters, 1888, to William James)

It is always a great misfortune, I think, when one has reached a certain age, that if one is living in a country not one's own and one is of anything of an ironic or critical disposition, one mistakes the inevitable reflections and criticisms that one makes, more and more as one grows older, upon life and human nature etc., for a judgment of that particular country, its natives, peculiarities, etc., to which, really, one has grown exceedingly accustomed. For myself, at any rate, I am deadly weary of the whole "international" state of mind—so that I *ache*, at times, with fatique at the way it is constantly forced upon me as a sort of virtue or obligation. I can't look at the English-American world, or feel about them, any more, save as a big Anglo-Saxon total, destined to such an amount of melting together that an insistence on their differences becomes more and more idle and pedantic; and that melting together will come the faster the more one takes it for granted and treats the life of the two countries as continuous or more or less convertible, or at any rate as simply different chapters of the same general subject. Literature, fiction in particular, affords a magnificent arm for such taking for granted, and one may so do an excellent work with it. I have not the least hesitation in saying that I aspire to write in such a way that it would be impossible to an outsider to say whether I am at a given moment an American writing about England or an Englishman writing about America (dealing as I do with both countries,) and so far from being ashamed of such an ambiguity I should be exceedingly proud of it, for it would be highly civilized.

11. the Western imagination

("American Letter," April 9, 1898)

As the novel in America multiplies, it will seek more room, I seem to foresee, by coming for inspiration to Europe; reversing in this manner, on another plane, oddly enough, a great historical fact. Just exactly for room these three centuries Europe has been crossing the ocean Westward. We may yet therefore find it sufficiently curious to see the Western imagination, so planted, come back. This imagination will find for a long time, to my sense —it will find doubtless always—its most interesting business in staying where it has grown; but if there is to be a great deal of it, it must obviously follow the fashion of other matters, seek all adventures and take all chances. Fiction as yet in the United States strikes me, none the less, as most curious when most confined and most local; this is so much the case that when it is even abjectly passive to surrounding conditions I find it capable of yielding an interest that almost makes me dread undue enlargement.

12. "business" plays a part in the United States

("American Letter," March 26, 1898)

I cannot but think that the American novel has in a special, far-reaching direction to sail much closer to the wind. "Business" plays a part in the United States that other interests dispute much less showily than they some-times dispute it in the life of European countries; in consequence of which the typical American figure is above all that "business man" whom the novelist and the dramatist have scarce yet seriously touched, whose song has still to be sung and his picture still to be painted. He is often an obscure, but not less often an epic, hero, seamed all over with the wounds of the market and the dangers of the field, launched into action and passion by the immensity and complexity of the general struggle, a boundless ferocity of battle—driven above all by the extraordinary, the unique relation in which he for the most part stands to the life of his lawful, his immitigable womankind, the wives and daughters who float, who splash on the surface and ride the waves, his terrific link with civilization, his social substitutes and representatives, while, like a diver for shipwrecked treasure, he gasps in the depths and breathes through an airtube.

This relation, even taken alone, contains elements that strike me as only yearning for their interpreter—elements, moreover, that would present the further merit of melting into the huge neighbouring province of the special situation of women in an order of things where to be a women at all—certainly to be a young one—constitutes in itself a social position. The difficulty, doubtless, is that the world of affairs, as affairs are understood in the panting cities, though around us all the while, before us, behind us, beside us, and under out feet, is as special and occult a one to the outsider as the world, say, of Arctic exploration—as impenetrable save as a result of special training. Those who know it are not the men to paint it; those who might attempt it are not the men who know it. The most energetic attempt at portrayal that we have anywhere had—L'Argent, of Emile Zola—is precisely a warning of the difference between false and true initiation. The subject there, though so richly imagined, is all too mechanically, if prodigiously, "got up." Meanwhile, accordingly, the American "business man" remains, thanks to the length and strength of the wires that move him, the magnificent theme en disponibilité. The romance of fact, indeed, has touched him in a way that quite puts to shame the romance of fiction. It gives his measure for purposes of art that it was he, essentially, who embarked in the great war of 1861-65, and who, carrying it on in the North to a triumphant conclusion, went back, since business was his standpoint, to his very "own" with an undimmed capacity to mind it. When, in imagination, you give the type, as it exists to-day, the benefit of its great double lustre—that of these recorded antecedents and that of its preoccupied, systematic and magnanimous abasement before the other sex—you will easily feel your sense of what may be done with its overflow.

To glance at that is, at the point to which the English-speaking world has brought the matter, to remember by the same stroke that if there be no virtue in any forecast of the prospect of letters, any sounding of their deeps and shallows that fails to take account of the almost predominant hand now exercised about them by women, the precaution is doubly needful in respect to the American situation. Whether the extraordinary dimensions of the public be a promise or a threat, nothing is more unmistakable than the sex of some of the largest masses. The longest lines are feminine—feminine, it may almost be said, the principal front. Both as readers and as writers on the other side of the Atlantic women have, in fine, "arrived" in numbers not equalled even in England, and they have succeeded in giving the pitch and marking the limits more completely than elsewhere. The public taste, as our fathers used to say, has become so largely *their* taste, their tone, their experiment, that nothing is at last more apparent than that the public cares little for anything that they cannot do. And what, after all, may the very finest opportunity of American literature be but just to show that they can do what the peoples will have ended by regarding as everything? The settlement of such a question, the ups and downs of such a process surely more than justify that sense of sport, in this direction, that I have spoken of as the privilege of the vigilant critic.

13. the acute sense of "Europe" . . . of the American mind

("The Story-Teller at Large: Mr. Henry Harland," 1898)

We receive now and then an impression that seems to hint at the advent of a time for looking more closely into the old notion that, to have a quality of his own, a writer must needs draw his sap from the soil of his origin. The great writers of the world have, as a general thing, struck us so as fed by their native air and furnished forth with things near and dear to them, that an author without a country would have come long ago—had any one ever presumed to imagine him—to be a figure as formless as an author without a pen, a publisher or a subject. Such would have been especially, to the inner vision, and for the very best reasons, the deep incongruity of the novelist at large. We are ridden by the influence of types established, and as the novelist is essentially a painter we assign him to his climate and circumstances as confidently as we assign Velasquez and Gainsborough to their schools. Does he not paint the things he knows? and are not the things he knows—knows best, of course—just the things for which he has the warrant of the local, the national consciousness? We settle the question easily—have settled it, that is, once for all; nothing being easier than to appeal for proof, with a fond and loyal glance, to Dickens, to Scott, to Balzac, to Hawthorne, respectively so English, so Scotch, so French, so American, particularly in the matter of subject, to which part of the business an analysis not prone to sin by excess of penetration has mainly found itself confined.

But if our analysis limps along as it may, the elements of the matter and the field of criticism so change and so extend themselves that an increase of refreshment will practically perhaps not be denied us even by the pace obtained. If it was perfectly true earlier in the century and in a larger world—I speak of the globe itself—that he was apt to paint best who painted nearest home, the case may well be, according to some symptoms, in course of modification. Who shall say, at the rate things are going, what is to be "near" home in the future and what is to be far from it? London, in the time of Fenimore Cooper, was fearfully—or perhaps only fortunately—far from Chicago, and Paris stood to London in a relation almost equally awkward for an Easter run, though singularly favourable, on either side, for concentration. The forces that are changing all this need scarce be mentioned at a moment when each day's breakfast-table—if the morning paper be part of its furniture—fairly bristles with revelations of them. The globe is fast shrinking, for the imagination, to the size of an orange that can be played with; the hurry to and fro over its surface is that of ants when you turn up a stone and there are times when we feel as if, as regards his habitat—and especially as regards *hers*, for women wander as they have never wandered—almost everyone must have changed place, and changed language, with everyone else. The ancient local concentration that was so involuntary in Dickens and Balzac is less and less a matter of course; and the period is calculably near when successfully to emulate it will figure to the critical eye as a rare and possibly beautiful *tour de force*.

The prospect, surely, therefore, is already interesting, and while it widens and the marks of it multiply we may watch the omens and wonder if they have a lesson for us. I find myself much prompted to some such speculation by Mr. Henry Harland's new volume of *Comedies and Errors;* though I confess that in reading into the influences behind it the idea of dispatriation I take a liberty for which, on its face, it opens no door. To speak of a writer as detached, one must at least know what he is detached from, and in this collection of curiously ingenious prose pieces there is not a single clear sound of the fundamental, the native note, not the tip of a finger held out indeed to any easy classifying. This very fact in itself perhaps constitutes the main scrap of evidence on behalf of a postulate of that particular set of circumstances—those of the trans-atlantic setting—that lends itself to being most unceremoniously, as it were, escaped from. There is not a single direct glance at American life in these pages, and only two or three implied; but the very oddity of the case is in our gradual impression, as we read, that conclusive proof resides most of all in what is absent, in the very quality that has dropped out. This quality, when it is present, is that of the bird in the cage or the branch on the tree—the fact of being confined, attached, continuous. Mr. Harland is at the worst in a cage of wires remarkably interspaced, and not on the tree save so far as we may suppose it to put forth branches of fantastic length. He is the branch broken off and converted to other useful and agreeable purposes—even in portions to that of giving out, in a state of combustion, charming red and blue flame.

To put it less indirectly, I have found half the interest of *Comedies and Errors* to be the peculiar intensity of that mark of the imagination that may best be described as the acute sense of the "Europe"—synthetic symbol!—

of the American mind, and that therefore, until Asia and Africa shall pour in their contingent of observers, we are reduced to regarding as almost the sharpest American characteristic. If it be not quite always the liveliest of all, it is certainly the liveliest on the showing of such work as I here consider, the author's maturest—work which probably gives quite the best occasion the critic in quest of an adventure can find to-day for sounding, by way of a change, the mystery of what nutrition may eventually be offered to those artistic spirits for whom the "countries" are committed to the process, that I have glanced at, of overlapping and getting mixed. A special instance is illuminating, and Mr. Harland is a distinguished one. He is the more of one that he has clearly thought out a form—of great interest and promise, a form that tempers the obscurity of our question by eliminating one danger. If we are to watch the "cosmopolitan" painter on trial, it will always be so much to the good for him that he has mastered a method and learned how to paint. *Then* we may, with all due exhilaration, set down all his shipwrecks to his unanchored state. . . .

It is a very wonderful thing, this Europe of the American in general and of the author of *Comedies and Errors* in particular—in particular, I say, because Mr. Harland tends, in a degree quite his own, to give it the romantic and tender voice, the voice of fancy pure and simple, without the disturbance of other elements, such as comparison and reaction, either violent or merciful. He is not even "international," which is, after all, but another way, perhaps, of being a slave to the "countries," possibly twice or even three times a jingo. It is a complete surrender of that province of the mind with which registration and subscription have to do. Thus is presented a disencumbered, sensitive surface for the wonderful Europe to play on. The question for the critic is that of the value of what this surface, so liberally, so artfully prepared, may give back. What strikes me as making the author of the volume before me a case to watch, as I have said, is that fact that he has a form so compact and an execution so light and firm. He is just yet, I think, a little too much everywhere, a trifle astray, as regards his inspiration, in the very wealth of his memories and the excess, even, of his wit—specimens of which I might gather, had I space, from the charming *Invisible Prince*, from *The Queen's Pleasure*, from *Flower o' the Clove*, from each indeed, I have noted as I read, of these compositions.

He is lost in the vision, all whimsical and picturesque, of palace secrets, rulers and pretenders and ministers of bewilderingly light comedy, in undiscoverable Balkan States, Bohemias of the seaboard, where the queens have platonic friendships with professional English, though not American, humourists; in the heavy, many-voiced air of the old Roman streets and of the high Roman saloons where cardinals are part of the furniture; in the hum of prodigious Paris, heard in corners of old cafés; in the sense of the deep English background as much as that of any of these; in a general facility of reference, in short, to the composite spectacle and the polyglot doom. Most of his situations are treated in the first person, and as they skip across frontiers and pop up in parks and palaces they give us the impression that, all suffused with youth as the whole thing seems, it is the play of a memory that has had half-a-dozen lives. Nothing is more charming in it than the reverberation of the old delicate, sociable France that the author loves most of all to conjure up and that fills the exquisite little picture of *Rooms* with an odour of faint lavender in wonderful bowls and a rustle of ancient silk on polished floors. But these, I dare say, are mere exuberances of curiosity and levities of independence. He has, as I have sufficiently hinted, the sense of subject and the sense of shape, and it is when, under the coercion of these things, he really stops and begins to dig that the critic will more attentively look out for him. Then we shall come back to the question of soil—the question with which I started—and of the possible ups and downs, as an artist, of the citizen of the world.

14. the American case and character

(*Letters*, 1912, to W. D. Howells)

They make a great array, a literature in themselves, your studies of American life, so acute, so direct, so disinterested, so preoccupied but with the fine truth of the case; and the more attaching to me, always, for their referring themselves to a time and an order when we knew together what American life *was*—or thought we did, deluded though we may have been! I don't pretend to measure the effect, or to sound the depths, if they be not the shallows, of the huge wholesale importations and so-called assimilations of this later time; I can only feel and speak for those conditions in which, as "quiet observers," as careful painters, as sincere artists, we could still, in our native, our human and social element, know more or less where we were and feel more or less what we had hold of. You knew and felt these things better than I; you had learnt them earlier and more intimately, and it was impossible, I think, to be in more instinctive and more informed possession of the general truth of your subject than you happily found yourself. The *real* affair of the American case and character, as it met your view and brushed your sensibility, that was what inspired and attached you, and, heedless of foolish flurries from other quarters, of all wild or weak slashings of the air and wavings in the void, you gave yourself to it with an incorruptible faith. You saw your field with a rare lucidity; you saw all it had to give in the way of the romance of the real and the interest and the thrill and the charm of the common, as one may put it; the character and the comedy, the point, the pathos, the tragedy, the particular home-grown humanity under your eyes and your hand and with which the life all about you was closely interknitted. Your hand reached out to these things with a fondness that was in itself a literary gift, and played with them as the artist only and always can play: freely, quaintly, incalculably, with all the assurance of his fancy and his irony, and yet with that fine taste for the truth and the pity and the meaning of the matter which keeps the temper of observation both sharp and sweet. To observe, by such an instinct and by such reflection, is to find work to one's hand and a challenge in every bush; and as the familiar American scene thus bristled about you, so, year by year, your vision more and more justly responded and swarmed. You put forth A Modern Instance, and The Rise of Silas Lapham, and A Hazard of New Fortunes, and The Landlord àt Lion's Head, and The Kentons (that perfectly classic illustration of your spirit and your form,) after having put forth in perhaps lighter-fingered prelude A Foregone Conclusion, and The Undiscovered Country, and The Lady of the Aroostook, and The Minister's Charge—to make of a long list too short a one; with the effect, again and again, of a feeling for the human relation, as the social climate of our country qualifies, intensifies, generally conditions and colours it, which, married in perfect felicity to the expression you found for its service, constituted the originality that we want to fasten upon you, as with silver nails, to-night. Stroke by stroke and book by book your work was to become, for this exquisite notation of our whole democratic light and shade and give and take, in the highest degree *documentary;* so that none other, through all your fine long season, could approach it in value and amplitude. None, let me say too, was to approach it in essential distinction; for you had grown master, by insidious practices best known to yourself, of a method so easy and so natural, so marked with the personal element of your humour and the play, not less personal, of your sympathy, that the critic kept coming on its secret connection with the grace of letters much as Fenimore Cooper's Leather-stocking—so knowing to be able to do it!— comes, in the forest, on the subtle tracks of Indian braves. However, these things take us far, and what I wished mainly to put on record is my sense of that unfailing, testifying truth in you which will keep you from ever being neglected. The critical intelligence—if any such fitful and discredited light may still be conceived as within our sphere—has not at all begun to render you its tribute. The more inquiringly and perceivingly it shall still be projected upon the American life we used to know, the more it shall be moved by the analytic and historic spirit, the more indispensable, the more a vessel of light, will you be found. It's a great thing to have used one's genius and done one's work with such quiet and robust consistency that they fall by their own weight into that happy service.

15. the old conditions of contrast and color

("Honoré de Balzac," 1913)

What makes Balzac so pre-eminent and exemplary that he was to leave the
novel a far other and a vastly more capacious and significant affair than he
found it, is his having felt his fellow-creatures (almost altogether for him
his contemporaries) as quite failing of reality, as swimming in the vague and
the void and the abstract, unless their social conditions, to the last particular,
their generative and contributive circumstances, of every discernible sort,
enter for all these are "worth" into his representative attempt. This great
compound of the total looked into and starting up in its element, as it always
does, to meet the eye of genius and patience half way, bristled for him with
all its branching connections, those thanks to which any figure could *be* a
figure but by showing for endlessly entangled in them. . . .

   . . . The later part of the eighteenth century, with the Revolution, the
Empire and the Restoration, had inimitably conspired together to scatter
abroad their separate marks and stigmas, their separate trails of character
and physiognomic hits—for which advantage he might have arrived too
late, as his hapless successors, even his more or less direct imitators, visibly
have done. The fatal fusions and uniformities inflicted on our newer generations, the running together of all the differences of form and tone, the ruinous
liquefying wash of the great industrial brush over the old conditions of
contrast and colour, doubtless still have left the painter of manners much
to do, but have ground him down to the sad fact that his ideals of differen-
tiation, those inherent oppositions from type to type, in which drama most
naturally resides, have well-nigh perished. They pant for life in a hostile
air; and we may surely say that their last successful struggle, their last bright
resistance to eclipse among ourselves, was in their feverish dance to the great
fiddling of Dickens. Dickens made them dance, we seem to see, caper and
kick their heels, wave their arms, and above all agitate their features, for the
simple reason that he couldn't make them stand or sit *at once* quietly and
expressively, couldn't make them look straight out as for themselves—quite
in fact as through his not daring to, not feeling he could afford to, in a
changing hour when ambiguities and the wavering line, droll and "dodgy"
dazzlements and the possibly undetected factitious alone, might be trusted
to keep him right with an incredibly uncritical public, a public blind to the
difference between a shade and a patch.

Chapter III

THE WRITER AND HIS EXPERIENCE

In 1891, James described in his Notebooks *what he called the "terrible law of the artist—the law of fructification, of fertilization, the law by which everything is grist to his mill—the law, in short, of the acceptance of all experience, of all suffering, of all life, of all suggestion and sensation and illumination" (see Chapter IV, "The Writer and his Imagination"). Over and over again, in getting at the sources of art, James used the terms experience, life, impressions, observation, perception. In "The Art of Fiction" and elsewhere he insisted that the end of the novel was to "represent life," and that there were no other restrictions: "The province of art is all life, all feeling, all observation, all vision . . . all experience."*

Perhaps James's most famous statement relating fiction to experience is from "The Art of Fiction": "A novel is . . . a personal, a direct impression of life: that, to begin with, constitutes its value, which is greater or less according to the intensity of the impression." The selections in Part A of this chapter are a kind of explication of this definition. James's comments on "impressions" included here are far too few to indicate how important the matter was to him —they became the law of the writer's life. In "The Art of Fiction" James said: "If experience consists of impressions, it may be said that impressions are experience, just as (have we not seen it?) they are the very air we breathe."

Impressions, in quantity and intensity, became for James the lifeblood of consciousness, and consciousness came to be for him not only a primary condition of art, but in fact a kind of religion. (In that curious essay "Is There a Life after Death?" included in F. O. Matthiessen's The James Family, *James links immortality to consciousness—or "creative awareness of things": "It is in a word the artistic consciousness and privilege in itself that thus shines as from immersion in the fountain of being. Into that fountain, to depths immeasurable, our spirit dips—to the effect of feeling itself, quâ imagination and aspiration, all scented with universal sources. What is that but an adventure of personality, and how can we after it hold complete disconnection likely?" Matthiessen explores the nature of James's "Religion of Consciousness" in a chapter of* Henry James: The Major Phase.)

In stressing personal impression, James was emphasizing his belief that all men see reality, or life, differently, uniquely, and that this difference and uniqueness constituted the value of the personal impression. *Indeed, James rejected the notion of kinds or schools of fiction, inasmuch as differences, not likenesses, made up the lifeblood of fiction. His favorite metaphor for the personal impression was the individual window through which the writer looked at the scene of life; there were as many windows as there were writers in the house of fiction (see Chapter XV, "Morality and Philosophy; Meaning and Theme," for other relevant passages). In stressing* direct *impression, James was avoiding endorsement of the second-hand impression or an "imitation of observation." When James pointed out (in discussing Maupassant) that we too seldom have the courage of our perceptions, he was perhaps saying in his own way what Hemingway meant later when he pointed out the difficulty of knowing how we really feel in contrast with the prevailing notions of how we are supposed to feel (see* Death in the Afternoon, *1932).*

In part B of this chapter are gathered together some specific examples of the writer's use of his impressions of life. In four separate instances, James describes how his novels emerged from a speech, a sense of place, a sense of character, and a striking action, all four of which came from experience in some sense. Impressions became seeds, were planted, and grew into novels. But perhaps more interesting than these accounts is the view of reality which pervades these pieces: life is all "inclusion and confusion"; it is a "thick jungle" or an endless and ladened "current" or an air that swarms with multitudes: "clumsy Life again at her stupid work." The personal impression, or seed, seized from the rushing torrent becomes the precious basis of art.

This chapter concludes with James's tribute to Balzac's allegiance to experience, which contains one of James's most brilliant descriptions of the rooting of fiction in life: "His [Balzac's] plan was to handle, primarily, not a world of ideas, animated by figures representing these ideas; but the packed and constituted, the palpable, provable world before him, by the study of which ideas would inevitably find themselves thrown up."

PART A: IMPRESSIONS, PERCEPTIONS, CONSCIOUSNESS

1. impressions never lost

(*Notebooks*, 1881)

It is too late to recover all those lost impressions—those of the last six years —that I spoke of in beginning; besides, they are not lost altogether, they are buried deep in my mind, they have become part of my life, of my nature.

2. *to catch and keep something of life*

(*Notebooks*, 1881)

If I should write here all that I might write, I should speedily fill this as yet unspotted blank-book, bought in London six months ago, but hitherto unopened. It is so long since I have kept any notes, taken any memoranda, written down my current reflections, taken a sheet of paper, as it were, into my confidence. Meanwhile so much has come and gone, so much that it is now too late to catch, to reproduce, to preserve. I have lost too much by losing, or rather by not having acquired, the note-taking habit. It might be of great profit to me; and now that I am older, that I have more time, that the labour of writing is less onerous to me, and I can work more at my leisure, I ought to endeavour to keep, to a certain extent, a record of passing impressions, of all that comes, that goes, that I see, and feel, and observe. To catch and keep something of life—that's what I mean.

3. *the great thing is to be saturated*

(*Letters*, 1888, to William James)

You are right in surmising that it must often be a grief to me not to get more time for reading—though not in supposing that I am "hollowed out inside" by the limitations my existence has too obstinately attached to that exercise, combined with the fact that I produce a great deal. At times I do read almost as much as my wretched little *stomach* for it literally will allow, and on the whole I get much more time for it as the months and years go by. I touched bottom, in the way of missing time, during the first half of my long residence in London—and traversed then a sandy desert, in that respect—where, however, I took on board such an amount of human and social information that if the same necessary alternatives were presented to me again I should make the same choice. One can read when one is middle-aged or old; but one can mingle in the world with fresh perceptions only when one is young. The great thing is to be *saturated* with something—that is, in one way or another, with life; and I chose the form of my saturation. Moreover you exaggerate the degree to which my writing takes it out of my mind, for I try to spend only the interest of my capital.

4. *impressions personal and unique (reality or illusion)*

("Guy de Maupassant," 1888)

He [Guy de Maupassant in Preface to *Pierre et Jean*] has said his say concisely and as if he were saying it once for all. In fine, his readers must be grateful to him for such a passage as that in which he remarks that whereas the public at large very legitimately says to a writer, "Console me, amuse me, terrify me, make me cry, make me dream, or make me think," what the sincere critic says is, "Make me something fine in the form that shall suit you best, according to your temperament." This seems to me to put into a nutshell the whole question of the different classes of fiction, concerning which there has recently been so much discourse. There are simply as many different kinds as there are persons practicing the art, for if a picture, a tale, or a novel be a direct impression of life (and that surely constitutes its interest and value), the impression will vary according to the plate that takes it, the particular structure and mixture of the recipient.

I am not sure that I know what M. de Maupassant means when he says, "The critic shall appreciate the result only according to the nature of the effort; he has no right to concern himself with tendencies." The second clause of that observation strikes me as rather in the air, thanks to the vagueness of the last word. But our author adds to the definiteness of his contention when he goes on to say that any form of the novel is simply a vision of the world from the standpoint of a person constituted after a certain fashion, and that it is therefore absurd to say that there is, for the novelist's use, only one reality of things. This seems to me commendable, not as a flight of metaphysics, hovering over bottomless gulfs of controversy, but, on the contrary, as a just indication of the vanity of certain dogmatisms. The particular way we see the world is our particular illusion about it, says M. de Maupassant, and this illusion fits itself to our organs and senses; our receptive vessel becomes the furniture of *our* little plot of the universal consciousness.

"How childish, moreover, to believe in reality, since we each carry our own in our thought and in our organs. Our eyes, our ears, our sense of smell, of taste, differing from one person to another, create as many truths as there are men upon earth. And our minds, taking instruction from these organs, so diversely impressed, understand, analyze, judge, as if each of us belonged to a different race. Each one of us, therefore, forms for himself an illusion of the world, which is the illusion poetic, or sentimental, or joyous, or melancholy, or unclean, or dismal, according to his nature. And the writer has no other mission than to reproduce faithfully this illusion, with all the contrivances of art that he has learned and has at his command. The illusion of beauty, which is a human convention! The illusion of ugliness, which is a changing opinion! The illusion of truth, which is never immutable! The illusion of the ignoble, which attracts so many! The great artists are those who make humanity accept their particular illusion. Let us, therefore, not get angry with any one theory, since every theory is the generalized expression of a temperament asking itself questions."

What is interesting in this is not that M. de Maupassant happens to hold that we have no universal measure of the truth, but that it is the last word on a question of art from a writer who is rich in experience and has had success in a very rare degree. It is of secondary importance that our impression should be called, or not called, an illusion; what is excellent is that our author has stated more neatly than we have lately seen it done that the value of the artist resides in the clearness with which he gives forth that impression. His particular organism constitutes a *case*, and the critic is intelligent in proportion as he apprehends and enters into that case. To quarrel with it because it is not another, which it could not possibly have been without a wholly different outfit, appears to M. de Maupassant a deplorable waste of time.

5. the courage of one's perceptions

("Guy de Maupassant," 1888)

What makes M. de Maupassant salient is two facts: the first of which is that his gifts are remarkably strong and definite, and the second that he writes directly *from* them, as it were: holds the fullest, the most uninterrupted—I scarcely know what to call it—the boldest communication with them. A case is poor when the cluster of the artist's sensibilities is small, or they themselves are wanting in keenness, or else when the personage fails to admit them— either through ignorance, or diffidence, or stupidity, or the error of a false ideal—to what may be called a legitimate share in his attempt. It is, I think, among English and American writers that this latter accident is most liable to occur; more than the French we are apt to be misled by some convention or other as to the sort of feeler we *ought* to put forth, forgetting that the best one will be the one that nature happens to have given us. We have doubtless often enough the courage of our opinions (when it befalls that we have opinions), but we have not so constantly that of our perceptions. There is a whole side of our perceptive apparatus that we in fact neglect, and there are probably many among us who would erect this tendency into a duty. M. de Maupassant neglects nothing that he possesses; he cultivates his garden with admirable energy; and if there is a flower you miss from the rich parterre, you may be sure that it could not possibly have been raised, his mind not containing the soil for it. He is plainly of the opinion that the first duty of the artist, and the thing that makes him most useful to his fellow-men, is to master his instrument, whatever it may happen to be.

6. the novelist is a particular window

(*Letters*, 1890, to W. D. Howells)

The novelist is a particular *window*, absolutely—and of worth in so far as he is one; and it's because you open so well and are hung so close over the street that I could hang out of it all day long. Your very value is that you choose your own street—heaven forbid I should have to choose it for you. If I should say I mortally dislike the people who pass in it, I should seem to be taking on myself that intolerable responsibility of selection which it is exactly such a luxury to be relieved of. Indeed I'm convinced that no readers above the rank of an idiot—this number is moderate, I admit— really fail to take any view that is really *shown* them—any gift (of subject) that's really given. The usual imbecility of the novel is that the showing and giving simply don't come off—the reader never touches the subject and the subject never touches the reader; the window is no window at all—but only childish *finta*, like the ornaments of our beloved Italy. This is why, as a triumph of *communication*, I hold the *Hazard* so rare and strong. You communicate in touches so close, so fine, so true, so droll, so frequent. I am writing too much (you will think me demented with chatter;) so that I can't go into specifications of success. . . .

7. experience conditioned, infinitely, in this personal way

("Mr. Kipling's Early Stories," 1891)

Mr. Kipling, then, has the character that furnishes plenty of play and of vicarious experience—that makes any perceptive reader foresee a rare luxury. He has the great merit of being a compact and convenient illustration of the surest source of interest in any painter of life—that of having an identity as marked as a window-frame. He is one of the illustrations, taken near at hand, that help to clear up the vexed question in the novel or the tale, of kinds, camps, schools, distinctions, the right way and the wrong way; so very positively does he contribute to the showing that there are just as many kinds, as many ways, as many forms and degrees of the "right," as there are personal points in view. It is the blessing of the art he practises that it is made up of experience conditioned, infinitely, in this personal way—the sum of the feeling of life as reproduced by innumerable natures; natures that feel through all their differences, testify through their diversities. These differences, which make the identity, are of the individual; they form the channel by which life flows through him, and how much he is able to give us of life— in other words, how much he appeals to us—depends on whether they form it solidly.

This hardness of the conduit, cemented with a rare assurance, is perhaps the most striking idiosyncrasy of Mr. Kipling; and what makes it more remarkable is that incident of his extreme youth which, if we talk about him at all, we cannot affect to ignore. I cannot pretend to give a biography or a chronology of the author of "Soldiers Three," but I cannot overlook the general, the importunate fact that, confidently as he has caught the trick and habit of this sophisticated world, he has not been long of it. His extreme youth is indeed what I may call his window-bar—the support on which he somewhat rowdily leans while he looks down at the human scene with his pipe in his teeth; just as his other conditions (to mention only some of them), are his prodigious facility, which is only less remarkable than his stiff selection; his unabashed temperament, his flexible talent, his smoking-room manner, his familiar friendship with India—established so rapidly, and so completely under his control; his delight in battle, his "cheek" about women —and indeed about men and about everything; his determination not to be duped, his "imperial" fibre, his love of the inside view, the private soldier and the primitive man.

8. imitation *of observation*

("Emile Zola," 1903)

Zola's own reply to all puzzlements would have been, at any rate, I take it, a straight summary of his inveterate professional habits. "It is all very simple —I produce, roughly speaking, a volume a year, and of this time some five months go to preparation, to special study. In the other months, with all my *cadres* established, I write the book. And I can hardly say which part of the job is stiffest."

The story was not more wonderful for him than that, nor the job more complex; which is why we must say of his whole process and its results that they constitute together perhaps the most extraordinary *imitation* of observation that we possess. Balzac appealed to "science" and proceeded by her aid; Balzac had *cadres* enough and a tabulated world, rubrics, relationships and genealogies; but Balzac affects us in spite of everything as personally overtaken by life, as fairly hunted and run to earth by it. He strikes us as struggling and all but submerged, as beating over the scene such a pair of wings as were not soon again to be wielded by any visitor of his general air and as had not at all events attached themselves to Zola's rounded shoulders. His bequest is in consequence immeasurably more interesting, yet who shall declare that his adventure was in its greatness more successful? Zola "pulled it off," as we say, supremely, in that he never but once found himself obliged to quit, to our vision, his magnificent treadmill of the pigeonholed and documented —the region we may qualify as that of experience by imitation. His splendid economy saw him through, he labored to the end within sight of his notes and his charts.

9. *the only way to know is to have lived*

(*Letters*, 1913, to Hugh Walpole)

I make out that you will then be in London again—I mean *by* November, though such a black gulf of time intervenes; and then of course I may look to you to come down to me for a couple of days. It will be the lowest kind of "jinks"—so halting is my pace; yet we shall somehow make it serve. Don't say to me, by the way, à propos of jinks—the "high" kind that you speak of having so wallowed in previous to leaving town—that I ever challenge you as to *why* you wallow, or splash or plunge, or dizzily and sublimely soar (into the jinks element,) or whatever you may call it: as if I ever remarked on anything but the absolute inevitability of it for you at your age and with your natural curiosities, as it were, and passions. It's good healthy exercise, when it comes but in bouts and brief convulsions, and it's always a kind of thing that it's good, and considerably final, to *have* done. We must know, as much as possible, in our beautiful art, yours and mine, what we are talking about—and the only way to know is to have lived and loved and cursed and floundered and enjoyed and suffered. I think I don't regret a single "excess" of my responsive youth—I only regret, in my chilled age, certain occasions and possibilities I didn't embrace. Bad doctrine to impart to a young idiot or a duffer, but in place for a young friend (pressed to my heart) with a fund of nobler passion, the preserving, the defying, the dedicating, and which always has the last word; the young friend who can dip and shake off and go his straight way again when it's time. But we'll talk of all this—it's absolutely late.

PART B: GERMS, SEEDS, PLANTS

1. *speech: the faint vague germ*

(*Letters*, 1901, to W. D. Howells)

I lately finished a tolerably long novel [*The Ambassadors*], and I've written a third of another—with still another begun and two or three more subjects awaiting me thereafter like carriages drawn up at the door and horses champing their bits. And à propos of the first named of these, which is in the hands of the Harpers, I have it on my conscience to let you know that the idea of the fiction in question had its earliest origin in a circumstance mentioned to me—years ago—in respect to no less a person than yourself. At Torquay, once, our young friend Jon. Sturges came down to spend some days near me, and, lately from Paris, repeated to me five words you had said to him one day on his meeting you during a call at Whistler's. I thought the words charming—you have probably quite forgotten them; and the whole incident suggestive—so far as it was an incident; and, more than this, they presently caused me to see in them the faint vague germ, the mere point of the *start*, of a subject. I noted them, to that end, as I note everything; and years afterwards (that is three or four) the subject sprang at me, one day, out of my notebook. I don't know if it be good; at any rate it has been treated, now, for whatever it is; and my point is that it had long before— it had in the very act of striking me as a germ—got away from *you* or from anything like you! had become impersonal and independent. Nevertheless your initials figure in my little note; and if you hadn't said the five words to Jonathan he wouldn't have had them (most sympathetically and interestingly) to relate, and I shouldn't have had them to work in my imagination. The moral is that you are responsible for the whole business. But I've had it, since the book was finished, much at heart to tell you so. May you carry the burden bravely!

2. *place: so the impressions worked*

(Preface to *The Princess Casamassima*, 1908)

The simplest account of the origin of "The Princess Casamassima" is, I think, that this fiction proceeded quite directly, during the first year of a long residence in London, from the habit and the interest of walking the streets. I walked a great deal—for exercise, for amusement, for acquisition, and above all I always walked home at the evening's end, when the evening had been spent elsewhere, as happened more often than not; and as to do this was to receive many impressions, so the impressions worked and sought an issue, so the book after a time was born. It is a fact that, as I look back, the attentive exploration of London, the assault directly made by the great city upon an imagination quick to react, fully explains a large part of it. There is a minor element that refers itself to another source, of which I shall presently speak; but the prime idea was unmistakeably the ripe round fruit of perambulation. One walked of course with one's eyes greatly open, and I hasten to declare that such a practice, carried on for a long time and over a considerable space, positively provokes, all round, a mystic solicitation, the urgent appeal, on the part of everything, to be interpreted and, so far as may be, reproduced. "Subjects" and situations, character and history, the tragedy and comedy of life, are things of which the common air, in such conditions, seems pungently to taste; and to a mind curious, before the human scene, of meanings and revelations the great grey Babylon easily becomes, on its face, a garden bristling with an immense illustrative flora. Possible stories, presentable figures, rise from the thick jungle as the observer moves, fluttering up like startled game, and before he knows it indeed he has fairly to guard himself against the brush of importunate wings. He goes on as with his head in a cloud of humming presences—especially during the younger, the initiatory time, the fresh, the sharply-apprehensive months or years, more or less numerous. We use our material up, we use up even the thick tribute of the London streets—if perception and attention but sufficiently light our steps. But I think of them as lasting, for myself, quite sufficiently long; I think of them as even still—dreadfully changed for the worse in respect to any romantic idea as I find them—breaking out on occasion into eloquence, throwing out deep notes from their vast vague murmur.

3. character: floated into our minds by the current of life

(Preface to *The Portrait of a Lady*, 1908)

Trying to recover here, for recognition, the germ of my idea, I see that it must have consisted not at all in any conceit of a "plot," nefarious name, in any flash, upon the fancy, of a set of relations, or in any one of those situations that, by a logic of their own, immediately fall, for the fabulist, into movement, into a march or a rush, a patter of quick steps; but altogether in the sense of a single character, the character and aspect of a particular engaging young woman, to which all the usual elements of a "subject," certainly of a setting, were to need to be super-added. Quite as interesting as the young woman herself, at her best, do I find, I must again repeat, this projection of memory upon the whole matter of the growth, in one's imagination, of some such apology for a motive. These are the fascinations of the fabulist's art, these lurking forces of expansion, these necessities of up-springing in the seed, these beautiful determinations, on the part of the idea entertained, to grow as tall as possible, to push into the light and the air and thickly flower there; and, quite as much, these fine possibilities of recovering, from some good standpoint on the ground gained, the intimate history of the business—of retracing and reconstructing its steps and stages. I have always fondly remembered a remark that I heard fall years ago from the lips of Ivan Turgénieff in regard to his own experience of the usual origin of the fictive picture. It began for him almost always with the vision of some person or persons, who hovered before him, soliciting him, as the active or passive figure, interesting him and appealing to him just as they were and by what they were. He saw them, in that fashion, as *disponibles*, saw them subject to the chances, the complications of existence, and saw them vividly, but then had to find for them the right relations, those that would most bring them out; to imagine, to invent and select and piece together the situations most useful and favorable to the sense of the creatures themselves, the complications they would be most likely to produce and to feel.

"To arrive at these things is to arrive at my 'story,' " he said, "and that's the way I look for it. The result is that I'm often accused of not having 'story' enough. I seem to myself to have as much as I need—to show my people, to exhibit their relations with each other; for that is all my measure. If I watch them long enough I see them come together, I see them *placed*, I see them engaged in this or that act and in this or that difficulty. How they look and move and speak and behave, always in the setting I have found for them, is my account of them—of which I dare say, alas, *que cela manque souvent d'architecture*. But I would rather, I think, have too little architecture than too much—when there's danger of its interfering with my measure of the truth. The French of course like more of it than I give—having by their own genius such a hand for it; and indeed one must give all one can. As for the origin of one's wind-blown germs themselves, who shall say, as you ask, where *they* come from? We have to go too far back, too far behind, to say. Isn't it all we can say that they come from every quarter of heaven, that they are *there* at almost any turn of the road? They accumulate, and we are always picking them over, selecting among them. They are the breath of life—by which I mean that life, in its own way, breathes them upon us. They are so, in a manner prescribed and imposed—floated into our minds by the current of life. That reduces to imbecility the vain critic's quarrel, so often, with one's subject, when he hasn't the wit to accept it. Will he point out then which other it should properly have been?—his office being, essentially *to* point out. *Il en serait bien embarrassé*. Ah, when he points out what I've done or failed to do with it, that's another matter : there he's on his ground. I give him up my 'architecture,' " my distinguished friend concluded, "as much as he will."

4. act: life all inclusion and confusion

(Preface to *The Spoils of Poynton*, 1908)

It was years ago, I remember, one Christmas Eve when I was dining with friends : a lady beside me made in the course of talk one of those allusions that I have always found myself recognising on the spot as "germs." The germ, wherever gathered, has ever been for me the germ of a "story," and most of the stories straining to shape under my hand have sprung from a single small seed, a seed as minute and wind-blown as that casual hint for "The Spoils of Poynton" dropped unwittingly by my neighbour, a mere floating particle in the stream of talk. What above all comes back to me with this reminiscence is the sense of the inveterate minuteness, on such happy occasions, of the precious particle—reduced, that is, to its mere fruitful essence. Such is the interesting truth about the stray suggestion, the wandering word, the vague echo, at touch of which the novelist's imagination winces as at the prick of some sharp point: its virtue is all in its needle-like quality, the power to penetrate as finely as possible. This fineness it is that communicates the virus of suggestion, anything more than the minimum of which spoils the operation. If one is given a hint at all designedly one is sure to be given too much; one's subject is in the merest grain, the speck of truth, of beauty, of reality, scarce visible to the common eye—since, I firmly hold, a good eye for a subject is anything but usual. Strange and attaching, certainly, the consistency with which the first thing to be done for the communicated and seized idea is to reduce almost to nought the form, the air as of a mere disjoined and lacerated lump of life, in which we may have happened to meet it. Life being all inclusion and confusion, and art being all discrimination and selection, the latter, in search of the hard latent *value* with which alone it is concerned, sniffs round the mass as instinctively and unerringly as a dog suspicious of some buried bone. The difference here, however, is that, while the dog desires his bone but to destroy it, the artist finds in *his* tiny nugget, washed free of awkward accretions and hammered into a sacred hardness, the very stuff for a clear affirmation, the happiest chance for the indestructible. It at the same time amuses him again and again to note how, beyond the first step of the actual case, the case that constitutes for him his germ, his vital particle, his grain of gold, life persistently blunders and deviates, loses herself in the sand. The reason is of course that life has no direct sense whatever for the subject and is capable, luckily for us, of nothing but splendid waste. Hence the opportunity for the sublime economy of art, which rescues, which saves, and hoards and "banks," investing and reinvesting these fruits of toil in wondrous useful "works" and thus making up for us, desperate spendthrifts that we all naturally are, the most princely of incomes. It is the subtle secrets of that system, however, that are meanwhile the charming study, with an endless attraction, above all, in the question—endlessly baffling indeed—of the method at the heart of the madness; the madness, I mean, of a zeal, among the reflective sort, so disinterested. If life, presenting us the germ, and left merely to herself in such a business, gives the case away, almost always, before we can stop her, what are the signs for our guidance, what the primary laws for a saving selection, how do we know when and where to intervene, where do we place the beginnings of the wrong or the right deviation? Such would be the elements of an enquiry upon which, I hasten to say, it is quite forbidden me here to embark: I but glance at them in evidence of the rich pasture that at every turn surrounds the ruminant critic. The answer may be after all that mysteries here elude us, that general considerations fail or mislead, and that even the fondest of artists need ask no wider range than the logic of the particular case. The particular case, or in other words his relation to a given subject, once the relation is established, forms in itself a little world of exercise and agitation. Let him hold himself perhaps supremely fortunate if he can meet half the questions with which that air alone may swarm.

So it was, at any rate, that when my amiable friend, on the Christmas Eve, before the table that glowed safe and fair through the brown London night, spoke of such an odd matter as that a good lady in the north, always well looked on, was at daggers drawn with her only son, ever hitherto exemplary, over the ownership of the valuable furniture of a fine old house just accruing to the young man by his father's death, I instantly became aware, with my "sense for the subject," of the prick of inoculation; the *whole* of the virus, as I have called it, being infused by that single touch. There had been but ten words, yet I had recognised in them, as in a flash, all the possibilities of the little drama of my "Spoils," which glimmered then and there into life; so that when in the next breath I began to hear of action taken, on the beautiful ground, by our engaged adversaries, tipped each, from that instant, with the light of the highest distinction, I saw clumsy Life again at her stupid work. For the action taken, and on which my friend, as I knew she would, had already begun all complacently and benightedly further to report, I had absolutely, and could have, no scrap of use; one had been so perfectly qualified to say in advance: "It's the perfect little workable thing, but she'll strangle it in the cradle, even while she pretends, all so cheeringly, to rock it; where-fore I'll stay her hand while yet there's time." I didn't, of course, stay her hand—there never *is* in such cases "time"; and I had once more the full demonstration of the fatal futility of Fact. The turn taken by the excel-lent situation—excellent, for development, if arrested in the right place, that is in the germ—had the full measure of the classic ineptitude; to which with the full measure of the artistic irony one could once more, and for the thousandth time, but take off one's hat. It was not, however, that this in the least mattered, once the seed had been transplanted to richer soil; and I dwell on that almost inveterate redundancy of the wrong, as opposed to the ideal right, in any free flowering of the actual, by reason only of its approach to calculable regularity.

5. collected experience: the palpable, provable world

("The Lesson of Balzac," 1905)

It is a question, you see, of *penetrating* into a subject; his [Balzac's] corridors always went further and further and further; which is but another way of expressing his inordinate passion for detail. It matters nothing—nothing for my present contention—that this extravagance is also his great fault; in spite, too, of its all being detail vivified and related, characteristic and constructive, essentially prescribed by the terms of his plan. The relations of parts to each other are at moments multiplied almost to madness—which is at the same time just why they give us the measure of his hallucination, make up the greatness of his intellectual adventure. His plan was to handle, primarily, not a world of ideas, animated by figures representing these ideas; but the packed and constituted, the palpable, provable world before him, by the study of which ideas would inevitably find themselves thrown up. If the happy fate is accordingly to *partake* of life, actively, assertively, not passively, narrowly, in mere sensibility and sufferance, the happiness has been greatest when the faculty employed has been largest. We employ different faculties— some of us only our arms and our legs and our stomach; Balzac employed most what he possessed in largest quantity. This is where his work ceases in a manner to mystify us—that is where we make out how he did quarry his material: it is the sole solution to an otherwise baffling problem. He collected his experience within himself; no other economy explains his achievement; this thrift alone, remarkable yet thinkable, embodies the necessary miracle. His system of cellular confinement, in the interest of the miracle, was positively that of a Benedictine monk, leading his life within the four walls of his convent and bent, the year round, over the smooth parch- ment on which, with wonderous illumination and enhancement of gold and crimson and blue, he inscribed the glories of the faith and the legends of the saints. Balzac's view of himself was indeed in a manner the monkish one; he was most at ease, while he wrought, in the white gown and cowl— an image of him that the friendly art of his time has handed down to us. Only, as happened, his subject of illumination was the legends not merely of the saints, but of the much more numerous uncanonized strugglers and sinners, an acquaintance with whose attributes was not all to be gathered in the place of piety itself; not even from the faintest ink of old records, the mild lips of old brothers, or the painted glass of church windows.

This is where envy does follow him, for to have so many other human cases, so many other personal predicaments to get into, up to one's chin, is verily to be able to get out of one's own box. And it was up to his chin, constantly, that he sank in his illusion—not, as the weak and timid in this line do, only up to his ankles or his knees. The figures he sees begin immedi- ately to bristle with all their characteristics. Every mark and sign, outward and inward, that they possess; every virtue and every vice, every strength and every weakness, every passion and every habit, the sound of their voices, the expression of their eyes, the tricks of feature and limb, the buttons on their clothes, the food on their plates, the money in their pockets, the furniture in their houses, the secrets in their breasts, are all things that interest, that concern, that command him, and that have, for the picture, significance, relation and value. It is a prodigious multiplication of values, and thereby a prodigious entertainment of the vision—on the condition the vision can bear it. Bearing it—that is *our* bearing it—is a serious matter; for the appeal is truly to that faculty of attention out of which we are educating ourselves, as hard as we possibly can; educating ourselves with such complacency, with such boisterous high spirits, that we may already be said to have practically lost it—with the consequence that any work of art or of criticism making a demand on it is by that fact essentially discredited. It takes attention not only to thread the labyrinth of the *Comédie Humaine*, but to keep our author himself in view, in the relations in which we thus image him. But if we can muster it, as I say, in sufficient quantity, we thus walk with him in the great glazed gallery of his thought; the long, lighted and pictured ambulatory where the endless series of windows, on one side, hangs over his revolution-ized, ravaged, yet partly restored and reinstated garden of France, and where, on the other, the figures and the portraits we fancy stepping down to meet him climb back into their frames, larger and smaller, and take up position and expression as he desired they shall look out and compose.

Chapter IV

THE WRITER AND HIS IMAGINATION

Although James always insisted on the primacy of experience in the writing of fiction, he also always insisted on the importance of the imagination: one without the other crippled the writer. In "The Art of Fiction," James made clear the relation of the two: "Experience is never limited, and it is never complete; it is an immense sensibility, a kind of huge spider-web of the finest silken threads suspended in the chamber of consciousness, and catching every airborne particle in its tissue. It is the very atmosphere of the mind; and when the mind is imaginative—much more when it happens to be that of a man of genius—it takes to itself the faintest hints of life, it converts the very pulses of the air into revelations."

When the mind is imaginative, a mystic conversion takes place. James's favorite metaphor for this process was the crucible, in which experience was transfigured by the imagination into the substance of fiction. Almost always James saw the process as one of mystery or magic. It took place most frequently outside the conscious mind, among the "dark-based pillars." The imagination was not subject to the individual will, but lived an independent life of its own.

Throughout his comments on the imagination (Part A of this chapter), James appears on the verge of locating the crucible of the imagination in the uncontrolled and teeming unconscious of the writer. In Part B are collected a series of passages in which James in fact does, directly or indirectly, describe the unconscious as an important and contributing attribute in the fictional process. It is a reservoir, into which an idea or germ may be dropped to mingle with other gathered and stored impressions, later to emerge with a "notable increase of weight."

In Part C, "The World of Creation," appears a selection of James's apostrophes to his art as a world into which he can enter and live a full life, or as a paradise to which he can surrender his whole being. Although these passages tend to be visionary and ecstatic, they suggest that James depended on such surrenders to bring him through the processes of growth and development in his fictions—processes that were less rational than imaginative, less conscious than unconscious: processes that fed and multiplied upon each other most richly and abundantly when the artist entered their world with total abandon.

But it would be a mistake to take these passages as an indication that

James used his art as an escape from reality. This superficial reading is denied by James's lifelong commitment to experience and life as the fundamental source of fiction. To the last he insisted (letter to H. G. Wells, 1915): "For myself I live, live intensely and am fed by life, and my value, whatever it be, is in my own kind of expression of that." In brief, James lived alternately and intensely in the two worlds, of reality and art, of life and creation, mediating between them and enriching each with the other.

In the final cluster of comments in this chapter, James touches on something of the inverse of the equation with which he by implication began: "Life makes art." Does art make life? Perhaps, in some sense, yes. Just as, in language or speech, expression always "penetrates" or "reacts creatively" on sense, the two becoming inseparable (see Chapters XIII and XIV, "Form" and "Style"), so form in art "fertilizes" subject. There is, in short, a sense in which the reality of a fiction derives not from life itself (which is all chaos and confusion) so much as from the art (or form) of the writer. A work of fiction, then, contains its own, created reality. Thus James could say to Wells, even when claiming to be fed intensely by life, that "it is art that makes life, makes interest, makes importance." In the random flow and ceaseless flux of experience itself, life does not of its own nature fall into focus or acquire form.

PART A: THE CRUCIBLE OF THE IMAGINATION

1. *the great stew pot or crucible of the imagination*

(*Letters*, 1911, to H. G. Wells)

There is, to my vision, no authentic, and no really interesting and no *beautiful*, report of things on the novelist's, the painter's part unless a particular detachment has operated, unless the great stewpot or crucible of the imagination, of the observant and recording and interpreting mind in short, has intervened and played its part—and this detachment, this chemical transmutation for the aesthetic, the representational, end is terribly wanting in autobiography brought, as the horrible phrase is, up to date.

2. *imagination guides his hand and modulates his touch*

("Ivan Turgénieff," 1874)

All rigid critical formulas are more or less unjust, and it is not a complete description of our author—it would be a complete description of no real

master of fiction—to say that he is simply a searching observer. M. Turgénieff's imagination is always lending a hand and doing work on its own
account. Some of this work is exquisite; nothing could have more of the
simple magic of picturesqueness than such tales as "The Dog," "The Jew,"
"Visions," "The Adventure of Lieutenant Jergounoff," "Three Meetings,"
a dozen episodes in the "Memoirs of a Sportsman." Imagination guides
his hand and modulates his touch, and makes the artist worthy of the observer.
In a word, he is universally sensitive. In susceptibility to the sensuous impressions of life—to colours and odours and forms, and the myriad ineffable
refinements and enticements of beauty—he equals, and even surpasses, the
most accomplished representatives of the French school of story-telling; and
yet he has, on the other hand, an apprehension of man's religious impulses,
of the *ascetic* passion, the capacity of becoming dead to colours and odours
and beauty, never dreamed of in the philosophy of Balzac and Flaubert,
Octave Feuillet and Gustave Droz. He gives us Lisa in "A Nest of Noblemen," and Madame Polosoff in "Spring-Torrents." This marks his range.
Let us add, in conclusion, that his merit of form is of the first order. He is
remarkable for concision; few of his novels occupy the whole of a moderate
volume, and some of his best performances are tales of thirty pages.

3. among the shadows and substructions, the dark-based pillars

(*Hawthorne*, 1879)

What had a development was his imagination—that delicate and penetrating
imagination which was always at play, always entertaining itself, always
engaged in a game of hide-and-seek in the region in which it seemed to him
that the game could best be played—among the shadows and substructions,
the dark-based pillars and supports of our moral nature. Beneath this movement and ripple of his imagination—as free and spontaneous as that of the
sea-surface—lay directly his personal affections. These were solid and strong,
but, according to my impression, they had the place very much to themselves.

4. in my imagination the clearing process

(*Notebooks*, 1891)

I interrupt myself, because suddenly, in my imagination the clearing process
takes place—the little click that often occurs when I begin to straighten
things out pen in hand, really tackle them, sit down and look them in the face.
I catch hold of the slip of a tail of my action—I see my little drama.

5. imagination (art) vs. observation (history)

("Honoré de Balzac," 1902)

He [Balzac] had indeed a striking good fortune, the only one he was to enjoy as an harassed and exasperated worker: the great garden of life presented itself to him absolutely and exactly in the guise of the great garden of France, a subject vast and comprehensive enough, yet with definite edges and corners. This identity of his universal with his local and national vision is the particular thing we should doubtless call his greatest strength were we preparing agreeably to speak of it also as his visible weakness. Of Balzac's weaknesses, however, it takes some assurance to talk; there is always plenty of time for them; they are the last signs we know him by—such things truly as in other painters of manners often come under the head of mere exuberance of energy. So little in short do they earn the invidious name even when we feel them as defects.

What he did above all was to read the universe, as hard and as loud as he could, *into* the France of his time; his own eyes regarding his work as at once the drama of man and a mirror of the mass of social phenomena the most rounded and registered, most organized and administered, and thereby most exposed to systematic observation and portrayal, that the world had seen. There are happily other interesting societies, but these are for schemes of such an order comparatively loose and incoherent, with more extent and perhaps more variety, but with less of the great enclosed and exhibited quality, less neatness and sharpness of arrangement, fewer categories, subdivisions, juxtapositions. Balzac's France was both inspiring enough for an immense prose epic and reducible enough for a report or a chart. To allow his achievement all its dignity we should doubtless say also treatable enough for a history, since it was as a patient historian, a Benedictine of the actual, the living painter of his living time, that he regarded himself and handled his material. All painters of manners and fashions, if we will, are historians, even when they least don the uniform: Fielding, Dickens, Thackeray, George Eliot, Hawthorne among ourselves. But the great difference between the great Frenchman and the eminent others is that, with an imagination of the highest power, an unequalled intensity of vision, he saw his subject in the light of science as well, in the light of the bearing of all its parts on each other, and under pressure of a passion for exactitude, an appetite, the appetite of an ogre, for *all* the kinds of facts. We find I think in the union here suggested something like the truth about his genius, the nearest approach to a final account of him. Of imagination on one side all compact, he was on the other an insatiable reporter of the immediate, the material, the current combination, and perpetually moved by the historian's impulse to fix, preserve and explain them. One asks one's self as one reads him what concern the poet has with so much arithmetic and so much criticism, so many statistics and documents, what concern the critic and the economist have with so many passions, characters and adventures. The contradiction is always before us; it springs from the inordinate scale of the author's two faces; it explains more than anything else his eccentricities and difficulties. It accounts for his want of grace, his want of the lightness associated with an amusing literary form, his bristling surface, his closeness of texture, so rough with richness, yet so productive of the effect we have in mind when we speak of not being able to see the wood for the trees.

A thorough-paced votary, for that matter, can easily afford to declare at once that his confounding duality of character does more things still, or does at least the most important of all—introduces us without mercy (mercy for ourselves I mean) to the oddest truth we could have dreamed of meeting in such a connection. It was certainly *a priori* not to be expected we should feel it of him, but our hero is after all not in his magnificence totally an artist: which would be the strangest thing possible, one must hasten to add, were not the smallness of the practical difference so made even stranger. His endowment and his effect are each so great that the anomaly makes at the most a difference only by adding to his interest for the critic. The critic worth his salt is indiscreetly curious and wants ever to know how and why— whereby Balzac is thus a still rarer case for him, suggesting that exceptional curiosity may have exceptional rewards. The question of what makes the artist on a great scale is interesting enough; but we feel it in Balzac's company to be nothing to the question of what on an equal scale frustrates him. The scattered pieces, the *disjecta membra* of the character are here so numerous and so splendid that they prove misleading; we pile them together and the help assuredly is monumental; it forms an overtopping figure. The genius this figure stands for, none the less, is really such a lesson to the artist as perfection itself would be powerless to give; it carries him so much further into the special mystery. Where it carries him, at the same time, I must not in this scant space attempt to say—which would be a loss of the fine thread of my argument. I stick to our point in putting it, more concisely, that the artist of the *Comédie Humaine* is half smothered by the historian. Yet it belongs as well to the matter also to meet the question of whether the historian himself may not be an artist—in which case Balzac's catastrophe would seem to lose its excuse. The answer of course is that the reporter, however philosophic, has one law, and the originator, however substantially fed, has another; so that the two laws can with no sort of harmony or congruity make, for the finer sense, a common household. Balzac's catastrophe— so to name it once again—was in this perpetual conflict and final impossibility, an impossibility that explains his defeat on the classic side and extends so far at times as to make us think of his work as, from the point of view of beauty, a tragic waste of effort.

What it would come to, we judge, is that the irreconcilability of the two kinds of law is, more simply expressed, but the irreconcilability of two different ways of composing one's effect. The principle of composition that his free imagination would have, or certainly might have, handsomely imposed on him is perpetually dislocated by the quite opposite principle of the earnest seeker, the inquirer to a useful end, in whom nothing is free but a born antipathy to his yokefellow.

6. the mystic process of the crucible

("The Lesson of Balzac," 1905)

We have lately had a literary case of the same general family as the case of Balzac, and in presence of which some of the same speculations come up: I had occasion, not long since, after the death of Emile Zola, to attempt an appreciation of *his* extraordinary performance—his series of the *Rougon-Macquart* constituting in fact, in the library of the fiction that can hope in some degree to live, a monument to the idea of plenitude, of comprehension and variety, second only to the *Comédie Humaine*. The question presented itself, in respect to Zola's ability and Zola's career, with a different proportion and value, I quite recognize, and wearing a much less distinguished face; but it was there to be met, none the less, on the very threshold, and all the more because this was just where he himself had placed it. His idea had been, from the first, in a word, to lose no time—as if one could have experience, even the mere amount requisite for showing others as having it, *without* losing time!—and yet the degree in which he too, so handicapped, has achieved valid expression is such as still to stagger us. He had had inordinately to simplify—had had to leave out the life of the soul, practically, and confine himself to the life of the instincts, of the more immediate passions, such as can be easily and promptly caught in the fact. He had had, in a word, to confine himself almost entirely to the impulses and agitations that men and women are possessed by in common, and to take them as exhibited in mass and number, so that, being writ larger, they might likewise be more easily read. He met and solved, in this manner, his difficulty—the difficulty of knowing, and of showing, of life, only what his "notes" would account for. But it is in the *waste*, I think, much rather—the waste of time, of passion, of curiosity, of contact—that true initiation resides; so that the most wonderful adventures of the artist's spirit are those, immensely quickening for his "authority," that are yet not reducible to his notes. It is exactly here that we get the difference between such a solid, square, symmetrical structure as Les *Rougon-Macquart*, vitiated, in a high degree, by its mechanical side, and the monument left by Balzac—without the example of which, I surmise, Zola's work would not have existed. The mystic process of the crucible, the transformation of the material under aesthetic heat, is, in the *Comédie Humaine*, thanks to an intenser and more submissive fusion, completer, and also finer; for if the commoner and more wayside passions and conditions are, in the various episodes there, at no time gathered into so large and so thick an illustrative bunch, yet on the other hand they are shown much more freely at play in the individual case—and the individual case it is that permits of supreme fineness. It is hard to say where Zola is fine; whereas it is often, for pages together, hard to say where Balzac is, even under the weight of his too ponderous personality, not. The most fundamental and general sign of the novel, from one desperate experiment to another, is its being everywhere an effort at *representation*—this is the beginning and the end of it: wherefore it was that one could say at last, with account taken of everything, that Zola's performance, on his immense scale, was an extraordinary show of *representation* imitated. The imitation, in places—notably and admirably, for instance, in *L'Assommoir*—breaks through into something that we take for reality; but, for the most part, the separating rift, the determining difference, holds its course straight, prevents the attempted process from becoming the sound, straight, whole thing that is given us by those who have really *bought* their information. This is where Balzac remains unshaken,—in our feeling that, with all his faults of pedantry, ponderosity, pretentiousness, bad taste and charmless form, his spirit has somehow paid for its knowledge. His subject is again and again the complicated human creature or human condition; and it is with these complications as if he knew them, as Shakespeare knew them, by his charged consciousness, by the history of his soul and the direct exposure of his sensibility. This source of supply he found, forever—and one may indeed say he mostly left—sitting at his fireside; where it constituted the company with which I see him shut up, and his practical intimacy with which, during such orgies and debauches of intellectual passion, might earn itself that name of high personal good fortune that I have applied.

7. *the independent life of the imagination*

(Preface to *What Maisie Knew*, 1908)

This [the foregoing history] must serve as my account of the origin of "The Pupil": it will commend itself, I feel, to all imaginative and projective persons who have had—and what imaginative and projective person hasn't? —any like experience of the suddenly-determined *absolute* of perception. The whole cluster of items forming the image is on these occasions born at once; the parts are not pieced together, they conspire and interdepend; but what it really comes to, no doubt, is that at a simple touch an old latent and dormant impression, a buried germ, implanted by experience and then forgotten, flashes to the surface as a fish, with a single "squirm," rises to the baited hook, and there meets instantly the vivifying ray. I remember at all events having no doubt of anything or anyone here; the vision kept to the end its ease and its charm; it worked itself out with confidence. These are minor matters when the question is of minor results; yet almost any assured and downright imaginative act is—granted the sort of record in which I here indulge—worth fondly commemorating. One cherishes, after the fact, any proved case of the independent life of the imagination; above all if by that faculty one has been appointed mainly to live. We are then *never* detached from the question of what it may out of simple charity do for us. Besides which, in relation to the poor Moreens, innumerable notes, as I have inti-mated, all equally urging their relevance, press here to the front. The general adventure of the little composition itself—for singular things were to happen to it, though among such importunities not the most worth noting now— would be, occasion favouring, a thing to live over; moving as one did, roundabout it, in I scarce know what thick and coloured air of slightly tar-nished anecdote, of dim association, of casual confused romance; a compound defying analysis, but truly, for the social chronicler, any student in especial of the copious "cosmopolite" legend, a boundless and tangled, but highly explorable, garden. Why, somehow—these were the intensifying questions —did one see the Moreens, whom I place at Nice, at Venice, in Paris, as of the special essence of the little old miscellaneous cosmopolite Florence, the Florence of other, of irrecoverable years, the restless yet withal so convenient scene of a society that has passed away for ever with all its faded ghosts and fragile relics; immaterial presences that have quite ceased to revisit (trust an old romancer's, an old pious observer's fine sense to have made sure of it!) walks and prospects once sacred and shaded, but now laid bare, gaping wide, despoiled of their past and unfriendly to any appreciation of it?—through which the unconscious Barbarians troop with the regularity and passivity of "supplies," or other promiscuous goods, prepaid and forwarded.

8. in the deeps of his imagination

(Preface to *The Spoils of Poynton*, 1908)

That points, I think, to a large part of the very source of interest for the artist : it resides in the strong consciousness of his seeing all for himself. He has to borrow his motive, which is certainly half the battle; and this motive is his ground, his site and his foundation. But after that he only lends and gives, only builds and piles high, lays together the blocks quarried in the deeps of his imagination and on his personal premises. He thus remains all the while in intimate commerce with his motive, and can say to himself—what really more than anything else inflames and sustains him—that he alone has the *secret* of the particular case, he alone can measure the truth of the direction to be taken by his developed data. There can be for him, evidently, only one logic for these things; there can be for him only one truth and one direction —the quarter in which his subject most completely expresses itself. The careful ascertainment of how it shall do so, and the art of guiding it with consequent authority—since this sense of "authority" is for the master-builder the treasure of treasures, or at least the joy of joys—renews in the modern alchemist something like the old dream of the secret of life.

9. a rare alchemy

(Preface to *The Lesson of the Master*, 1909)

The subject of "The Coxon Fund," published in "The Yellow Book" in 1894, had long been with me, but was, beyond doubt, to have found its interest clinched by my perusal, shortly before the above date, of Mr. J. Dyke Campbell's admirable monograph on S. T. Coleridge. The wondrous figure of that genius had long haunted me, and circumstances into which I needn't here enter had within a few years contributed much to making it vivid. Yet it's none the less true that the Frank Saltram of "The Coxon Fund" pretends to be of his great suggester no more than a dim reflexion and above all a free rearrangement. More interesting still than the man—for the dramatist at any rate—is the S. T. Coleridge *type*; so what I was to do was merely to recognise the type, to borrow it, to re-embody and freshly place it; an ideal under the law of which I could but cultivate a free hand. I proceeded to do so; I reconstructed the scene and the figures—I had my own idea, which required, to express itself, a new set of relations—though, when all this is said, it had assuredly taken the recorded, transmitted person, the image embalmed in literary history, to fertilise my fancy. What I should, for that matter, like most to go into here, space serving, is the so interesting question —for the most part, it strikes me, too confusedly treated—of the story-teller's "real person" or actual contemporary transplanted and exhibited. But this pursuit would take us far, such radical revision do the common laxities of the case, as generally handled, seem to call for. No such process is *effectively* possible, we must hold, as the imputed act of transplanting; an act essentially not mechanical, but thinkable rather—so far as thinkable at all—in chemical, almost in mystical terms. We can surely account for nothing in the novelist's work that hasn't passed through the crucible of his imagination, hasn't, in that perpetually simmering cauldron his intellectual *pot-au-feu*, been reduced to savoury fusion. We here figure the morsel, of course, not as boiled to nothing, but as exposed, in return for the taste it gives out, to a new and richer saturation. In this state it is in due course picked out and served, and a meagre esteem will await, a poor importance attend it, if it doesn't speak most of its late genial medium, the good, the wonderful company it has, as I hint, aesthetically kept. It has entered, in fine, into new relations, it emerges for new ones. Its final savour has been constituted, but its prime identity destroyed—which is what was to be demonstrated. Thus it has become a different and, thanks to a rare alchemy, a better thing. Therefore let us have here as little as possible about its "being" Mr. This or Mrs. That. If it adjusts itself with the least truth to its new life it can't possibly be either. If it gracelessly refers itself to either, if it persists as the impression not artistically dealt with, it shames the honour offered it and can only be spoken of as having ceased to be a thing of fact and yet not become a thing of truth.

PART B: THE UNCONSCIOUS

1. the dim underworld of fiction

("The Middle Years," 1893)

He [the novelist, Dencombe] dived once more into his story and was drawn down, as by a siren's hand, to where, in the dim underworld of fiction, the great glazed tank of art, strange silent subjects float. He recognised his motive and surrendered to his talent. Never probably had that talent, such as it was, been so fine. His difficulties were still there, but what was also there, to his perception, though probably, alas! to nobody's else, was the art that in most cases had surmounted them. In his surprised enjoyment of this ability he had a glimpse of a possible reprieve. Surely its force wasn't spent—there was life and service in it yet. It hadn't come to him easily, it had been backward and roundabout. It was the child of time, the nursling of delay; he had struggled and suffered for it, making sacrifices not to be counted, and now that it was really mature was it to cease to yield, to confess itself brutally beaten? There was an infinite charm for Dencombe in feeling as he had never felt before that diligence *vincit omnia*. The result produced in his little book was somehow a result beyond his conscious intention: it was as if he had planted his genius, had trusted his method, and they had grown up and flowered with this sweetness.

      •   •   •   •   •

". . . We work in the dark—we do what we can—we give what we have. Our doubt is our passion and our passion is our task. The rest is the madness of art."

2. begin it — and it will grow

(*Notebooks*, 1899)

How, through all hesitations and conflicts and worries, *the* thing, the desire to get back only to the *big* (scenic, constructive 'architectural' effects) seizes me and carries me off my feet: making me feel that it's a far deeper economy of time to sink, at *any* moment, into the evocation and ciphering out of *that*, than into any other *small* beguilement at all. Ah, once more, to let myself go! The very thought of it soothes and sustains, lays a divine hand on my nerves, and lights, so beneficently, my uncertainties and obscurities. *Begin* it —and it will grow. Put in now some strong short novel, and come back from the continent, with it all figured out. I must have a long *tête à tête* with myself, a long ciphering bout, on it, before I really start. *Basta*. I've other work to do this a.m. and I only just now overflowed into this from a little gust of restless impatience. I'm somehow haunted with the *American* family represented to me by Mrs. Cameron (*à propos* of the 'Lloyd Bryces') last summer. Yet that is a large, comprehensive picture, and I long to represent an *action:* I mean a rapid, concrete action is what I desire, yearn, just now, to put in: to build, construct, teach myself a mastery of. But *basta* again. *A bientôt.*

3. the deep well of unconscious cerebration

(Preface to *The American*, 1907)

I was charmed with my idea, which would take, however, much working out; and precisely because it had so much to give, I think, must I have dropped it for the time into the deep well of unconscious cerebration: not without the hope, doubtless, that it might eventually emerge from that reservoir, as one had already known the buried treasure to come to light, with a firm iridescent surface and a notable increase of weight.

4. themes break loose to roam and hunt

(Preface to *What Maisie Knew*, 1908)

I have already elsewhere noted, I think, that the memory of my own work preserves for me no theme that, at some moment or other of its development, and always only waiting for the right connexion or chance, hasn't

THE WRITER AND HIS IMAGINATION 87

signally refused to remain humble, even (or perhaps all the more resentfully) when fondly selected for its conscious and hopeless humility. Once "out," like a house-dog of a temper above confinement, it defies the mere whistle, it roams, it hunts, it seeks out and "sees" life; it can be brought back but by hand and then only to take its futile thrashing.

5. the triumph of intentions never entertained

(Preface to *The Awkward Age*, 1908)

The little ideas one wouldn't have treated save for the design of keeping them small, the developed situations that one would never with malice prepense have undertaken, the long stories that had thoroughly meant to be short, the short subjects that had underhandedly plotted to be long, the hypocrisy of modest beginings, the audacity of misplaced middles, the triumph of intentions never entertained—with these patches, as I look about, I see my experience paved: an experience to which nothing is wanting save, I confess, some grasp of its final lesson.

6. the Story is just the spoiled child of art

(Preface to *The Ambassadors*, 1909)

There is always, of course, for the story-teller, the irresistible determinant and the incalculable advantage of his interest in the story *as such;* it is ever, obviously, overwhelmingly, the prime and precious thing (as other than this I have never been able to see it); as to which what makes for it, with whatever headlong energy, may be said to pale before the energy with which it simply makes for itself. It rejoices, none the less, at its best, to seem to offer itself in a light, to seem to know, and with the very last knowledge, what it's about—liable as it yet is at moments to be caught by us with its tongue in its cheek and absolutely no warrant but its splendid impudence. Let us grant then that the impudence is always there—there, so to speak, for grace and effect and *allure;* there, above all, because the Story is just the spoiled child of art, and because, as we are always disappointed when the pampered don't "play up," we like it, to that extent, to look all its character. It probably does so, in truth, even when we most flatter ourselves that we negotiate with it by treaty.

Part C: The World of Creation

1. *the luminous paradise of art*

(*Notebooks*, 1891)

Meanwhile the soothing, the healing, the sacred and salutary refuge from all these vulgarities and pains is simply to lose myself in this quiet, this blessed and uninvaded workroom in the inestimable effort and refreshment of art, in resolute and beneficent production. I come back to it with a treasure of experience, of wisdom, of acquired material, of (it seems to me) seasoned fortitude and augmented capacity. Purchased by disgusts enough, it is at any rate a boon that now that I hold it, I feel I wouldn't, I oughtn't, to have missed. Ah, the terrible law of the artist—the law of fructification, of fertilization, the law by which everything is grist to his mill—the law, in short, of the acceptance of all experience, of all suffering, of *all* life, of *all* suggestion and sensation and illumination. To keep at it—to strive toward the perfect, the ripe, the only best; to go on, by one's own clear light, with patience, courage and continuity, to live with the high vision and effort, to justify one's self —and, oh, so greatly!—all in time: this and this alone can be my only lesson from *anything*. Vague and weak are these words, but the experience and the purpose are of welded gold and adamant. The consolation, the dignity, the joy of life are that discouragements and lapses, depressions and darknesses come to one only as one stands *without*—I mean without the luminous paradise of art. As soon as I really re-enter it—cross the loved threshold— stand in the high chamber, and the gardens divine—the whole realm widens out again before me and around me—the air of life fills my lungs—the light of achievement flushes over all the place, and I believe, I see, I *do*.

2. *to live in the world of creation*

(*Notebooks*, 1891)

To live *in* the world of creation—to get into it and stay in it—to frequent it and haunt it—to *think* intently and fruitfully—to woo combinations and inspirations into being by a depth and continuity of attention and meditation —this is the only thing—and I neglect it, far and away too much; from indolence, from vagueness, from inattention, and from a strange nervous fear of letting myself go. If I vanquish that nervousness, the world is mine.

3. the refuge, the asylum

(Notebooks, 1893)

I have been worrying at the dramatic, the unspeakably theatric form for a long time, but I am in possession now of some interposing days (the reasons for which I needn't go into here—they are abundantly chronicled elsewhere), during which I should like to dip my pen into the *other* ink—the sacred fluid of fiction. Among the delays, the disappointments, the *déboires* of the horrid theatric trade nothing is so soothing as to remember that literature sits patient at my door, and that I have only to lift the latch to let in the exquisite little form that is, after all, nearest to my heart and with which I am so far from having done. I let it in and the old brave hours come back; I live them over again—I add another little block to the small literary monument that it has been given to me to erect. The dimensions don't matter—one must cultivate one's garden. To do many—and do them perfect: that is the refuge, the asylum. I must *always* have one on the stocks. It will be there—it will be started—and little by little it will grow. I have among the rough notes of this old book ½ a dozen decent starting-points. I don't say to myself, here, a 10th of the things I might—but it isn't necessary. So deeply I know them and feel them.

4. to surrender one's self

(Notebooks, 1895)

I have my head, thank God, full of visions. One has never too many—one has never enough. Ah, just to let one's self go—at last: to surrender one's self to what through all the long years one has (quite heroically, I think) hoped for and waited for—the mere potential, and relative, increase of *quantity* in the material act—act of application and production. One has prayed and hoped and waited, in a word, to be able to work *more*. And now, toward the end, it seems, within its limits, to have come. That is all I ask. Nothing else in the world. I bow down to Fate, equally in submission and in gratitude. This time it's gratitude; but the form of the gratitude, to be real and adequate, must be large and confident action—splendid and supreme creation. *Basta.*

PART D: FERTILIZATION OF SUBJECT BY FORM

1. expression . . . makes the reality

("Gustave Flaubert," 1902)

His [Flaubert's] own sense of all this, as I have already indicated, was that beauty comes with expression, that expression is creation, that it *makes* the reality, and only in the degree in which it *is*, exquisitely, expression; and that we move in literature through a world of different values and relations, a blessed world in which we know nothing except by style, but in which also everything is saved by it, and in which the image is thus always superior to the thing itself. . . .

. . . What but the "doing" makes the thing, he would have asked, and how can a positive result from a mere iteration of negatives, or wealth proceed from the simple addition of so many instances of penury? We should here, in closer communion with him, have got into his highly characteristic and suggestive view of the fertilization of subject by form, penetration of the sense, ever, by the expression—the latter reacting creatively on the former; a conviction in the light of which he appears to have wrought with real consistency and which borrows from him thus its high measure of credit.

2. *literary deeds vs. social deeds*

(Preface to *The Golden Bowl*, 1909)

All of which amounts doubtless but to saying that as the whole conduct of life consists of things done, which do other things in their turn, just so our behaviour and its fruits are essentially one and continuous and persistent and unquenchable, so the act has its way of abiding and showing and testifying, and so, among our innumerable acts, are no arbitrary, no senseless separations. The more we are capable of acting the less gropingly we plead such differences; whereby, with any capability, we recognise betimes that to "put" things is very exactly and responsibly and interminably to do them. Our expression of them, and the terms on which we understand that, belong as nearly to our conduct and our life as every other feature of our freedom; these things yield in fact some of its most exquisite material to the religion of doing. More than that, our literary deeds enjoy this marked advantage over many of our acts, that, though they go forth into the world and stray even in the desert, they don't to the same extent lose themselves; their attachment and reference to us, however strained, needn't necessarily lapse— while of the tie that binds us to *them* we may make almost anything we like. We are condemned, in other words, whether we will or no, to abandon and outlive, to forget and disown and hand over to desolation, many vital or social performances—if only because the traces, records, connexions, the very memorials we would fain preserve, are practically impossible to rescue for that purpose from the general mixture. We give them up even when we wouldn't—it is not a question of choice. Not so on the other hand our really "done" things of this superior and more appreciable order—which leave us indeed all licence of disconnexion and disavowal, but positively impose on us no such necessity. Our relation to them is essentially traceable, and in that fact abides, we feel, the incomparable luxury of the artist. It rests altogether with himself not to break with his values, not to "give away" his importances. Not to *be* disconnected, for the tradition of behaviour, he has but to feel that he is not; by his lightest touch the whole chain of relation and responsibility is reconstituted. Thus if he is always doing he can scarce, by his own measure, ever have done. All of which means for him conduct with a vengeance, since it is conduct minutely and publicly attested. Our noted behaviour at large may show for ragged, because it perpetually escapes our control; we have again and again to consent to its appearing in undress—that is in no state to brook criticism. But on all the ground to which the pretension of performance by a series of exquisite laws may apply there reigns one sovereign truth—which decrees that, as art is nothing if not exemplary, care nothing if not active, finish nothing if not consistent, the proved error is the base apologetic deed, the helpless regret is the barren commentary, and "connexions" are employable for finer purposes than mere gaping contrition.

3. *it is art that* makes *life*

(*Letters*, 1915, to H. G. Wells)

Of course for myself I live, live intensely and am fed by life, and my value, whatever it be, is in my own kind of expression of that. . . . Meanwhile I absolutely dissent from the claim that there are any differences whatever in the amenability to art of forms of literature aesthetically determined, and hold your distinction between a form that is (like) painting and a form that is (like) architecture for wholly null and void. There is no sense in which architecture is aesthetically "for use" that doesn't leave any other art whatever exactly as much so; and so far from that of literature being irrelevent to the literary report upon life, and to its being made as interesting as possible, I regard it as relevant in a degree that leaves everything else behind. It is art that *makes* life, makes interest, makes importance, for our consideration and application of these things, and I know of no substitute whatever for the force and beauty of its process.

Chapter V

DEFINITIONS AND DISCRIMINATIONS

Although Henry James never attempted comprehensive definition of the forms and modes of literature, he inevitably touched on and even formulated such definitions in the process of writing about writers and about his own fiction. These definitions lie scattered throughout his work and are brought together here in the systematic form that James never attempted; his suspicions were too easily aroused by neat formulas and tidy categories. The fragmentary nature of this chapter results from James's recurring preference, when drawn by abstraction, to return to the particular case, the specific example.

James provided two famous definitions of the novel in "The Art of Fiction," and these definitions lie at the heart of all his discussions of fiction: "The only reason for the existence of a novel is that it does attempt to represent life." And again: "A novel is in its broadest definition a personal, a direct impression of life: that, to begin with, constitutes its value, which is greater or less according to the intensity of the impression." These definitions are deceptively simple, as was shown in Chapter III by James's extended comments on the writer's relation to life and experience. But though simple, they are able to withstand the pressures of intensive exploration, as James demonstrates here and elsewhere. James's statements are direct, but his words are charged with complexity.

In Part A of this chapter, James's discriminations among novel, poem, and play are brought together for mutual illumination. His most frequent and extended comments are, of course, on fiction. But when he touches on the other forms, it generally is to attempt discrimination. In "The Lesson of Balzac" (1905), he writes: "The Poet is most the Poet when he is preponderantly lyrical, when he speaks, laughing or crying, most directly from his individual heart, which throbs under the impressions of life. It is not the image of life that he thus expresses, so much as life itself, in its sources—so much as his own intimate, essential states and feelings. By the time he has begun to collect anecdotes, to tell stories, to represent scenes, to concern himself, that is, with the states and feelings of others, he is well on the way not to be the Poet pure and simple." Again, in "The New Novel," James writes: "The play, as distinguished from the novel, lives exclusively on the spoken word— not on the report of the thing said but, directly and audibly, on that very thing. . . . the order in which the drama simply says things gives it all its form."

In Part B are assembled definitions of some of the elements of fiction together with discriminations between the shorter forms. It is important to note that James's vocabulary was never rigidly fixed, and he could easily allow—as any good writer does—the context to suggest shifting meanings for words. But James did come to divide short stories into types—the picture and the anecdote, or some combination of the two with one predominant. And he came to discriminate between a narrative idea that was "anecdotic," which made the short story, and the idea that was "developmental," that turned into the nouvelle—defined in one passage as "a complicated thing with a strong brevity."

In Part C of this chapter James has his say on the non-realistic modes that fascinated him most, especially the fairy tale and the ghost story. In writing about R. L. Stevenson's work, James noted: "The novelist who leaves the extraordinary out of his account is liable to awkward confrontations, as we are compelled to reflect in this age of newspapers and of universal publicity." Of course James included the extraordinary in his own work, in a series of ghostly tales that continue to fascinate and puzzle. His ventures in that form confirm his commitment to the total freedom of the novelist. He said in his essay on Stevenson: "The breath of the novelist's being is his liberty, and the incomparable virtue of the form he uses is that it leads itself to views innumerable and diverse, to every variety of illustration."

PART A: NOVEL, POEM, PLAY

1. to represent life

("Alphonse Daudet," 1883)

I should say that the main object of the novel is to represent life. I cannot understand any other motive for interweaving imaginary incidents, and I do not perceive any other measure of the value of such combinations. The *effect* of a novel—the effect of any work of art—is to entertain; but that is a very different thing. The success of a work of art, to my mind, may be measured by the degree to which it produces a certain illusion; that illusion makes it appear to us for the time that we have lived another life—that we have had a miraculous enlargement of experience. The greater the art the greater the miracle, and the more certain also the fact that we have been entertained —in the best meaning of that word, at least, which signifies that we have been living at the expense of some one else. I am perfectly aware that to say the object of a novel is to represent life does not bring the question to a point so fine as to be uncomfortable for any one. It is of the greatest importance that there should be a very free appreciation of such a question, and the definition I have hinted at gives plenty of scope for that. For, after all, may not people differ infinitely as to what constitutes life—what constitutes representation?

2. a picture of life vs. a moralised fable

("The Life of George Eliot," 1885)

[For George Eliot, the novel] was not primarily a picture of life, capable of deriving a high value from its form, but a moralised fable, the last word of a philosophy endeavouring to teach by example.

3. a direct impression of life

(*Selected Letters*, 1889, to The Deerfield Summer School)

To tell the truth, I can't help thinking that we already talk too much about the novel, about and around it, in proportion to the quantity of it having any importance that we produce. What I should say to the nymphs and swains who propose to converse about it under the great trees at Deerfield is: "Oh, do something from your point of view; an ounce of example is worth a ton of generalities; do something with the great art and the great form; do something with life. Any point of view is interesting that is a direct impression of life. You each have an impression colored by your individual conditions; make that into a picture, a picture framed by your own personal wisdom, your glimpse of the American world. The field is vast for freedom, for study, for observation, for satire, for truth." I don't think I really do know what you mean by "materializing tendencies" any more than I should by "spiritualizing" or "etherealizing." There are no tendencies worth anything but to see the actual or the imaginative, which is just as visible, and to paint it. I have only two little words for the matter remotely approaching to rule or doctrine; one is life and the other freedom. Tell the ladies and gentlemen, the ingenious inquirers, to consider life directly and closely, and not to be put off with mean and puerile falsities, and be conscientious about it. It is infinitely large, various and comprehensive. Every sort of mind will find what it looks for in it, whereby the novel becomes truly multifarious and illustrative. That is what I mean by liberty; give it its head and let it range. If it is in a bad way, and the English novel is, I think, nothing but absolute freedom can refresh it and restore its self-respect.

4. how little "story" is required

("Matilde Serao," 1901)

Let me further not fail to register my admiration for the curious cluster of scenes that, in "Il Romanzo," bears the title of "Nella Lava." Here frankly, I take it, we have the real principle of "naturalism"—a consistent present-ment of the famous "slice of life." The slices given us—slices of shabby hungry maidenhood in small cockney circles—are but sketchily related to the volcanic catastrophe we hear rumbling behind them, the undertone of all the noise of Naples; but they have the real artistic importance of showing us how little "story" is required to hold us when we get, before the object evoked and in the air created, the impression of the real thing. Whatever thing—interesting inference—has but effectively to *be* real to constitute in itself story enough. There is no story without it, none that is not rank hum-bug; whereas with it the very desert blooms.

5. a capacious vessel

("Emile Zola," 1903)

There then [in Zola's *Les Rougon-Macquart*], provisionally at least, we touch bottom; we get a glimpse of the pliancy and variety, the ideal of vivid-ness, on behalf of which our equivocal form may appeal to a strong head. In the name of what ideal on its own side, however, does the strong head yield to the appeal? What is the logic of its so deeply committing itself? Zola's case seems to tell us, as it tells us other things. The logic is in its huge freedom of adjustment to the temperament of the worker, which it carries, so to say, as no other vehicle can do. It expresses fully and directly the whole man, and big as he may be it can still be big enough for him without becoming false to its type. We see this truth made strong, from beginning to end, in Zola's work; we see the temperament, we see the whole man, with his size and all his marks, stored and packed away in the huge hold of *Les Rougon-Macquart* as a cargo is packed away on a ship. His personality is the thing that finally pervades and prevails, just as so often on a vessel the pres-ence of the cargo makes itself felt for the assaulted senses. What has most come home to me in reading him over is that a scheme of fiction so con-ducted is in fact a capacious vessel. It can carry anything—with art and force in the stowage; nothing in this case will sink it. And it is the only form for which such a claim can be made. All others have to confess to a smaller scope—to selection, to exclusion, to the danger of distortion, explosion, combustion. The novel has nothing to fear but sailing too light. It will take aboard all we bring in good faith to the dock.

6. novelist vs. poet: image of life vs. life . . . in its sources

("The Lesson of Balzac," 1905)

When I am tempted, on occasion, to ask myself why we should, after all, so much as talk about the Novel, the wanton fable, against which, in so many ways, so showy an indictment may be drawn, I seem to see that the simplest plea is not to be sought in any attempted philosophy, in any abstract reason for our perversity or our levity. The real gloss upon these things is reflected from some great practitioner, some concrete instance of the art, some ample cloak under which we may gratefully crawl. It comes back, of course, to the example and the analogy of the Poet—with the abatement, however, that the Poet is most the Poet when he is preponderantly lyrical, when he speaks, laughing or crying, most directly from his individual heart, which throbs under the impressions of life. It is not the *image* of life that he thus expresses, so much as life itself, in its sources—so much as his own intimate, essential states and feelings. By the time he has begun to collect anecdotes, to tell stories, to represent scenes, to concern himself, that is, with the states and feelings of others, he is well on the way not to be the Poet pure and simple. The lyrical element, all the same, abides in him, and it is by this element that he is connected with what is most splendid in his expression. The lyrical instinct and tradition are immense in Shakespeare; which is why, great story-teller, great dramatist and painter, great lover, in short, of the image of life though he was, we need not press the case of his example. The lyrical element is not great, is in fact not present at all, in Balzac, in Scott (the Scott of the voluminous prose), nor in Thackeray, nor in Dickens—which is precisely why they are so essentially novelists, so almost exclusively lovers of the image of life. It *is* great, or it is at all events largely present, in such a writer as George Sand—which is doubtless why we take her for a novelist in a much looser sense than the others we have named. It is considerable in that bright particular genius of our own day, George Meredith, who so strikes us as hitching winged horses to the chariot of his prose—steeds who prance and dance and caracole, who strain the traces, attempt to quit the ground, and yearn for the upper air. Balzac, with huge feet fairly plowing the sand of our desert, is on the other hand the very type and model of the projector and creator; so that when I think, either with envy or with terror, of the nature and the effort of the Novelist, I think of something that reaches its highest expression in him. That is why those of us who, as fellow-craftsmen, have once caught a glimpse of this value in him, can never quite rest from hanging about him; that is why he seems to have all that the others have to tell us, with more, besides, that is all his own. He lived and breathed in his medium, and the fact that he was able to achieve in it, as man and as artist, so crowded a career, remains for us one of the most puzzling problems—I scarce know whether to say of literature or of life. He is himself a figure more extraordinary than any he drew, and the fascination may still be endless of all the questions he puts to us and of the answers for which we feel ourselves helpless.

7. novel vs. play

("The New Novel," 1914)

We need of course scarce expressly note that the play, as distinguished from the novel, lives exclusively on the spoken word—not on the report of the thing said but, directly and audibly, on that very thing; that it thrives by its law on the exercise under which the novel hopelessly collapses when the attempt is made disproportionately to impose it. There is no danger for the play of the cart before the horse, no disaster involved in it; that form being *all* horse and the interest itself mounted and astride, and not, as that of the novel, dependent in the first instance on wheels. The order in which the drama simply says things gives it all its form, while the story told and the picture painted, as the novel at the pass we have brought it to embraces them, reports of an infinite diversity of matters, gathers together and gives out again a hundred sorts, and finds its order and its structure, its unity and its beauty, in the alternation of parts and the adjustment of differences. It is no less apparent that the novel may be fundamentally *organized*—such things as *The Egoist* and *The Awkward Age* are there to prove it; but in this case it adheres unconfusedly to that logic and has nothing to say to any other.

8. drama: a masterly structure

("Tennyson's Drama," 1875–77)

The dramatic form seems to me of all literary forms the very noblest. I have so extreme a relish for it that I am half afraid to trust myself to praise it, lest I should seem to be merely rhapsodizing. But to be really noble it must be quite itself, and between a poor drama and a fine one there is, I think, a wider interval than anywhere else in the scale of success. A sequence of speeches headed by proper names—a string of dialogues broken into acts and scenes—does not constitute a drama; not even when the speeches are very clever and the dialogue bristles with "points."

The fine thing in a real drama, generally speaking, is that, more than any other work of literary art, it needs a masterly structure. It needs to be shaped and fashioned and laid together, and this process makes a demand upon an artist's rarest gifts. He must combine and arrange, interpolate and eliminate, play the joiner with the most attentive skill; and yet at the end effectually bury his tools and his sawdust, and invest his elaborate skeleton with the smoothest and most polished integument. The five-act drama—serious or humourous, poetic or prosaic—is like a box of fixed dimensions and inelastic material, into which a mass of precious things are to be packed away. It is a problem in ingenuity and a problem of the most interesting kind. The precious things in question seem out of all proportion to the compass of the receptacle; but the artist has an assurance that with patience and skill a place may be made for each, and that nothing need be clipped or crumpled, squeezed or damaged. The false dramatist either knocks out the sides of his box, or plays the deuce with the contents; the real one gets down on his knees, disposes of his goods tentatively, this, that, and the other way, loses his temper but keeps his ideal, and at last rises in triumph, having packed his coffer in the one way that is mathematically right. It closes perfectly, and the lock turns with a click; between one object and another you cannot insert the point of a penknife.

To work successfully beneath a few grave, rigid laws, is always a strong man's highest ideal of success. The reader cannot be sure how deeply conscious Mr. Tennyson has been of the laws of the drama, but it would seem as if he had not very attentively pondered them. In a play, certainly, the subject is of more importance than in any other work of art. Infelicity, triviality, vagueness of subject, may be outweighed in a poem, a novel, or a picture, by charm of manner, by ingenuity of execution; but in a drama the subject is of the essence of the work—it *is* the work. If it is feeble, the work can have no force; if it is shapeless, the work must be amorphous.

Queen Mary, I think, has this fundamental weakness; it would be very hard to say what its subject is. Strictly speaking, the drama has none. To the statement, "It is the reign of the elder daughter of Henry VIII.," it seems to me very nearly fair to reply that that is not a subject. I do not mean to say that a consummate dramatist could not resolve it into one, but the presumption is altogether against it. It cannot be called an intrigue, nor treated as one; it tends altogether to expansion; whereas a genuine dramatic subject should tend to concentration.

Madame Ristori, that accomplished tragédienne, has for some years been carrying about the world with her a piece of writing, punctured here and there with curtain-falls, which she presents to numerous audiences as a tragedy embodying the history of Queen Elizabeth. The thing is worth mentioning only as an illustration; it is from the hand of a prolific Italian purveyor of such wares, and is as bad as need be. Many of the persons who read these lines will have seen it, and will remember it as a mere bald sequence of anecdotes, roughly cast into dialogue. It is not incorrect to say that, as regards form, Mr. Tennyson's drama is of the same family as the historical tragedies of Signor Giacometti. It is simply a dramatised chronicle, without an internal structure, taking its material in pieces, as history hands them over, and working each one up into an independent scene—usually with rich ability. It has no shape; it is cast into no mould; it has neither beginning, middle, nor end, save the chronological ones.

PART B: PICTURE, ANECDOTE, SHORT STORY, NOUVELLE

1. *picture vs. story*

("Anthony Trollope," 1883)

His [Trollope's] stories, in spite of their great length, deal very little in the surprising, the exceptional, the complicated; as a general thing he has no great story to tell. The thing is not so much a story as a picture; if we hesitate to call it a picture it is because the idea of composition is not the controlling one and we feel that the author would regard the artistic, in general, as a kind of affectation. There is not even much description, in the sense which the present votaries of realism in France attach to that word. The painter lays his scene in a few deliberate, not especially pictorial strokes, and never dreams of finishing the piece for the sake of enabling the reader to hand it up. The finish, such as it is, comes later, from the slow and somewhat clumsy accumulation of small illustrations. These illustrations are sometimes of the commonest; Trollope turns them out inexhaustibly, repeats them freely, unfolds them without haste and without rest.

2. *short story: detached incident vs. impression of a complexity or continuity*

("The Story-Teller at Large: Mr. Henry Harland," 1898)

Mr. Harland's method [Henry Harland in *Comedies and Errors*] is that of the "short story" which has of late become an object of such almost extravagant dissertation. If it has awaked to consciousness, however, it has doubtless only done what most things are doing in an age of organized talk. It took itself, in the comparatively silent years, less seriously, and there was perhaps a more general feeling that you both wrote and read your short story best when you did so in peace and patience. To turn it out, at any rate, as well as possible, by private, and almost diffident, instinct and reflection, was a part of the general virtue of the individual, the kind of virtue that shunned the high light of the public square. The public square is now the whole city, and, taking us all in, has acoustic properties so remarkable that thoughts barely whispered in a corner are heard all over the place. Therefore each of us already knows what every other of us thinks of the short story, though he knows perhaps at the same time that not every other can write it. Anything we may say about it is at best but a compendium of the current wisdom. It is a form delightful and difficult, and with one of these qualities—as, for that matter, one of them almost everywhere is—the direct reason of the other. It is an easy thing, no doubt, to do a little with, but the interest quickens at a high rate on an approximation to that liberal *more* of which we speedily learn it to be capable. The charm I find in Mr. Harland's tales is that he is always trying for the more, for the extension of the picture, the full and vivid summary, and trying with an art of ingenuity, an art of a reflective order, all alive with felicities and delicacies.

Are there not two quite distinct effects to be produced by this rigour of brevity—the two that best make up for the many left unachieved as requiring a larger canvas? The one with which we are most familiar is that of the detached incident, single and sharp, as clear as a pistol-shot; the other, of rarer performance, is that of the impression, comparatively generalised—simplified, foreshortened, reduced to a particular perspective—of a complexity or a continuity. The former is an adventure comparatively safe, in which you have, for the most part, but to put one foot after the other. It is just the risks of the latter, on the contrary, that make the best of the sport. These are naturally—given the general reduced scale—immense, for nothing is less intelligible than bad foreshortening, which, if it fails to mean everything intended, means less than nothing. It is to Mr. Harland's honour that he always "goes in" for the risks. *The Friend of Man*, for instance, is an attempt as far removed as possible from the snap of the pistol-shot; it is an excellent example of the large in a small dose, the smaller form put on its mettle and trying to do—by sharp selection, composition, presentation and the sacrifice of verbiage—what the longer alone is mostly supposed capable of. It is the picture of a particular figure—eccentric, comic, pathetic, tragic—disengaged from old remembrances, encounters, accidents, exhibitions and exposures, and resolving these glimpses and patches into the unity of air and feeling that makes up a character. It is all a matter of odds and ends recovered and interpreted. The "story" is nothing, the subject everything, and the manner in which the whole thing becomes expressive strikes me as an excellent specimen of what can be done on the minor scale when art comes in. There are, of course, particular effects that insist on space, and the thing, above all, that the short story has to renounce is the actual *pursuit* of a character. Temperaments and mixtures, the development of a nature, are shown us perforce in a tale, as they are shown us in life, only by illustration more or less copious and frequent; and the drawback is that when the tale is

short the figure, before we have had time to catch up with it, gets beyond
and away, dips below the horizon made by the little square of space that we
have accepted.

Yet, in the actual and prospective flood of fiction, the greatest of all the
streams that empty into the sea of the verbose, the relief may still be immense
that comes even from escapes for which we pay by incidental losses. We
are often tempted to wonder if almost any escape is not better than mere
submersion. *Petit-Bleu*, in this volume, *Cousin Rosalys*, *Tirala-Tirala*,
Rooms, all show the same love of evocation for evocation's sake, if need be;
the successful suggestion of conditions, states, circumstances, aspects; the
suggestion of the feeling of things in youth, of the remembrance of this
feeling in age; the suggestion, above all, of that most difficult of all things
for the novelist to render, the duration of time, the drag and friction of its
passage, the fact that things have not taken place, as the fashionable fables
of our day, with their terrific abuse of dialogue and absence of composition, seem to have embraced the mission of representing, just in the hour
or two it may take to estimate the manner of the book. The feeling of things
—in especial of the particular place, of the lost and regretted period and
chance, always, to fond fancy, supremely charming and queer and exquisite
—is, in fact, Mr. Harland's general subject and most frequent inspiration.
And what I find characteristic and curious in this is that the feeling is, in the
most candid way in the world, but with new infatuations and refinements,
the feeling of the American for his famous Europe.

3. *short story: anecdote or picture*

(Preface to *The Spoils of Poynton*, 1908)

A short story, to my sense and as the term is used in magazines, has to choose
between being either an anecdote or a picture and can but play its part strictly
according to its kind. I rejoice in the anecdote, but I revel in the picture;
though having doubtless at times to note that a given attempt may place
itself near the dividing-line. This is in some degree the case with "The Chaperon," in which, none the less, on the whole, picture ingeniously prevails;
picture aiming at those richly summarised and foreshortened effects—the
opposite pole again from expansion inorganic and thin—that refer their
terms of production, for which the magician has ever to don his best cap
and gown, to the inner compartment of our box of tricks. From *them*
comes the true grave close consistency in which parts hang together even
as the interweavings of a tapestry. "The Chaperon" has perhaps, so far as
it goes, something of that texture.

4. anecdote: something that has oddly happened to some one

(Preface to *The Reverberator*, 1908)

The anecdote consists, ever, of something that has oddly happened to some one, and the first of its duties is to point directly to the person whom it so distinguishes. He may be you or I or any one else, but a condition of our interest—perhaps the principal one—is that the anecdote shall know him, and shall accordingly speak of him, as its subject.

5. like the hard, shining sonnet

(Preface to *The Author of Beltraffio*, 1909)

The merit of the thing ["Europe," James's short story] is in the feat, once more, of the transfusion; the receptacle (of form) being so exiguous, the brevity imposed so great. I undertook the brevity, so often undertaken on a like scale before, and again arrived at it by the innumerable repeated chemical reductions and condensations that tend to make of the very short story, as I risk again noting, one of the costliest, even if, like the hard, shining sonnet, one of the most indestructible, forms of composition in general use. I accepted the rigour of its having, all sternly, in this case, to treat so many of its most appealing values as waste; and I now seek my comfort perforce in the mere exhibited result, the union of whatever fulness with whatever clearness.

6. the idea anecdotal vs. the idea developmental

(Preface to *The Author of Beltraffio*, 1909)

To get it ["The Middle Years"] right was to squeeze my subject into the five or six thousand words I had been invited to make it consist of—it consists, in fact, should the curious care to know, of some 5550—and I scarce perhaps recall another case, with the exception I shall presently name, in which my struggle to keep compression rich, if not, better still, to keep accretions compressed, betrayed for me such community with the anxious effort of some warden of the insane engaged at a critical moment in making fast a victim's straitjacket. The form of "The Middle Years" is not that of the *nouvelle*, but that of the concise anecdote; whereas the subject treated would perhaps seem one comparatively demanding "developments"—if indeed, amid these mysteries, distinctions were so absolute. (There is of course neither close not fixed measure of the reach of a development, which in some connexions seems almost superfluous and then in others to represent the whole sense of the matter; and we should doubtless speak more thoroughly by book had we some secret for exactly tracing deflexions and returns.) However this may be, it was as an anecdote, an anecdote only, that I was determined my little situation here should figure; to which end my effort was of course to follow it as much as possible from its outer edge in, rather than from its centre outward. That fond formula, I had alas already discovered, may set as many traps in the garden as its opposite may set in the wood; so that after boilings and reboilings of the contents of my small cauldron, after added pounds of salutary sugar, as numerous as those prescribed in the choicest recipe for the thickest jam, I well remember finding the whole process and act (which, to the exclusion of everything else, dragged itself out for a month) one of the most expensive of its sort in which I had ever engaged.

But I recall, by good luck, no less vividly how much finer a sweetness than any mere spooned-out saccharine dwelt in the fascination of the questions involved. Treating a theme that "gave" much in a form that, at the best, would give little, might indeed represent a peck of troubles; yet who, none the less, beforehand, was to pronounce with authority such and such an idea anecdotic and such and such another developmental? One had, for the vanity of *a priori* wisdom here, only to be so constituted that to see any form of beauty, for a particular application, proscribed or even questioned, was forthwith to covet that form more than any other and to desire the benefit of it exactly there. One had only to be reminded that for the effect of quick roundness the small smooth situation, though as intense as one will, is prudently indicated, and that for a fine complicated entangled air nothing will serve that doesn't naturally swell and bristle—one had only, I say, to be so warned off or warned on, to see forthwith no beauty for the simple thing that shouldn't, and even to perversity, enrich it, and none for the other, the comparatively intricate, that shouldn't press it out as a mosaic. After which fashion the careful craftsman would have prepared himself the special inviting treat of scarce being able to say, at his highest infatuation, before any series, which might be the light thing weighted and which the dense thing clarified.

7. short story vs. nouvelle

(Preface to *The Lesson of the Master*, 1909)

I was invited, and all urgently, to contribute to the first number [of "The Yellow Book"], and was regaled with the golden truth that my composition might absolutely assume, might shamelessly parade in, its own organic form. It was disclosed to me, wonderfully, that—so golden the air pervading the enterprise—any projected contribution might conform, not only unchallenged but by this circumstance itself the more esteemed, to its true intelligible nature. For any idea I might wish to express I might have space, in other words, elegantly to express it—an offered licence that, on the spot, opened up the millennium to the "short story." One had so often known this product to struggle, in one's hands, under the rude prescription of brevity at any cost, with the opposition so offered to its really becoming a story, that my friend's emphasised indifference to the arbitrary limit of length struck me, I remember, as the fruit of the finest artistic intelligence. We had been at one—that we already knew—on the truth that the forms of wrought things, in this order, *were*, all exquisitely and effectively, the things; so that, for the delight of mankind, form might compete with form and might correspond to fitness; might, that is, in the given case, have an inevitability, a marked felicity. Among forms, moreover, we had had, on the dimensional ground—for length and breadth—our ideal, the beautiful and blest *nouvelle;* the generous, the enlightened hour for which appeared thus at last to shine. It was under the star of the *nouvelle* that, in other languages, a hundred interesting and charming results, such studies on the minor scale as the best of Turgénieff's, of Balzac's, of Maupassant's, of Bourget's, and just lately, in our own tongue, of Kipling's, had been, all economically, arrived at—thanks to their authors', as "contributors," having been able to count, right and left, on a wise and liberal support. It had taken the blank misery of our Anglo-Saxon sense of such matters to organise, as might be said, the general indifference to this fine type of composition. In that dull view a "short story" was a "short story," and that was the end of it. Shades and differences, varieties and styles, the value above all of the idea happily *developed*, languished, to extinction, under the hard-and-fast rule of the "from six to eight thousand words"—when, for one's benefit, the rigour was a little relaxed. For myself, I delighted in the shapely *nouvelle*—as, for that matter, I had from time to time and here and there been almost encouraged to show.

8. the nouvelle: a complicated thing with a strong brevity

(Preface to *The Lesson of the Master*, 1909)

I am tempted to add that this recommemorative strain might easily woo me to another light step or two roundabout "The Coxon Fund." For I find myself look at it most interestedly to-day, after all, in the light of a significance quite other than that just noted. A marked example of the possible scope, at once, and the possible neatness of the *nouvelle*, it takes its place for me in a series of which the main merit and sign is the effort to do the complicated thing with a strong brevity and lucidity—to arrive, on behalf of the multiplicity, at a certain science of control. Infinitely attractive—though I risk here again doubtless an effect of reiteration—the question of how to exert this control in accepted conditions and how yet to sacrifice no real value; problem ever dearest to any economic soul desirous to keep renewing, and with a frugal splendour, its ideal of economy. Sacred altogether to memory, in short, such labours and such lights. Thus "The Coxon Fund" is such a complicated thing that if it still seems to carry itself—by which I mean if its clearness still rules here, or still serves—some pursued question of how the trick was played would probably not be thankless.

Part C: Allegory, The Extraordinary, Romance, Fairy Tale, Ghost Story

1. allegory with the deeper psychology

(Hawthorne, 1879)

Hawthorne, in his metaphysical moods, is nothing if not allegorical, and allegory, to my sense, is quite one of the lighter exercises of the imagination. Many excellent judges, I know, have a great stomach for it; they delight in symbols and correspondences, in seeing a story told as if it were another and very different story. I frankly confess that I have, as a general thing, but little enjoyment of it, and that it has never seemed to me to be, as it were, a first-rate literary form. It has produced assuredly some first-rate works; and Hawthorne in his younger years had been a great reader and devotee of Bunyan and Spenser, the great masters of allegory. But it is apt to spoil two good things—a story and a moral, a meaning and a form; and the taste for it is responsible for a large part of the forcible-feeble writing that has been inflicted upon the world. The only cases in which it is endurable is when it is extremely spontaneous, when the analogy presents itself with eager promptitude. When it shows signs of having been groped and fumbled for, the needful illusion is of course absent, and the failure complete. Then the machinery alone is visible, and the end to which it operates becomes a matter of indifference. There was but little literary criticism in the United States at the time Hawthorne's earlier works were published; but among the reviewers Edgar Poe perhaps held the scales the highest. He, at any rate, rattled them loudest, and pretended, more than any one else, to conduct the weighing-process on scientific principles. Very remarkable was this process of Edgar Poe's, and very extraordinary were his principles; but he had the advantage of being a man of genius, and his intelligence was frequently great. His collection of critical sketches of the American writers flourishing in what M. Taine would call his *milieu* and *moment*, is very curious and interesting reading, and it has one quality which ought to keep it from ever being completely forgotten. It is probably the most complete and exquisite specimen of *provincialism* ever prepared for the edification of men. Poe's judgments are pretentious, spiteful, vulgar; but they contain a great deal of sense and discrimination as well, and here and there, sometimes at frequent intervals, we find a phrase of happy insight imbedded in a patch of the most fatuous pedantry. He wrote a chapter upon Hawthorne, and spoke of him, on the whole, very kindly; and his estimate is of sufficient value to make it noticeable that he should express lively disapproval of the large part allotted to allegory in his tales—in defence of which, he says, "however, or for whatever object employed, there is scarcely one respectable word to be said. . . . The deepest emotion," he goes on, "aroused within us by the happiest allegory *as* allegory, is a very, *very* imperfectly satisfied sense of the writer's ingenuity in overcoming a difficulty we should have preferred his not having attempted to overcome. . . . One thing is clear, that if allegory ever establishes a fact, it is by dint of overturning a fiction;" and Poe has furthermore the courage to remark that the *Pilgrim's Progress* is a "ludicrously overrated book." Certainly, as a general thing, we are struck with the ingenuity and felicity of Hawthorne's analogies and correspondences; the idea appears to have made itself at home in them easily. Nothing could be better in this respect than *The Snow Image* (a little masterpiece), or *The Great Carbuncle*, or *Doctor Heidegger's Experiment*, or *Rappacini's Daughter*. But in such things as *The Birth-Mark* and *The Bosom-Serpent* we are struck with something stiff and mechanical, slightly incongruous, as if the kernel had not assimilated its envelope. But these are matters of light impression, and there would be a want of tact in pretending to discriminate too closely among things which all, in one way or another, have a charm. The charm—the great charm—is that they are glimpses of a great field, of the whole deep mystery of man's soul and conscience. They are moral, and their interest is moral; they deal with something more than the mere accidents and conventionalities, the surface occurrences of life. The fine thing in Hawthorne is that he cared for the deeper psychology, and that, in his way, he tried to become familiar with it. This natural, yet fanciful, familiarity with it; this air, on the author's part, of being a confirmed *habitué* of a region of mysteries and subtleties, constitutes the originality of his tales. And then they have the further merit of seeming, for what they are, to spring up so freely and lightly. The author has all the ease, indeed, of a regular dweller in the moral, psychological realm; he goes to and fro in it, as a man who knows his way. His tread is a light and modest one, but he keeps the key in his pocket.

2. *the extraordinary: psychology added*

("Robert Louis Stevenson," 1888)

Mr. Stevenson has a theory of composition in regard to the novel on which he is to be congratulated, as any positive and genuine conviction of this kind is vivifying so long as it is not narrow. The breath of the novelist's being is his liberty, and the incomparable virtue of the form he uses is that it lends itself to views innumerable and diverse, to every variety of illustration. There is certainly no other mould of so large a capacity. The doctrine of M. Zola himself, so jejune if literally taken, is fruitful, inasmuch as in practice he romantically departs from it. Mr. Stevenson does not need to depart, his individual taste being as much to pursue the romantic as his principle is to defend it. Fortunately, in England to-day, it is not much attacked. The triumphs that are to be won in the portrayal of the strange, the improbable, the heroic, especially as these things shine from afar in the credulous eye of youth, are his strongest, most constant incentive. On one happy occasion, in relating the history of *Doctor Jekyll*, he has seen them as they present themselves to a maturer vision. *Doctor Jekyll* is not a "boy's book," nor yet is *Prince Otto;* the latter, however, is not, like the former, an experiment in mystification—it is, I think, more than anything else, an experiment in style, conceived one summer's day when the author had given the reins to his high appreciation of Mr. George Meredith. It is perhaps the most literary of his works, but it is not the most natural. It is one of those coquetries, as we may call them for want of a better word, which may be observed in Mr. Stevenson's activity—a kind of artful inconsequence. It is easy to believe that if his strength permitted him to be a more abundant writer he would still more frequently play this eminently literary trick—that of dodging off in a new direction—upon those who might have fancied they knew all about him. I made the reflection, in speaking of *Will of the Mill*, that there is a kind of anticipatory malice in the subject of that fine story: as if the writer had intended to say to his reader "You will never guess, from the unction with which I describe the life of a man who never stirred five miles from home, that I am destined to make my greatest hits in treating of the rovers of the deep." Even here, however, the author's characteristic irony would have come in; for—the rare chances of life being what he most keeps his eye on—the uncommon belongs as much to the way the inquiring Will sticks to his door-sill as to the incident, say, of John Silver and his men, when they are dragging Jim Hawkins to his doom, hearing in the still woods of Treasure Island the strange hoot of the maroon.

The novelist who leaves the extraordinary out of his account is liable to awkward confrontations, as we are compelled to reflect in this age of newspapers and of universal publicity. The next report of the next divorce case (to give an instance) shall offer us a picture of astounding combinations of circumstance and behaviour, and the annals of any energetic race are rich in curious anecdote and startling example. That interesting compilation *Vicissitudes of Families* is but a superficial record of strange accidents: the family (taken of course in the long piece), is as a general thing a catalogue of odd specimens and tangled situations, and we must remember that the most singular products are those which are not exhibited. Mr. Stevenson leaves so wide a margin for the wonderful—it impinges with easy assurance upon the text—that he escapes the danger of being brought up by cases he has not allowed for. When he allows for Mr. Hyde he allows for everything, and one feels moreover that even if he did not wave so gallantly the flag of the imaginative and contend that the improbable is what has most character, he would still insist that we ought to make believe. He would say we ought to make believe that the extraordinary is the best part of life even if it were not, and to do so because the finest feelings—suspense, daring, decision, passion, curiosity, gallantry, eloquence, friendship—are involved in it, and it is of infinite importance that the tradition of these precious things should not perish. He would prefer, in a word, any day in the week, Alexandre Dumas to Honoré de Balzac, and it is indeed my impression that he prefers the author of *The Three Musketeers* to any novelist except Mr. George Meredith. I should go so far as to suspect that his ideal of the delightful work of fiction would be the adventures of Monte Cristo related by the author of *Richard Feverel*. There is some magnanimity in his esteem for Alexandre Dumas, inasmuch as in *Kidnapped* he has put into a fable worthy of that inventor a closeness of notation with which Dumas never had anything to do. He makes us say, Let the tradition live, by all means, since it was delightful; but at the same time he is the cause of our perceiving afresh that a tradition is kept alive only by something being added to it. In this particular case—in *Doctor Jekyll* and *Kidnapped*—Mr. Stevenson has added psychology.

3. romance and realism: the cable cut

(Preface to *The American*, 1907)

The only *general* attribute of projected romance that I can see, the only one that fits all its cases, is the fact of the kind of experience with which it deals —experience liberated, so to speak; experience disengaged, disembroiled, disencumbered, exempt from the conditions that we usually know to attach to it and, if we wish so to put the matter, drag upon it, and operating in a medium which relieves it, in a particular interest, of the inconvenience of a *related*, a measurable state, a state subject to all our vulgar communities. The greatest intensity may so be arrived at evidently—when the sacrifice of community, of the "related" sides of situations, has not been too rash. It must to this end not flagrantly betray itself; we must even be kept if possible, for our illusion, from suspecting any sacrifice at all. The balloon of experience is in fact of course tied to the earth, and under that necessity we swing, thanks to a rope of remarkable length, in the more or less commodious car of the imagination; but it is by the rope we know where we are, and from the moment that cable is cut we are at large and unrelated: we only swing apart from the globe—though remaining as exhilarated, naturally, as we like, especially when all goes well. The art of the romancer is, "for the fun of it," insidiously to cut the cable, to cut it without our detecting him. What I have recognised then in "The American," much to my surprise and after long years, is that the experience here represented is the disconnected and uncontrolled experience—uncontrolled by our general sense of "the way things happen"—which romance alone more or less successfully palms off on us. It is a case of Newman's own intimate experience all, that being my subject, the thread of which, from beginning to end, is not once exchanged, however momentarily, for any other thread; and the experience of others concerning us, and concerning him, only so far as it touches him and as he recognises, feels or divines it. There is our general sense of the way things happen—it abides with us indefeasibly, as readers of fiction, from the moment we demand that our fiction shall be intelligible; and there is our particular sense of the way they don't happen, which is liable to wake up unless reflexion and criticism, in us, have been skilfully and successfully drugged. There are drugs enough, clearly—it is all a question of applying them with tact; in which case the way things don't happen may be artfully made to pass for the way things do.

4. fairy tales: anecdote vs. improvisation

(Preface to The Aspern Papers, 1908)

Yet the fairy-tale belongs mainly to either of two classes, the short and sharp and single, charged more or less with the compactness of anecdote (as to which let the familiars of our childhood, Cinderella and Blue-Beard and Hop o'my Thumb and Little Red Riding Hood and many of the gems of the Brothers Grimm directly testify), or else the long and loose, the copious, the various, the endless, where, dramatically speaking, roundness is quite sacrificed—sacrificed to fullness, sacrificed to exuberance, if one will: witness at hazard almost any one of the Arabian Nights. The charm of all these things for the distracted modern mind is in the clear field of experience, as I call it, over which we are thus led to roam; an annexed but independent world in which nothing is right save as we rightly imagine it. We have to do that, and we do it happily for the short spurt and in the smaller piece, achieving so perhaps beauty and lucidity; we flounder, we lose breath, on the other hand—that is we fail, not of continuity, but of an agreeable unity, of the "roundness" in which beauty and lucidity largely reside—when we go in, as they say, for great lengths and breadths. And this, oddly enough, not because "keeping it up" isn't abundantly within the compass of the imagination appealed to in certain conditions, but because the finer interest depends just on *how* it is kept up.

Nothing is so easy as improvisation, the running on and on of invention; it is sadly compromised, however, from the moment its stream breaks bounds and gets into flood. Then the waters may spread indeed, gathering houses and herds and crops and cities into their arms and wrenching off, for our amusement, the whole face of the land—only violating by the same stroke our sense of the course and the channel, which is our sense of the uses of a stream and the virtue of a story. Improvisation, as in the Arabian Nights, may keep on terms with encountered objects by sweeping them in and floating them on its breast; but the great effect it so loses—that of keeping on terms with itself. This is ever, I intimate, the hard thing for the fairy-tale; but by just so much as it struck me as hard did it in "The Turn of the Screw" affect me as irresistibly prescribed. To improvise with extreme freedom and yet at the same time without the possibility of ravage, without the hint of a flood; to keep the stream, in a word, on something like ideal terms with itself: that was here my definite business. The thing was to aim at absolute singleness, clearness and roundness, and yet to depend on an imagination working freely, working (call it) with extravagance; by which law it wouldn't be thinkable except as free and wouldn't be amusing except as controlled.

5. ghost stories: direct presentation vs. impact on a consciousness

(Preface to *The Altar of the Dead*, 1909)

Such compositions as "The Jolly Corner," printed here not for the first time, but printed elsewhere only as I write and after my quite ceasing to expect it; "The Friends of the Friends," to which I here change the colourless title of "The Way It Came" (1896), "Owen Wingrave" (1893), "Sir Edmund Orme" (1891), "The Real Right Thing" (1900), would obviously never have existed but for that love of "a story as a story" which had from far back beset and beguiled their author. To this passion, the vital flame at the heart of any sincere attempt to lay a scene and launch a drama, he flatters himself he has never been false; and he will indeed have done his duty but little by it if he has failed to let it, whether robustly or quite insidiously, fire his fancy and rule his scheme. He has consistently felt it (the appeal to wonder and terror and curiosity and pity and to the delight of fine recognitions, as well as to the joy, perhaps sharper still, of the mystified state) the very source of wise counsel and the very law of charming effect. He has revelled in the creation of alarm and suspense and surprise and relief, in all the arts that practise, with a scruple for nothing but any lapse of application, on the credulous soul of the candid or, immeasurably better, on the seasoned spirit of the cunning, reader. He has built, rejoicingly, on that blest faculty of wonder just named, in the latent eagerness of which the novelist so finds, throughout, his best warrant that he can but pin his faith and attach his car to it, rest in fine his monstrous weight and his queer case on it, as on a strange passion planted in the heart of man for his benefit, a mysterious provision made for him in the scheme of nature. He has seen this particular sensibility, the need and the love of wondering and the quick response to any pretext for it, as the beginning and the end of his affair—thanks to the innumerable ways in which that chord may vibrate. His prime care has been to master those most congruous with his own faculty, to make it vibrate as finely as possible—or in other words to the production of the interest appealing most (by its kind) to himself. This last is of course the particular clear light by which the genius of representation ever best proceeds—with its beauty of adjustment to any strain of attention whatever. Essentially, meanwhile, excited wonder must have a subject, must face in a direction, must be, increasingly, *about* something. Here comes in then the artist's bias and his range—determined, these things, by his own fond inclination. About what, good man, does he himself most wonder? for upon that, whatever it may be, he will naturally most abound. Under that star will he gather in what he shall most seek to represent; so that if you follow thus his range of representation you will know how, you will see where, again, good man, he for himself most aptly vibrates.

All of which makes a desired point for the little group of compositions here placed together; the point that, since the question has ever been for me but of wondering and, with all achievable adroitness, of causing to wonder, so the whole fairy-tale side of life has used, for its tug at my sensibility, a cord all its own. When we want to wonder there's no such good ground for it as the wonderful—premising indeed always, by an induction as prompt, that this element can but be at best, to fit its different cases, a thing of appreciation. What is wonderful in one set of conditions may quite fail of its spell in another set; and, for that matter, the peril of the unmeasured strange, in fiction, being the silly, just as its strength, when it saves itself, is the charming, the wind of interest blows where it lists, the surrender of attention persists where it can. The ideal, obviously, on these lines, is the straight fairy-tale, the case that has purged in the crucible all its *bêtises* while keeping all its grace. It may seem odd, in a search for the amusing, to try to steer wide of the silly by hugging close the "supernatural"; but one man's amusement is at the best (we have surely long had to recognise) another's desolation; and I am prepared with the confession that the "ghost-story," as we for convenience call it, has ever been for me the most possible form of the fairy-tale. It enjoys, to my eyes, this honour by being so much the neatest— neat with that neatness without which *representation*, and therewith beauty, drops. One's working of the spell is of course—decently and effectively— but by the represented thing, and the grace of the more or less closely represented state is the measure of any success; a truth by the general smug neglect of which it's difficult not to be struck. To begin to wonder, over a case, I must begin to believe—to begin to give out (that is to attend) I must begin to take in, and to enjoy *that* profit I must begin to see and hear and feel. This wouldn't seem, I allow, the general requirement—as appears from the fact that so many persons profess delight in the picture of marvels and prodigies which by any, even the easiest, critical measure *is* no picture; in the recital of wonderful horrific or beatific things that are neither represented nor, so far as one makes out, seen as representable: a weakness not invalidating, round about us, the most resounding appeals to curiosity. The main condition of interest—that of some appreciable rendering of sought effects— is absent from them; so that when, as often happens, one is asked how one "likes" such and such a "story" one can but point responsively to the lack of material for a judgement.

The apprehension at work, we thus see, would be of certain projected conditions, and its first need therefore is that these appearances be constituted in some other and more colourable fashion than by the author's answering for them on his more or less gentlemanly honour. This isn't enough; *give me your elements, treat me your subject*, one has to say—I must wait till then to tell you how I like them. I might "rave" about them all were they given and treated; but there is no basis of opinion in such matters without a basis of vision, and no ground for that, in turn, without some communicated closeness of truth. There are portentous situations, there are prodigies and marvels and miracles as to which this communication, whether by necessity or by chance, works comparatively straight—works, by our measure, to some convincing consequence; there are others as to which the report, the picture, the plea, answers no tithe of the questions we would put. Those questions *may* perhaps then, by the very nature of the case, be unanswerable —though often again, no doubt, the felt vice is but in the quality of the provision made for them: on any showing, my own instinct, even in the service of great adventures, is all for the best *terms* of things; all for ground on which touches and tricks may be multiplied, the greatest number of questions answered, the greatest appearance of truth conveyed. With the preference I have noted for the "neat" evocation—the image, of any sort, with fewest attendant vaguenesses and cheapnesses, fewest loose ends dangling and fewest features missing, the image kept in fine the most susceptible of intensity—with this predilection, I say, the safest arena for the play of moving accidents and mighty mutations and strange encounters, or whatever odd matters, is the field, as I may call it, rather of their second than of their first exhibition. By which, to avoid obscurity, I mean nothing more cryptic than I feel myself show them best by showing almost exclusively the way they are felt, by recognising as their main interest some impression strongly made by them and intensely received. We but too probably break down, I have ever reasoned, when we attempt the prodigy, the appeal to mystification, in itself; with its "objective" side too emphasised the report (it is ten to one) will practically run thin. We want it clear, goodness knows, but we also want it thick, and we get the thickness in the human consciousness that entertains and records, that amplifies and interprets it. That indeed, when the question is (to repeat) of the "supernatural," constitutes the only thickness we do get; here prodigies, when they come straight, come with an effect imperilled; they keep all their character, on the other hand, by looming through some other history—the indispensable history of somebody's *normal* relation to something. It's in such connexions as these that they most interest, for what we are then mainly concerned with is their imputed and borrowed dignity. Intrinsic values they have none—as we feel for instance in such a matter as the would-be portentous climax of Edgar Poe's "Arthur Gordon Pym," where the indispensable history is absent, where the phenomena evoked, the moving accidents, coming straight, as I say, are immediate and flat, and the attempt is all at the horrific in itself. The result is that, to my sense, the climax fails—fails because it stops short, and stops short for want of connexions. There *are* no connexions; not only, I mean, in the sense of further statement, but of our own further relation to the elements, which hang in the void: whereby we see the effect lost, the imaginative effort wasted.

I dare say, to conclude, that whenever, in quest, as I have noted, of the amusing, I have invoked the horrific, I have invoked it, in such air as that of "The Turn of the Screw," that of "The Jolly Corner," that of "The Friends of the Friends," that of "Sir Edmund Orme," that of "The Real Right Thing," in earnest aversion to waste and from the sense that in art economy is always beauty. The apparitions of Peter Quint and Miss Jessel, in the first of the tales just named, the elusive presence nightly "stalked" through the New York house by the poor gentleman in the second, are matters as to which in themselves, really, the critical challenge (essentially nothing ever but the spirit of fine attention) may take a hundred forms—and a hundred felt or possibly proved infirmities is too great a number. Our friends' respective minds about them, on the other hand, are a different matter—challengeable, and repeatedly, if you like, but never challengeable without some consequent further stiffening of the whole texture. Which proposition involves, I think, a moral. The moving accident, the rare conjunction, whatever it be, doesn't make the story—in the sense that the story is our excitement, our amusement, our thrill and our suspense; the human emotion and the human attestation, the clustering human conditions we expect presented, only make it. The extraordinary is most extraordinary in that it happens to you and me, and it's of value (of value for others) but so far as visibly brought home to us. At any rate, odd though it may sound to pretend that one feels on safer ground in tracing such an adventure as that of the hero of "The Jolly Corner" than in pursuing a bright career among pirates or detectives, I allow that composition to pass as the measure or limit, on my own part, of any achievable comfort in the "adventure-story"; and this not because I may "render"—well, what my poor gentleman attempted and suffered in the New York house—better than I may render detectives or pirates or other splendid desperadoes, though even here too there would be something to say; but because the spirit engaged with the forces of violence interests me most when I can think of it as engaged most deeply, most finely and most "subtly" (precious term!). For then it is that, as with the longest and firmest prongs of consciousness, I grasp and hold the throbbing subject; *there* it is above all that I find the steady light of the picture.

Chapter VI

SUBJECTS: THE WHOLE HUMAN CONSCIOUSNESS

One of the most frequently quoted and widely misunderstood of James's passages in "The Art of Fiction" is that dealing with subject: "Of course it is of execution that we are talking—that being the only point of a novel that is open to contention. . . . We must grant the artist his subject, his idea, his donnée: our criticism is applied only to what he makes of it." This statement, taken in isolation, has led many readers to assume that James believed the "subject" to be unimportant. On the contrary, he adds in "The Art of Fiction": "The idea, the subject . . . . matters, to my sense, in the highest degree, and if I might put up a prayer it would be that artists should select none but the richest."

Over and over again, James insisted on the complete and total freedom of the writer to choose as his subject any experience: "The province of art is all life, all feeling, all observation, all vision" ("The Art of Fiction"). He wrote in "The Future of the Novel": "The novel is of all pictures the most comprehensive and the most elastic. It will stretch anywhere—it will take in absolutely anything. All it needs is a subject and a painter. But for its subject, magnificently, it has the whole human consciousness."

In this chapter, Part A, are gathered passages that elaborate and explicate these principles. James appears at times to declare the subject off critical limits primarily because its roots and origins lie too deep within the writer to detect. In 1904 he wrote: "We . . . never play the fair critical game with an author, never get into relation with him at all, unless we grant him his postulates. His subject is what is given him—given him by influences, by a process, with which we have nothing to do; since what art, what revelation can ever really make such a mystery, such a passage in the private life of the intellect, adequately traceable for us?"

At other times, James appears to take an almost deterministic view of the artist's selection of his subject. In the Preface to Lady Barbarina he wrote: "One never really chooses one's general range of vision—the experience from which ideas and themes and suggestions spring: this proves ever what it has had to be, this is one with the very turn one's life has taken. . . . The subject thus pressed upon the artist is the necessity of his case and the fruit of his consciousness; which truth makes and has ever made of any quarrel with his subject, any stupid attempt to go behind that, *the true stultification of criticism."*

Perhaps the key phrase here is that the artist's subject is "the necessity of his case and the fruit of his consciousness": his experience is in some sense determined, but his consciousness is free to wither or nourish whatever it catches from the flux and flow of experience. Thus James may see subjects as having "degrees of merit," some thin, others rich, some frail and spindly, others flourishing and luxuriant in splendid growth and tangled undergrowth. And, moreover, James could see subjects as having an independent growth of their own—which, indeed, is the primary "Lesson of Balzac" (1905). Balzac had "respect for the liberty of the subject": "Such a witness to the human comedy fairly holds his breath for fear of arresting or diverting that natural license."

In Part B of this chapter, James comments in various passages on "the common, the vulgar, the ugly" as subjects in fiction. It has sometimes been observed that James appears to have been committed to treating only the special and the precious, and particularly the privileged classes, in his fiction. This kind of critical judgment, based on the subject of James's fiction, is precisely the kind he over and over again proscribed. If we follow James's own argument, we recognize that the limitations of James's subject were largely determined simply by the limitations of his experience. In the passages gathered here, James over and over again welcomed the extension of the subject of the novel to social levels and human activities well outside his own experience and beyond the limits of his own fiction (or, for that matter, the fiction generally of England and America.)

James's comments on sex as a subject in fiction are so voluminous as to make up an entire chapter all by themselves: see Chapter VII, "Sex: An Immense Omission." No account of James's view of subject in fiction can be complete without some attention to James's remarkably liberal views on the possibilities of sex as a subject.

PART A: SUBJECTS: GIVEN, IMPORTANT, FREE

1. the folly of quarreling with an artist over his subject

("Henrik Ibsen," 1891)

The demonstration is complete and triumphant, but it does not conceal from us—on the contrary—that his drama is essentially that supposedly undramatic thing, the picture not of an action but of a condition. It is the portrait of a nature, the story of what Paul Bourget would call an *état d' âme,* and of a state of nerves as well as of soul, a state of temper, of health, of chagrin, of despair. *Hedda Gabler* is, in short, the study of an exasperated woman; and it may certainly be declared that the subject was not in advance, as a theme for scenic treatment, to be pronounced promising. There could in fact, however, be no more suggestive illustration of the folly of quarrelling with an artist over his subject. Ibsen has had only to take hold of this one in earnest to make it, against every presumption, live with an intensity of life. One can doubtless imagine other ways, but it is enough to say of this one that, put to the test, it imposes its particular spectacle. Something might have been gained, entailing perhaps a loss in another direction, by tracing the preliminary stages, showing the steps in Mrs. Tesman's history which led to the spasm, as it were, on which the curtain rises and of which the breathless duration—ending in death—is the period of the piece. But a play is above everything a work of selection, and Ibsen, with his curious and beautiful passion for the unity of time (carried in him to a point which almost always implies also that of place), condemns himself to admirable rigors. We receive Hedda ripe for her catastrophe, and if we ask for antecedents and explanations we must simply find them in her character. Her motives are just her passions. What the four acts show us is these motives and that character— complicated, strange, irreconcilable, infernal—playing themselves out. We know too little why she married Tesman, we see too little why she ruins Lövborg; but we recognize that she is infinitely perverse, and Heaven knows that, as the drama mostly goes, the crevices we are called upon to stop are singularly few. That Mrs. Tesman is a perfectly ill-regulated person is a matter of course, and there are doubtless spectators who would fain ask whether it would not have been better to represent in her stead a person totally different. The answer to this sagacious question seems to me to be simply that no one can possibly tell. There are many things in the world that are past finding out, and one of them is whether the subject of a work had not better have been another subject. We shall always do well to leave that matter to the author (*he* may have some secret for solving the riddle); so terrible would his revenge easily become if we were to accept a responsibility for his theme.

2. *his subject is what is given him*

("Gabriele D'Annunzio," 1904)

Autobiographic in form, *L'Innocente* [by D'Annunzio] sticks closely to its theme, and though the form is on the whole a disadvantage to it the texture is admirably close. The question is of nothing less than a young husband's relation to the illegitimate child of his wife, born confessedly as such, and so born, marvellous to say, in spite of the circumstance that the wife adores him, and of the fact that, though long grossly, brutally false to her, he also adores his wife. To state these data is sufficiently to express the demand truly made by them for superiority of treatment; they require certainly two or three almost impossible postulates. But we of course never play the fair critical game with an author, never get into relation with him at all, unless we grant him his postulates. His subject is what is given him—given him by influences, by a process, with which we have nothing to do; since what art, what revelation, can ever really make such a mystery, such a passage in the private life of the intellect, adequately traceable for us? His treatment of it, on the other hand, is what he actively gives; and it is with what he gives that we are critically concerned. If there is nothing in him that effectually induces us to make the postulate, he is then empty for us altogether, and the sooner we have done with him the better; little as the truly curious critic enjoys, as a general thing, having publicly to throw up the sponge.

3. one never really chooses one's general range of vision

(Preface to *Lady Barbarina*, 1908)

The great truth in the whole connexion, however, is, I think, that one never really chooses one's general range of vision—the experience from which ideas and themes and suggestions spring: this proves ever what it has *had* to be, this is one with the very turn one's life has taken; so that whatever it "gives," whatever it makes us feel and think of, we regard very much as imposed and inevitable. The subject thus pressed upon the artist is the necessity of his case and the fruit of his consciousness; which truth makes and has ever made of any quarrel with his subject, any stupid attempt to go behind *that*, the true stultification of criticism. The author of these remarks has in any case felt it, from far back, quite his least stupid course to meet halfway, as it were, the turn taken and the perceptions engendered by the tenor of his days. Here it is that he has never pretended to "go behind"—which would have been for him a deplorable waste of time. The thing of profit is to *have* your experience—to recognise and understand it, and for this almost any will do; there being surely no absolute ideal about it beyond getting from it all it has to give. The artist—for it is of this strange brood we speak—has but to have his honest sense of life to find it fed at every pore even as the birds of the air are fed; with more and more to give, in turn, as a consequence, and, quite by the same law that governs the responsive affection of a kindly-used animal, in proportion as more and more is confidently asked.

4. the importance of the subject

("*The Prophet. A Tragedy.* by Bayard Taylor," 1875)

We believe greatly, for our own part, in the importance of the subject; a large one, to our mind, promises more than a small one, and when a poet has secured for a hero a veritable prophet, with the bloom not yet rubbed off by literature, he has our heartiest congratulations. It perturbs our faith a little to learn that the prophet is Mr. Joe Smith, and the *dénouement* is to be the founding of Salt Lake City by Mr. Brigham Young; we reflect that there is a magic in associations, and we are afraid we scent vulgarity in these. But we are anxious to see what the author makes of them, and we grant that the presumption is in favor of his audacity. . . .

. . . If his book has no atmosphere, the fault is not only Mr. Taylor's but his subject's. It is very well to wish to poetize common things, but here as much as ever, more than ever, one must choose. There are things inherently vulgar, things to which no varnish will give a gloss, and on which the fancy contents only grudgingly to rest her eyes. Mormonism is one of these; an attempt to import Joseph Smith into romance, even very much diluted and arranged, must in the nature of things fall flat. The reason why is the reason the rhymist didn't like Doctor Fell. His associations are fatal to him and to all his companions.

5. the general complexity of life

(*Letters*, 1897, to Miss Grace Norton)

Rudyard [Kipling] and his wife and offspring depart presently for South Africa. They have settled upon a small propriété at Rottingdean near the [Burne-Jones's], and the South Africa is but a parenthetic family picnic. It would do as well as anything else, perhaps, if one still felt, as one used to, that everything is grist to his mill. I don't, however, think that everything is, as the affair is turning out, at all; I mean as to the general complexity of life. His *Ballad* future may still be big. But my view of his prose future has much shrunken in the light of one's increasingly observing how little of life he can make use of. Almost nothing civilised save steam and patriotism— and the latter only in verse, where I *hate* it so, especially mixed up with God and goodness, that that half spoils my enjoyment of his great talent. Almost nothing of the complicated soul or of the female form or of any question of *shades*—which latter constitute, to my sense, the real formative literary discipline. In his earliest time I thought he perhaps contained the seeds of an English Balzac; but I have quite given that up in proportion as he has come steadily from the less simple in subject to the more simple—from the Anglo-Indians to the natives, from the natives to the Tommies, from the Tommies to the quadrupeds, from the quadrupeds to the fish, and from the fish to the engines and screws. . . .

6. *degrees of merit in subjects*

(Preface to *The Ambassadors*, 1909)

For I think, verily, that there are degrees of merit in subjects—in spite of the fact that to treat even one of the most ambiguous with due decency we must for the time, for the feverish and prejudiced hour, at least figure its merit and its dignity as *possibly* absolute. What it comes to, doubtless, is that even among the supremely good—since with such alone is it one's theory of one's honour to be concerned—there is an ideal *beauty* of goodness the invoked action of which is to raise the artistic faith to its maximum. Then truly, I hold, one's theme may be said to shine, and that of "The Ambassadors," I confess, wore this glow for me from beginning to end. Fortunately thus I am able to estimate this as, frankly, quite the best, "all round," of my productions; any failure of that justification would have made such an extreme of complacency publicly fatuous.

7. *the liberty of the subject*

("The Lesson of Balzac," 1905)

Let me say, definitely, that I hold several of his [Balzac's] faults to be grave, and that if there were any question of time for it I should like to speak of them; but let me add, as promptly, that they are faults, on the whole, of execution, flaws in the casting, accidents of the process: they never come back to that fault in the artist, in the novelist, that amounts most completely to a failure of dignity, the absence of saturation with his idea. When saturation fails no other presence really avails; as when, on the other hand, it operates, no failure of method fatally interferes. There is never in Balzac that damning interference which consists of the painter's not seeing, not possessing, his image; not having fixed and held his creature and his creature's conditions. "Balzac aime sa Valérie," says Taine, in his great essay,—so much the finest thing ever written on our author,—speaking of the way in which the awful little Madame Marneffe of *Les Parents Pauvres* is drawn, and of the long

rope, for her acting herself out, that her creator's participation in her reality
assures her. He has been contrasting her, as it happens, with Thackeray's
Becky Sharp or rather with Thackeray's attitude toward Becky, and the
marked jealousy of her freedom that Thackeray exhibits from the first. I
remember reading at the time of the publication of Taine's study—though it
was long, long ago—a phrase in an English review of the volume which
seemed to my limited perception, even in extreme youth, to deserve the
highest prize ever bestowed on critical stupidity undisguised. If Balzac loved
his Valérie, said this commentator, that only showed Balzac's extraordinary
taste; the truth being really, throughout, that it was just through this love of
each seized identity, and of the sharpest and liveliest identities most, that
Madame Marneffe's creator was able to marshal his array at all. The love,
as we call it, the joy in their communicated and exhibited movement, in
their standing on their feet and going of themselves and acting out their
characters, was what rendered possible the saturation I speak of; what
supplied him, through the inevitable gaps of his preparation and the crevices
of his prison, his long prison of labor, a short cut to the knowledge he
required. It was by loving them—as the terms of his subject and the nuggets
of his mine—that he knew them; it was not by knowing them that he loved.

He at all events robustly loved the sense of another explored, assumed,
assimilated identity—enjoyed it as the hand enjoys the glove when the glove
ideally fits. My image indeed is loose; for what he liked was absolutely to
get into the constituted consciousness, into all the clothes, gloves and whatever else, into the very skin and bones, of the habited, featured, colored,
articulated form of life that he desired to present. How do we know given
persons, for any purpose of demonstration, unless we know their situation
for themselves, unless we see it from their point of vision, that is, from their
point of pressing consciousness or sensation?—without our allowing for
which there is no appreciation. Balzac loved his Valérie then as Thackeray
did not love his Becky, or his Blanche Amory in *Pendennis*. But his prompting was not to expose her; it could only be, on the contrary,—intensely aware
as he was of all the lengths she might go to, and paternally, maternally
alarmed about them—to cover her up and protect her, in the interest of her
special genius and freedom. All his impulse was to *la faire valoir*, to give her
all her value, just as Thackeray's attitude was the opposite one, a desire
positively to expose and desecrate poor Becky—to follow her up, catch her
in the act, and bring her to shame: though with a mitigation, an admiration,
an inconsequence, now and then wrested from him by an instinct finer, in
his mind, than the so-called "moral" eagerness. The English writer wants
to make sure, first of all, of your moral judgment; the French is willing,
while it waits a little, to risk, for the sake of his subject and its interest, your
spiritual salvation. Madame Marneffe, detrimental, fatal as she is, is
"exposed," so far as anything in life, or in art, may be, by the working-out

of the situation and the subject themselves; so that when they have done what they would, what they logically had to, with her, we are ready to take it from them. We do not feel, very irritatedly, very lecturedly, in other words with superflous edification, that she has been sacrificed. Who can say, on the contrary, that Blanche Amory, in *Pendennis*, with the author's lash about her little bare white back from the first—who can feel that she has *not* been sacrificed, or that her little bareness and whiteness, and all the rest of her, have been, by such a process, presented as they had a right to demand?

It all comes back, in fine, to that respect for the liberty of the subject which I should be willing to name as *the* great sign of the painter of the first order. Such a witness to the human comedy fairly holds his breath for fear of arresting or diverting that natural license; the witness who begins to breathe so uneasily in presence of it that his respiration not only warns off the little prowling or playing creature he is supposed to be studying, but drowns, for our ears, the ingenuous sounds of the animal, as well as the general, truthful hum of the human scene at large—this demonstrator has no sufficient warrant for his task. And if such an induction as this is largely the moral of our renewed glance at Balzac, there is a lesson, of a more essential sort, I think, folded still deeper within—the lesson that there is no convincing art that is not ruinously expensive. I am unwilling to say, in the presence of such of his successors as George Eliot and Tolstoy and Zola (to name, for convenience, only three of them), that he was the last of the novelists to do the thing handsomely; but I will say that we get the impression at least of his having had more to spend. Many of those who have followed him affect us as doing it, in the vulgar phrase, "on the cheap"; by reason mainly, no doubt, of their having been, all helplessly, foredoomed to cheapness. Nothing counts, of course, in art, but the excellent; nothing exists, however briefly, for estimation, for appreciation, but the superlative—always in its kind; and who shall declare that the severe economy of the vast majority of those apparently emulous of the attempt to "render" the human subject and the human scene proceeds from anything worse than the consciousness of a limited capital? This flourishing frugality operates happily, no doubt—given all the circumstances—for the novelist; but it has had terrible results for the novel, so far as the novel is a form with which criticism may be moved to concern itself. Its misfortune, its discredit, what I have called its bankrupt state among us, is the not unnatural consequence of its having ceased, for the most part, to be artistically interesting. It has become an object of easy manufacture, showing on every side the stamp of the machine; it has become the article of commerce, produced in quantity, and as we so see it we inevitably turn from it, under the rare visitations of the critical impulse, to compare it with those more precious products of the same general nature that we used to think of as belonging to the class of the hand-made.

PART B: THE COMMON, THE VULGAR, THE UGLY

1. the stragglers on life's march

("Ivan Turgénieff," 1874)

M. Turgénieff lacks, as regards form, as we have said, this immense charm of absorbed inventiveness; but in the way of substance there is literally almost nothing he does not care for. Every class of society, every type of character, every degree of fortune, every phase of manners, passes through his hands; his imagination claims its property equally, in town and country, among rich and poor, among wise people and idiots, *dilettanti* and peasants, the tragic and the joyous, the probable and the grotesque. He has an eye for all our passions, and a deeply sympathetic sense of the wonderful complexity of our souls. He relates in "Mumu" the history of a deaf-and-dumb serf and a lap-dog, and he portrays in "A Strange Story" an extraordinary case of religious fanaticism. He has a passion for shifting his point of view, but his object is constantly the same—that of finding an incident, a person, a situation, *morally* interesting. This is his great merit, and the underlying harmony of his apparently excessive attention to detail. He believes the intrinsic value of "subject" in art; he holds that there are trivial subjects and serious ones, that the latter are much the best, and that their superiority resides in their giving us absolutely a greater amount of information about the human mind. Deep into the mind he is always attempting to look, though he often applies his eye to very dusky apertures. There is perhaps no better evidence of his minutely psychological attitude than the considerable part played in his tales by simpletons and weak-minded persons. There are few novelists who have not been charmed by the quaintness and picturesqueness of mental invalids; but M. Turgénieff is attracted by something more—by the opportunity of watching the machinery of character, as it were, through a broken window-pane. One might collect from his various tales a perfect regiment of incapables, of the stragglers on life's march. Almost always, in the background of his groups of well-to-do persons there lurks some grotesque, under-witted poor relation, who seems to hover about as a vague memento, in his scheme, of the instability both of fortune and of human cleverness. Such, for instance, is Uvar Ivanovitsch, who figures as a kind of inarticulate chorus in the tragedy of "Hélène." He sits about, looking very wise and opening and closing his fingers, and in his person, in this attitude, the drama capriciously takes leave of us. Perhaps the most moving of all the author's tales—moving, not in the sense that it makes us shed easy tears, but as reminding us vividly of the solidarity, as we may say, of all human weakness—has for its hero a person made imbecile by suffering. The admirable little story of "The Brigadier" can only be spoilt by an attempt to retail it; we warmly recommend it to the reader, in the French version. Never did Romance stoop over a lowlier case of moral decomposition, but never did she gather more of the perfume of human truth.

2. the commoner stuff of human nature

(Hawthorne, 1879)

Like almost all people who possess in a strong degree the story-telling faculty, Hawthorne had a democratic strain in his composition, and a relish for the commoner stuff of human nature. Thoroughly American in all ways, he was in none more so than in the vagueness of his sense of social distinctions, and his readiness to forget them if a moral or intellectual sensation were to be gained by it. He liked to fraternise with plain people, to take them on their own terms, and put himself, if possible, into their shoes. His Note-Books, and even his tales, are full of evidence of this easy and natural feeling about all his unconventional fellow-mortals—this imaginative interest and contemplative curiosity; and it sometimes takes the most charming and graceful forms. Commingled as it is with his own subtlety and delicacy, his complete exemption from vulgarity, it is one of the points in his character which his reader comes most to appreciate—that reader I mean for whom he is not, as for some few, a dusky and malarious genius.

3. the common . . . a large part of the truth

("William Dean Howells," 1886)

He [Howells] is animated by a love of the common, the immediate, the familiar and vulgar elements of life, and holds that in proportion as we move into the rare and strange we become vague and arbitrary; that truth of representation, in a word, can be achieved only so long as it is in our power to test and measure it. He thinks scarcely anything too paltry to be interesting, that the small and the vulgar have been terribly neglected, and would rather see an exact account of a sentiment or a character he stumbles against every day than a brilliant evocation of a passion or a type he has never seen and does not even particularly believe in. He adores the real, the natural, the colloquial, the moderate, the optimistic, the domestic, and the democratic; looking askance at exceptions and perversities and superiorities, at surprising and incongruous phenomena in general. One must have seen a great deal before one concludes; the world is very large, and life is a mixture of many things; she by no means eschews the strange, and often risks combinations and effects that make one rub one's eyes. Nevertheless, Mr. Howells' standpoint is an excellent one for seeing a large part of the truth, and even if it were less advantageous, there would be a great deal to admire in the firmness with which he has planted himself.

4. that vast, dim section of society

("Guy de Maupassant," 1888)

The author's choice of a *milieu* [Maupassant's in *Pierre et Jean*], moreover, will serve to English readers as an example of how much more democratic contemporary French fiction is than that of his own country. The greater part of it—almost all the work of Zola and of Daudet, the best of Flaubert's novels, and the best of those of the brothers De Goncourt—treat of that vast, dim section of society which, lying between those luxurious walks on whose behalf there are easy presuppositions and that darkness of misery which, in addition to being picturesque, brings philanthropy also to the writer's aid, constitutes really, in extent and expressiveness, the substance of any nation. In England, where the fashion of fiction still sets mainly to the country house and the hunting-field, and yet more novels are published than anywhere else in the world, that thick twilight of mediocrity of condition has been little explored. May it yield triumphs in the years to come!

5. treating of low life and of primitive man

("Mr. Kipling's Early Stories," 1891)

Nothing is more refreshing than this [Kipling's] active, disinterested sense of the real; it is doubtless the quality for the want of more of which our English and American fiction has turned so wofully stale. We are ridden by the old conventionalities of type and small proprieties of observance—by the foolish baby-formula (to put it sketchily) of the picture and the subject. Mr. Kipling has all the air of being disposed to lift the whole business off the nursery carpet, and of being perhaps even more able than he is disposed. One must hasten of course to parenthesise that there is not, intrinsically, a bit more luminosity in treating of low life and of primitive man than of those whom civilisation has kneaded to a finer paste: the only luminosity in either case is in the intelligence with which the thing is done. But it so happens that, among ourselves, the frank, capable outlook, when turned upon the vulgar majority, the coarse, the receding edges of the social perspective, borrows a charm from being new; such a charm as, for instance, repetition has already despoiled it of among the French—the hapless French who pay the penalty as well as enjoy the glow of living intellectually so much faster than we. It is the most inexorable part of our fate that we grow tired of everything, and of course in due time we may grow tired even of what explorers shall come back to tell us about the great grimy condition, or, with unprecedented items and details, about the gray middle state which darkens into it. But the explorers, bless them! may have a long day before that; it is early to trouble about reactions, so that we must give them the benefit of every presumption. We are thankful for any boldness and any sharp curiosity, and that is why we are thankful for Mr. Kipling's general spirit and for most of his excursions.

6. *impressions of homely country life*

("Turgenev and Tolstoy," 1897)

...*A Sportsman's Sketches*, published in two volumes in 1852. This admirable collection of impressions of homely country life, as the old state of servitude had made it, is often spoken of as having borne to the great decree of Alexander II the relation borne by Mrs. Beecher Stowe's famous novel to the emancipation of the Southern slaves. Incontestably, at any rate, Turgenev's rustic studies sounded, like *Uncle Tom's Cabin*, a particular hour: with the difference, however, of not having at the time produced an agitation—of having rather presented the case with an art too insidious for instant recognition, an art that stirred the depths more than the surface.

7. *to recognize the vulgar*

("London Notes," July, 1897)

The English novel has as a general thing kept so desperately, so nervously clear of it [the vulgar], whisking back compromised skirts and bumping frantically against obstacles to retreat, that we welcome as the boldest of adventurers a painter who has faced it and survived. We have had low life in plenty, for, with its sores and vices, its crimes and penalties, misery has colour enough to open the door to any quantity of artistic patronage. We have shuddered in the dens of thieves and the cells of murderers, and have dropped the inevitable tear over tortured childhood and purified sin. We have popped in at the damp cottage with my lady and heard the quaint rustic, bless his simple heart, commit himself for our amusement. We have fraternised on the other hand with the peerage and the county families, staying at fine old houses till exhausted nature has, for this source of intoxication, not a wink of sociability left. It has grown, the source in question, as stale as the sweet biscuit with pink enhancements in that familiar jar of the refreshment counter from which even the attendant young lady in black, with admirers and a social position, hesitates to extract it. We have recognised the humble, the wretched, even the wicked; also we have recognised the "smart." But save under the immense pressure of Dickens we have never done anything so dreadful as to recognise the vulgar. We have at the very most recognised it as the extravagant, the grotesque. The case of Dickens was absolutely special; he dealt intensely with "lower middle," with "lowest" middle, elements, but he escaped the predicament of showing them as vulgar by showing them only as prodigiously droll. When his people are not funny who shall dare to say what they are? The critic may draw breath as from a responsibility averted when he reflects that they almost always *are* funny. They belong to a walk of life that we may be ridiculous but never at all serious about. We may be tragic, but that is often but a form of humour. I seem to hear Mr. Gissing say: "Well, dreariness for dreariness, let us try Brondesbury and Pinner; especially as in the first place I know them so well; as in the second they are the essence of England; and as in the third they are, artistically speaking, virgin soil. Behold them glitter in the morning dew."

8. *the appeal of ugly things*

("Emile Zola," 1903)

Grant—and the generalization may be emphatic—that the shallow and the simple are *all* the population of his [Zola's] richest and most crowded pictures, and that his "psychology," in a psychologic age, remains thereby comparatively coarse, grant this and we but get another view of the miracle. We see enough of the superficial among novelists at large, assuredly, without deriving from it, as we derive from Zola at his best, the concomitant impression of the solid. It is in general—I mean among the novelists at large—the impression of the *cheap*, which the author of *Les Rougon-Macquart*, honest man, never faithless for a moment to his own stiff standard, manages to spare us even in the prolonged sandstorm of *Vérité*. The Common is another matter; it is one of the forms of the superficial—pervading and consecrating all things in such a book as *Germinal*—and it only adds to the number of our critical questions. How in the world is it made, this deplorable democratic malodorous Common, so strange and so interesting? How is it taught to receive into its loins the stuff of the epic and still, in spite of that association with poetry, never depart from its nature? It is in the great lusty game he plays with the shallow and the simple that Zola's mastery resides, and we see of course that when values are small it takes innumerable items and combinations to make up the sum. In *L'Assommoir* and in *Germinal*, to some extent even in *La Débâcle*, the values are all, morally, personally, of the lowest—the highest is poor Gervaise herself, richly human in her generosities and follies—yet each is as distinct as a brass-headed nail.

What we come back to accordingly is the unprecedented case of such a combination of parts. Painters, of great schools, often of great talent, have responded liberally on canvas to the appeal of ugly things, of Spanish beggars, squalid and dusty-footed, of martyred saints or other convulsed sufferers, tortured and bleeding, of boors and louts soaking a Dutch proboscis in perpetual beer; but we had never before had to reckon with so literary a treatment of the mean and vulgar. When we others of the Anglo-Saxon race are vulgar we are, handsomely and with the best conscience in the world, vulgar all through, too vulgar to be in any degree literary, and too much so therefore to be critically reckoned with at all. The French are different—they separate their sympathies, multiply their possibilities, observe their shades, remain more or less outside of their worst disasters. They mostly contrive to get the *idea*, in however dead a faint, down into the lifeboat. They may lose sight of the stars, but they save in some such fashion as that their intellectual souls.

Chapter VII

SEX: AN IMMENSE OMISSION

For a writer who has been accused of ignoring the more rudimentary passions of life, James wrote an immense amount about sex as a subject in fiction. There are important passages on the matter in both "The Art of Fiction" and "The Future of the Novel." In "The Art of Fiction" he points to the Anglo-American novelist's "moral timidity" which consists of his "aversion to face the difficulties with which on every side the treatment of reality bristles." In "The Future of the Novel" he prophesies that this "most superstitiously closed" window might well one day be smashed by the very individuals in whose name it was originally sealed—the women, who more and more were taking to the pen.

James's handling of sex in his fiction has been distorted by his detractors. It would be difficult to find franker and yet more delicate treatment of sexual passion in Victorian fiction than James gives us in the illicit relations in The Wings of the Dove, The Ambassadors, *and* The Golden Bowl. *What* Maisie Knew *is even more astonishing in its treatment of the sexual drama. In still other works—*The Bostonians, *"The Pupil," "The Author of Beltraffio," and "The Turn of the Screw," for example, James dealt obliquely and indirectly with sexual complexity (or "deviation"). Thanks now to the Leon Edel biography, we know more about James's important attachments—such as that to the writer, Constance Fenimore Woolson, and the sculptor, Hendrik Anderson—and we are aware of his attitude toward such sexually ambivalent or sensational figures as Oscar Wilde and J. A. Symonds (who served as a model for the writer in "The Author of Beltraffio").*

All of this is to say that only now has the sex in James's fiction and his life fallen into a kind of focus, and it is therefore appropriate that we now come to realize that James, far from eschewing or decrying sex as a subject, was in advance of his time in attempting to open the window so tightly closed to this area of experience. Part of James's attitude was clearly shaped by his intimate familiarity with the French writers, who suffered under no such subject-restrictions as did the English and American. In coming to terms with the French, James discovered the principles of his own position somewhere between the imposed taboos and silences of English fiction and the obsessive and narrowing licence of the French.

In this chapter James's observations on sexual passion as the focus of

fiction are placed in chronological order. James may sometimes seem squeam-
ish, but he is almost always generous in his judgments. And he sticks to his
principle of granting the writer his subject. When he criticizes adversely, it
is usually on grounds of execution. Of Zola he says: "It is not his choice of
subject that has shocked us, it is the melancholy dryness of his execution."
Of Matilde Serao, the female Italian novelist, he says: "It is not in short at
all the moral but the fable itself that in the exclusively sexual light breaks
down and fails us." It is perhaps some such criticism as this that could be
directed at many modern writers, now enjoying the freedoms that James called
for, who have succeeded astonishingly in making sex dull.

James closes his discussion of Maupassant by addressing those who would
censor or restrict his subject: "A healthy, living and growing art, full of
curiosity and fond of exercise, has an indefeasible mistrust of rigid prohibi-
tions. Let us leave this magnificent art of the novelist to itself and to its
perfect freedom."

1. portrayal of passion

("George Sand," 1877)

We have delayed too long to say how far it [the pendulum of criticism]
had swung in the first direction [against George Sand]; and we have delayed
from the feeling that it is difficult to say it. We have seen that George
Sand was by the force of heredity projected into this field with a certain
violence; she took possession of a portion of it as a conqueror, and she
was never compelled to retreat. The reproach brought against her by her
critics is that, as regards her particular advocacy of the claims of the heart,
she has for the most part portrayed vicious love, not virtuous love. But
the reply to this, from her own side, would be that she has at all events portrayed something which those who disparage her activity have not portrayed.
She may claim that although she has the critics against her, the writers of her
own class who represent virtuous love have not pushed her out of the field.
She has the advantage that she has portrayed a *passion*, and those of the other
group have the disadvantage that they have not. In English literature, which,
we suppose, is more especially the region of virtuous love, we do not "go
into" the matter, as the phrase is (we speak of course of English prose). We
have agreed among our own confines that there is a certain point at which
elucidation of it should stop short; that among the things which it is possible
to say about it, the greater number had on the whole better not be said. It
would be easy to make an ironical statement of the English attitude, and it
would be, if not easy, at least very possible, to make a sound defence of it.

The thing with us, however, is not a matter of theory; it is above all a matter of practice, and the practice has been that of the leading English novelists. Miss Austen and Sir Walter Scott, Dickens and Thackeray, Hawthorne and George Eliot, have all represented young people in love with each other; but no one of them has, to the best of our recollection, described anything that can be called a passion—put it into motion before us and shown us its various paces. To say this is to say at the same time that these writers have spared us much that we consider "objectionable," and that George Sand has not spared us; but it is to say furthermore that few persons would resort to English prose fiction for any information concerning the ardent forces of the heart—for any ideas upon them. It is George Sand's merit that she has given us ideas upon them—that she has enlarged the novel-reader's conception of them and proved herself in all that relates to them an authority. This is a great deal. From this standpoint Miss Austen, Walter Scott and Dickens will appear to have omitted the erotic sentiment altogether, and George Eliot will seem to have treated it with singular austerity. Strangely loveless, seen in this light, are those large, comprehensive fictions "Middlemarch" and "Daniel Deronda." They seem to foreign readers, probably, like vast, cold, commodious, respectable rooms, through whose window-panes one sees a snow-covered landscape, and across whose acres of sober-hued carpet one looks in vain for a fireplace or a fire.

The distinction between virtuous and vicious love is not particularly insisted upon by George Sand. In her view love is always love, is always divine in its essence and ennobling in its operation. The largest life possible is to hold one's self open to an unlimited experience of this improving passion. This, I believe, was Madame Sand's practice, as it was certainly her theory—a theory to the exposition of which one of her novels, at least, is expressly dedicated. "Lucrezia Floriani" is the history of a lady who, in the way of love, takes everything that comes along, and who sets forth her philosophy of the matter with infinite grace and felicity. It is probably fortunate for the world that ladies of Lucrezia Floriani's disposition have not as a general thing her argumentative brilliancy. About all this there would be much more to say than these few pages afford space for. Madame Sand's plan was to be open to *all* experience, all emotions, all convictions; only to keep the welfare of the human race, and especially of its humbler members, well in mind, and to trust that one's moral and intellectual life would take a form profitable to the same. One was therefore not only to extend a great hospitality to love, but to interest one's self in religion and politics. This Madame Sand did with great activity during the whole of the reign of Louis Philippe. She had broken utterly with the Church of course, but her disposition was the reverse of sceptical. Her religious feeling, like all her feelings, was powerful and voluminous, and she had an ideal of a sort of etherealized and liberated Christianity, in which unmarried but affectionate couples might find an element friendly to their "expansion." Like all her feelings, too, her religious sentiment was militant; her ideas about love were an attack upon marriage; her faith was an attack upon the Church and the clergy; her social-istic sympathies were an attack upon all present political arrangements. These things all took hold of her by turn—shook her hard, as it were, and dropped her, leaving her to be played upon by some new inspiration; then, in some cases, returned to her, took possession of her afresh and sounded another tune. M. Renan, in writing of her at the time of her death, used a fine phrase about her; he said that she was "the Aeolian harp of our time;" he spoke of her "sonorous soul." This is very just; there is nothing that belonged to her time that she had not a personal emotion about—an emotion intense enough to produce a brilliant work of art—a novel that had bloomed as rapidly and perfectly as the flower that the morning sun sees open on its stem. In her care about many things during all these years, in her expenditure of passion, reflection, and curiosity, there is something quite unprecedented. Never had philosophy and art gone so closely hand in hand. Each of them suffered a good deal; but it had appeared up to that time that their mutual concessions must be even greater. Balzac was a far superior artist; but he was incapable of a lucid reflection.

We have already said that mention has been made of George Sand's analogy with Goethe, who claimed for his lyrical poems the merit of being each the result of a particular incident in his life. It was incident too that prompted Madame Sand to write; but what it produced in her case was not a short copy of verses, but an elaborate drama, with a plot and a dozen characters. It will help us to understand this extraordinary responsiveness of mind and fertility of imagination to remember that inspiration was often embodied in a concrete form; that Madame Sand's "incidents" were usually clever, eloquent, suggestive men. "Le style c'est l'homme"—of her, it has been epigramatically said, that is particularly true. Be this as it may, these influences were strikingly various, and they are reflected in works which may be as variously labelled: amatory tales, religious tales, political, aesthetic, pictor-ial, musical, theatrical, historical tales. And it is to be noticed that in what-ever the author attempted, whether or no she succeeded, she appeared to lose herself. The "Lettres d'un Voyageur" read like a writer's single book. This melancholy, this desolation and weariness, might pass as the complete distil-lation of a soul. In the same way "Spiridion" is exclusively religious and theological. The author might, in relation to this book, have replied to such of her critics as reproach her with being too erotic, that she had performed the very rare feat of writing a novel not only containing no love save divine love, but containing not one woman's figure. We can recall but one rival to "Spiridion" in this respect—Godwin's "Caleb Williams."

But if other things come and go with George Sand, amatory disquisition is always there. It is of all kinds, sometimes very noble and sometimes very disagreeable. Numerous specimens of the two extremes might be cited. There is to our taste a great deal too much of it; the total effect is displeasing. The author illuminates and glorifies the divine passion, but she does something which may be best expressed by saying that she cheapens it. She handles it too much; she lets it too little alone. Above all she is too positive, too explicit, too business-like; she takes too technical a view of it. Its various signs and tokens and stages, its ineffable mysteries, are all catalogued and tabulated in her mind, and she whisks out her references with the nimbleness with which the doorkeeper at an exhibition hands you back your umbrella in return for a check. In this relation, to the English mind, discretion is a great point—a virtue so absolute and indispensable that it speaks for itself and cannot be analysed away; and George Sand is judged from our point of view by one's saying that, for her, discretion is simply non-existent. Its place is occupied by a sort of benevolent, an almost conscientious disposition to sit down, as it were, and "talk over" the whole matter. The subject fills her with a motherly loquacity; it stimulates all her wonderful and beautiful self-sufficiency of expression—the quality that we have heard a hostile critic call her "glibness."

We can hardly open a volume of George Sand without finding an example of what we mean. We glance at a venture into "Teverino," and we find Lady G., who has left her husband at the inn and gone out to spend a day with the more fascinating Léonce, "passing her beautiful hands over the eyes of Léonce, *peut-être par tendresse naïve*, perhaps to convince herself that it was really tears she saw shining in them." The *peut-être* here, the *tendresse naïve*, the alternatives, the impartial way in which you are given your choice, are extremely characteristic of Madame Sand. They remind us of the heroine of "Isidora," who alludes in conversation to "une de mes premières fautes." In the list of Madame Sand's more technically amatory novels, however, there is a distinction to be made; the earlier strike us as superior to the later. The fault of the earlier—the fact that passion is too intellectual, too pedantic, too sophistical, too much bent upon proving itself abnegation and humility, maternity, fraternity, humanity, or some fine thing that it really is not and that it is much simpler and better for not pretending to be—this fault is infinitely exaggerated in the tales written after "Lucrezia Floriani." "Indiana," "Valentine," "Jacques," and "Mauprat" are, comparatively speaking, frankly and honestly passionate; they do not represent the love that declines to compromise with circumstances as a sort of eating of one's cake and having it too—an eating it as a pleasure and a having it as virtue. But the stories of the type of "Lucrezia Floriani," which indeed is the most argumentative, have an indefinable falsity of tone. Madame Sand had here begun to play with her topic intellectually; the first freshness of her interest in it had gone, and invention had taken the place of conviction. To acquit one's self happily of such experiments, one must certainly have all the gifts that George Sand possessed. But one must also have two or three that she lacked. Her sense of delicacy was certainly defective. This is a brief statement, but it means a great deal, and of what it means there are few of her novels that do not contain a number of illustrations.

2. *a question of taste*

("Nana," 1880)

Reality is the object of M. Zola's efforts, and it is because we agree with him in appreciating it highly that we protest against its being discredited. In a time when literary taste has turned, to a regrettable degree, to the vulgar and the insipid, it is of high importance that realism should not be compromised. Nothing tends more to compromise it than to represent it as necessarily allied to the impure. That the pure and the impure are for M. Zola, as conditions of taste, vain words, and exploded ideas, only proves that his advocacy does more to injure an excellent cause than to serve it. It takes a very good cause to carry a *Nana* on its back, and if realism breaks down, and the conventional comes in again with a rush, we may know the reason why. The real has not a single shade more affinity with an unclean vessel than with a clean one, and M. Zola's system, carried to its utmost expression, can dispense as little with taste and tact as the floweriest mannerism of a less analytic age. Go as far as we will, so long as we abide in literature, the thing remains always a question of taste, and we can never leave taste behind without leaving behind, by the same stroke, the very grounds on which we appeal, the whole human side of the business. Taste, in its intellectual applications, is the most human faculty we possess, and as the novel may be said to be the most human form of art, it is a poor speculation to put the two things out of conceit of each other. Calling it naturalism will never make it profitable. . . .
. . . What will strike the English reader of M. Zola at large, however, and what will strike the English reader of *Nana*, if he have stoutness of stomach enough to advance in the book, is the extraordinary absence of humour, the dryness, the solemnity, the air of tension and effort. M. Zola disapproves greatly of wit; he thinks it is an impertinence in a novel, and he would probably disapprove of humour if he *knew* what it is. There is no indication in all his works that he has a suspicion of this; and what tricks the absence of a sense of it plays him! . . . It is not his choice of subject that has shocked us; it is the melancholy dryness of his execution, which gives us all the bad taste of a disagreeable dish and none of the nourishment.

3. half of life is a sealed book

("Nana," 1880)

A novelist with a system, a passionate conviction, a great plan—incontest-able attributes of M. Zola—is not now to be easily found in England or the United States, where the storyteller's art is almost exclusively feminine, is mainly in the hands of timid (even when very accomplished) women, whose acquaintance with life is severely restricted, and who are not conspicuous for general views. The novel, moreover, among ourselves, is almost always addressed to young unmarried ladies, or at least always assumes them to be a large part of the novelist's public. . . . Half of life is a sealed book to young unmarried ladies, and how can a novel be worth anything that deals only with half of life? How can a portrait be painted (in any way to be recogniz-able) of half a face? It is not in one eye, but in the two eyes together that the expression resides, and it is the combination of features that constitutes the human identity. These objections are perfectly valid, and it may be said that our English system is a good thing for virgins and boys, and a bad thing for the novel itself, when the novel is regarded as something more than a simple *jeu d' esprit*, and considered as a composition that treats of life at large and helps us to *know*.

4. tactile sensibility

("Pierre Loti," 1888)

A writer of the ability of Alphonse Daudet, of that of Guy de Maupassant, or of that of the brothers De Goncourt, can never fail to be interesting by virtue of that ability, the successive manifestations of which keep our curiosity alive; but this curiosity is never so great as after we have noted, as I think we almost inveterately do, that the strongest gift of each of them is the strongest gift of all: a remarkable art of expressing the life, of picturing the multitu-dinous, adventurous experience, of the senses. We recognize this accomplish-ment with immense pleasure as we read—a pleasure so great that it is not for some time that we make the other observation that inevitably follows on its heels. That observation is somewhat to this effect: that in comparison the deeper, stranger, subtler inward life, the wonderful adventures of the soul, are so little pictured that they may almost be said not to be pictured at all. We end with an impression of want of equilibrium and proportion, and by asking ourselves (so coercive are the results of comparative criticism) whether such a sacrifice be quite obligatory. The value of the few words in the letter I just cited is simply that they offer a fresh, direct, almost startled measure of the intensity of the sacrifice, accompanied with the conviction that it must sooner or later be paid for, like every other extravagance, and that if the payment be on the scale of the aberration it will make an eddy of which those who are wise in time should keep clear. This profuse development of the external perceptions—those of the appearance, the sound, the taste, the material presence and pressure of things, will at any rate, I think, not be denied to be the master-sign of the novel in France as the first among the younger talents show it to us to-day. They carry into the whole business of looking, seeing, hearing, smelling, into all kinds of tactile sensibility and into noting, analyzing and expressing the results of these acts, a seriousness much greater than that of any other people. Their tactile sensibility is immense, and it may be said in truth to have produced a literature. They are so strong on this side that they seem to me to be easily masters, and I cannot imagine that their supremacy should candidly be contested.

5. *a precocity of depravity*

("Pierre Loti," 1888)

If our author's [Pierre Loti's] ruling passion is the appreciation of the exotic, it is not in his first works that he confines his quest to funny calls on nervous mandarins, to the twilight gloom of rheumatic old sailors or the vulgar pranks of reckless young ones. "Le Roman d'un Spahi," "Ayizadé," and "Rarahu" each contain the history of a love-affair with a primitive woman or a combination of primitive women. There is a kind of complacent animalism in them which makes it difficult to speak of them as the perfection of taste, and I profess to be able to defend them on the ground of taste only so long as they are not attacked. The great point is that they will not be attacked by any one who is capable of feeling the extraordinary power of evocation of (for instance) "Le Mariage de Loti" (another name for "Rarahu"), at the same time that he recognizes the abnormal character of such a performance, a character the more marked as the feeling of youth is strong in these early volumes, and the young person has rarely M. Loti's assurance as a *viveur*. He betrays a precocity of depravity which is disconcerting. I write the gross word depravity because we must put the case against him (so many English readers would feel it that way) as strongly as it can be put. It doesn't put it strongly enough to say that the serene surrender to polygamous practices among coral-reefs and in tepid seas is a sign much rather of primitive innocence, for there is an element in the affair that vitiates the argument. This is simply that the serenity (which, I take it, most makes the innocence) cannot under the circumstances be adequate. The pen, the talent, the phrase, the style, the note-book take care of that and change the whole situation;

they invalidate the plea of the primitive. They introduce the conscious element, and that is the weak side of Loti's spontaneities and pastorals. What saves him is that his talent never falters, and this is but another illustration of his interesting double nature. His customs and those of his friends at Tahiti, at Stamboul, on the east coast of the Adriatic, or again, according to his latest work, at Nagasaki, are not such as we associate in the least with high types; and yet when we close these various records of the general activity known as the attitude of "conquest," the impression that abides with us is one of surpassing delicacy. The facts are singularly vulgar, in spite of the exotic glow that wraps them up; but the subjective side of the business, the author's imagination, has an extraordinary light. Few things could suggest more the value that we instinctively attach to a high power of evocation—the degree to which we regard it as precious in itself.

What makes the facts vulgar, what justifies us in applying to Loti's picture of himself an ironic epithet or two, is his almost inveterate habit of representing the closest and most intimate personal relations as unaccompanied with any moral feeling, any impulse of reflection or reaction. He has so often the air of not seeming to talk of affection when he talks of love—that oddest of all French literary characteristics, and one to which we owe the circumstance that whole volumes have been written on the latter of these principles without an allusion to the former. There is a moral feeling in the singular friendship of which "Mon Frère Yves" is mainly a masterly commemoration, and also a little in the hindered passion which at last unites, for infinite disaster, alas! the hero and heroine of "Pêcheur d'Islande." These are the exceptions; they are admirable and reassuring. The closer, the more intimate is a personal relation the more we look in it for the human drama, the variations and complications, the note of responsibility for which we appeal in vain to the loves of the quadrupeds. Failing to satisfy us in this way, such a relation is not, as Mr. Matthew Arnold says of American civilization, *interesting*. M. Pierre Loti is too often guilty of the simplicity of assuming that when exhibited on his own part it *is* interesting.

6. omission of life of the spirit

("Pierre Loti," 1888)

If it be then a matter of course in France that a fresh talent should present its possessor mainly as one more *raffiné* in the observation of external things, and also, I think I may add, as one more pessimist in regard to the nature of man and of woman, and if such a presumption appears to have been confirmed by an examination of Pierre Loti, in spite of the effort of poor Yves to cultivate his will and of the mutual tenderness of Yann and Gaud, our conclusion, all the same, will not have escaped the necessity of taking into account the fact that there still seems an inexhaustible life for writers who obey this particular inspiration. The Nemesis remains very much what I attempted to suggest its being at the beginning of these remarks, but somehow the writers over whom it hovers enjoy none the less remarkable health on the side on which they are strong. If they have almost nothing to show us in the way of the operation of character, the possibilities of conduct, the part played in the world by the *idea* (you would never guess, either from Pierre Loti or from M. Guy de Maupassant, that the idea has any force or any credit in the world); if man, for them, is the simple sport of fate, with suffering for his main sign—either suffering or one particular satisfaction, always the same —their affirmation of all this is still, on the whole, the most complete affirmation that the novel at present offers us. They have on their side the accident, if accident it be, that they never cease to be artists. They will keep this advantage till the optimists of the hour, the writers for whom the life of the soul is equally real and visible (lends itself to effects and triumphs, challenges the power to "render"), begin to seem to them formidable competitors. On that day it will be very interesting to see what line they take, whether they will throw up the battle, surrendering honorably, or attempt a change of base. Many intelligent persons hold that for the French a change of base is impossible and that they are either what they incessantly show themselves or nothing. This view, of course, derives sanction from that awkward condition which I have mentioned as attached to the work of those among them who are most conspicuous—the fact that their attempts to handle the life of the spirit are comparatively so ineffectual. On the other hand, it is terribly compromising when those who do handle the life of the spirit with the manner of experience fail to make *their* affirmation complete, fail to make us take them seriously as artists, and even go so far (some of them are capable of that) as to introduce the ruinous suggestion that there is perhaps some essential reason (I scarcely know how to say it) why observers who are of that way of feeling should be a little weak in the conjuring line. To be even a little weak in representation is, of course, practically and for artistic purposes, to be what schoolboys call a duffer, and I merely glance, shuddering, at such a possibility. What would be *their* Nemesis, what penalty would such a group have incurred in their failure to rebut triumphantly so damaging an imputation? Who would then have to stand from under? It is not Pierre Loti, at any rate, who makes the urgency of these questions a matter only for the materialists (as it is convenient to call them) to consider. He only adds to our suspicion that, for good or for evil, they have still an irrepressible life, and he does so the more notably that, in his form and seen as a whole, he is a renovator, and, as I may say, a refresher. He plays from his own bat, imitating no one, not even nearly or remotely, to my sense—though I have heard the charge made—Châteaubriand. He arrives with his bundle of impressions, but they have been independently gathered in the world, not in the school, and it is a coincidence that they are of the same order as the others, expressed in their admirable personal way and with an indifference to the art of transitions which is at once one of the most striking cases of literary irresponsibility that I know and one of the finest of ingratiation. He has settled the question of his own *superficies* (even in the pathos of the sacred reunion of his lovers in "Pêcheur d'Islande" there is something inconvertibly carnal), but he has not settled the other, the general question of how long and how far accomplished and exclusive—practically exclusive—impressionism will yet go, with its vulture on its back and feeding on it. I hope I appear not to speak too apocalyptically in saying that the problem is still there to minister to our interest and perhaps even a little to our anxiety.

7. *the empire of the sexual sense*

("Guy de Maupassant," 1888)

As regards the other sense [other than the "visual sense"], the sense *par excellence*, the sense which we scarcely mention in English fiction, and which I am not very sure I shall be allowed to mention in an English periodical, M. de Maupassant speaks for that, and of it, with extraordinary distinctness and authority. To say that it occupies the first place in his picture is to say too little; it covers in truth the whole canvas, and his work is little else but a report of its innumerable manifestations. These manifestations are not, for him, so many incidents of life; they are life itself, they represent the standing answer to any question that we may ask about it. He describes them in detail, with a familiarity and a frankness which leave nothing to be added; I should say with singular truth, if I did not consider that in regard to this article he may be taxed with a certain exaggeration. M. de Maupassant would doubtless affirm that where the empire of the sexual sense is concerned, no exaggeration is possible: nevertheless it may be said that whatever depths may be discovered by those who dig for them, the impression of the human spectacle for him who takes it as it comes has less analogy with that of the monkeys' cage than this admirable writer's account of it. I speak of the human spectacle as we Anglo-Saxons see it—as we Anglo-Saxons pretend we see it, M. de Maupassant would possibly say.

At any rate, I have perhaps touched upon this peculiarity sufficiently to explain my remark that his point of view is almost solely that of the senses. If he is a very interesting case, this makes him also an embarrassing one, embarrassing and mystifying for the moralist. I may as well admit that no writer of the day strikes me as equally so. To find M. de Maupassant a lion in the path—that may seem to some people a singular proof of want of courage; but I think the obstacle will not be made light of by those who have really taken the measure of the animal. We are accustomed to think, we of the English faith, that a cynic is a living advertisement of his errors, especially in proportion as he is a thoroughgoing one; and M. de Maupassant's cynicism, unrelieved as it is, will not be disposed of off-hand by a critic of a competent literary sense. Such a critic is not slow to perceive, to his no small confusion, that though, judging from usual premises, the author of *Bel-Ami* ought to be a warning, he somehow is not. His baseness, as it pervades him, ought to be written all over him; yet somehow there are there certain aspects—and those commanding, as the house agents say—in which it is not in the least to be perceived. It is easy to exclaim that if he judges life only from the point of view of the senses, many are the noble and exquisite things that he must leave out. What he leaves out has no claim to get itself considered till after we have done justice to what he takes in. It is this positive side of M. de Maupassant that is most remarkable—the fact that his literary character is so complete and edifying. "Auteur à peu près irréprochable dans un genre qui ne l'est pas," as that excellent critic M. Jules Lemaître says of him, he disturbs us by associating a conscience and a high standard with a temper long synonymous, in our eyes, with an absence of scruples. The situation would be simpler certainly if he were a bad writer; but none the less it is possible, I think, on the whole, to circumvent him, even without attempting to prove that after all he is one.

8. the sexual vs. the reflective side of man

("Guy de Maupassant," 1888)

It may seem that I have claimed little for M. de Maupassant, so far as English readers are concerned with him, in saying that after publishing twenty improper volumes he has at last published a twenty-first, which is neither indecent nor cynical. It is not this circumstance that has led me to dedicate so many pages to him, but the circumstance that in producing all the others he yet remained, for those who are interested in these matters, a writer with whom it was impossible not to reckon. This is why I called him, to begin with, so many ineffectual names: a rarity, a "case," an embarrassment, a lion in the path. He is still in the path as I conclude these observations, but I think that in making them we have discovered a legitimate way round. If he is a master of his art and it is discouraging to find what low views are compatible with mastery, there is satisfaction, on the other hand, in learning on what particular condition he holds his strange success. This condition, it seems to me, is that of having totally omitted one of the items of the problem, an omission which has made the problem so much easier that it may almost be described as a short cut to a solution. The question is whether it be a fair cut. M. de Maupassant has simply skipped the whole reflective part of his men and women—that reflective part which governs conduct and produces character. He may say that he does not see it, does not know it; to which the answer is, "So much the better for you, if you wish to describe life without it. The strings you pull are by so much the less numerous, and you can therefore pull those that remain with greater promptitude, consequently with greater firmness, with a greater air of knowledge." Pierre Roland, I repeat, shows a capacity for reflection, but I cannot think who else does, among the thousand figures who compete with him—I mean for reflection addressed to anything higher than the gratification of an instinct. We have an impression that M. d'Apreval and Madame de Cadour reflect, as they trudge back from their mournful excursion, but that indication is not pushed very far. An aptitude for this exercise is a part of disciplined manhood, and disciplined manhood M. de Maupassant has simply not attempted to represent. I can remember no instance in which he sketches any considerable capacity for conduct, and his women betray that capacity as little as his men. I am much mistaken if he has once painted a gentleman, in the English sense of the term. His gentlemen, like Paul Brétigny and Gontran de Ravenel, are guilty of the most extraordinary deflections. For those who are conscious of this element in life, look for it and like it, the gap will appear to be immense. It will lead them to say, "No wonder you have a contempt if that is the way you limit the field. No wonder you judge people roughly if that is the way you see them. Your work, on your premisses, remains the admirable thing it is, but is your 'case' not adequately explained?"

The erotic element in M. de Maupassant, about which much more might have been said, seems to me to be explained by the same limitation, and explicable in a similar way wherever else its literature occurs in excess. The carnal side of man appears the most characteristic if you look at it a great deal; and you look at it a great deal if you do not look at the other, at the side by which he reacts against his weaknesses, his defeats. The more you look at the other, the less the whole business to which French novelists have ever appeared to English readers to give a disproportionate place—the business, as I may say, of the senses—will strike you as the only typical one. Is not this the most useful reflection to make in regard to the famous question of the morality, the decency, of the novel? It is the only one, it seems to me, that will meet the case as we find the case today. Hard and fast rules, *a priori* restrictions, mere interdictions (you shall not speak of this, you shall not look at that) have surely served their time, and will in the nature of the case never strike an energetic talent as anything but arbitrary. A healthy, living and growing art, full of curiosity and fond of exercise, has an indefeasible mistrust of rigid prohibitions. Let us then leave this magnificent art of the novelist to itself and to its perfect freedom, in the faith that one example is at good as another, and that our fiction will always be decent enough if it be sufficiently general. Let us not be alarmed at this prodigy (though prodigies are alarming) of M. de Maupassant, who is at once so licentious and so impeccable, but gird ourselves up with the conviction that another point of view will yield another perfection.

9. a moralist of the sexual passion

("Dumas the Younger," 1896)

He [Dumas the Younger] had in relation to his special gift, his mastery of the dramatic form, a faculty of imagination as contracted as that of the author of "Monte Cristo" was boundless, but his moral sense on the other hand, as distinguished from that of his parent, was of the liveliest, was indeed of the most special and curious kind. The moral sense of the parent was to be found only in his good humour and his good health—the moral sense of a musketeer in love. This lack of adventurous vision, of the long flight and the joy of motion, was in the younger genius quite one of the conditions of his strength and luck, of his fine assurance, his sharp edge, his high emphasis, his state untroubled above all by things not within his too irregularly conditioned ken. The things close about him were the things he saw—there were alternatives, differences, opposites, of which he lacked so much as the suspicion. Nothing contributes more to the prompt fortune of an artist than some such positive and exclusive temper, the courage of his convictions, as we usually call it, the power to neglect something thoroughly, to abound aggressively in his own sense and express without reserve his own saturation. The saturation of the author of "Le Demi-Monde" was never far to seek. He was as native to Paris as a nectarine to a south wall. He would have fared ill if he had not had a great gift and Paris had not been a great city.

It was another element of the happy mixture that he came into the world at the moment in all our time that was for a man of letters the most amusing and beguiling—the moment exactly when he could see the end of one era and the beginning of another and join hands luxuriously with each. This was an advantage to which it would have taken a genius more elastic to do full justice, but which must have made him feel himself both greatly related and inspiringly free. He sprang straight from the lap of full-grown romanticism; he was a boy, a privileged and initiated youth, when his father, when Victor Hugo, when Lamartine and Musset and Scribe and Michelet and Balzac and George Sand were at the high tide of production. He saw them all, knew them all, lived with them and made of them his profit, tasting just enough of the old concoction to understand the proportions in which the new should be mixed. He had above all in his father, for the purpose that was in him, a magnificent springboard—a background to throw into relief, as a ruddy sunset seems to make a young tree doubly bristle, a profile of another type. If it was not indispensable it was at any rate quite poetic justice that the successor to the name should be, in his conditions, the great casuist of the theatre. He had seen the end of an age of imagination, he had seen all that could be done and shown in the way of mere illustration of the passions. That the passions are always with us is a fact he had not the smallest pretension to shut his eyes to—they were to constitute the almost exclusive subject of his study. But he was to study them not for the pleasure, the picture, the poetry they offer; he was to study them in the interest of something quite outside of them, about which the author of "Antony" and "Kean," about which Victor Hugo and Musset, Scribe and Balzac and even George Sand had had almost nothing to say. He was to study them from the point of view of the idea of the right and the wrong, of duty and conduct, and he was to this end to spend his artistic life with them and give a new turn to the theatre. He was in short to become, on the basis of a determined observation of the manners of his time and country, a professional moralist.

There can scarcely be a better illustration of differences of national habit and attitude than the fact that while among his own people this is the character, as an operative force, borne by the author of "Le Demi-Monde" and "Les Idées de Madame Aubray," so among a couple of others, in the proportion in which his reputation there has emerged from the vague, his most definite identity is that of a mere painter of indecent people and indecent doings. There are, as I have hinted, several reasons for the circumstance already noted, the failure of the attempt to domesticate him on the English-speaking stage; but one states the case fairly, I think, in saying that what accounts for half of it is our passion, in the presence of a work of art, for confounding the object, as the philosophers have it, with the subject, for losing sight of the idea in the vehicle, of the intention in the fable. Dumas is a dramatist as to whom nine playgoers out of ten would precipitately exclaim: "Ah, but you know, isn't he dreadfully immoral?" Such are the lions in the path of reputation, such the fate, in an alien air, of a master whose main reproach in his native clime is the importunity and the rigour of his lesson. The real difference, I take it, is that whereas we like to be good the French like to be better. We like to be moral, they like to moralise. This helps us to understand the number of our innocent writers—writers innocent even of reflection, a practice of course essentially indelicate, inasmuch as it speedily brings us face to face with scandal and even with evil. It accounts doubtless also for the number of writers on the further side of the Channel who have made the journey once for all and to whom, in the dangerous quarter they have reached, it appears of the very nature of scandal and evil to be inquired about. The whole undertaking of such a writer as Dumas is, according to his light, to carry a particular, an esthetic form of investigation as far as it will stretch—to study, and study thoroughly, the bad cases. These bad cases were precisely what our managers and adapters, our spectators and critics would have nothing to do with. It defines indeed the separation that they should have been, in the light in which he presented them, precisely what made them for his own public exceptionally edifying. One of his great contentions is, for instance, that seduced girls should under all circumstances be married—by somebody or other, failing the seducer. This is a contention that, as we feel, barely concerns us, shut up as we are in the antecedent conviction that they should under no circumstances be seduced. He meets all the cases that, as we see him, we feel to have been spread out before him; meets them successively, systematically, at once with a great earnestness and a great wit. He is exuberantly sincere: his good faith sometimes obscures his humour, but nothing obscures his good faith. So he gives us in their order the unworthy brides who must be denounced, the prenuptial children who must be adopted, the natural sons who must be avenged, the wavering ladies who must be saved, the credulous fiancés who must be enlightened, the profligate wives who must be shot, the merely blemished ones who must be forgiven, the too vindictive ones who must be humoured, the venal young men who must be exposed, the unfaithful husbands who must be frightened, the frivolous fathers who must be pulled up and the earnest sons who must pull them. To enjoy his manner of dealing with such material we must grant him in every connection his full premise: that of the importunity of the phenomenon, the ubiquity of the general plight, the plight in which people are left by an insufficient control of their passions. We must grant him in fact for his didactic and dramatic purpose a great many things. These things, taken together and added to some others, constitute the luxurious terms on which I have spoken of him as appearing to the alien admirer to have practised his complicated art.

When we speak of the passions in general we really mean, for the most part, the first of the number, the most imperious in its action and the most interesting in its consequences, the passion that unites and divides the sexes. It is the passion, at any rate, to which Dumas as dramatist and pamphleteer mainly devoted himself: his plays, his prefaces, his manifestos, his few tales roll exclusively on the special relation of the man to the woman and the woman to the man, and on the dangers of various sorts, even that of ridicule, with which this relation surrounds each party. This element of danger is what I have called the general plight, for when our author considers the sexes as united and divided it is with the predominance of the division that he is principally struck. It is not an unfair account of him to say that life presented itself to him almost wholly as a fierce battle between the woman and the man. He sides now with one and now with the other; the former combatant, in her own country, however, was far from pronouncing him sympathetic. His subject at all events is what we of English race call the sexes and what they in France call the sex. To talk of love is to talk, as we have it, of men and women; to talk of love is, as the French have it, to *parler femmes*. From every play of our author's we receive the impression that to *parler femmes* is its essential and innermost purpose. It is not assuredly singular that a novelist, a dramatist *should* talk of love, or even should talk of nothing else: what, in addition to his adroitness and his penetration, makes the position special for Dumas is that he talks of it—and in the form of address most associated with pure diversion—altogether from the anxious point of view of the legislator and the citizen.

10. a conspiracy of silence

("Matilde Serao," 1901)

Few attentive readers, I take it, would deny that the English novelist—from whom, in this case, there happens to be even less occasion than usual for distinguishing the American—testifies in his art much more than his foreign comrade, from whatever quarter, to the rigour of convention. There are whole sides of life about which he has as little to say as possible, about which he observes indeed in general a silence that has visibly ended by becoming for the foreign comrade his great characteristic. He strikes the spectator as having with a misplaced humility consented once for all to be admonished as to what he shall or shall not "mention"—and to be admonished in especial by an authority altogether indefinite. He subscribes, when his turn comes round, to an agreement in the drawing-up of which he has had no hand; he sits down to his task with a certain received canon of the "proper" before his eyes. The critic I am supposing reproaches him, naturally, in this critic's way, with a marked failure ever to challenge, much less to analyse, that conception; with having never, as would appear, so much as put to himself in regard to most of the matters of which he makes his mystery the simple question "Proper to what?" How can any authority, even the most embodied, asks the exponent of other views, decide for us in advance what shall in any case be proper—with the consequent implication of impropriety—to our given subject?

The English novelist would, I imagine, even sometimes be led on to finding that he has practically had to meet such an overhauling by a further admission, though an admission still tacit and showing him not a little shy of the whole discussion—principles and formulas being in general, as we know, but little his affair. Would he not, if off his guard, have been in peril of lapsing into the doctrine—suicidal when reflected upon—that there may be also an *a priori* rule, a "Thou shalt not," if not a "Thou shalt," as to treatable subjects themselves? Then it would be that his alien foe might fairly revel in the sense of having him in a corner, laughing an evil laugh to hear him plead in explanation that it is exactly *most* as to the subject to be treated that he feels the need laid upon him to conform. What is he to do when he has an idea to embody, we might suspect him rashly to inquire, unless, frankly to ask himself in the first place of *all* if it be proper? Not indeed —we catch the reservation—that he is consciously often accessible to ideas for which that virtue may not be claimed. Naturally, however, still, such a plea only brings forth for his interlocutor a repetition of the original appeal: "Proper to what?" There is only one propriety the painter of life can ask of his morsel of material: Is it, or is it not, of the stuff of life? So, in simplified terms at any rate, I seem to hear the interchange; to which I need listen no longer than thus to have derived from it a word of support for my position. The question of our possible rejoinder to the scorn of societies otherwise affected I must leave for some other connection. The point is—if point I may expect to obtain any countenance to its being called—that, in spite of our great Dickens and, in a minor degree, of our great George Eliot, the limitations of our practice are elsewhere than among ourselves pretty well held to have put us out of court. The thing least conceded to us moreover is that we handle at all frankly—if we put forward such a claim—even our own subject-matter or in other words our own life. "Your own is all we want of you, all we should like to see. But that your system really touches your own is exactly what we deny. Never, never!" For what it really comes to is that practically we, of all people in the world, are accused of a system. Call this system a conspiracy of silence, and the whole charge is upon us.

The fact of the silence, whether or no of the system, is fortunately all that at present concerns us. Did this not happen to be the case nothing could be more interesting, I think, than to follow somewhat further several of the bearings of the matter, which would bring us face to face with some wonderful and, I hasten to add, by no means doubtless merely disconcerting truths about ourselves. It has been given us to read a good deal, in these latter days, about *l'âme Française* and *l'âme Russe*—and with the result, in all probability, of our being rather less than more penetrated with the desire, in emulation of these opportunities, to deliver ourselves upon the English or the American soul. There would appear to be nothing we are totally conscious of that we are less eager to reduce to the mere expressible, to hand over to publicity, current journalistic prose aiding, than either of these fine essences; and yet incontestably there are neighbourhoods in which we feel ourselves within scent and reach of them by something of the same sense that in thick forests serves the hunter of great game. He may not quite touch the precious presence, but he knows when it is near. So somehow we know that the "Anglo-Saxon" soul, the modern at least, is not far off when we frankly consider the practice of our race—comparatively recent though it be—in taking for granted the "innocence" of literature.

Our perhaps a trifle witless way of expressing our conception of this innocence and our desire for it is, characteristically enough, by taking refuge in another vagueness, by invoking the allowances that we understand works of imagination and of criticism to make to the "young." I know not whether it has ever officially been stated for us that, given the young, given literature, and given, under stress, the need of sacrificing one or the other party, it is not certainly by our sense of "style" that our choice would be determined: no great art in the reading of signs and symptoms is at all events required for a view of our probable instinct in such a case. That instinct, however, has too many deep things in it to be briefly or easily disposed of, and there would be no greater mistake than to attempt too simple an account of it. The account most likely to be given by a completely detached critic would be that we are as a race better equipped for action than for thought, and that to let the art of expression go by the board is through that very fact to point to the limits of what we mostly have to express. If we accept such a report we shall do so, I think, rather from a strong than from a weak sense of what may easily be made of it; but I glance at these things only as at objects almost too flooded with light, and come back after my parenthesis to what more immediately concerns me: the plain reflection that, if the element of compromise—compromise with fifty of the "facts of life"—be the common feature of the novel of English speech, so it is mainly indebted for this character to the sex comparatively without a feeling for logic.

11. the exclusively sexual light

("Matilde Serao," 1901)

The effect then, we discover, of the undertaking to give *passione* its whole place is that by the operation of a singular law no place speedily appears to be left for anything else; and the effect of that in turn is greatly to modify, first, the truth of things, and second, with small delay, what may be left them of their beauty. We find ourselves wondering after a little whether there may not really be more truth in the world misrepresented according to our own familiar fashion than in such a world as that of Madame Serao's exuberant victims of Venus. It is not only that if Venus herself is notoriously beautiful her altar, as happens, is by no means always proportionately august;

it is also that we draw, in the long run, small comfort from the virtual suppression, by any painter, of whatever skill—and the skill of this particular one fails to rise to the height—of every relation in life but that over which Venus presides. In "Fior di Passione" and the several others of a like connection that I have named the suppression is really complete; the common humanities and sociabilities are wholly absent from the picture.

The effect of this is extraordinarily to falsify the total show and to present the particular affair—the intimacy in hand for the moment, though the moment be but brief—as taking place in a strange false perspective, a denuded desert which experience surely fails ever to give us the like of and the action of which on the faculty of observation in the painter is anything but favourable. It strikes at the root, in the impression producible and produced, of discrimination and irony, of humour and pathos. Our present author would doubtless contend on behalf of the works I have mentioned that pathos at least does abound in them—the particular bitterness, the inevitable despair that she again and again shows to be the final savour of the cup of *passione*. It would be quite open to her to urge—and she would be sure to do so with eloquence—that if we pusillanimously pant for a moral, no moral really can have the force of her almost inveterate evocation of the absolute ravage of Venus, the dry desolation that in nine cases out of ten Venus may be perceived to leave behind her. That, however, but half meets our argument—which bears by no means merely on the desolation behind, but on the desolation before, beside and generally roundabout. It is not in short at all the moral but the fable itself that in the exclusively sexual light breaks down and fails us. Love, at Naples and in Rome, as Madame Serao exhibits it, is simply unaccompanied with any interplay of our usual conditions—with affection, with duration, with circumstances or consequences, with friends, enemies, husbands, wives, children, parents, interests, occupations, the manifestation of tastes. Who are these people, we presently ask ourselves, who love indeed with fury—though for the most part with astonishing brevity—but who are so without any suggested situation in life that they can only strike us as loving for nothing and in the void, to no gain of experience and no effect of a felt medium or a breathed air. We know them by nothing but their convulsions and spasms, and we feel once again that it is not the passion of hero and heroine that gives, that can ever give, the heroine and the hero interest, but that it is they themselves, with the ground they stand on and the objects enclosing them, who give interest to their passion. This element touches us just in proportion as we see it mixed with other things, with all the things with which it has to reckon and struggle. There is moreover another reflection with which the pathetic in this connection has to count, even though it undermine not a little the whole of the tragic effect of the agitations of *passione*. Is it, ruthlessly speaking, certain that the effect most consonant, for the spectator, with truth is half as tragic as it is something else? Should not the moral be sought in the very different quarter where the muse of comedy rather would have the last word? The ambiguity and the difficulty are, it strikes me, of a new growth, and spring from a perverse desire on the part of the erotic novelist to secure for the adventures he depicts a dignity that is not of the essence. To compass this dignity he has to cultivate the high pitch and beat the big drum, but when he has done so he has given everything the wrong accent and the whole the wrong extravagance. Why see it all, we ask him, as an extravagance of the solemn and the strained? Why make *such* an erotic a matter of tears and imprecations, and by so doing render so poor a service both to pleasure and to pain? Since by your own free showing it is pre-eminently a matter of folly, let us at least have folly with her bells, or when these must—since they must —sound knells and dirges, leave them only to the light hand of the lyric poet, who turns them at the worst to music. Matilde Serao is in this connection constantly lugubrious; even from the little so-called pastels of "Gli Amanti" she manages, with an ingenuity worthy of a better cause, to expunge the note of gaiety.

This dismal *parti pris* indeed will inevitably, it is be feared, when all the emancipations shall have said their last word, be that of the ladies. Yet perhaps too, whatever such a probability, the tone scarce signifies—in the presence, I mean, of the fundamental mistake from which the author before us warns us off. That mistake, we gather from her warning, would be to encourage, after all, any considerable lowering of the level of our precious fund of reserve. When we come to analyse we arrive at a final impression of what we pay, as lovers of the novel, for such a chartered state as we have here a glimpse of; and we find it to be an exposure, on the intervention at least of such a literary temperament as the one before us, to a new kind of vulgarity. We have surely as it is kinds enough. The absence of the convention throws the writer back on tact, taste, delicacy, discretion, subjecting these principles to a strain from which the happy office of its presence is, in a considerable degree and for performers of the mere usual endowment, to relieve him. When we have not a very fine sense the convention appears in a manner to have it on our behalf. And how frequent to-day, in the hurrying herd of brothers and sisters of the pen, *is* a fine sense—of *any* side of their affair? Do we not approach the truth in divining that only an eminent individual here and there may be trusted for it? Here—for the case is our very lesson—is this robust and wonderful Serao who is yet not to be trusted at all. Does not the dim religious light with which we surround its shrine do more, on the whole, for the poetry of *passione* than the flood of flaring gas with which, in her pages, and at her touch, it is drenched? Does it not shrink, as a subject under treatment, from such expert recognitions and easy discussions, from its so pitiless reduction to the category of the familiar? It issues from the ordeal with the aspect with which it might escape from a noisy family party ·or alight from a crowded omnibus. It is at the category of the familiar that vulgarity begins. There may be a cool virtue therefore even for "art," and an appreciable distinction even for truth, in the grace of hanging back and the choice of standing off, in that shade of the superficial which we best defend by simply practising it in season. A feeling revives at last, after a timed intermission, that we may not immediately be quite able, quite assured enough, to name, but which, gradually clearing up, soon defines itself almost as a yearning. We turn round in obedience to it—unmistakably we turn round again to the opposite pole, and there before we know it have positively laid a clinging hand on dear old Jane Austen.

12. *sex shut out from the rest of life*

("Gabriele D'Annunzio," 1904)

Here at all events we put our finger, I think, on the very point at which his (D'Annunzio's) aesthetic plenitude meets the misadventure that discredits it. We see just where it "joins on" with vulgarity. That sexual passion from which he extracts such admirable detached pictures insists on remaining for him *only* the act of a moment, beginning and ending in itself and disowning any representative character. From the moment it depends on itself alone for its beauty it endangers extremely its distinction, so precarious at the best. For what it represents, precisely, is it poetically interesting; it finds its extension and consummation only in the rest of life. Shut out from the rest of life, shut out from all fruition and assimilation, it has no more dignity than—to use a homely image—the boots and shoes that we see, in the corridors of promiscuous hotels, standing, often in double pairs, at the doors of rooms. Detached and unassociated these clusters of objects present, however obtruded, no importance. What the participants do with their agitation, in short, or even what it does with them, *that* is the stuff of poetry, and it is never really interesting save when something finely contributive in themselves makes it so. It is this absence of anything finely contributive in themselves, on the part of the various couples here concerned, that is the open door to the trivial. I have said, with all appreciation, that they present the great "relation", for intimacy, as we shall nowhere else find it presented; but to see it related, in its own turn, to nothing in the heaven above or the earth beneath, this undermines, we definitely learn, the charm of that achievement.

Chapter VIII

PLOTS, ACTIONS, CENTERS

Ever since Aristotle defined a tragedy as an imitation of an action, and proclaimed the primacy of plot, the critical question has been debated as to the place of events, happenings, actions, or adventures in narrative literary works. In the nineteenth century, an ascendant view (expressed by such critics as Walter Besant) was that fictions lived by their "stories," and that stories were above all else "adventures" or actions. We have become so accustomed to "adventure-less" fiction in the twentieth century that we sometimes forget that there once prevailed a rule that adventures were supreme. By "adventures" was generally meant external events or actions. Today a fiction is as likely to be organized around an "internal reaction" as around an external action— and for this development we owe much, perhaps most, to Henry James.

In "The Art of Fiction" (James's reply to Walter Besant), James rejected the common distinction between a novel of character and a novel of incident: "What is character but the determination of incident? What is incident but the illustration of character? . . . It is an incident for a woman to stand up with her hand resting on a table and look out at you in a certain way; or if it be not an incident I think it will be hard to say what it is." Moreover, James rejected the idea that there was "a part of a novel which is the story and part of it which for mystical reasons is not." In discussing Besant's demand for "adventure," James—in typical fashion—renders the demand pointless by expanding the definition of "adventure" to include what was generally designated adventure-less ("It is an adventure—an immense one—for me to write this little article"), and then clinches his argument by insisting on the suitability for fiction of psychological "events": "A psychological reason is, to my imagination, an object adorably pictorial; to catch the tint of its complexion—I feel as if that idea might inspire one to Titianesque efforts."

It is possible, of course, to view James's conception of psychological drama as simply "internal action," and thus to render Aristotle's view of plot-primacy relevant. To do so, however, is to gloss over some of the persistent questions that James himself raises. What is an "incident" in a plot, and when does psychological inaction become action in the Aristotelian sense? But more important than these questions is the nature of unity in a literary work: Aristotle seems to place the source of unity in the combination of events to make a plot. It was perhaps James's greatest contribution to fiction that he

151

came to see the possibilities of locating the source of unity not in the events themselves, nor in some focal character (as we have seen, he rejected the idea of a "novel of character"), but rather in the drama of a consciousness.

It is important to distinguish between this discovery and contribution and James's concern for point of view (to which a later chapter is devoted). Of course James made major contributions to the discovery that a writer might consciously choose the "best" perspective on his subject (idea, story, donnée) by carefully choosing the character or characters to "go behind." But identifying the center of a work in the unfolding of a consciousness is more than merely locating the point of view. It is, indeed, making a commitment to psychological drama. It is to render the conventional plot of external events quite subordinate to a psychological plot of internal actions and reactions, musings and meditations.

The result in effect is two "plots," external and internal, but only one—the internal—is the fiction's center. Misunderstanding on this score has caused the recurring complaint that nothing much ever happens in a James novel. The truth is that such complaints arise because the reader or critic has focused his attention in the wrong place—on the events themselves rather than on the dramatized consciousness interacting with the events.

In Part A of this chapter, "Diffusion and Concentration," appear a succession of James's statements ranging in time from the beginning to the end of his career, attacking diffuseness and disunity in fiction, and demonstrating the need for concentration, for centers, for selection. In Part B, "Stories, Adventures, Ados," are gathered statements more directly addressed (in the quest for unity) to the nature of actions—stories, adventures—and ultimately developing a vocabulary for talking about psychological "plots" as sources of a fiction's unity, introducing such terms as "subjective adventure" and "drama of consciousness." The end of James's progression results in turning the reader's gaze away from outer experience to inner transactions, from external acts to internal feelings and movements.

PART A: DIFFUSION AND CONCENTRATION

1. *diffusiveness vs. concentration*

("George Eliot's *Middlemarch*," 1873)

Middlemarch is at once one of the strongest and one of the weakest of English novels. Its predecessors as they appeared might have been described in the same terms; *Romola* is especially a rare masterpiece, but the least *entraînant* masterpieces. *Romola* sins by excess of analysis; there is too much description and too little drama; too much reflection (all certainly of a highly imaginative sort) and too little creation. Movement lingers in the story, and with it attention stands still in the reader. The error in *Middlemarch* is not precisely of a similar kind, but it is equally detrimental to the total aspect of the work. We can well remember how keenly we wondered, while its earlier chapters unfolded themselves, what turn in the way of form the story would take—that of an organized, molded, balanced composition, gratifying the reader with a sense of design and construction, or a mere chain of episodes, broken into accidental lengths and unconscious of the influence of a plan. We expected the actual result, but for the sake of English imaginative literature which, in this line is rarely in need of examples, we hoped for the other. If it had come we should have had the pleasure of reading, what certainly would have seemed to us in the immediate glow of attention, the first of English novels. But that pleasure has still to hover between prospect and retrospect. *Middlemarch* is a treasure-house of detail, but it is an indifferent whole.

Our objection may seem shallow and pedantic, and may even be represented as a complaint that we have had the less given us rather than the more. Certainly the greatest minds have the defects of their qualities, and as George Eliot's mind is preëminently contemplative and analytic, nothing is more natural than that her manner should be discursive and expansive. "Concentration" would doubtless have deprived us of many of the best things in the book —of Peter Featherstone's grotesquely expectant legatees, of Lydgate's medical rivals, and of Mary Garth's delightful family. The author's purpose was to be a generous rural historian, and this very redundancy of touch, born of abundant reminiscence, is one of the greatest charms of her work. It is as if her memory was crowded with antique figures, to whom for very tenderness she must grant an appearance. Her novel is a picture—vast, swarming, deep-colored, crowded with episodes, with vivid images, with lurking master-strokes, with brilliant passages of expression; and as such we may freely accept it and enjoy it. It is not compact, doubtless; but when was a panorama compact? And yet, nominally, *Middlemarch* has a definite subject—the subject indicated in the eloquent preface. An ardent young girl was to have been the central figure, a young girl framed for a larger moral life than circumstance often affords, yearning for a motive for sustained spiritual effort and only wasting her ardor and soiling her wings against the meanness of opportunity. The author, in other words, proposed to depict the career of an obscure St. Theresa. Her success has been great, in spite of serious drawbacks. Dorothea Brooke is a genuine creation, and a most remarkable one when we consider the delicate material in which she is wrought. . . . To the end we care less about Fred Vincy than appears to be expected of us. In so far as the writer's design has been to reproduce the total sum of life in an English village forty years ago, this commonplace young gentleman, with his somewhat meager tribulations and his rather neutral egotism, has his proper place in the picture; but the author narrates his fortunes with a fullness of detail which the reader often finds irritating. . . .

. . . Many of the discursive portions of *Middlemarch* are, as we may say, too clever by half. The author wishes to say too many things, and to say them too well; to recommend herself to a scientific audience. Her style, rich and flexible as it is, is apt to betray her on these transcendental flights; we find, in our copy, a dozen passages marked "obscure." *Silas Marner* was a delightful tinge of Goldsmith—we may almost call it: *Middlemarch* is too often an echo of Messrs. Darwin and Huxley. In spite of these faults—which it seems graceless to indicate with this crude rapidity—it remains a very splendid performance. It sets a limit, we think, to the development of the old-fashioned English novel. Its diffuseness, on which we have touched, makes it too copious a dose of pure fiction. If we write novels so, how shall we write History? But it is nevertheless a contribution of the first importance to the rich imaginative department of our literature.

2. *life without art vs. art without life*

("Daniel Deronda: A Conversation," 1876)

Pulcheria. All that is very fine, but you cannot persuade me that *Deronda* [by George Eliot] is not a very ponderous and ill-made story. It has nothing that one can call a subject. A silly young girl and a solemn, sapient young man who doesn't fall in love with her! That is the *donnée* of eight monthly volumes. I call it very flat. Is that what the exquisite art of Thackeray and Miss Austen and Hawthorne has come to? I would as soon read a German novel outright.

Theodora. There is something higher than form—there is spirit.

Constantius. I am afraid Pulcheria is sadly aesthetic. She had better confine herself to Mérimée.

Pulcheria. I shall certainly to-day read over *La Double Méprise.*

Theodora. Oh, my dear, *y pensez-vous?*

Constantius. Yes, I think there is little art in *Deronda*, but I think there is a vast amount of life. In life without art you can find your account; but art without life is a poor affair. The book is full of the world.

3. *a subject's logical centre*

(*Letters*, 1899, to Mrs. Humphry Ward)

And may I say (as I *can* read nothing, if I read it at all, save in the light of how one would *one's self* proceed in tackling the same *data!*) just two other things? One is that I think your material suffers a little from the fact that the reader feels you approach your subject too *immediately*, show him its elements, the cards in your hand, too bang off from the first page—so that a wait to begin to guess *what and whom the thing is going to be about* doesn't impose itself: the antechamber or two and the crooked corridor before he is already in the Presence. The other is that you don't give him a positive sense of dealing with your subject from its logical centre. This centre I gathered to be, from what you told me in Rome (and one gathers it also from the title,) the consciousness of Eleanor—to which all the rest (Manisty, Lucy, the whole phantasmagoria and drama) is presented by life. I should have urged you: "Make that consciousness full, rich, universally prehensile and *stick* to it—don't shift—and don't shift *arbitrarily*—how, otherwise, do you get your unity of subject or keep up your reader's sense of it?" To which, if you say: How then do I get *Lucy's* consciousness, I impudently retort: "By that magnificent and masterly *indirectness* which means the *only* dramatic straightness and intensity. You get it, in other words, by Eleanor." "And how does Eleanor get it?" "By *Everything!* By Lucy, by Manisty, by every pulse of the action in which she is engaged and of which she is the fullest—and exquisite—register. Go behind *her*—miles and miles; don't go behind the others, or the subject—*i.e.* the unity of impression—goes to smash." But I am going too far—and this is more than you will have bargained for. On these matters there is far too much to say.

4. *the* objective *unity of subjects*

(*Letters*, 1899, to Mrs. Humphry Ward)

I beg you not to believe that if you elicit a reply from me—to your so interesting letter just received—you do so at any cost to any extreme, or uncomfortable pressure that I'm just now under. I am always behind with everything—and it's no worse than usual. Besides I shall be very brief.* But I must say two or three words—not only because these are the noblest speculations that can engage the human mind, but because—to a degree that distresses me—you labour under two or three mistakes as to what, the other day, I at all wanted to express. I don't myself, for that matter, recognise what you mean by any "old difference" between us on *any* score—and least of all when you appear to glance at it as an opinion of mine (if I understand you, that is,) as to there being but *one general* "hard and fast rule of *presentation*." I protest that I have never had with you any difference—consciously —on any such point, and rather resent, frankly, your attributing to me a judgment so imbecile. I hold that there are five million such "rules" (or

*Later !!!! Latest. Don't rejoin!—*don't!*

as many as there are subjects in all the world—I fear the subjects are *not* 5,000,000!) only each of them imposed, artistically, by the particular case—involved in the writer's repsonsibility to it; and each *then*—and then only—"hard and fast" with an immitigable hardness and fastness. I don't see, *without* this latter condition, where any work of art, any artistic *question* is, or any artistic probity. Of course, a 1000 times, there are as many magnificent and imperative cases as you like of presenting a thing by "going behind" as many forms of consciousness as you like—all Dickens, Balzac, Thackeray, Tolstoi (save when they use the autobiographic dodge,) are huge illustrations of it. But they are illustrations of extreme and calculated selection, or singleness, too, whenever that has been, by the case, imposed on them. My own immortal works, for that matter, if I may make bold, are recognizable instances of all the variation. I "go behind" right and left in "The Princess Casamassima," "The Bostonians," "The Tragic Muse," just as I do the same but singly in "The American" and "Maisie," and just as I do it consistently *never at all* (save for a false and limited *appearance*, here and there, of doing it a *little*, which I haven't time to explain) in "The Awkward Age." So far from not seeing what you mean in *Pêcheur d'Islande*, I see it as a most beautiful example—a crystal-clear one. It's a picture of a *relation* (a *single* relation) and that relation isn't given at all unless given on both sides, because, practically, there are no other relations to make *other* feet for the situation to walk withal. The logic jumps at the eyes. Therefore acquit me, please, *please*, of anything so abject as putting forward anything at once specific and *a priori*. "Then why," I hear you ask, "do you pronounce for *my book* a priori?" Only because of a mistake, doubtless, for which I do here humble penance—that of assuming too precipitately, and with the freedom of an inevitably too-foreshortened letter, that I was dealing with it *a posteriori!*—and *that* on the evidence of only those few pages and of a somewhat confused recollection of what, in Rome, you told me of your elements. Or rather—more correctly—I was giving way to my irresistible need of wondering how, *given* the subject, one could best work one's self into the presence of it. And, lo and behold, the subject isn't (of course, in so scant a show and brief a piece) "given" at all—I have doubtless simply, with violence and mutilation, *stolen* it. It is of the nature of that violence that I'm a wretched person to *read* a novel—I begin so quickly and concomitantly, *for myself*, to write it rather—even before I know clearly what it's about! The novel I can *only* read, I can't read at all! And I had, to be just with me, one attenuation—I thought I gathered from the pages already absorbed that your *parti pris* as to your process with "Eleanor" was already defined—and defined as "dramatic"—and that was a kind of *lead:* the people all, as it were, phenomenal to a particular imagination (hers) and that imagination, with all its contents, phenomenal to the reader. I, in fine, just rudely and egotistically thrust forward the beastly

way *I* should have done it. But there is too much to say about these things
—and I am writing too much—and yet haven't said half I want to—
and, above all, there *being* so much, it is doubtless better not to attempt to
say pen in hand what one can say but so partially. And yet I *must* still add
one or two things more. What I said above about the "rule" of presentation
being, in each case, hard and fast, *that* I will go to the stake and burn with
slow fire for—the slowest that will burn at all. I hold the artist must
(infinitely!) know how he is doing it, or he is not doing it at all. I hold he
must have a perception of the interests of his subject that grasps him as in a
vise, and that (the subject being of course formulated in his mind) he sees
as sharply the way that most presents it, and presents most of it, as against
the ways that comparatively give it away. And he must there choose and
stick and be consistent—and that is the hard-and-fastness and the vise. I am
afraid I *do* differ with you if you mean that the picture can get any *objective*
unity from any other source than that; can get it from, e.g., the "personality
of the author." From the personality of the author (which, however enchanting, is a thing for the reader only, and not for the author himself, without humiliating abdications, to my sense, to count in at all) it can get
nothing but a unity of execution and of tone. There is no short cut for the
subject, in other words, out of the process, which, having made out most
what it (the subject) is, *treats* it most, handles it, in that relation, with the
most consistent economy. May I say, to exonerate myself a little, that when,
e.g., I see you make Lucy "phenomenal" to Eleanor (one has to express it
briefly and somehow,) I find myself supposing completely that you "know
how you're doing it," and enjoy, as critic, the sweet peace that comes with
that sense. But I haven't the sense that you "know how you're doing it"
when, at the point you've reached, I see you make Lucy phenomenal, even
for one attempted stroke, to the little secretary of embassy. And the reason
of this is that Eleanor counts as presented, and thereby *is* something to
go behind. The secretary *doesn't* count as presented (and isn't he moreover
engaged, at the very moment—*your* moment—in being phenomenal himself,
to Lucy?) and is therefore, practically, *nothing* to go behind. The promiscuous shiftings of standpoint and centre of Tolstoi and Balzac for instance
(which come, to my eye, from their being not so much big dramatists as big
painters—as Loti is a painter,) are the inevitable result of the *quantity of
presenting* their genius launches them in. With the complexity they pile up
they *can* get no clearness without trying again and again for new centres.
And they don't *always* get it. However, I don't mean to say they don't get
enough. And I hasten to add that you have—I wholly recognise—every right
to reply to me: "Cease your intolerable chatter and dry up your preposterous
deluge. If you will have the decent civility to *wait*, you will see that *I* 'present'
also—*anch' io!*—enough for *every* freedom I use with it!"—And with my
full assent to that, and my profuse prostration in the dust for this extrava-

gant discourse, with all faith, gratitude, appreciation and affection, I *do* cease, dear Mrs. Ward, I dry up! and am yours most breathlessly.

5. *slice of life vs. centre of consciousness*

("The Novel in 'The Ring and the Book,' " 1912)

The question of the whereabouts of the unity of a group of data subject to be wrought together into a thing of art, the question in other words of the point at which the various implications of interest, no matter how many, *most* converge and interfuse, becomes always, by my sense of the affair, quite the first to be answered; for according to the answer shapes and fills itself the very vessel of that beauty—the beauty, exactly, *of* interest, of maximum interest, which is the ultimate extract of any collocation of facts, any picture of life, and the finest aspect of any artistic work. Call a novel a picture of life as much as we will; call it, according to one of our recent fashions, a slice, or even a chunk, even a "bloody" chunk, of life, a rough excision from that substance as superficially cut and as summarily served as possible, it still fails to escape this exposure to appreciation, or in other words to criticism, that it has had to be selected, selected under some sense for something; and the unity of the exhibition should meet us, does meet us if the work be done, at the point at which that sense is most patent. If the slice or the chunk, or whatever we call it, if *it* isn't "done," as we say—and as it so often declines to be—the work itself of course isn't likely to be; and there we may dismiss it.

The first thing we do is to cast about for some centre in our field [the story in Browning's *The Ring and the Book*]; seeing that, for such a purpose as ours, the subject might very nearly go a-begging with none more definite than the author has provided for it. I find that centre in the embracing consciousness of Caponsacchi, which, coming to the rescue of our question of treatment, of our search for a point of control, practically saves everything, and shows itself moreover the only thing that *can* save.

6. *slice of life vs. selection*

("The New Novel," 1914)

If those remarks represent all the while, further, that the performances we have glanced at [the new novelists of saturation, Wells, Bennett et al.], with others besides, lead our attention on, we hear ourselves the more

naturally asked what it is then that we expect or want, confessing as we do
that we have been in a manner interested, even though, from case to case,
in a varying degree, and that Thackeray, Turgénieff, Balzac, Dickens, Anatole
France, no matter who, can not do more than interest. Let us therefore concede to the last point that small mercies are better than none, that there are
latent within the critic numberless liabilities to being "squared" (the extent
to which he may on occasion betray his price!) and so great a preference for
being pleased over not being, that you may again and again see him assist
with avidity at the attempt of the slice of life to butter itself thick. Its explanation that it *is* a slice of life and pretends to be nothing else figures for us,
say, while we watch, the jam superadded to the butter. For since the jam,
on this system, descends upon our desert, in its form of manna, from quite
another heaven than the heaven of method, the mere demonstration of its
agreeable presence is alone sufficient to hint at our more than one chance of
being supernaturally fed. The happy-go-lucky fashion of it is indeed not then,
we grant, an objection so long as we do take in refreshment: the meal may
be of the last informality and yet produce in the event no small sense of
repletion. The slice of life devoured, the butter and the jam duly appreciated,
we are ready, no doubt, on another day, to trust ourselves afresh to the desert.
We break camp, that is, and face toward a further stretch of it, all in the
faith that we shall be once more provided for. We take the risk, we enjoy
more or less the assistance—more or less, we put it, for the vision of a possible
arrest of the miracle or failure of our supply never wholly leaves us. The
phenomenon is too uncanny, the happy-go-lucky, as we know it in general,
never *has* been trustable to the end; the absence of the last true touch in the
preparation of its viands becomes with each renewal of the adventure a more
sensible fact. By the last true touch we mean of course the touch of the hand
of selection; the principle of selection having been involved at the worst or
the least, one would suppose, in any approach whatever to the loaf of life
with the *arrière-pensée* of a slice. There being no question of a slice upon
which the further question of where and how to cut it does not wait, the
office of method, the idea of choice and comparison, have occupied the ground
from the first. This makes clear, to a moment's reflection, that there can be
no such thing as an amorphous slice, and that any waving aside of inquiry
as to the sense and value of a chunk of matter has to reckon with the simple
truth of its having been *born* of naught else but measured excision. Reasons
have been the fairies waiting on its cradle, the possible presence of a bad fairy
in the form of a bad reason to the contrary notwithstanding. It has thus had
connections at the very first stage of its detachment that are at no later stage
logically to be repudiated; let it lie as lumpish as it will—for adoption, we
mean, of the ideal of the lump—it has been tainted from too far back with
the hard liability to form, and thus carries in its very breast the hapless contradiction of its sturdy claim to have none. This claim has the inevitable

challenge at once to meet. How can a slice of life be anything but illustrational of the loaf, and how can illustration not immediately bristle with every sign of the extracted and related state? The relation is at once to what the thing comes from and to what it waits upon—which last is our act of recognition. We accordingly appreciate it in proportion as it so accounts for itself; the quantity and the intensity of its reference are the measure of our knowledge of it. This is exactly why illustration breaks down when reference, otherwise application, runs short, and why before any assemblage of figures or aspects, otherwise of samples and specimens, the question of what these are, extensively, samples and specimens *of* declines not to beset us—why, otherwise again, we look ever for the supreme reference that shall avert the bankruptcy of sense.

7. saturation vs. application

("The New Novel," 1914)

The act of squeezing out to the utmost the plump and more or less juicy orange of a particular acquainted state and letting this affirmation of energy, however directed or undirected, constitute for them [the new novelists, Bennett, Wells et al.] the "treatment" of a theme—*that* is what we remark them as mainly engaged in, after remarking the example so strikingly, so originally set, even if an undue subjection to it be here and there repudiated. Nothing is further from our thought than to undervalue saturation and possession, the fact of the particular experience, the state and degree of acquaintance incurred, however such a consciousness may have been determined; for these things represent on the part of the novelist, as on the part of any painter of things seen, felt or imagined, just one half of his authority—the other half being represented of course by the application he is inspired to make of them. Therefore that fine secured half is so much gained at the start, and the fact of its brightly being there may really by itself project upon the course so much colour and form as to make us on occasion, under the genial force, almost not miss the answer to the question of application.

PART B: STORIES, ADVENTURES, ADOS:
THE DRAMA OF CONSCIOUSNESS

1. he hates a "story"

("William Dean Howells," 1886)

He [Howells] hates a "story," and (this private feat is not impossible) has probably made up his mind very definitely as to what the pestilent thing consists of. In this respect he is more logical than M. Emile Zola, who partakes of the same aversion, but has greater lapses as well as greater audacities. Mr. Howells hates an artificial fable and a *dénouement* that is pressed into service; he likes things to occur as they occur in life, where the manner of a great many of them is not to occur at all. He has observed that heroic emotion and brilliant opportunity are not particularly interwoven with our days, and indeed, in the way of omission, he *has* often practiced in his pages a very considerable boldness. It has not, however, made what we find there any less interesting and less human.

2. the question of what constitutes a "story"

("Guy de Maupassant," 1888)

M. de Maupassant tells us that he has imbibed many of his principles from Gustave Flaubert, from the study of his works as well as, formerly, the enjoyment of his words. It is in *Une Vie* that Flaubert's influence is most directly traceable, for the thing has a marked analogy with *L'Education sentimentale*. That is, it is the presentation of a simple piece of a life (in this case a long piece), a series of observations upon an episode *quelconque*, as the French say, with the minimum of arrangement of the given objects. It is an excellent example of the way the impression of truth may be conveyed by that form, but it would have been a still better one if in his search for the effect of dreariness (the effect of dreariness may be said to be the subject of *Une Vie*, so far as the subject is reducible) the author had not eliminated excessively. He has arranged, as I say, as little as possible; the necessity of a "plot" has in no degree imposed itself upon him, and his effort has been to give the uncomposed, unrounded look of life, with its accidents, its broken rhythm, its queer resemblance to the famous description of "Bradshaw"—a compound of trains that start but don't arrive, and trains that arrive but don't start. It is almost an arrangement of the history of poor Mme. de Lamare to have left so many things out of it, for after all she is described in very few of the relations of life. The principal ones are there certainly; we see her as a daughter, a wife, and a mother, but there is a certain accumulation of secondary experience that marks any passage from youth to old age which is a wholly absent element in M. de Maupassant's narrative, and the suppression of which gives the thing a tinge of the arbitrary. It is in the power of this secondary experience to make a great difference, but nothing makes any difference for Jeanne de Lamare as M. de Maupassant puts her before us. Had she no other points of contact than those he describes?—no friends, no phases, no episodes, no chances, none of the miscellaneous *remplissage* of life? No doubt M. de Maupassant would say that he has had to select, that the most comprehensive enumeration is only a condensation, and that, in accordance with the very just principles enunciated in that preface to which I have perhaps too repeatedly referred, he has sacrificed what is uncharacteristic to what is characteristic. It characterizes the career of this French country lady of fifty years ago that its long gray expanse should be seen as peopled with but five or six figures. The essence of the matter is that she was deceived in almost every affection, and that essence is given if the persons who deceived her are given.

The reply is doubtless adequate, and I have only intended my criticism to suggest the degree of my interest. What it really amounts to is that if the subject of this artistic experiment had been the existence of an English lady, even a very dull one, the air of verisimilitude would have demanded that she should have been placed in a denser medium. *Une Vie* may after all be only a testimony to the fact of the melancholy void of the coast of Normandy, even within a moderate drive of a great seaport, under the Restoration and Louis Philippe. It is especially to be recommended to those who are interested in the question of what constitutes a "story," offering as it does the most definite sequences at the same time that it has nothing that corresponds to the usual idea of a plot, and closing with an implication that finds us prepared. The picture again in this case is much more dominant than the idea, unless it be an idea that loneliness and grief are terrible. The picture, at any rate, is full of truthful touches, and the work has the merit and the charm that it is the most delicate of the author's productions and the least hard. In none other has he occupied himself so continuously with so innocent a figure as his soft, bruised heroine; in none other has he paid our poor blind human history the compliment (and this is remarkable, considering the flatness of so much of the particular subject) of finding it so little *bête*. He may think it, here, but comparatively he does not say it. He almost betrays a sense of moral things. Jeanne is absolutely passive, she has no moral spring, no active moral life, none of the edifying attributes of character (it costs her apparently as little as may be in the way of a shock, a complication of feeling, to discover, by letters, after her mother's death, that this lady has not been the virtuous woman she has supposed); but her chronicler has had to handle the immaterial forces of patience and renunciation, and this has given the book a certain purity, in spite of two or three "physiological" passages that come in with violence —a violence the greater as we feel it to be a result of selection. It is very much a mark of M. de Maupassant that on the most striking occasion, with a single exception, on which his picture is not a picture of libertinage it is a picture of unmitigated suffering. Would he suggest that these are the only alternatives?

3. action . . . is . . . a question of terms

("Mrs. Humphry Ward," 1892)

Life, for Mrs. Humphry Ward, as the subject of a large canvas, means predominantly the life of the thinking, the life of the sentient creature, whose chronicler at the present hour, so little is he in fashion, it has been almost an originality on her part to become. The novelist is often reminded that he must put before us an action; but it is, after all, a question of terms. There are actions and actions, and Mrs. Ward was capable of recognizing possibilities of palpitation without number in that of her hero's passionate conscience, that of his relentless faith. Just so in her admirable appreciation of the strange and fascinating Amiel, she found in his throbbing stillness a quantity of life that she would not have found in the snapping of pistols.

4. centre of interest as drama of consciousness

(Preface to *Roderick Hudson*, 1907)

My subject [in *Roderick Hudson*], all blissfully, in face of difficulties, had defined itself—and this in spite of the title of the book—as not directly, in the least, my young sculptor's adventure. This it had been but indirectly, being all the while in essence and in final effect another man's, his friend's and patron's, view and experience of him. One's luck was to have felt one's subject right—whether instinct or calculation, in those dim days, most served; and the circumstance even amounts perhaps to a little lesson that when this has happily occurred faults may show, faults may disfigure, and yet not upset the work. It remains in equilibrium by having found its centre, the point of command of all the rest. From this centre the subject has been treated, from this centre the interest has spread, and so, whatever else it may do or may not do, the thing has acknowledged a principle of composition and contrives at least to hang together. We see in such a case why it should so hang; we escape that dreariest displeasure it is open to experiments in this general order to inflict, the sense of any hanging-together precluded as by the very terms of the case.

The centre of interest throughout "Roderick" is in Rowland Mallet's consciousness, and the drama is the very drama of that consciousness—which I had of course to make sufficiently acute in order to enable it, like a set and lighted scene, to hold the play. By making it acute, meanwhile, one made its own movement—or rather, strictly, its movement in the particular connexion—interesting; this movement really being quite the stuff of one's thesis. It had, naturally, Rowland's consciousness, not to be *too* acute—which would have disconnected it and made it superhuman: the beautiful little problem was to keep it connected, connected intimately, with the general human exposure, and thereby bedimmed and befooled and bewildered, anxious, restless, fallible, and yet to endow it with such intelligence that the appearances reflected in it, and constituting together there the situation and the "story," should become by that fact intelligible. Discernible from the first the joy of such a "job" as this making of his relation to everything involved a sufficiently limited, a sufficiently pathetic, tragic, comic, ironic, personal state to be thoroughly natural, and yet at the same time a sufficiently clear medium to represent a whole. This whole was to be the sum of what "happened" to him, or in other words his total adventure; but as what happened to him was above all to feel certain things happening to others, to Roderick, to Christina, to Mary Garland, to Mrs. Hudson, to the Cavaliere, to the Prince, so the beauty of the constructional game was to preserve in everything its especial value for *him*.

5. *subjective adventure and scenic law*

(Preface to "What Maisie Knew," 1908)

My central spirit [heroine in "In the Cage"], in the anecdote, is, for verisimilitude, I grant, too ardent a focus of divination; but without this excess the phenomena detailed would have lacked their principle of cohesion. The action of the drama is simply the girl's "subjective" adventure—that of her quite definitely winged intelligence; just as the catastrophe, just as the solution, depends on her winged wit. Why, however, should I explain further —for a case that, modestly as it would seem to present itself, has yet already whirled us so far? A course of incident complicated by the intervention of winged wit—which is here, as I say, confessed to—would be generally expected, I judge, to commit me to the explanation of everything. But from that undertaking I shrink, and take refuge instead, for an instant, in a much looser privilege.

If I speak, as just above, of the *action* embodied, each time, in these so "quiet" recitals, it is under renewed recognition of the inveterate instinct with which they keep conforming to the "scenic" law. They demean themselves for all the world—they quite insist on it, that is, whenever they have a chance—as little constituted dramas, little exhibitions founded on the logic of the "scene," the unit of the scene, the general scenic consistency, and knowing little more than that. To read them over has been to find them on this ground never at fault. The process repeats and renews itself, moving in the light it has once for all adopted. These finer idiosyncrasies of a literary form seem to be regarded as outside the scope of criticism—small reference to them do I remember ever to have met; such surprises of re-perusal, such recoveries of old fundamental intention, such moments of almost ruefully independent discrimination, would doubtless in that case not have waylaid my steps. Going over the pages here placed together has been for me, at all events, quite to watch the scenic system at play. The treatment by "scene" regularly, quite rhythmically recurs; the intervals between, the massing of the elements to a different effect and by a quite other law, remain, in this fashion, all preparative, just as the scenic occasions in themselves become, at a given moment, illustrative, each of the agents, true to its function, taking up the theme from the other very much as the fiddles, in an orchestra, may take it up from the cornets and flutes, or the wind-instruments take it up from the violins. The point, however, is that the scenic passages are *wholly* and logically scenic, having for their rule of beauty the principle of the "conduct," the organic development, of a scene—the entire succession of values that flower and bear fruit on ground solidly laid for them. The great advantage for the total effect is that we feel, with the definite alternation, how the theme *is* being treated. That is we feel it when, in such tangled connexions, we happen to care. I shouldn't really go on as if this were the case with many readers.

6. centre of subject: a single consciousness

(Preface to *The Portrait of a Lady*, 1908)

The point is, however, that this single small corner-stone, the conception of a certain young woman affronting her destiny, had begun with being all my outfit for the large building of "The Portrait of a Lady." It came to be a square and spacious house—or has at least seemed so to me in this going over it again; but, such as it is, it had to be put up round my young woman while she stood there in perfect isolation. That is to me, artistically speaking, the circumstance of interest; for I have lost myself once more, I confess, in the curiosity of analysing the structure. By what process of logical accretion was this slight "personality," the mere slim shade of an intelligent but presumptuous girl, to find itself endowed with the high attributes of a Subject? —and indeed by what thinness, at the best, would such a subject not be vitiated? Millions of presumptuous girls, intelligent or not intelligent, daily affront their destiny, and what is it open to their destiny to *be*, at the most, that we should make an ado about? The novel is of its very nature an "ado," an ado about something, and the larger the form it takes the greater of course the ado. Therefore, consciously, that was what one was in for—for positively organising an ado about Isabel Archer. . . .

   . . . There is always the escape from any close account of the weak agent of such spells by using as a bridge for evasion, for retreat and flight, the view of her relation to those surrounding her. Make it predominantly a view of *their* relation and the trick is played: you give the general sense of her effect, and you give it, so far as the raising on it of a superstructure goes, with the maximum of ease. Well, I recall perfectly how little, in my now quite established connexion, the maximum of ease appealed to me, and how I seemed to get rid of it by an honest transposition of the weights in the two scales. "Place the centre of the subject in the young woman's own consciousness," I said to myself, "and you get as interesting and as beautiful a difficulty as you could wish. Stick to *that*—for the centre; put the heaviest weight into *that* scale, which will be so largely the scale of her relation to herself. Make her only interested enough, at the same time, in the things that are not herself, and this relation needn't fear to be too limited. Place meanwhile in the other scale the lighter weight (which is usually the one that tips the balance of interest): press least hard, in short, on the consciousness of your heroine's satellites, especially the male; make it an interest contributive only to the greater one. See, at all events, what can be done in this way. What better field could there be for a due ingenuity? The girl hovers, inextinguishable, as a charming creature, and the job will be to translate her into the highest terms of that formula, and as nearly as possible moreover into *all* of them. To depend upon her and her little concerns wholly to see you through will necessitate, remember, your really 'doing' her."

7. mystic conversion: mild adventures into the stuff of drama

(Preface to *The Portrait of a Lady*, 1908)

I do at least seem to catch the key to a part of this abundance of small anxious, ingenious illustration as I recollect putting my finger, in my young woman's [Isabel Archer in *The Portrait of a Lady*] interest, on the most obvious of her predicates. "What will she 'do'? Why, the first thing she'll do will be to come to Europe; which in fact will form, and all inevitably, no small part of her principal adventure. Coming to Europe is even for the 'frail vessels,' in this wonderful age, a mild adventure; but what is truer than that on one side—the side of their independence of flood and field, of the moving accident, of battle and murder and sudden death—her adventures are to be mild? Without her sense of them, her sense *for* them, as one may say, they are next to nothing at all; but isn't the beauty and the difficulty just in showing their mystic conversion by that sense, conversion into the stuff of drama or, even more delightful word still, of 'story'?" It was all as clear, my contention, as a silver bell. Two very good instances, I think, of this effect of conversion, two cases of the rare chemistry, are the pages in which Isabel, coming into the drawing-room at Gardencourt, coming in from a wet walk or whatever, that rainy afternoon, finds Madame Merle in possession of the place, Madame Merle seated, all absorbed but all serene, at the piano, and deeply recognises, in the striking of such an hour, in the presence there, among the gathering shades, of this personage, of whom a moment before she had never so much as heard, a turning-point in her life. It is dreadful to have too much, for any artistic demonstration, to dot one's i's and insist on one's intentions, and I am not eager to do it now; but the question here was that of producing the maximum of intensity with the minimum of strain.

The interest was to be raised to its pitch and yet the elements to be kept in their key; so that, should the whole thing duly impress, I might show what an "exciting" inward life may do for the person leading it even while it remains perfectly normal. And I cannot think of a more consistent application of that ideal unless it be in the long statement, just beyond the middle of the book, of my young woman's extraordinary meditative vigil on the occasion that was to become for her such a landmark. Reduced to its essence, it is but the vigil of searching criticism; but it throws the action further forward than twenty "incidents" might have done. It was designed to have all the vivacity of incident and all the economy of picture. She sits up, by her dying fire, far into the night, under the spell of recognitions on which she finds the last sharpness suddenly wait. It is a representation simply of her motionlessly *seeing*, and an attempt withal to make the mere still lucidity of her act as "interesting" as the surprise of a caravan or the identification of a pirate. It represents, for that matter, one of the identifications dear to the novelist, and even indispensable to him; but it all goes on without her being approached by another person and without her leaving her chair. It is obviously the best thing in the book, but it is only a supreme illustration of the general plan.

8. adventure: a matter of relation and appreciation

(Preface to *Daisy Miller*, 1909)

It is, not surprisingly, one of the rudiments of criticism that a human, a personal "adventure" is no *a priori*, no positive and absolute and inelastic thing, but just a matter of relation and appreciation—a name we conveniently give, after the fact, to any passage, to any situation, that has added the sharp taste of uncertainty to a quickened sense of life. Therefore the thing is, all beautifully, a matter of interpretation and of the particular conditions; without a view of which latter some of the most prodigious adventures, as one has often had occasion to say, may vulgarly show for nothing.

Chapter IX

RENDERING: EXECUTION

Although James wrote often and much about the nature and finding of subjects, and proclaimed frequently the urgency of finding the center of subjects, he wrote probably even more about the presentation of subjects —the representation, the rendering, the execution. His Notebooks and Prefaces are devoted largely to this matter in specific instances of his own work. And he turned to the matter in "The Art of Fiction," using his favorite term borrowed from painting—rendering: the writer (like the painter) "competes with life . . . in his attempt to render the look of things, the look that conveys their meaning, to catch the color, the relief, the expression, the surface, the substance of the human spectacle. . . . All life solicits him, and to 'render' the simplest surface, to produce the most momentary illusion, is a very complicated business."

How complicated the business is, James goes on to point out by stressing the complex interrelationship of such fictional elements usually dealt with as separate entities—dialogue, incident, description: "I cannot imagine composition existing in a series of blocks, nor conceive, in any novel worth discussing at all, of a passage of description that is not in its intention narrative, a passage of dialogue that is not in its intention descriptive." But however complicated the business, it must command the primary attention of the critic—as James points out in one of the most quoted remarks from "The Art of Fiction": "Of course it is of execution that we are talking—that being the only point of a novel that is open to contention. . . . We must grant the artist his subject, his idea, his donnée: our criticism is applied only to what he makes of it."

Critics of James, disturbed by the absence of sensational action in his fictions, and puzzled by the stress he placed on execution in his criticism, have placed him in the "school" that James ridiculed in "The Art of Fiction": "There is surely no 'school'—Mr. Besant speaks of a school—which urges that a novel should be all treatment and no subject. There must assuredly be something to treat. . . . The story and the novel, the idea and the form, are the needle and thread, and I never heard of a guild of tailors who recommended the use of the thread without the needle, or the needle without the thread."

The "needlework" of fiction was, for James, endlessly fascinating, not only in his own work but in the work of others that he encountered. In this

*chapter are gathered numerous passages in which he explored various facets
of the needlework.*

In Part A, "Art," are brought together some general comments on the need
for art after the finding of a subject. The general comments, emphasizing the
complexities confronted by a writer in imposing the order of art on the infinite
complexities of life ("relations stop nowhere"), are concluded with a specific
example from James's own work—the complications of "rendering" he confronted in evoking a vision of evil, without exact specification, in "*The Turn
of the Screw.*"

Part B, "Presence of the Author," presents a number of important comments
(arranged chronologically) on the intricate question of the place of the author
in his own work. Because in "The Art of Fiction" and elsewhere James
scolded Trollope for his intrusions and his asides in his novels, it has been
widely assumed that James argued for an impersonal or authorless fiction.
On the contrary. He scolded Trollope not for his appearance in his novels,
but for his continual assertions that he was only "making believe"—therefore
violating verisimilitude. In fact, James over and over again pointed to the
author's presence in his own work, stressed its inevitability, and tried to
discriminate the various ways the presence was felt by the reader. The point
is important for James's own work, where his presence is indeed felt clearly
as a part of James's major intention.

In Part C, "Picture, Preparation, Scene, Drama," James has his say about
a variety of methods of representation or rendering. In his discussions, James
tended to pose the pictorial (descriptive, static) against the dramatic (scenic,
conversational). In the latter part of his career he came to think of his work
as rhythmically progressive through preparation, scene, preparation, scene—
with great emphasis on the dramatic tension of the scenes. Although James
came to believe in the supremacy (in its effect) of scene, with its dominance
of dialogue, he came also to believe that some of his greatest passages were in
picture, or the non-scenic form, in which he achieved "representational effect"
—that is, the non-dramatic that gave the dramatic effect. This belief is, of
course, related to his development (simultaneously with his movement in the
direction of the dramatic) of greater and greater interest in psychological
"action." He perhaps sensed a conflict between his passion for presenting his
action, essentially "interior," in the "exterior" dramatic form. And he sought
his greatest triumphs in rendering the interior tensions and conflicts dramatically vivid without drama.

Part D of this chapter, "Foreshortening; Time-Sequence; Dialogue,"
reveals how deeply intertwined James repeatedly found these vital elements of
fiction. "Foreshortening," another borrowing from the painter's craft, James
found the greatest challenge of the novelist, for it was only through it—a
"figuring synthetically"—that reality could be rendered at all. And closely
allied to the technique of foreshortening was the problem of conveying the

"*sense of duration, of the lapse and accumulation of time.*" *And both of these elements imposed controls or limits on the use of dialogue. Any notion, then, that good novels were made simply by the injection of abundant dialogue was exposed as naive. In brief, James found the question of dialogue intimately bound up with other intricate questions of rendering and evoking.*

Part A: Art

1. after "finding" the subject: the "process" of art

(Preface to The Ambassadors, 1909)

No privilege of the teller of tales and the handler of puppets is more delightful, or has more of the suspense and the thrill of a game of difficulty breathlessly played, than just this business of looking for the unseen and the occult, in a scheme half-grasped, by the light or, so to speak, by the clinging scent, of the gage already in hand. No dreadful old pursuit of the hidden slave with bloodhounds and the rag of association can ever, for "excitement," I judge, have bettered it at its best. For the dramatist always, by the very law of his genius, believes not only in a possible right issue from the rightly-conceived tight place; he does much more than this—he believes, irresistibly, in the necessary, the precious "tightness" of the place (whatever the issue) on the strength of any respectable hint. It being thus the respectable hint that I had with such avidity picked up, what would be the story to which it would most inevitably form the centre? It is part of the charm attendant on such questions that the "story," with the omens true, as I say, puts on from this stage the authenticity of concrete existence. It then *is*, essentially—it begins to be, though it may more or less obscurely lurk; so that the point is not in the least what to make of it, but only, very delightfully and very damnably, where to put one's hand on it.

In which truth resides surely much of the interest of that admirable mixture for salutary application which we know as art. Art deals with what we see, it must first contribute full-handed that ingredient; it plucks its material, otherwise expressed, in the garden of life—which material elsewhere grown is stale and uneatable. But it has no sooner done this than it has to take account of a *process*—from which only when it's the basest of the servants of man, incurring ignominious dismissal with no "character," does it, and whether under some muddled pretext of morality or on any other, pusillanimously edge away. The process, that of the expression, the literal squeezing-out, of value is another affair—with which the happy luck of mere finding has little to do. The joys of finding, at this stage, are pretty well over; that quest of the subject as a whole by "matching," as the ladies say at the shops, the big piece with the snippet, having ended, we assume, with a capture. The subject is found, and if the problem is then transferred to the ground of what to do with it the field opens out for any amount of doing. This is precisely the infusion that, as I submit, completes the strong mixture. It is on the other hand the part of the business that can least be likened to the chase with horn and hound. It's all a sedentary part—involves as much ciphering, of sorts, as would merit the highest salary paid to a chief accountant. Not, however, that the chief accountant hasn't *his* gleams of bliss; for the felicity, or at least the equilibrium, of the artist's state dwells less, surely, in the further delightful complications he can smuggle in than in those he succeeds in keeping out. He sows his seed at the risk of too thick a crop; wherefore yet again, like the gentlemen who audit ledgers, he must keep his head at any price.

2. *the execution of a work of art is a part of its very essence*

("William Dean Howells," 1886)

The execution of a work of art is a part of its very essence, and that, it seems to me, must have mattered in all ages in exactly the same degree, and be destined always to do so. I can conceive of no state of civilization in which it shall not be deemed important, though of course there are states in which executants are clumsy. I should . . . venture to express a certain regret that Mr. Howells . . . should appear increasingly to hold composition too cheap— by which I mean, should neglect the effect that comes from alternation, distribution, relief. He has an increasing tendency to tell his story altogether in conversations, so that a critical reader sometimes wishes, not that the dialogue might be suppressed (it is too good for that), but that it might be distributed, interspaced with narrative and pictorial matter. The author forgets sometimes to paint, to evoke the conditions and appearances, to build in the subject. He is doubtless afraid of doing these things in excess, having seen in other hands what disastrous effects that error may have; but all the same I cannot help thinking that the divinest thing in a valid novel is the compendious, descriptive, pictorial touch, *a la Daudet*.

3. *relations stop nowhere*

(Preface to *Roderick Hudson*, 1907)

Really, universally, relations stop nowhere, and the exquisite problem of the artist is eternally but to draw, by a geometry of his own, the circle within which they shall happily *appear* to do so. He is in the perpetual predicament that the continuity of things is the whole matter, for him, of comedy and tragedy; that this continuity is never, by the space of an instant or an inch, broken, and that, to do anything at all, he has at once intensely to consult and intensely to ignore it. All of which will perhaps pass but for a supersubtle way of pointing the plain moral that a young embroiderer of the canvas of life soon began to work in terror, fairly, of the vast expanse of that surface, of the boundless number of its distinct perforations for the needle, and the tendency inherent in his many-coloured flowers and figures to cover and consume as many as possible of the little holes. The development of the flower, of the figure, involved thus an immense counting of holes and a careful selection among them. That would have been, it seemed to him, a brave enough process, were it not the very nature of the holes so to invite, to solicit, to persuade, to practise positively a thousand lures and deceits. The prime effect of so sustained a system, so prepared a surface, is to lead on and on; while fascination of following resides, by the same token, in the presumability *somewhere* of a convenient, of a visibly-appointed stopping-place. Art would be easy indeed if, by a fond power disposed to "patronise" it, such conveniences, such simplifications, had been provided. We have, as the case stands, to invent and establish them, to arrive at them by a difficult, dire process of selection and comparison, of surrender and sacrifice. The very meaning of expertness is acquired courage to brace one's self for the cruel crisis from the moment one sees it grimly loom.

4. the rigour of his artistic need

(Preface to *Daisy Miller*, 1909)

These in fact are the saving sanities of the dramatic poet's always rather mad undertaking—the rigour of his artistic need to cultivate almost at any price variety of appearance and experiment, to dissimulate likenesses, samenesses, stalenesses, by the infinite play of a form pretending to a life of its own. There are not so many quite distinct things in his field, I think, as there are sides by which the main masses may be approached; and he is after all but a nimble besieger or nocturnal sneaking adventurer who perpetually plans, watches, circles for penetrable places.

5. vision of evil: lack of specification

(Preface to *The Aspern Papers*, 1908)

Here it was—in the use made of them [Peter Quint and Miss Jessel in "The Turn of the Screw"]—that I felt a high degree of art really required; and here it is that, on reading the tale over, I find my precautions justified. The essence of the matter was the villainy of motive in the evoked predatory creatures; so that the result would be ignoble—by which I mean would be trivial— were this element of evil but feebly or inanely suggested. Thus arose on behalf of my idea the lively interest of a possible suggestion and process of *adumbration;* the question of how best to convey that sense of the depths of the sinister without which my fable would so woefully limp. Portentous evil—how was I to save that, as an intention on the part of my demon-spirits, from the drop, the comparative vulgarity, inevitably attending, throughout the whole range of possible brief illustration, the offered example, the imputed vice, the cited act, the limited deplorable presentable instance? To bring the bad dead back to life for a second round of badness is to warrant them as indeed prodigious, and to become hence as shy of specifications as of a waiting anti-climax. One had seen, in fiction, some grand form of wrong-doing, or better still of wrong-being, imputed, seen it promised and announced as by the hot breath of the Pit—and then, all lamentably, shrink to the compass of some particular brutality, some particular immorality, some particular infamy portrayed : with the result, alas, of the demonstration's falling sadly short. If *my* bad things, for "The Turn of the Screw," I felt, should succumb to this danger, if they shouldn't seem sufficiently bad, there would be nothing for me but to hang my artistic head lower than I had ever known occasion to do.

The view of that discomfort and the fear of that dishonour, it accordingly must have been, that struck the proper light for my right, though by no means easy, short cut. What, in the last analysis, had I to give the sense of? Of their being, the haunting pair, capable, as the phrase is, of everything—that is of exerting, in respect to the children, the very worst action small victims so conditioned might be conceived as subject to. What would *be* then, on reflexion, this utmost conceivability?—a question to which the answer all admirably came. There is for such a case no eligible *absolute* of the wrong; it remains relative to fifty other elements, a matter of appreciation, speculation, imagination—these things moreover quite exactly in the light of the spectator's, the critic's, the reader's experience. Only make the reader's general vision of evil intense enough, I said to myself—and that already is a charming job— and his own experience, his own imagination, his own sympathy (with the children) and horror (of their false friends) will supply him quite sufficiently with all the particulars. Make him *think* the evil, make him think it for himself, and you are released from weak specifications. This ingenuity I took pains—as indeed great pains were required—to apply; and with a success apparently beyond my liveliest hope. Droll enough at the same time, I must add, some of the evidence—even when most convincing—of this success. How can I feel my calculation to have failed, my wrought suggestion not to have worked, that is, on my being assailed, as has befallen me, with the charge of a monstrous emphasis, the charge of all indecently expatiating? There is not only from beginning to end of the matter not an inch of expatiation, but my values are positively all blanks save so far as an excited horror, a promoted pity, a created expertness—on which punctual effects of strong causes no writer can ever fail to plume himself—proceed to read into them more or less fantastic figures. Of high interest to the author meanwhile —and by the same stroke a theme for the moralist—the artless resentful reaction of the entertained person who has abounded in the sense of the situation. He visits his abundance, morally, on the artist—who has but clung to an ideal of faultlessness. Such indeed, for this latter, are some of the observations by which the prolonged strain of that clinging may be enlivened!

PART B: PRESENCE OF THE AUTHOR

1. *the autobiographical form of composition*

("Autobiography in Fiction," 1865)

Reminiscences of this period [childhood] are always gossip at the best, and it is curious to see how commonly novelists, even poor novelists, excel in them. A writer who has brought his hero through his school-days very prettily and successfully, often fails of inspiration at the threshold of worldly life. This kind of retrospection makes poets and romancers of the dullest of us, and the professional writer gets the benefit of our common tendency. The autobiographical form of composition enables him to carry this tendency to its furthest limits. It is for this reason that it is so popular. It has indeed great advantages in the way of allowing a writer to run on, as we may call it; but it has the prime disadvantage of being the most dramatic form possible. The author not only puts off his own personality, but he assumes that of another, and in proportion as the imaginary hero is different from himself, his task becomes difficult. Hence the merit of most fictitious autobiographies is that they give you a tolerably fair reflection of the writer's character. To project yourself into the consciousness of a person essentially your opposite requires the audacity of great genius; and even men of genius are cautious in approaching the problem. Mr. Browning the great master of the art in these days never assumes the burden of its solution but for a few pages at a time.

2. *situations speak for themselves*

("Ivan Turgénieff," 1874)

In this tale ["A Nest of Noblemen"], as always with our author, the drama is quite uncommented; the poet never plays chorus; situations speak for themselves. When Lavretzky reads in the *chronique* of a French newspaper that his wife is dead, there is no description of his feelings, no portrayal of his mental attitude. The living, moving narrative has so effectually put us in the way of feeling with him that we can be depended upon. He had been reading in bed before going to sleep, had taken up the paper and discovered the momentous paragraph. He "threw himself into his clothes," the author simply says, "went out into the garden, and walked up and down till morning in the same alley." We close the book for a moment and pause, with a sense of personal excitement.

3. little slaps at credulity

("Anthony Trollope," 1883)

I may take occasion to remark here upon a very curious fact—the fact that there are certain precautions in the way of producing that illusion dear to the intending novelist which Trollope not only habitually scorned to take, but really, as we may say, asking pardon for the heat of the thing, delighted wantonly to violate. He took a suicidal satisfaction in reminding the reader that the story he was telling was only, after all, a make-believe. He habitually referred to the work in hand (in the course of that work) as a novel, and to himself as a novelist, and was fond of letting the reader know that this novelist could direct the course of events according to his pleasure. Already, in *Barchester Towers*, he falls into this pernicious trick. In describing the wooing of Eleanor Bold by Mr. Arabin he has occasion to say that the lady might have acted in a much more direct and natural way than the way he attributes to her. But if she had, he adds, "where would have been my novel?" The last chapter of the same story begins with the remark, "The end of a novel, like the end of a children's dinner party, must be made up of sweetmeats and sugar-plums." These little slaps at credulity (we might give many more specimens) are very discouraging, but they are even more inexplicable; for they are deliberately inartistic, even judged from the point of view of that rather vague consideration of form which is the only canon we have a right to impose upon Trollope. It is impossible to imagine what a novelist takes himself to be unless he regard himself as an historian and his narrative as a history. It is only as an historian that he has the smallest *locus standi*. As a narrator of fictitious events he is nowhere; to insert into his attempt a backbone of logic, he must relate events that are assumed to be real. This assumption permeates, animates all the work of the most solid storytellers; we need only mention (to select a single instance) the magnificent historical tone of Balzac, who would as soon have thought of admitting to the reader that he was deceiving him, as Garrick or John Kemble would have thought of pulling off his disguise in front of the footlights. Therefore, when Trollope suddenly winks at us and reminds us that he is telling us an arbitrary thing, we are startled and shocked in quite the same way as if Macaulay or Motley were to drop the historic mask and intimate that William of Orange was a myth or the Duke of Alva an invention.

4. *impersonality and personal presence of the author*

("Guy de Maupassant," 1888)

The latter part of his introduction to *Pierre et Jean* [by Maupassant] is less felicitous than the beginning, but we learn from it—and this is interesting—that he regards the analytic fashion of telling a story, which has lately begotten in his own country some such remarkable experiments (few votaries as it has attracted among ourselves), as very much less profitable than the simple epic manner which "avoids with care all complicated explanations, all dissertations upon motives, and confines itself to making persons and events pass before our eyes." M. de Maupassant adds that in his view "psychology should be hidden in a book, as it is hidden in reality under the facts of existence. The novel conceived in this manner gains interest, movement, color, the bustle of life." When it is a question of an artistic process, we must always mistrust very sharp distinctions, for there is surely in every method a little of every other method. It is as difficult to describe an action without glancing at its motive, its moral history, as it is to describe a motive without glancing at its practical consequence. Our history and our fiction are what we do; but it surely is not more easy to determine where what we do begins than to determine where it ends—notoriously a hopeless task. Therefore it would take a very subtle sense to draw a hard and fast line on the borderland of explanation and illustration. If psychology be hidden in life, as, according to M. de Maupassant, it should be in a book, the question immediately comes up, "From whom is it hidden?" From some people, no doubt, but very much less from others; and all depends upon the observer, the nature of one's observation, and one's curiosity. For some people motives, reasons, relations, explanations, are a part of the very surface of the drama, with the footlights beating full upon them. For me an act, an incident, an attitude, may be a sharp, detached, isolated thing, of which I give a full account in saying that in such and such a way it came off. For you it may be hung about with implications, with relations, and conditions as necessary to help you to recognize it as the clothes of your friends are to help you know them in the street. You feel that they would seem strange to you without petticoats and trousers.

M. de Maupassant would probably urge that the right thing is to know, or to guess, how events come to pass, but to say as little about it as possible. There are matters in regard to which he feels the importance of being explicit, but that is not one of them. The contention to which I allude strikes me as rather arbitrary, so difficult is it to put one's finger upon the reason why, for instance, there should be so little mystery about what happened to Christiane Andermatt, in *Mont-Oriol*, when she went to walk on the hills with Paul Brétigny, and so much, say, about the forces that formed her for that gentleman's convenience, or those lying behind any other odd collapse that our author may have related. The rule misleads, and the best rule certainly is the tact of the individual writer, which will adapt itself to the material as the material comes to him. The cause we plead is ever pretty sure to be the cause of our idiosyncrasies, and if M. de Maupassant thinks meanly of "explanations," it is, I suspect, that they come to him in no great affluence. His view of the conduct of man is so simple as scarcely to require them; and indeed so far as they are needed he *is*, virtually, explanatory. He deprecates reference to motives, but there is one, covering an immense ground in his horizon, as I have already hinted, to which he perpetually refers. If the sexual impulse be not a moral antecedent, it is none the less the wire that moves almost all M. de Maupassant's puppets, and as he has not hidden it, I cannot see that he has eliminated analysis or made a sacrifice to discretion. His pages are studded with that particular analysis; he is constantly peeping behind the curtain, telling us what he discovers there. The truth is that the admirable system of simplification which makes his tales so rapid and so concise (especially his shorter ones, for his novels in some degree, I think, suffer from it) strikes us as not in the least a conscious intellectual effort, a selective, comparative process. He tells us all he knows, all he suspects, and if these things take no account of the moral nature of man, it is because he has no window looking in that direction, and not because artistic scruples have compelled him to close it up. The very compact mansion in which he dwells presents on that side a perfectly dead wall.

This is why, if his axiom that you produce the effect of truth better by painting people from the outside than from the inside has a large utility, his example is convincing in a much higher degree. A writer is fortunate when his theory and his limitations so exactly correspond, when his curiosities may be appeased with such precision and promptitude. M. de Maupassant contends that the most that the analytic novelist can do is to put himself—his own peculiarities—into the costume of the figure analyzed. This may be true, but if it applies to one manner of representing people who are not ourselves, it applies also to any other manner. It is the limitation, the difficulty of the novelist, to whatever clan or camp he may belong. M. de Maupassant is remarkably objective and impersonal, but he would go too far if he were to entertain the belief that he has kept himself out of his books. They speak of him eloquently, even if it only be to tell us how easy—how easy, given his talent of course—he has found this impersonality. Let us hasten to add that in the case of describing a character it is doubtless more difficult to convey the impression of something that is not one's self (the constant effort, however delusive at bottom, of the novelist) than in the case of describing some object more immediately visible. The operation is more delicate, but that circumstance only increases the beauty of the problem.

5. Flaubert: everywhere felt but nowhere seen

("Gustave Flaubert," 1893)

"May I be skinned alive," he [Flaubert] writes in 1854, "before I ever turn my private feelings to literary account." His constant refrain in his letters is the impersonality, as he calls it, of the artist, whose work should consist exclusively of his subject and his style, without an emotion, an idiosyncrasy that is not utterly transmuted. Quotation does but scanty justice to his rage for this idea; almost all his feelings were such a rage that we wonder what form they would have borrowed from a prevision of such posthumous betrayal. "It's one of my principles that one must never write down *one's self*. The artist must be present in his work like God in Creation, invisible and almighty, everywhere felt but nowhere seen." Such was the part he allotted to form, to that rounded detachment which enables the perfect work to live by its own life, that he regarded as indecent and dishonourable the production of any impression that was not intensely calculated. "Feelings" were necessarily crude because they were inevitably unselected, and selection (for the picture's sake) was Flaubert's highest morality.

6. the spiritual presence of the author

("The Lesson of Balzac," 1905)

There would be much to say, I think, had we only a little more time, on this question of the projected light of the individual strong temperament in fiction—the color of the air with which this, that or the other painter of life (as we call them all), more or less unconsciously suffuses his picture. I say unconsciously because I speak here of an effect of atmosphere largely, if not wholly, distinct from the effect sought on behalf of the special subject to be treated; something that proceeds from the contemplative mind itself, the very complexion of the mirror in which the material is reflected. This is of the nature of the man himself—an emanation of his spirit, temper, history; it springs from his very presence, his spiritual presence, in his work, and is, in so far, not a matter of calculation and artistry. All a matter of his own, in a word, for each seer of visions, the particular tone of the medium in which each vision, each clustered group of persons and places and objects, is bathed. Just how, accordingly, does the light of the world, the projected, painted, peopled, poetized, realized world, the furnished and fitted world into which we are beguiled for the holiday excursion, cheap trips or dear, of the eternally amusable, eternally dupeable voyaging mind— just how does this strike us as different in Fielding and in Richardson, in Scott and in Dumas, in Dickens and in Thackeray, in Hawthorne and in Meredith, in George Eliot and in George Sand, in Jane Austen and in Charlotte Bronte? Do we not feel the general landscape evoked by each of the more or less magical wands to which I have given name, not to open itself under the same sun that hangs over the neighboring scene, not to receive the solar rays at the same angle, not to exhibit its shadows with the same intensity or the same sharpness; not, in short, to seem to belong to the same time of day or same state of the weather? Why is it that the life that over- flows in Dickens seems to me always to go on in the morning, or in the very earliest hours of the afternoon at most, and in a vast apartment that appears to have windows, large, uncurtained, and rather unwashed windows, on all sides at once? Why is it that in George Eliot the sun sinks forever to the west, and the shadows are long, and the afternoon wanes, and the trees vaguely rustle, and the color of the day is much inclined to yellow? Why is it that in Charlotte Brontë we move through an endless autumn? Why is it that in Jane Austen we sit quite resigned in an arrested spring? Why does Hawthorne give us the afternoon hour later than any one else? —oh, late, late, quite uncannily late, and as if it were always winter outside? But I am wasting the very minutes I pretended, at the start, to cherish, and am only sustained though my levity by seeing you watch for the time of day or season of the year or state of the weather that I shall fasten upon the complicated clockface of Thackeray. I do, I think, see his light also— see it very much as the light (a different thing from the mere dull dusk) of rainy days in "residential" streets; but we are not, after all, talking of him, and, though Balzac's waiting power has proved itself, this half-century, immense, I must not too much presume upon it.

The question of the color of Balzac's air and the time of *his* day would indeed here easily solicit our ingenuity—were I at liberty to say more than one thing about it. It is rich and thick, the mixture of sun and shade diffused through the *Comédie Humaine*—a mixture richer and thicker and represent- ing an absolutely greater quantity of "atmosphere," than we shall find prevailing within the compass of any other suspended frame. That is how we see him, living in his garden, and it is by reason of the restless energy with which he circulated there that I hold his fortune and his privilege, in spite of the burden of his toil and the brevity of his immediate reward, to have been before any others enviable. It is strange enough, but what most abides with us, as we follow his steps, is a sense of the intellectual luxury he enjoyed. To focus him at all, for a single occasion, we have to simplify, and this wealth of his vicarious experience forms the side, moreover, on which he is most attaching for those who take an interest in the real play of the imagination. From the moment our imagination plays at all, of course, and from the moment we try to catch and preserve the pictures it throws off, from that moment we too, in our comparatively feeble way, live vicariously— succeed in opening a series of dusky passages in which, with a more or less childlike ingenuity, we can romp to and fro. Our passages are mainly short and dark, however; we soon come to the end of them—dead walls, without resonance, in presence of which the candle goes out and the game stops, and we have only to retrace our steps. Balzac's luxury, as I call it, was in the extraordinary number and length of his radiating and ramifying corridors— the labyrinth in which he finally lost himself. What it comes back to, in other words, is the intensity with which we live—and his intensity is recorded for us on every page of his work.

Part C: Picture, Preparation, Scene, Drama

1. the scenic method

(*Notebooks*, 1896)

I realise—none too soon—that the *scenic* method is my absolute, my imperative, my *only* salvation. The *march of an action* is the thing for me to, more and more, *attach* myself to : it is the only thing that really, for *me*, at least, will *produire* l'oeuvre, and l'oeuvre is, before God, what I'm going in for. Well, the scenic scheme is the only one that *I* can trust, with my tendencies, to stick to the march of an action. How reading Ibsen's splendid *John Gabriel* a day or two ago (in proof) brought that, FINALLY AND FOR- EVER, home to me! I must now, I fully recognize, have a splendid recourse to it to see me out of the wood, at all, of this interminable little *Maisie*; *10,000 more words* of which I have still to do. They can be magnificent in movement if I resolutely and triumphantly take this course with them, and *only if I do so*.

2. *dramatic form vs. "going behind"*

(Preface to *The Awkward Age*, 1908)

The beauty of the conception [in *The Awkward Age*] was in this approximation of the respective divisions of my form to the successive Acts of a Play—as to which it was more than ever a case for charmed capitals. The divine distinction of the act of a play—and a greater than any other it easily succeeds in arriving at—was, I reasoned, in its special, its guarded objectivity. This objectivity, in turn, when achieving its ideal, came from the imposed absence of that "going behind," to compass explanations and amplifications, to drag out odds and ends from the "mere" storyteller's great property shop of aids to illusion: a resource under denial of which it was equally perplexing and delightful, for a change, to proceed. Everything, for that matter, becomes interesting from the moment it has closely to consider, for full effect positively to bestride, the law of its kind. "Kinds" are the very life of literature, and truth and strength come from the complete recognition of them, from abounding to the utmost in their respective senses and sinking deep into their consistency. I myself have scarcely to plead the cause of "going behind," which is right and beautiful and fruitful in its place and order; but as the confusion of kinds is the inelegance of letters and the stultification of values, so to renounce that line utterly and do something quite different instead may become in another connexion the true course and the vehicle of effect. Something in the very nature, in the fine rigour, of this special sacrifice (which is capable of affecting the form-lover, I think, as really more of a projected form than any other) lends it moreover a coercive charm; a charm that grows in proportion as the appeal to it tests and stretches and strains it, puts it powerfully to the touch. To make the presented occasion tell all its story itself, remain shut up in its own presence and yet on that patch of staked-out ground become thoroughly interesting and remain thoroughly clear, is a process not remarkable, no doubt, so long as a very light weight is laid on it, but difficult enough to challenge and inspire great adroitness so soon as the elements to be dealt with begins at all to "size up."

The disdainers of the contemporary drama deny, obviously, with all promptness, that the matter to be expressed by its means—richly and successfully expressed that is—*can* loom with any largeness; since from the moment it does one of the conditions breaks down. The process simply collapses under pressure, they contend, proves its weakness as quickly as the office laid on it ceases to be simple. "Remember," they say to the dramatist, "that you have to be, supremely, three things: you have to be true to your form, you have to be interesting, you have to be clear. You have in other words to prove yourself adequate to taking a heavy weight. But we defy you really to conform to your conditions with any but a light one. Make the thing you have to convey, make the picture you have to paint, at all rich and complex, and you cease to be clear. Remain clear—and with the clearness required by the infantine intelligence of any public consenting to see a play— and what becomes of the 'importance' of your subject? If it's important by any other critical measure than the little foot-rule the 'produced' piece has to conform to, it is predestined to be a muddle. When it has escaped being a muddle the note it has succeeded in striking at the furthest will be recognised as one of those that are called high but by the courtesy, by the intellectual provinciality, of theatrical criticism, which, as we can see for ourselves any morning, is—well, an abyss even deeper than the theatre itself. Don't attempt to crush us with Dumas and Ibsen, for such values are from any informed and enlightened point of view, that is measured by other high values, literary, critical, philosophic, of the most moderate order. Ibsen and Dumas are precisely cases of men, men in their degree, in their poor theatrical straight-jacket, speculative, who have *had* to renounce the finer thing for the coarser, the thick, in short, for the thin and the curious for the self-evident. What earthly intellectual distinction, what 'prestige' of achievement, would have attached to the substance of such things as 'Denise,' as 'Monsieur Alphonse,' as 'Francillon' (and we take the Dumas of the sup- posedly subtler period) in any other form? What virtues of the same order would have attached to 'The Pillars of Society,' to 'An Enemy of the People,' to 'Ghosts,' to 'Rosmersholm' (or taking also Ibsen's 'subtler period') to 'John Gabriel Borkmann,' to 'The Master-Builder'? Ibsen is in fact wonderfully a case in point, since from the moment he's clear, from the moment he's 'amusing,' it's on the footing of a thesis as simple and super- ficial as that of 'A Doll's House'—while from the moment he's by apparent intention comprehensive and searching it's on the footing of an effect as confused and obscure as 'The Wild Duck.' From which you easily see *all* the conditions can't be met. The dramatist has to choose but those he's most capable of, and by that choice he's known."

So the objector concludes, and never surely without great profit from his having been "drawn." His apparent triumph—if it be even apparent—still leaves, it will be noted, convenient cover for retort in the riddled face of the opposite stronghold. The last word in these cases is for nobody who can't pretend to an *absolute* test. The terms here used, obviously, are matters of appreciation, and there is no short cut to proof (luckily for us all round) either that "Monsieur Alphonse" develops itself on the highest plane of irony or that "Ghosts" simplifies almost to excruciation. If "John Gabriel Borkmann" is but a pennyworth of effect as to a character we can imagine much more amply presented, and if "Hedda Gabler" makes an appeal enfeebled by remarkable vagueness, there is by the nature of the case no catching the convinced, or call him the deluded, spectator or reader in the act of a mistake. He is to be caught at the worst in the act of attention, of the very greatest attention, and that is all, as a precious preliminary at least, that the playwright asks of him, besides being all the very divinest poet can get. I remember rejoicing as much to remark this, after getting launched in "The Awkward Age," as if I were in fact constructing a play; just as I may doubtless appear now not less anxious to keep the philosophy of the dramatist's course before me than if I belonged to his order. I felt, certainly, the support he feels, I participated in his technical amusement, I tasted to the full the bitter-sweetness of his draught—the beauty and the difficulty (to harp again on that string) of escaping poverty *even though* the references in one's action can only be, with intensity, to each other, to things exactly on the same plane of exhibition with themselves. Exhibition may mean in a "story" twenty different ways, fifty excursions, alternatives, excrescences, and the novel, as largely practised in English, is the perfect paradise of the loose end. The play consents to the logic of but one way, mathematically right, and with the loose end as gross an impertinence on its surface, and as grave a dishonour, as the dangle of a snippet of silk or wool on the right side of a tapestry. We are shut up wholly to cross-relations, relations all within the action itself; no part of which is related to anything but some other part—save of course by the relation of the total to life. And, after invoking the protection of Gyp, I saw the point of my game all in the problem of keeping these conditioned relations crystalline at the same time that I should, in emulation of life, consent to their being numerous and fine and characteristic of the London world (as the London world was in this quarter and that to be deciphered). All of which was to make in the event for complications.

3. *picture vs. drama*

(Preface to *The Wings of the Dove*, 1909)

I haven't the heart now, I confess, to adduce the detail of so many lapsed importances; the explanation of most of which, after all, I take to have been in the crudity of a truth beating full upon me through these reconsiderations, the odd inveteracy with which picture, at almost any turn, is jealous of drama, and drama (though on the whole with a greater patience, I think) suspicious of picture. Between them, no doubt, they do much for the theme; yet each baffles insidiously the other's ideal and eats round the edges of its position; each is too ready to say "I can take the thing for 'done' only when done in *my* way." The residuum of comfort for the witness of these broils is of course meanwhile in the convenient reflexion, invented for him in the twilight of time and the infancy of art by the Angel, not to say by the Demon, of Compromise, that nothing is so easy to "do" as not to be thankful for almost any stray help in its getting done.

4. picture as preparation for scene

(Preface to *The Ambassadors*, 1909)

The material of "The Ambassadors," conforming in this respect exactly to that of "The Wings of the Dove," published just before it, is taken absolutely for the stuff of drama; so that, availing myself of the opportunity given me by this edition for some prefatory remarks on the latter work, I had mainly to make on its behalf the point of its scenic consistency. It disguises that virtue, in the oddest way in the world, by just *looking*, as we turn its pages, as little scenic as possible; but it sharply divides itself, just as the composition before us does, into the parts that prepare, that tend in fact to over-prepare, for scenes, and the parts, or otherwise into the scenes, that justify and crown the preparation. It may definitely be said, I think, that everything in it that is not scene (not, I of course mean, complete and functional scene, treating *all* the submitted matter, as by logical start, logical turn, and logical finish) is discriminated preparation, is the fusion and synthesis of picture. These alternations propose themselves all recogniseably, I think, from an early stage, as the very form and figure of "The Ambassadors"; so that, to repeat, such an agent as Miss Gostrey, pre-engaged at a high salary, but waits in the draughty wing with her shawl and her smelling-salts. Her function speaks at once for itself, and by the time she has dined with Strether in London and gone to a play with him her intervention as a *ficelle* is, I hold, expertly justified. Thanks to it we have treated scenically, and scenically alone, the whole lumpish question of Strether's "past," which has seen us more happily on the way than anything else could have done; we have strained to a high lucidity and vivacity (or at least we hope we have) certain indispensable facts; we have seen our two or three immediate friends all conveniently and profitably in "action"; to say nothing of our beginning to descry others, of a remoter intensity, getting into motion, even if a bit vaguely as yet, for our further enrichment. Let my first point be here that the scene in question, that in which the whole situation at Woollett and the complex forces that have propelled my hero to where this lively extractor of his value and distiller of his essence awaits him, is normal and entire, is really an excellent *standard* scene; copious, comprehensive, and accordingly never short, but with its office as definite as that of the hammer on the gong of the clock, the office of expressing *all that is in* the hour.

5. non-scenic form with representational effect

(Preface to The Ambassadors, 1909)

I am moved to add after so much insistence on the scenic side of my labour that I have found the steps of re-perusal almost as much waylaid here by quite another style of effort in the same signal interest—or have in other words not failed to note how, even so associated and so discriminated, the finest proprieties and charms of the non-scenic may, under the right hand for them, still keep their intelligibility and assert their office. Infinitely suggestive such an observation as this last on the whole delightful head, where representation is concerned, of possible variety, of effective expressional change and contrast. One would like, at such an hour as this, for critical license, to go into the matter of the noted inevitable deviation (from too fond an original vision) that the exquisite treachery even of the straightest execution may ever be trusted to inflict even on the most mature plan— the case being that, though one's last reconsidered production always seems to bristle with that particular evidence, "The Ambassadors," would place a flood of such light at my service. I must attach to my final remark here a different import; noting in the other connexion I just glanced at that such passages as that of my hero's first encounter with Chad Newsome, absolute attestations of the non-scenic form though they be, yet lay the firmest hand too—so far at least as intention goes—on representational effect. To report at all closely and completely of what "passes" on a given occasion is inevit- ably to become more or less scenic; and yet in the instance I allude to, *with* the conveyance, expressional curiosity and expressional decency are sought and arrived at under quite another law. The true inwardness of this may be at bottom but that one of the suffered treacheries has consisted precisely, for Chad's whole figure and presence, of a direct presentability diminished and compromised—despoiled, that is, of its *proportional* advantage; so that, in a word, the whole economy of his author's relation to him has at impor- tant points to be redetermined. The book, however, critically viewed, is touchingly full of these disguised and repaired losses, these insidious re- coveries, these intensely redemptive consistencies. The pages in which Mamie Pocock gives her appointed and, I can't but think, duly felt lift to the whole action by the so inscrutably-applied side-stroke or short-cut of our just watching, and as quite at an angle of vision as yet untried, her single hour of suspense in the hotel salon, in our partaking of her concentrated study of the sense of matters bearing on her own case, all the bright warm Paris after- noon, from the balcony that overlooks the Tuileries garden—these are as marked an example of the representational virtue that insist here and there on being, for the charm of opposition and renewal, other than the scenic. It wouldn't take much to make me further argue that from an equal play of such oppositions the book gathers an intensity that fairly adds to the dramatic —though the latter is supposed to be the sum of all intensities; or that has at any rate nothing to fear from juxtaposition with it. I consciously fail to shrink in fact from that extravagance—I risk it, rather, for the sake of the moral involved; which is not that the particular production before us exhausts the interesting questions it raises, but that the Novel remains still, under the right persuasion, the most independent, most elastic, most prodigious of literary forms.

PART D: FORESHORTENING; TIME-SEQUENCE; DIALOGUE

1. Gissing: foreshortening, time, dialogue

("London Notes," July, 1897)

It is form above all that is talent, and if Mr. Gissing's were proportionate to his knowledge, to what may be called his possession, we should have a larger force to reckon with. That—not to speak of the lack of intensity in his imagination—is the direction in which one would wish him to go further. Our Anglo-Saxon tradition of these matters remains surely in some respects the strangest. After the perusal of such a book as "The Whirlpool" I feel as if I had almost to explain that by "these matters" I mean the whole question of composition, of foreshortening, of the proportion and relation of parts. Mr. Gissing, to wind up my reserves, overdoes the ostensible report of spoken words; though I hasten to add that this abuse is so general a sign, in these days, of the English and the American novel as to deprive a challenge of every hope of credit. It is attended visibly—that is visibly to those who can see—with two or three woeful results. If it had none other it would still deserve arraignment on the simple ground of what it crowds out—the golden blocks themselves of the structure, the whole divine exercise and mystery of the exquisite art of presentation.

The ugliest trick it plays at any rate is its effect on that side of the novelist's effort—the side of most difficulty and thereby of most dignity—which consists in giving the sense of duration, of the lapse and accumulation of time. This is altogether to my view the stiffest problem that the artist in fiction has to tackle, and nothing is more striking at present than the blankness, for the most part, of his indifference to it. The mere multiplication of quoted remarks is the last thing to strengthen his hand. Such an expedient works exactly to the opposite end, absolutely minimising, in regard to time, our impression of lapse and passage. That is so much the case that I can think of no novel in which it prevails as giving at all the sense of the gradual and the retarded—the stretch of the years in which developments really take place. The picture is nothing unless it be a picture of the conditions, and the conditions are usually hereby quite omitted. Thanks to this perversity everything dealt with in fiction appears at present to occur simply on the occasion of a few conversations about it; there is no other constitution of it. A few hours, a few days seem to account for it. The process, the "dark backward and abysm," is really so little reproduced. We feel tempted to send many an author, to learn the rudiments of this secret, back to his Balzac again, the most accomplished master of it. He will learn also from Balzac while he is about it that nothing furthermore, as intrinsic effect, so much discounts itself as this abuse of the element of colloquy.

"Dialogue," as it is commonly called, is singularly suicidal from the moment it is not directly illustrative of something given us by another method, something constituted and presented. It is impossible to read work even as interesting as Mr. Gissing's without recognising the impossibility of making people both talk "all the time" and talk with the needful differences. The thing, so far as we have got, is simply too hard. There is always at the best the author's voice to be kept out. It can be kept out for occasions, it can not be kept out always. The solution therefore is to leave it its function, for it has the supreme one. This function, properly exercised, averts the disaster of the blight of the colloquy really in place—illustrative and indispensable. Nothing is more inevitable than such a blight when antecedently the general effect of the process has been undermined. We then want the report of the spoken word—want that only. But, proportionately, it doesn't come, doesn't count. It has been fatally cheapened. There is no effect, no relief.

2. Balzac: foreshortening, time, dialogue

("The Lesson of Balzac," 1905)

Add to this, then, that the fusion of all the elements of the picture, under his [Balzac's] hand, is complete—of what people are with what they do, of what they do with what they are, of the action with the agents, of the medium with the action, of all the parts of the drama with each other. Such a production as Le Père Goriot for example, or as Eugénie Grandet, or as Le Curé de Village, has, in respect to this fusion, a kind of inscrutable perfection. The situation sits shrouded in its circumstances, and then, by its inner expansive force, emerges from them, the action marches, to the rich rustle of this great tragic and ironic train, the embroidered heroic mantle, with an art of keeping together that makes of Le Père Goriot in especial a supreme case of composition, a model of that high virtue that we know as economy of effect, economy of line and touch. An inveterate sense of proportion was not, in general, Balzac's distinguishing mark; but with great talents one has great surprises, and the effect of this large handling of the conditions was more often than not to make the work, whatever it might be, appear admirably composed. Of all the costly charms of a "story" this interest derived from composition is the costliest—and there is perhaps no better proof of our present penury than the fact that, in general, when one makes a plea for it, the plea might seemingly (for all it is understood!) be for trigonometry or osteology. "Composition?—what may that happen to *be*, and, whatever it is, what has it to do with the matter?" I shall take for granted here that every one perfectly knows, for without that assumption I shall not be able to wind up, as I must immediately do. The presence of the conditions, when really presented, when made vivid, provides for the action—which is, from step to step, constantly implied in them; whereas the process of suspending the action in the void and dressing it there with the tinkling bells of what is called dialogue only makes no provision at all for the other interest. There are two elements of the art of the novelist which, as they present, I think, the greatest difficulty, tend thereby most to fascinate us: in the first place that mystery of the foreshortened procession of facts and figures, of appearances of whatever sort, which is in some lights but another name for the picture governed by the principle of composition, and which has at any rate as little as possible in common with the method now usual among us, the juxtaposition of items emulating the column of numbers of a schoolboy's sum in addition. It is the art of the brush, I know, as opposed to the art of the slate-pencil; but to the art of the brush the novel must return, I hold, to recover whatever may be still recoverable of its sacrificed honor.

The second difficulty that I commend for its fascination, at all events, the most attaching when met and the most rewarding when triumphantly met,—though I hasten to add that it also strikes me as not only the least "met," in general, but the least suspected,—this second difficulty is that of representing, to put it simply, the lapse of time, the duration of the subject: representing it, that is, more subtly than by a blank space, or a row of stars, on the historic page. With the blank space and the row of stars Balzac's genius had no affinity, and he is therefore as unlike as possible those narrators—so numerous, all round us, it would appear, today in especial —the succession of whose steps and stages, the development of whose action, in the given case, affects us as occupying but a week or two. No one begins, to my sense, to handle the time-element and produce the time-effect with the authority of Balzac in his amplest sweeps—by which I am far from meaning in his longest passages. That study of the foreshortened image, of the neglect of which I suggest the ill consequence, is precisely the enemy of the tiresome procession of would-be narrative items, seen all in profile, like the rail-heads of a fence; a substitute for the baser device of accounting for the time-quantity by mere quantity of statement. Quality and manner of statement account for it in a finer way—always assuming, as I say, that unless it is accounted for nothing else really is. The fashion of our day is to account for it almost exclusively by an inordinate abuse of the colloquial resource, of the report, from page to page, from chapter to chapter, from beginning to end, of the talk, between the persons involved, in which situation and action may be conceived as registered. Talk between persons is perhaps, of all the parts of the novelist's plan, the part that Balzac most scrupulously weighed and measured and kept in its place; judging it, I think, —though he perhaps even had an undue suspicion of its possible cheapness, as feeling it the thing that can least afford to be cheap,—a precious and supreme resource, the very flower of illustration of the subject and thereby not to be inconsiderately discounted. It was his view, discernibly, that the flower must keep its bloom, or in other words not be too much handled, in order to have a fragrance when nothing but its fragrance will serve.

It was his view indeed positively that there is a *law* in these things, and that, admirable for illustration, functional for illustration, dialogue has its function perverted, and therewith its life destroyed, when forced, all clumsily, into the constructive office. It is in the drama, of course, that it is constructive; but the drama lives by a law so different, verily, that everything that is right for it seems wrong for the prose picture, and everything that is right for the prose picture addressed directly, in turn, to the betrayal of the "play." These are questions, however, that bore deep—if I have successfully braved the danger that they absolutely do bore; so that I must content myself, as a glance at this point, with the claim for the author of Le Père Goriot that colloquial illustration, in his work, suffers less, on the whole, than in any other I know, from its attendant, its besetting and haunting penalty of springing, unless watched, a leak in its effect. It is as if the master of the ship were keeping his eye on the pump; the pump, I mean, of relief and alternation, the pump that keeps the vessel free of too much water. We must always remember that, save in the cases where "dialogue" is organic, is the very law of the game—in which case, as I say, the game is another business altogether— it is essentially the fluid element: as, for instance (to cite, conveniently, Balzac's most eminent prose contemporary) was strikingly its character in the elder Dumas: just as its character in the younger, the dramatist, illustrates supremely what I call the other game. The current, in old Dumas, the large, loose, facile flood of talked movement, talked interest, as much as you will, is, in virtue of this fluidity, a current indeed, with so little of wrought texture that we float and splash in it; feeling it thus resemble much more some capacious tepid tank than the figured tapestry, all overscored with objects in fine perspective, which symbolizes to me (if one may have a symbol) the last word of the achieved fable. Such a tapestry, with its wealth of expression of its subject, with its myriad ordered stitches, its harmonies of tone and felicities of taste, is a work, above all, of closeness—and therefore the more pertinent image here, as it is in the name of closeness that I am inviting you to let Balzac once more appeal to you.

It will strike you perhaps that I speak as if we all, as if you all, without exception were novelists, haunting the back shop, the laboratory, or, more nobly expressed, the inner shrine of the temple; but such assumptions, in this age of print—if I may not say this age of poetry—are perhaps never too wide of the mark, and I have at any rate taken your interest sufficiently for granted to ask you to close up with me for an hour at the feet of the master of us all. Many of us may stray, but he always remains—he is fixed by virtue of his weight. Do not look too knowing at that—as a hint that you were already conscious he is heavy, and that if this is what I have mainly to suggest my lesson might have been spared. He is, I grant, too heavy to be moved; many of us may stray and straggle, as I say—since we have not his inaptitude largely to circulate. There is none the less such an odd condition as circulating without motion, and I am not so sure that even in our own way we do move. We do not, at any rate, get away from him; he is behind us, at the worst, when he is not before, and I feel that any course about the country we explore is ever best held by keeping him, through the trees of the forest, in sight. So far as we do move, we move round him; every road comes back to him; he sits there, in spite of us, so massively, for orientation. "Heavy" therefore if we like, but heavy because weighted with his fortune; the extraordinary fortune that has survived all the extravagance of his career, his twenty years of royal intellectual spending, and that has done so by reason of the rare value of the original property—the high, prime genius so tied-up from him that that was safe. And "that," through all that has come and gone, has steadily, has enormously appreciated. Let us then also, if we see him, in the sacred grove, as our towering idol, see him as gilded thick, with so much gold—plated and burnished and bright, in the manner of towering idols. It is for the lighter and looser and poorer among us to be gilded thin!

3. time-schemes and foreshortening

(Preface to Roderick Hudson, 1907)

To re-read "Roderick Hudson" was to find one remark so promptly and so urgently prescribed that I could at once only take it as pointing almost too stern a moral. It stared me in the face that the time-scheme of the story is quite inadequate, and positively to that degree that the fault but just fails to wreck it. The thing escapes, I conceive, with its life: the effect sought is fortunately more achieved than missed, since the interest of the subject bears down, auspiciously dissimulates, this particular flaw in the treatment Everything occurs, none the less, too punctually and moves too fast: Roderick's disintegration, a gradual process, and of which the exhibitional interest is exactly that it *is* gradual and occasional, and thereby traceable and watchable, swallows two years in a mouthful, proceeds quite *not* by years, but by weeks and months, and thus renders the whole view the disservice of appearing to present him as a morbidly special case. The very claim of the fable is naturally that he *is* special, that his great gift makes and keeps him highly exceptional; but that is not for a moment supposed to preclude his appearing typical (of the general type) as well; for the fictive hero successfully appeals to us only as an eminent instance, as eminent as we like, of our own conscious kind. My mistake on Roderick's behalf—and not in the least of conception, but of composition and expression—is that, at the rate at which he falls to pieces, he seems to place himself beyond our understanding and our sympathy. These are not our rates, we say; we ourselves certainly, under like pressure,—for what is it after all?—would make more of a fight. We conceive going to pieces—nothing is easier, since we see people do it, one way or another, all round us; but this young man must either have had less of the principle of development to have had so much of the principle of collapse, or less of the principle of collapse to have had so much of the principle of development. "On the basis of so great a weakness," one hears the reader say, "where was your idea of the interest? On the basis of so great an interest, where is the provision for so much weakness?" One feels indeed, in the light of this challenge, on how much too scantly projected and suggested a field poor Roderick and his large capacity for ruin are made to turn round. It has all begun too soon, as I say, and too simply, and the determinant function attributed to Christina Light, the character of well-nigh sole agent of his catastrophe that this unfortunate young woman has forced upon her, fails to commend itself to our sense of truth and proportion.

It was not, however, that I was at ease on this score even in the first fond good faith of composition; I felt too, all the while, how many more ups and downs, how many more adventures and complications my young man would have had to know, how much more experience it would have taken, in short, either to make him go under or to make him triumph. The greater complexity, the superior truth was all more or less present to me; only the question was, too dreadfully, how make it present to the reader? How boil down so many facts in the alembic, so that the distilled result, the produced appearance, should have intensity, lucidity, brevity, beauty, all the merits required for my effect? How, when it was already so difficult, as I found, to proceed even as I *was* proceeding? It didn't help, alas, it only maddened, to remember that Balzac would have known how, and would have yet asked no additional credit for it. All the difficulty I could dodge still struck me, at any rate, as leaving more than enough; and yet I was already consciously in presence, here, of the most interesting question the artist has to consider. To give the image and the sense of certain things while still keeping them subordinate to his plan, keeping them in relation to matters more immediate and apparent, to give all the sense, in a word, without all the substance or all the surface, and so to summarise and foreshorten, so to make values both rich and sharp, that the mere procession of items and profiles is not only, for the occasion, superseded, but is, for essential quality, almost "compromised"—such a case of delicacy proposes itself at every turn to the painter of life who wishes both to treat his chosen subject and to confine his necessary picture. It is only by doing such things that art becomes exquisite, and it is only by positively becoming exquisite that it keeps clear of becoming vulgar, repudiates the coarse industries that masquerade in its name. This eternal time-question is accordingly, for the novelist, always there and always formidable; always insisting on the *effect* of the great lapse and passage, of the "dark backward and abysm," by the terms of truth, and on the effect of compression, of composition and form, by the terms of literary arrangement. It is really a business to terrify all but stout hearts into abject omission and mutilation, though the terror would indeed be more general were the general consciousness of the difficulty greater. It is not by consciousness of difficulty, in truth, that the story-teller is mostly ridden; so prodigious a number of stories would otherwise scarce get themselves (shall it be called?) "told." None was ever very well told, I think, under the law of mere elimination—inordinately as that device appears in many quarters to be depended on. I remember doing my best not to be reduced to it for "Roderick," at the same time that I did so helplessly and consciously beg a thousand questions. What I clung to as my principle of simplification was the precious truth that I was dealing, after all, essentially with an Action, and that no action, further, was ever made historically vivid without a certain factitious compactness; though this logic indeed opened up horizons and abysses of its own. But into these we must plunge on some other occasion.

4. foreshortening: *the art of figuring synthetically*

(Preface to *The Tragic Muse*, 1908)

Not the least imperative of one's conditions was thus that one should have really, should have finely and (given one's scale) concisely treated one's subject, in spite of there being so much of the confounded irreducible quantity still to treat. If I spoke just now, however, of the "exasperated" charm of supreme difficulty, that is because the challenge of economic representation so easily becomes, in any of the arts, intensely interesting to meet. To put all that is possible of one's idea into a form and compass that will contain and express it only by delicate adjustments and an exquisite chemistry, so that there will at the end be neither a drop of one's liquor left nor a hair's breadth of the rim of one's glass to spare—every artist will remember how often that sort of necessity has carried with it its particular inspiration. Therein lies the secret of the appeal, to his mind, of the successfully *fore-shortened* thing, where representation is arrived at, as I have already elsewhere had occasion to urge, not by the addition of items (a light that has for its attendant shadow a possible dryness) but by the art of figuring synthetically, a compactness into which the imagination may cut thick, as into the rich density of wedding-cake.

5. *dialogue*

(Preface to *The Awkward Age*, 1908)

One had noted this reader as perverse and inconsequent in respect to the absorption of "dialogue"—observed the "public for fiction" consume it, in certain connexions, on the scale and with the smack of lips that mark the consumption of bread-and-jam by a children's school-feast, consume it even at the theatre, so far as our theatre ever vouchsafes it, and yet as flagrantly reject it when served, so to speak, *au naturel*. One had seen good solid slices of fiction, well endued, one might surely have thought, with this easiest of lubrications, deplored by editor and publisher as positively not, for the general gullet as known to *them*, made adequately "slick." " 'Dialogue', always 'dialogue'!" I had seemed from far back to hear them mostly cry: "We can't have too much of it, we can't have enough of it, and no excess of it, in the form of no matter what savourless dilution, or what boneless dispersion, ever began to injure a book so much as even the very scantest claim put in for form and substance." This wisdom had always been in one's ears; but it had at the same time been equally in one's eyes that really constructive dialogue, dialogue organic and dramatic, speaking for itself, representing and embodying substance and form, is among us an uncanny and abhorrent thing, not to be dealt with on any terms. A comedy or a tragedy may run for a thousand nights without prompting twenty persons in London or in New York to desire that view of its text which is so desired in Paris, as soon as a play begins to loom at all large, that the number of copies of the printed piece in circulation far exceeds at last the number of performances. But as with the printed piece our own public, infatuated as it may be with the theatre, refuses all commerce—though indeed this can't but be, without cynicism, very much through the infirmity the piece, *if* printed, would reveal —so the same horror seems to attach to any typographic hint of the proscribed playbook or any insidious plea for it. The immense oddity resides in the almost exclusively typographic order of the offence. . . . dishonour would await me if, proposing to treat the different faces of my subject in the most completely instituted colloquial form, I should evoke the figure and affirm the presence of participants by the repeated and prefixed name rather than by the recurrent and *affixed* "said he" and "said she." All I have space to go into here—much as the funny fact I refer to might seem to invite us to dance hand in hand round it—is that I was at any rate duly admonished, that I took my measures accordingly, and that the manner in which I took them has lived again for me ever so arrestingly, so amusingly, on re-examination of the book.

6. foreshortening

(Preface to *Daisy Miller*, 1909)

Any real art of representation is, I make out, a controlled and guarded accept-ance, in fact a perfect economic mastery, of that conflict: the general sense of the expansive, the explosive principle in one's material thoroughly noted, adroitly allowed to flush and colour and animate the disputed value, but with its other appetites and treacheries, its characteristic space-hunger and space-cunning, kept down. The fair flower of this artful compromise is to my sense the secret of "foreshortening"—the particular economic device for which one must have a name and which has in its single blessedness and its determined pitch, I think, a higher price than twenty other clustered loosenesses; and just because full-fed statement, just because the picture of as many of the condi-tions as possible made and kept proportionate, just because the surface irides-cent, even in the short piece, by what is beneath it and what throbs and gleams through, are things all conducive to the only compactness that has a charm, to the only spareness that has a force, to the only simplicity that has a grace—those, in each order, that produce the *rich* effect.

Chapter X

CHARACTERS

Although James over and over again suggested the impossibility of separating in any absolute way the various elements of fiction, he continued to talk about individual elements—and he probably talked more frequently about character than any other element. This should not be surprising in a writer who came to\ believe that interior or psychological action had a primacy over exterior happenings and events, and who organized his own fictions as dramas of con- / sciousness rather than as complications of actions.

In the "Art of Fiction" and elsewhere James attacked as simplistic the notion that there was some kind of distinction between a "novel of character" and a "novel of incident": "What is character but the determination of incident? What is incident but the illustration of character? What is either a picture or a novel that is not of character?" Having demolished the distinction to his own satisfaction, James proceeded often in his criticism of his own and others' work to discuss characters as fundamental to the life of any fiction.

James was clear in his own mind as to why he could talk at such length about character in a novelist like Trollope. In his essay on Trollope (1883), James cited Trollope's "extreme interest in character" as the quality which will "preserve his best work." Trollope, indeed, "gave his practical testimony in favor of the idea that the interest of a work of fiction is great in proportion as the people stand on their feet." The tribute to the dominance—even the primacy —of character in fiction James goes on to justify by demonstrating how character is intimately linked with—in fact, in some sense, is—the other contending elements: "Character, in any sense in which we can get at it, is action, and action is plot, and any plot which hangs together, even if it pretend to interest us only in the fashion of a Chinese puzzle, plays upon our emotion, our suspense, by means of personal references. We care what happens to people⟩ only in proportion as we know what people are."

James's rather voluminous remarks on character in fiction presented here are not all he made by any means, but they represent the range and complexity of his concept of the place or role of character in fiction. Part A, "The Dominance of Characters," presents a number of passages which reveal the supreme importance James attached to this element. Most revealing, perhaps, is the fact that James's discussions of his most highly regarded and beloved novelists, Balzac and Turgénieff, resolved into discussions of characters, their living

195

people. Over and over again we witness James discovering (as he discovered later in the Prefaces of his own novels) that novels by these writers have their "starting-point in character." And the reader departs the work of these and other successful writers with a vivid memory of a multitude of specific characters.

In Part B, "Fiction and Fact," are passages in which James touches upon the relation of characters to real people. James had strong feelings on this matter, as he had to reply (in a passage included here) to his brother's accusation, on the publication of the The Bostonians, that the fictional Miss Birdseye was a portrait of the actual Miss Peabody of Boston. Of course James did not deny that the novelist drew from life (as he indeed must, as impression-gatherer and observer), but he explained that the reality always underwent transmutation in the writer's consciousness under the pressure and heat of his imagination. But there were other aspects of the question of the factual background of fictional characters that drew the attention of James's sharp critical eye.

By far the longest section of this chapter is Part C, "Creation of Characters," in which passages dealing with the problems of creating living, breathing people are brought together. James's favorite (but by no means consistent) distinction is between characters and figures, the former successful creations, the latter more wooden than living (a distinction clearly related to but not equatable with E. M. Forster's later distinction between flat and round characters in Aspects of the Novel, 1927). It should be noted, incidentally, that James's use of the term "puppets" in referring to a novelist's characters is not meant to be derogatory.

In Part D, "Special Problems; Special Characters," are gathered together a great variety of comments, ranging from the problem of naming characters (reminding one that in his Notebooks James frequently jotted down long lists of possible names) to the concept of the ficelle—the minor or secondary character who belongs more to the treatment than to the substance of a fiction. Here are some of James's most interesting observations on such topics as the artist as a character, or the difficulties encountered in creating a sick protagonist. It was such questions and problems that fascinated James, and which he frequently chose to confront in his own fiction.

PART A: THE DOMINANCE OF CHARACTERS

1. starting-point in character

("Ivan Turgénieff," 1874)

The story of "Rudin," ["A Russian Hamlet"], which followed soon after, is perhaps the most striking example of his preference for a theme which takes its starting-point in character—if need be, in morbid character. We have had no recent opportunity to refresh our memory of the tale, but we have not forgotten the fine quality of its interest—its air of psychological truth, unencumbered with the usual psychological apparatus. The theme is one which would mean little enough to a coarse imagination—the exhibition of a character peculiarly unrounded, unmoulded, unfinished, inapt for the regular romantic attitudes. Dmitri Rudin is a moral failure, like many of the author's heroes—one of those fatally complex natures who cost their friends so many pleasures and pains; who might, and yet, evidently, might not, do great things; natures strong in impulse, in talk, in responsive emotion, but weak in will, in action, in the power to feel and do singly. Madame Sand's "Horace" is a broad, free study of this type of person, always so interesting to imaginative and so intolerable to rational people; M. Turgénieff's hero is an elaborate miniature-portrait. Without reading "Rudin" we should not know just how fine a point he can give to his pencil. But M. Turgénieff, with his incisive psychology, like Madame Sand, with her expansive synthesis, might often be a vain demonstrator and a very dull novelist if he were not so constantly careful to be a dramatist. Everything, with him, takes the dramatic form; he is apparently unable to conceive anything independently of it, he has no recognition of unembodied ideas; an idea, with him, is such and such an individual, with such and such a nose and chin, such and such a hat and waistcoat, bearing the same relation to it as the look of a printed word does to its meaning. Abstract possibilities immediately become, to his vision, concrete situations, as elaborately defined and localized as an interior by Meissonier. In this way, as we read, we are always looking and listening; and we seem, indeed, at moments, for want of a running thread of explanation, to see rather more than we understand.

2. *Turgénieff: strong female characters*

("Ivan Turgénieff," 1874)

American readers of Turgénieff have been struck with certain points of resemblance between American and Russian life. The resemblance is generally superficial; but it does not seem to us altogether fanciful to say that Russian young girls, as represented by Lisa, Tatiana, Maria Alexandrovna, have to our sense a touch of the faintly acrid perfume of the New England temperament—a hint of Puritan angularity. It is the women and young girls in our author's tales who mainly represent strength of will—the power to resist, to wait, to attain. Lisa represents it in all that heroic intensity which says so much more to M. Turgénieff's imagination than feline grace. The character conspicuous in the same tale ["A Nest of Noblemen"] for feline grace

—Varvara Pavlovna, Lavretzky's heartless wife—is conspicuous also for her moral flimsiness. In the integrity of Lisa, of Hélène, even of the more dimly shadowed Maria Alexandrovna—a sort of finer distillation, as it seems, of masculine honour—there is something almost formidable: the strongest men are less positive in their strength. In the keenly pathetic scene in which Maria Timofievna (the most delightful of the elderly maiden aunts of fiction) comes to Lisa in her room and implores her to renounce her project of entering a convent, we feel that there are depths of purpose in the young girl's deferential sweetness that nothing in the world can overcome. She is intensely religious, as she ought to be for psychological truth, and nothing could more effectually disconnect her from the usual *ingénue* of romance than our sense of the naturalness of her religious life. Her love for Lavretzky is a passion in its essence half renunciation. The first use she makes of the influence with him which his own love gives her is to try and reconcile him with his wife; and her foremost feeling, on learning that the latter is not dead, as they had believed, is an irremissible sense of pollution. The dusky, antique consciousness of sin in this tender, virginal soul is a combination which we seem somehow to praise amiss in calling it picturesque, but which it would be still more inexact to call didactic. Lisa is altogether a most remarkable portrait, and one that readers of the heroine's own sex ought to contemplate with some complacency. They have been known to complain on the one hand that romancers abuse them, and on the other that they insufferably patronise them. Here is a picture drawn with all the tenderness of a lover, and yet with an indefinable—an almost unprecedented—respect.

3. *Balzac: the portraiture of people*

("Honoré de Balzac," 1875)

This latter [the portraiture of people] is Balzac's strongest gift, and is so strong that it easily distances all competition. Two other writers in this line have gone very far, but they suffer by comparison with him. Dickens often sets a figure before us with extraordinary vividness; but the outline is fantastic and arbitrary; we but half believe in it, and feel as if we were expected but half to believe in it. It is like a silhouette in cut paper, in which the artist has allowed great license to his scissors.

If Balzac had a rival, the most dangerous rival would be Turgénieff. With the Russian novelist the person represented is equally definite—or meant to be equally definite; and the author's perception of idiosyncrasies is sometimes even more subtle. With Turgénieff as with Balzac the whole person springs into being at once; the character is never left shivering for its fleshly envelope, its face, its figure, its gestures, its tone, its costume, its name, its bundle of antecedents. But behind Balzac's figures we feel a certain heroic pressure that drives them home to our credence—a contagious illusion on the author's own part. The imagination that produced them is working at a greater heat; they seem to proceed from a sort of creative infinite and they help each other to be believed in. It is pictorially a larger, sturdier, more systematic style of portraiture than Turgénieff's. This is altogether the most valuable element in Balzac's novels; it is hard to see how the power of physical evocation can go farther. In future years, if people find his tales, as a whole, too rugged and too charmless, let them take one up occasionally and, turning the leaves, read simply the portraits. In Balzac every one who is introduced is minutely described; if the individual is to say but three words he has the honours of a complete enumeration. Portraits shape themselves under his pen as if in obedience to an irresistible force; while the effort with most writers is to collect the material—to secure the model—the effort with Balzac is to disintegrate his visions, to accept only one candidate in the dozen. And it is not only that his figures are so definite, but they are so plausible, so real, so characteristic, so recognisable.

4. Trollope: character is . . . action

("Anthony Trollope," 1883)

The source of his (Trollope's) success in describing the life that lay nearest to him, and describing it without any of those artistic perversions that come, as we have said, from a powerful imagination, from a cynical humor or from a desire to look, as George Eliot expresses it, for the suppressed transitions that unite all contrasts, the essence of this love of reality was his extreme interest in character. This is the fine and admirable quality in Trollope, this is what will preserve his best works in spite of those flatnesses which keep him from standing on quite the same level as the masters. Indeed this quality is so much one of the finest (to my mind at least), that it makes me wonder the more that the writer who had it so abundantly and so naturally should not have just that distinction which Trollope lacks, and which we find in his three brilliant contemporaries. If he was in any degree a man of genius (and I hold that he was), it was in virtue of this happy, instinctive perception of human varieties. His knowledge of the stuff we are made of, his observation of the common behavior of men and women, was not reasoned nor acquired, not even particularly studied. All human doings deeply interested him, human life, to his mind, was a perpetual story; but he never attempted to take the so-called scientific view, the view which has lately found ingenious advocates amoung the countrymen and successors of Balzac. He had no airs of being able to tell you *why* people in a given situation would conduct themselves in a particular way; it was enough for him that he felt their feelings and struck

the right note, because he had, as it were, a good ear. If he was a knowing psychologist he was so by grace; he was just and true without apparatus and
without effort. He must have had a great taste for the moral question; he evidently believed that this is the basis of the interest of fiction. We must be
careful, of course, in attributing convictions and opinions to Trollope, who,
as I have said, had as little as possible of the pedantry of his art, and whose
occasional chance utterances in regard to the object of the novelist and his
means of achieving it are of an almost startling simplicity. But we certainly
do not go too far in saying that he gave his practical testimony in favor of
the idea that the interest of a work of fiction is great in proportion as the
people stand on their feet. His great effort was evidently to make them stand
so; if he achieved this result with as little as possible of a flourish of the hand
it was nevertheless the measure of his success. If he had taken sides on the
droll, bemuddled opposition between novels of character and novels of plot,
I can imagine him to have said (except that he never expressed himself in
epigrams), that he preferred the former class, inasmuch as character in itself
is plot, while plot is by no means character. It is more safe indeed to believe
that his great good sense would have prevented him from taking an idle
controversy seriously. Character, in any sense in which we can get at it, is
action, and action is plot, and any plot which hangs together, even if it pretend to interest us only in the fashion of a Chinese puzzle, plays upon our
emotion, our suspense, by means of personal references. We care what happens
to people only in proportion as we know what people are. Trollope's great
apprehension of the real, which was what made him so interesting, came to
him through his desire to satisfy us on this point—to tell us what certain
people were and what they did in consequence of being so. That is the purpose
of each of his tales; and if these things produce an illusion it comes from
the gradual abundance of his testimony as to the temper, the tone, the
passions, the habits, the moral nature, of a certain number of contemporary
Britons.

5. the germ of a story: character, not plot

("Ivan Turgénieff," 1884)

Nothing that Turgénieff had to say could be more interesting that his talk
about his own work, his manner of writing. What I have heard him tell of
these things was worthy of the beautiful results he produced; of the deep
purpose, pervading them all, to show us life itself. The germ of a story, with
him, was never an affair of plot—that was the last thing he thought of: it
was the representation of certain persons. The first form in which a tale
appeared to him was as the figure of an individual, or a combination of individuals, whom he wished to see in action, being sure that such people must

do something very special and interesting. They stood before him definite, vivid, and he wished to know, and to show, as much as possible of their nature. The first thing was to make clear to himself what he did know, to begin with; and to this end, he wrote out a sort of biography of each of his characters, and everything that they had done and that had happened to them up to the opening of the story. He had their *dossier*, as the French say, and as the police has of that of every conspicuous criminal. With this material in his hand he was able to proceed; the story all lay in the question, What shall I make them do? He always made them do things that showed them completely; but, as he said, the defect of his manner and the reproach that was made him was his want of "architecture"—in other words, of composition. The great thing, of course, is to have architecture as well as precious material, as Walter Scott had them, as Balzac had them. If one reads Turgénieff's stories with the knowledge that they were composed—or rather that they came into being—in this way, one can trace the process in every line. Story, in the conventional sense of the word—a fable constructed, like Wordsworth's phantom, "to startle and waylay"—there is as little as possible. The thing consists of the motions of a group of selected creatures, which are not the result of a preconceived action, but a consequence of the qualities of the actors. Works of art are produced from every possible point of view, and stories, and very good ones, will continue to be written in which the evolution is that of a dance—a series of steps the more complicated and lively the better, of course, determined from without and forming a figure. This figure will always, probably, find favour with many readers, because it reminds them enough, without reminding them too much, of life. On opposition many young talents in France are ready to rend each other, for there is a numerous school on either side. We have not yet in England and America arrived at the point of treating such questions with passion, for we have not yet arrived at the point of feeling them intensely, or indeed, for that matter, of understanding them very well. It is not open to us as yet to discuss whether a novel had better be an excision from life or a structure built up of picture-cards, for we have not made up our mind as to whether life in general may be described. There is evidence of a good deal of shyness on this point—a tendency rather to put up fences than to jump over them. Among us, therefore, even a certain ridicule attaches to the consideration of such alternatives. But individuals may feel their way, and perhaps even pass unchallenged, if they remark that for them the manner in which Turgénieff worked will always seem the most fruitful. It has the immense recommendation that in relation to any human occurrence it begins, as it were, further back. It lies in its power to tell us the most about men and women. Of course it will but slenderly satisfy those numerous readers among whom the answer to this would be, "Hang it, we don't care a straw about men and women: we want a good story!"

And yet, after all, *Elena* is a good story, and *Lisa* and *Virgin Soil* are good stories. Reading over lately several of Turgénieff's novels and tales, I was struck afresh with their combination of beauty and reality. One must never forget, in speaking of him, that he was both an observer and a poet. The poetic element was constant, and it had great strangeness and power. It inspired most of the short things that he wrote during the last few years of his life, since the publication of *Virgin Soil*, things that are in the highest degree fanciful and exotic. It pervades the frequent little reveries, visions, epigrams of the *Senilia*. It was no part of my intention, here, to criticise his writings, having said my say about them, so far as possible, some years ago. But I may mention that in re-reading them I find in them all that I formerly found of two other elements—their richness and their sadness. They give one the impression of life itself, and not of an arrangement, a *réchauffé* of life. I remember Turgénieff's once saying in regard to Homais, the little Norman country apothecary, with his pedantry of "enlightened opinions," in *Madame Bovary*, that the great strength of such a portrait consisted in its being at once an individual, of the most concrete sort, and a type. This is the great strength of his own representations of character; they are so strangely, fascinatingly particular, and yet they are so recognisably general. Such a remark as that about Homais makes me wonder why it was that Turgénieff should have rated Dickens so high, the weakness of Dickens being in regard to just that point. If Dickens fail to live long, it will be because his figures are particular without being general; because they are individuals without being types; because we do not feel their continuity with the rest of humanity—see the matching of the pattern with the piece out of which all the creations of the novelist and the dramatist are cut. I often meant, but accidently neglected, to put Turgénieff on the subject of Dickens again, and ask him to explain his opinion. I suspect that his opinion was in a large measure merely that Dickens diverted him, as well he might. That complexity of the pattern was in itself fascinating.

6. *character expressed and exposed*

("Turgenev and Tolstoy," 1897)

Character, character expressed and exposed, is in all these things what we inveterately find. Turgenev's sense of it was the great light that artistically guided him; the simplest account of him is to say that the mere play of it constitutes in every case his sufficient drama. No one has had a closer vision, or a hand at once more ironic and more tender, for the individual figure. He sees it with its minutest signs and tricks—all its heredity of idiosyncrasies, all its particulars of weakness and strength, of ugliness and beauty, of oddity and charm; and yet it is of his essence that he sees it in the general flood of life, steeped in its relations and contacts, struggling or submerged, a hurried particle in the stream. This gives him, with his quiet method, his extraordinary breadth; dissociates his rare power to particularize from dryness or hardness, from any peril of caricature. He understands so much that we almost wonder he can express anything; and his expression is indeed wholly in absolute projection, in illustration, in giving of everything the unexplained and irresponsible specimen. He is of a spirit so human that we almost wonder at his control of his matter; of a pity so deep and so general that we almost wonder at his curiosity. The element of poetry in him is constant, and yet reality stares through it without the loss of a wrinkle. No one has more of that sign of the born novelist which resides in a respect unconditioned for the freedom and vitality, the absoluteness when summoned, of the creatures he invokes; or is more superior to the strange and second-rate policy of explaining or presenting them by reprobation or apology,—of taking the short cuts and anticipating the emotions and judgments about them that should be left, at the best, to the perhaps not most intelligent reader. And yet his system, as it may summarily be called, of the mere particularized report, has a lucidity beyond the virtue of the cruder moralist.

If character, as I say, is what he gives us at every turn, I should speedily add that he offers it not in the least as a synonym, in our Western sense, of resolution and prosperity. It wears the form of the almost helpless detachment of the short-sighted individual soul; and the perfection of his exhibition of it is in truth too often but the intensity of what, for success, it just does not produce. What works in him most is the question of the will; and the most constant induction he suggests, bears upon the sad figure that principle seems mainly to make among his countrymen. He had seen—he suggests to us—its collapse in a thousand quarters; and the most general tragedy, to his view, is that of its desperate adventures and disasters, its inevitable abdication and defeat. But if the men, for the most part, let it go, it takes refuge in the other sex; many of the representatives of which, in his pages, are supremely strong —in wonderful addition, in various cases, to being otherwise admirable. This is true of such a number—the younger women, the girls, the "heroines" in especial—that they form in themselves, on the ground of moral beauty, of the finest distinction of soul, one of the most striking groups the modern novel has given us. They are heroines to the letter, and of a heroism obscure and undecorated: it is almost they alone who have the energy to determine and to act. Elena, Lisa, Tatyana, Gemma, Marianna—we can write their names and call up their images, but I lack space to take them in turn. It is by a succession of the finest and tenderest touches that they live; and this, in all Turgenev's work, is the process by which he persuades and succeeds.

It was his own view of his main danger that he sacrificed too much to detail; was wanting in composition, in the gift that conduces to unity of impression. But no novelist is closer and more cumulative; in none does distinction spring from a quality of truth more independent of everything but the subject, but the idea itself. This idea, this subject, moreover,—a spark kindled by the innermost friction of things,—is always as interesting as an unopened telegram. The genial freedom—with its exquisite delicacy—of his approach to this "innermost" world, the world of our finer consciousness, has in short a side that I can only describe and commemorate as nobly disinterested; a side that makes too many of his rivals appear to hold us in comparison by violent means, and introduce us in comparison to vulgar things.

Part B: Characters: Fiction and Fact

1. *persons plus imagination: characters*

(*Hawthorne*, 1879)

There is no strictness in the representation by novelists of persons who have struck them in life, and there can in the nature of things be none. From the moment the imagination takes a hand in the game, the inevitable tendency is to divergence, to following what may be called new scents. The original gives hints, but the writer does what he likes with them, and imports new elements into the picture.

2. *evolved . . . from my moral consciousness*

(*Letters*, 1885, to William James)

I should be very sorry—in fact deadly sick, or fatally ill—if I thought Miss Peabody *herself* supposed I intended to represent her [as Miss Birdseye in *The Bostonians*]. I absolutely had no shadow of such an intention. I have not seen Miss P. for twenty years, I never had but the most casual observation of her, I didn't know whether she was alive or dead, and she was not in the smallest degree my starting-point or example. Miss Birdseye was evolved entirely from my moral consciousness, like every other person I have ever drawn, and originated in my desire to make a figure who should embody in a sympathetic, pathetic, picturesque, and at the same time grotesque way, the humanitary and ci-devant transcendental tendencies which I thought it highly probable I should be accused of treating in a contemptuous manner in so far as they were otherwise represented in the tale. I wished to make this figure a woman, because so it would be more touching, and an old, weary, battered, and simple-minded woman because that deepened the same effect. I elaborated her in my mind's eye—and after I had got going reminded myself that my creation would perhaps be identified with Miss Peabody—*that* I freely admit. So I have in mind the sense of being careful, at the same time that I didn't see what I could do but go my way, according to my own fancy, and make my image as living as I saw it. The one definite thing about which I had a scruple was some touch about Miss Birdseye's spectacles—I remembered that Miss Peabody's were always in the wrong place; but I didn't see, really, why I should deprive myself of an effect (as regards this point) which is common to a thousand old people. So I thought no more about Miss P. *at all*, but simply strove to realize my vision. If I have made my old woman *live* it is my misfortune, and the thing is doubtless a rendering, a vivid rendering, of my idea. If it is at the same time a rendering of Miss P. I am absolutely irresponsible—and extremely sorry for the accident. If there is any chance of its being represented to *her* that I have undertaken to reproduce her in a novel I will immediately write to her, in the most respectful manner, to say that I have done nothing of the kind, that an old survivor of the New England Reform period was an indispensable personage in my story, that my paucity of data and not my repletion is the faulty side of the whole picture, that, as I went, I had no sight or thought of her, but only of an imaginary figure which was much nearer to me, and that in short I have the vanity to claim that Miss Birdseye is a creation.

3. *historic vs. fictional great people*

(Preface to *The Aspern Papers*, 1908)

My friend's ["a highly critical friend"] argument bore then—at the time and afterward—on my vicious practice, as he maintained, of postulating for the purpose of my fable celebrities who not only *hadn't* existed in the conditions I imputed to them, but who for the most part (and in no case more markedly than in that of Jeffrey Aspern) couldn't possibly have done so. The stricture was to apply itself to a whole group of short fictions in which I had, with whatever ingenuity, assigned to several so-called eminent figures positions absolutely unthinkable in our actual encompassing air, an air definitely unfavourable to certain forms of eminence. It was vicious, my critic contended, to flourish forth on one's page "great people," public persons, who shouldn't more or less square with our quite definite and calculable array of such notabilities; and by this rule I was heavily incriminated. The rule demanded that the "public person" portrayed should be at least of the tradition, of the general complexion, of the face-value, exactly, of some past or present producible counterfoil. Mere private figures, under one's hand, might correspond with nobody, it being of their essence to be but narrowly known; the represented state of being conspicuous, on the other hand, involved before anything else a recognition—and none of my eminent folk were recogniseable. It was all very well for instance to have put one's self at such pains for Miriam Rooth in "The Tragic Muse"; but *there* was misapplied zeal, there a case of pitiful waste, crying aloud to be denounced. Miriam is offered not as a young person passing unnoticed by her age—like the Biddy Dormers and Julia Dallows, say, of the same book, but as a high rarity, a time-figure of the scope inevitably attended by other commemorations. Where on earth would be then Miriam's inscribed "counterfoil," and in what conditions of the contemporary English theatre, in what conditions of criticism, of appreciation, under what conceivable Anglo-Saxon star, might we take an artistic value of this order either for produced or for recognised? We are, as a "public," chalk-marked by nothing, more unmistakeably, than by the truth that we know nothing of such values—any more than, as my friend was to impress on me, we are susceptible of consciousness of such others (these in the sphere of literary eminence) as my Neil Paraday in "The Death of the Lion," as my Hugh Vereker in "The Figure in the Carpet," as my Ralph Limbert, above all, in "The Next Time," as sundry unprecedented and unmatched heroes and martyrs of the artistic ideal, in short, elsewhere exemplified in my pages. We shall come to these objects of animadversion in another hour, when I shall have no difficulty in producing the defence I found for them—since, obviously, I hadn't cast them into the world *all* naked and ashamed; and I deal for the moment but with the stigma in general as Jeffrey Aspern carries it.

The charge being that I foist upon our early American annals a distinguished presence for which they yield me absolutely no warrant—"Where, within them, gracious heaven, were we to look for so much as an approach to the social elements of habitat and climate of birds of that note and plumage?"—I find his link with reality then just in the tone of the picture wrought round him. What was that tone but exactly, but exquisitely, calculated, the harmless hocus-pocus under cover of which we might suppose him to have existed? This tone is the tone, artistically speaking of "amusement," the current floating that precious influence home quite as one of those high tides watched by the smugglers of old might, in case of their boat's being boarded, be trusted to wash far up the strand the cask of foreign liquor expertly committed to it. If through our lean prime Western period no dim and charming ghost of an adventurous lyric genius might by a stretch of fancy flit, if the time was really too hard to "take," in the light form proposed, the elegant reflexion, then so much the worse for the time—it was all one could say! The retort to that of course was that such a plea represented no "link" with reality—which was what was under discussion—but only a link, and flimsy enough too, with the deepest depths of the artificial: the restrictive truth exactly contended for, which may embody my critic's last word rather of course than my own. My own, so far as I shall pretend in that especial connexion to report it, was that one's warrant, in such a case, hangs essentially on the question of whether or no the false element imputed would have borne that test of further development which so exposes the wrong and so consecrates the right. My last word was, heaven forgive me, that, occasion favouring, I could have perfectly "worked out" Jeffrey Aspern. The boast remains indeed to be verified when we shall arrive at the other challenged cases.

4. Americans: young females and business men

(Preface to The Reverberator, 1908)

I need scarcely point out that "round" Francie Dosson [in The Reverberator] the tale is systematically constructed; with which fact was involved for me the clear sense that if I didn't see the Francie Dossons (by whom I mean the general quaint sisterhood, perfectly distinguishable then, but displaced, disfeatured, "discounted" to-day, for all I know) as always and at any cost —at whatever cost of repetition, that is—worth saving, I might as well shut up my international department. For practically—as I have said already more than enough to convey—they were what the American branch of that equation constantly threw me back upon; by reason indeed of a brace of conditions only one of which strictly inhered in the show itself.

In the heavy light of "Europe" thirty or forty years ago, there were more of the Francie Dossons and the Daisy Millers and the Bessie Aldens and the Pandora Days than of all the other attested American objects put together —more of them, of course I mean, from the moment the weird harvester was at all preoccupied with charm, or at all committed to "having to have" it. But quite apart from that truth was always the stiff fact, against which I might have dashed myself in vain, that I hadn't the data for a right approach to the minor quantities, such as they might have been made out to be. The minor quantities appeared, consistently, but in a single light—that of promiscuous obscure attendance on the Daisies and Bessies and Francies; a generalized crepuscular state at best, even though yielding little by little a view of dim forms and vague differences. These adumbrations, sufficient tests once applied, claimed identities as fathers, mothers, even sometimes as satellites more directly "engaged"; but there was always, for the author of this record, a prompt and urgent remark to be made about them—which placed him, when all was said, quite at his ease. The men, the non-European, in these queer clusters, the fathers, brothers, playmates, male appendages of

208 THEORY OF FICTION: HENRY JAMES

whatever presumption, were visible and thinkable only as the American "business-man"; and before the American business-man, as I have been prompt to declare, I was absolutely and irredeemably helpless, with no fibre of my intelligence responding to his mystery. No approach I could make to him on his "business side" really got near it. That is where I was fatally incompetent, and this in turn—the case goes into a nutshell—is so obviously why, for any decent documentation, I was simply shut up to what was left me. It takes but a glance to see how the matter was in such a fashion simpli-fied. With the men wiped out, at a stroke, so far as any grasp of the principle of their activity was concerned (what in the name of goodness did I, or could I, know, to call know, about the very alphabet of their activity?), it wasn't the *elder* woman I could take, on any reckoning, as compen-satory: her inveterate blankness of surface had a manner all its own of defying the imagination to hover or to hope. There was really, as a rule, nothing whatever to be done with the elder woman; not only were reason and fancy alike forewarned not to waste their time, but any attempt upon her, one somehow felt, would have been indecorous and almost monstrous. She wasn't so much as in question; since if one could work it out for the men that the depreciated state with which *they* vaguely and, as it were, somno-lently struggled, was perhaps but casual and temporary, might be regarded in fact as the mere state of the medal with its right face accidentally turned down, this redemption never glimmered for the wife and mother, in whom nothing was in eclipse, but everything rather (everything there was at all) straight in evidence, and to whom therefore any round and complete em-bodiment had simply been denied.

5. artist characters: from the depths of the designer's own mind

(Preface to *The Lesson of the Master*, 1909)

In putting them [stories of "the literary life": "The Death of the Lion," "The Coxon Fund," "The Next Time"] sundry such critical questions so much after the fact I find it interesting to make out—critically interesting of course, which is all our interest here pretends to be—that whereas any anecdote about life pure and simple, as it were, proceeds almost as a matter of course from some good jog of fond fancy's elbow, some pencilled note on somebody else's case, so the material for any picture of personal states so specifically complicated as those of my hapless friends in the present volume will have been drawn preponderantly from the depths of the designer's own mind. This, amusingly enough, is what, on the evidence before us, I seem critically, as I say, to gather—that the states represented, the embarassments and predicaments studied, the tragedies and comedies recorded, can be intelligibly fathered but on his own intimate experience. I have already mentioned the particular rebuke once addressed me on all this ground, the question of where on earth, where roundabout us at this hour, I had "found" my Neil Paradays, my Ralph Limberts, my Hugh Verekers and other such supersubtle fry. I was reminded then, as I have said, that these represented eminent cases fell to the ground, as by their foolish weight, unless I could give chapter and verse for the eminence. I was reduced to confessing I couldn't, and yet must repeat again here how little I was so abashed. On going over these things I see, to our critical edification, exactly why— which was because I was able to plead that my postulates, my animating presences, were all, to their great enrichment, their intensification of value, ironic; the strength of applied irony being surely in the sincerities, the lucidities, the utilities that stand behind it. When it's not a campaign, of a sort, on behalf of the something better (better than the obnoxious, the pro- voking object) that blessedly, as is assumed, *might* be, it's not worth speaking of. But this is exactly what we mean by operative irony. It implies and pro- jects the possible other case, the case rich and edifying where the actuality is pretentious and vain. So it plays its lamp; so, essentially, it carries that smoke- less flame, which makes clear, with all the rest, the good cause that guides it. My application of which remarks is that the studies here collected have their justification in the ironic spirit, the spirit expressed by my being able to reply promptly enough to my friend: "If the life about us for the last thirty years refuses warrant for these examples, then so much the worse for that life. The *constatation* would be so deplorable that instead of making it we must dodge it: there are decencies that in the name of the general self-respect we must take for granted, there's a kind of rudimentary intellectual honour to which we must, in the interest of civilisation, at least pretend." But I must really reproduce the whole passion of my retort.

PART C: CREATION OF CHARACTERS

1. describing vs. expressing: fingering puppets to death

("Miss Prescott's 'Azarian,' " 1865)

When a very little girl becomes the happy possessor of a wax-doll, she testifies her affection for it by a fond manipulation of its rosy visage. If the nose, for instance, is unusually shapely and pretty, the fact is made patent by a constant friction of the finger-tips; so that poor dolly is rapidly smutted out of recognition. In a certain sense we would compare Miss Prescott [Harriet Elizabeth Prescott, in *Azarian: An Episode*] to such a little girl. She fingers her puppets to death. "Good heavens, Madam!" we are forever on the point of exclaiming, "let the poor things speak for themselves. What? are you afraid they can't stand alone?" Even the most clearly defined character would succumb beneath this repeated posing, attitudinizing, and changing of costume. Take any breathing *person* from the ranks of fiction,—Hetty in "Adam Bede", or Becky Sharp the Great (we select women advisedly, for it is known that they can endure twenty times more than men in this respect),—place her for a few pages in Miss Prescott's charge, and what will be the result? Adieu, dear familiar friend; you melt like wax in a candle. Imagine Thackeray forever pulling Rebecca's curls and settling the folds of her dress.

This bad habit of Miss Prescott's is more than an offence against art. Nature herself resents it. It is an injustice to men and women to assume that the fleshly element carries such weight. In the history of a loving and breaking heart, is that the only thing worth noticing? Are the external signs and accidents of passion the only points to be detailed? What we want is Passion's self,—her language, her ringing voice, her gait, the presentment of her deeds. What do we care about the beauty of man or woman in comparison with their humanity? In a novel we crave the spectacle of that of which we may feel that we *know* it. The only lasting fictions are those which have spoken to the reader's heart, and not to his eye; those which have introduced him to an atmosphere in which it was credible that human beings might exist, and to human beings with whom he might feel tempted to claim kinship.

When once a work of fiction may be classed as a novel, its foremost claim to merit, and indeed the measure of its merit, is its *truth*,—its truth to something, however questionable that thing may be in point of morals or of taste. "Azarian" is true to nothing. No one ever looked like Azarian, talked like him, nor, on the whole, acted like him; for although his specific deeds, as related in the volume before us, are few and far between, we find it difficult to believe that any one ever pursued a line of conduct so utterly meaningless as that which we are invited, or rather allowed, to attribute to him.

We have called Miss Prescott's manner the descriptive manner; but in so doing we took care to distinguish it from the famous realistic system which has asserted itself so largely in the fictitious writing of the last few years. It is not a counsel we would indiscriminately bestow,—on the contrary, we would gladly see the vulgar realism which governs the average imagination leavened by a little old-fashioned idealism,—but Miss Prescott, if she hopes to accomplish anything worth accomplishing, must renounce new-fashioned idealism for a while, and diligently study the canons of the so-called realist school. We gladly admit that she has the talent to profit by such a discipline. But to be real in writing is to describe; such is the popular notion. Were this notion correct, Miss Prescott would be a very good realist,—none better. But for this fallacious axiom we propose to substitute another, which, if it does not embrace the whole truth, comes several degrees nearer to it: to be real in writing is to express; whether by description or otherwise is of secondary importance.

2. characters vs. figures: bundles of eccentricities

("Our Mutual Friend," 1865)

"Our Mutual Friend" is, to our perception, the poorest of Mr. Dickens's works. And it is poor with the poverty not of momentary embarrassment, but of permanent exhaustion. It is wanting in inspiration. For the last ten years it has seemed to us that Mr. Dickens has been unmistakably forcing himself. "Bleak House" was forced; "Little Dorrit" was labored; the present work is dug out, as with a spade and pickaxe. Of course—to anticipate the usual argument—who but Dickens could have written it? Who, indeed? Who else would have established a lady in business in a novel on the admirably solid basis of her always putting on gloves and tying a handkerchief 'round her head in moments of grief, and of her habitually addressing her family with "Peace! Hold!" It is needless to say that Mrs. Reginald Wilfer is first and last the occasion of considerable true humor. When, after conducting her daughter to Mrs. Boffin's carriage, in sight of all the envious neighbors, she is described as enjoying her triumph during the next quarter of an hour by airing herself on the doorstep "in a kind of splendidly serene trance," we laugh with as uncritical a laugh as could be desired of us. We pay the same tribute to her assertions, as she narrates the glories of the society she enjoyed at her father's table, that she has known as many as three copper-plate engravers exchanging the most exquisite sallies and retorts there at one time. But when to these we have added a dozen more happy examples of the humor which was exhaled from every line of Mr. Dickens's earlier writings, we shall have closed the list of the merits of the work before us. To say that the conduct of the story, with all its complications, betrays a long-practiced hand, is to pay no compliment worthy the author. If this were, indeed, a compliment, we should be inclined to carry it further, and congratulate him on his success in what we should call the manufacture of fiction; for in so doing we should express a feeling that has attended us throughout the book. Seldom, we reflected, had we read a book so intensely *written*, so little seen, known, or felt.

In all Mr. Dickens's works the fantastic has been his great resource; and while his fancy was lively and vigorous it accomplished great things. But the fantastic, when the fancy is dead, is a very poor business. The movement of Mr. Dickens's fancy in Mrs. Wilfer and Mr. Boffin and Lady Tippins, and Lammles and Miss Wren, and even in Eugene Wrayburn, is, to our mind, a movement lifeless, forced, mechanical. It is the letter of his old humor without the spirit. It is hardly too much to say that every character here put before us is a mere bundle of eccentricities, animated by no principle of nature whatever. In former days there reigned in Mr. Dickens's extravagances a comparative consistency; they were exaggerated statements of types that really existed. We had, perhaps, never known a Newman Noggs, nor a Pecksniff, nor a Micawber; but we had known persons of whom these figures were but the strictly logical consummation. But among the grotesque creatures who occupy the pages before us, there is not one whom we can refer to as an existing type. In all Mr. Dickens's stories, indeed, the reader has been called upon, and has willingly consented, to accept a certain number of figures or creatures of pure fancy, for this was the author's poetry. He was, moreover, always repaid for his concession by a peculiar beauty or power in these exceptional characters. But he is now expected to make the same concession with a very inadequate reward. What do we get in return for accepting Miss Jenny Wren as a possible person? This young lady is the type of a certain class of characters of which Mr. Dickens has made a specialty, and with which he has been accustomed to draw alternate smiles and tears, according as he pressed one spring or another. But this is very cheap merriment and very cheap pathos. Miss Jenny Wren is a poor little dwarf, afflicted, as she constantly reiterates, with a "bad back" and "queer legs," who makes doll's dresses, and is forever pricking at those with whom she converses, in the air, with her needle, and assuring them that she knows their "tricks and their manners." Like all Mr. Dickens's pathetic characters, she is a little monster; she is deformed, unhealthy, unnatural; she belongs to the troop of hunchbacks, imbeciles, and precocious children who have carried on the sentimental business in all Mr. Dickens's novels; the little Nells, the Smikes, the Paul Dombeys.

Mr. Dickens goes as far out of the way for his wicked people as he does for his good ones. Rogue Riderhood, indeed, in the present story, is villainous with a sufficiently natural villainy; he belongs to that quarter of society in which the author is most at his ease. But was there ever such wickedness as that of the Lammles and Mr. Fledgeby? Not that people have not been as mischievous as they; but was any one ever mischievous in that singular fashion? Did a couple of elegant swindlers ever take such particular pains to be aggressively inhuman?—for we can find no other word for the gratuitous distortions to which they are subjected. The word *humanity* strikes us as strangely discordant, in the midst of these pages; for, let us boldly declare it, there is no humanity here. Humanity is nearer home than the Boffins, and the Lammles, and the Wilfers, and the Veneerings. It is in what men have in common with each other, and not in what they have in distinction. The people just named have nothing in common with each other, except the fact that they have nothing in common with mankind at large. What a world were this world if the world of "Our Mutual Friend" were an honest reflection of it! But a community of eccentrics is impossible. Rules alone are consistent with each other; exceptions are inconsistent. Society is maintained by natural sense and natural feeling. We cannot conceive a society in which these principles are not in some manner represented. Where in these pages are the depositaries of that intelligence without which the movement of life would cease? Who represents nature? Accepting half of Mr. Dickens's persons as intentionally grotesque, where are those exemplars of sound humanity who should afford us the proper measure of their companion's variations? We ought not, in justice to the author, to seek them among his weaker—that is, his mere conventional—characters; in John Harmon, Lizzie Hexam, or Mortimer Lightwood; but we assuredly cannot find them among his stronger —that is, his artificial creations. Suppose we take Eugene Wrayburn and Bradley Headstone. They occupy a half-way position between the habitual probable of nature and the habitual impossible of Mr. Dickens. A large portion of the story rests upon the enmity borne by Headstone to Wrayburn, both being in love with the same woman. Wrayburn is a gentleman, and Headstone is one of the people. Wrayburn is wellbred, careless, elegant, sceptical, and idle: Headstone is a high-tempered, hard-working, ambitious young schoolmaster There lay in the opposition of these two characters a very good story. But the prime requisite was that they should *be* characters: Mr. Dickens, according to his usual plan, has made them simply figures, and between them the story that was to be, the story that should have been, has evaporated. Wrayburn lounges about with his hands in his pockets, smoking a cigar, and talking nonsense. Headstone strides about, clenching his fists and biting his lips and grasping his stick. There is one scene in which Wrayburn chaffs the schoolmaster with easy insolence, while the latter writhes impotently under his well-bred sarcasm. This scene is very clever, but it is very insufficient. If the majority of readers were not so very timid in the use of words we should call it vulgar. By this we do not mean to indicate the conventional impropriety of two gentlemen exchanging lively personalities; we mean to emphasize the essentially small character of these personalities. In other words, the moment, dramatically, is great, while the author's conception is weak. The friction of two *men*, of two characters, of two passions, produces stronger sparks than Wrayburn's boyish repartees and Headstone's melodramatic commonplaces. Such scenes as this are useful in fixing the limits of Mr. Dickens's insight. Insight is, perhaps, too strong a word; for we are convinced that it is one of the chief conditions of his genius not to see beneath the surface of things. If we might hazard a definition of his literary character, we should, accordingly, call him the greatest of superficial novelists. We are aware that this definition confines him to an inferior rank in the department of letters which he adorns; but we accept this consequence of our proposition. It were, in our opinion, an offense against humanity to place Mr. Dickens among the greatest novelists. For, to repeat what we have already intimated, he has created nothing but figures. He has added nothing

to our understanding of human character. He is master of but two alternatives: he reconciles us to what is commonplace, and he reconciles us to what
is odd. The value of the former service is questionable; and the manner in
which Mr. Dickens performs it sometimes conveys a certain impression
of charlatanism. The value of the latter service is incontestable, and here
Mr. Dickens is an honest, an admirable artist. But what is the condition of
the truly great novelist? For him there are no alternatives, for him there are
no oddities, for him there is nothing outside of humanity. He cannot shirk
it; it imposes itself upon him. For him alone, therefore, there is a true and
a false; for him alone it is possible to be right, because it is possible to be
wrong. Mr. Dickens is a great observer and a great humorist, but he is
nothing of a philosopher. Some people may hereupon say, so much the better;
we say, so much the worse. For a novelist very soon has need of a little
philosophy. In treating of Micawber, and Boffin, and Pickwick, *et hoc genus
omne*, he can, indeed, dispense with it, for this—we say it with all deference—is not serious writing. But when he comes to tell the story of a passion,
a story like that of Headstone and Wrayburn, he becomes a moralist as well
as an artist. He must know *man* as well as *men*, and to know man is to be
a philosopher. The writer who knows men alone, if he have Mr. Dickens's
humor and fancy, will give us figures and pictures for which we cannot be
too grateful, for he will enlarge our knowledge of the world. But when he
introduces men and women whose interest is preconceived to lie not in the
poverty, the weakness, the drollery of their natures, but in their complete
and unconscious subjection to ordinary and healthy human emotions, all
his humor, all his fancy, will avail him nothing if, out of the fullness of his
sympathy, he is unable to prosecute those generalizations in which alone
consists the real greatness of a work of art. This may sound like very subtle
talk about a very simple matter; it is rather very simple talk about a very
subtle matter. A story based upon those elementary passions in which alone
we seek the true and final manifestation of character must be told in a spirit
of intellectual superiority to those passions. That is, the author must understand what he is talking about. The perusal of a story so told is one of the most
elevating experiences within the reach of the human mind. The perusal of
a story which is not so told is infinitely depressing and unprofitable.

3. *characters vs. representatives*

(*Hawthorne*, 1879)

The faults of the book [*The Scarlet Letter*] are, to my sense, a want of reality
and an abuse of the fanciful element—of a certain superficial symbolism.
The people strike me not as characters, but as representatives, very pictur-

esquely arranged, of a single state of mind; and the interest of the story lies, not in them, but in the situation, which is insistently kept before us, with little progression, though with a great deal, as I have said, of a certain stable variation; and to which they, out of their reality, contribute little that helps it to live and move.

4. characters vs. figures

(Hawthorne, 1879)

They [characters in *The House of the Seven Gables*] are all figures rather than characters—they are all pictures rather than persons. But if their reality is light and vague, it is sufficient, and it is in harmony with the low relief and dimness of outline of the objects that surrounded them. They are all types, to the author's mind, of something general, of something that is bound up with the history, at large, of families and individuals, and each of them is the centre of a cluster of those ingenious and meditative musings, rather melancholy, as a general thing, than joyous, which melt into the current and texture of the story and give it a kind of moral richness.

5. perception of character

("Anthony Trollope," 1883)

He [Trollope] accepted all the common restrictions, and found that even within the barriers there was plenty of material. He attaches a preface to one of his novels—*The Vicar of Bullhampton*, before mentioned—for the express purpose of explaining why he has introduced a young woman who may, in truth, as he says, be called a "castaway"; and in relation to this episode he remarks that it is the object of the novelist's art to entertain the young people of both sexes. Writers of the French school would, of course, protest indignantly against such a formula as this, which is the only one of the kind that I remember to have encountered in Trollope's pages. It is meager, assuredly; but Trollope's practice was really much larger than so poor a theory. And indeed any theory was good which enabled him to pro-duce the works which he put forth between 1856 and 1869, or later. In spite of his want of doctrinal richness I think he tells us, on the whole, more about life than the "naturalists" in our sister republic. I say this with a full consciousness of the opportunities an artist loses in leaving so many corners unvisited, so many topics untouched, simply because I think his perception of character was naturally more just and liberal than that of the naturalists.

This has been from the beginning the good fortune of our English providers of fiction, as compared with the French. They are inferior in audacity, in neatness, in acuteness, in intellectual vivacity, in the arrangement of material, in the art of characterizing visible things. But they have been more at home in the moral world; as people say today they know their way about the conscience.

6. a charm of mystery and poetry and oddity

("Dumas the Younger," 1896)

His [Dumas the Younger's] characters are all pointed by observation, they are clear notes in the concert, but not one of them has known the little invisible push that, even when shyly and awkwardly administered, makes the puppet, in spite of the string, walk off by himself and quite "cut," if the mood take him, that distant relation his creator. They are always formal with this personage and thoroughly conscious and proud of him; there is a charm of mystery and poetry and oddity, a glory of unexpectedness, that they consistently lack. Their life, and that, in each case, of the whole story (quite the most wonderful part of this) is simply the author's own life, his high vitality, his very presence and temperament and voice. They do more for him even than they do for the subject, and he himself is at last accordingly the most vivid thing in every situation. He keeps it at arm's length because he has the instinct of the dramatist and the conscience of the artist, but we feel all the while that his face is bigger than his mask. Nothing about his work is more extraordinary than this manner in which his personality pervades without spoiling it the most detached and most impersonal of literary forms.

7. specify, localise . . .

(*Letters*, 1899, to Mrs. Humphry Ward)

I return the proofs of *Eleanor*, in a separate cover from this, and as I think it wise to *register* them I must wait till to-morrow a.m. to do that, and this, therefore, will reach you first. Let me immediately say that I don't light (and I've read carefully every word, and many two or three times, as Mr. Bellasis would say—and is Mr. B., by the way, naturally—as it were—H. J. ? ? ? ! ! !) on any peccant particular spots in the aspect of Lucy F. that the American reader would challenge. I do think he, or she, may be likely, at first, to think her more English than American—to say, I mean: "Why, this isn't *us*—it's English 'Dissent.' " For it's well—generally—to keep in mind how very different a thing that is (socially, aesthetically &c.) from the American free (and easy) multitudinous churches that, practically, in any community, are like so many (almost) clubs or Philharmonics or amateur theatrical companies. I *don't* quite think the however obscure American girl I gather you to conceive would have any shockability about Rome, the Pope, St. Peter's, kneeling, or anything of that sort—least of all any girl whose concatenations *could*, by any possibility of social handing-on, land her in the milieu you present at Albano. She would probably be either a Unitarian or "Orthodox" (which is, I believe, "Congregational," though in New England always called "Orthodox") and in either case as Emersonized, Hawthornized, J. A. Symondsized, and as "frantic" to *feel* the Papacy &c, as one could well represent her. And this, I mean, even were she of any provincial New England circle whatever that one could conceive as ramifying, however indirectly, into Villa Barb. This particularly were her father a college professor. In that case I should say "The bad clothes &c, oh yes; as much as you like. The beauty &c, *scarcely*. The offishness to Rome —as a spectator &c.— almost not at all." All this, roughly and hastily speaking. But there is no false note of surface, beyond this, I think, that you need be uneasy about at all. Had I looked over your shoulder I should have said: "*Specify*, localise, a little more—give her a *definite* Massachusetts, or Maine, or whatever, habitation—imagine a country-college-town—invent, if need be, a name, and stick to that." This for smallish, but appreciable reasons that I haven't space to develop—but after all not imperative. For the rest the chapters you send me are, as a beginning, to my vision very charming and interesting and pleasing—full of promise of strong elements—as your beginnings always are.

8. *a matter of detail*

(*Letters*, 1903, to Howard Sturgis)

I am a bad person, really, to expose "fictitious work" to—I, as a battered producer and "technician" myself, have long since inevitably ceased to read with *naïveté*; I can only read critically, constructively, *re*constructively, writing the thing over (if I can swallow it at all) *my* way, and looking at it, so to speak, from within. But even thus I "pass" your book very—tenderly! There is only one thing that, as a matter of detail, I am moved to say— which is that I feel you have a great deal increased your difficulty by screwing up the "social position" of all your people so very high. When a man is an English Marquis, even a lame one, there are whole masses of Marquisate things and items, a multitude of inherent detail in his existence, which it isn't open to the painter *de gaieté de coeur* not to make some picture of.

And yet if I mention this because it is *the* place where people will challenge you, and to suggest to you therefore to expect it—if I do so I am probably after all quite wrong. No one notices or understands *anything*, and no one will make a single intelligent or intelligible observation about your work. They will make plenty of others. What I applaud is your sticking to the real line and centre of your theme—the consciousness and view of Sainty himself, and your dealing with things, with the whole fantasmagoria, as presented to him only, not otherwise going behind them.

9. *the* conditions *of the creatures*

("The Lesson of Balzac," 1905)

The lesson of Balzac, under this comparison, is extremely various, and I should prepare myself much too large a task were I to attempt a list of the separate truths he brings home. I have to choose among them, and I choose the most important; the three or four that more or less include the others. In reading him over, in opening him almost anywhere today, what immediately strikes us is the part assigned by him, in any picture, to the *conditions* of the creatures with whom he is concerned. Contrasted with him other prose painters of life scarce seem to see the conditions at all. He clearly held pretended portrayals as nothing, as less than nothing, as a most vain thing, unless it should be, in spirit and intention, the art of complete representation. "Complete" is of course a great word, and there is no art at all, we are often reminded, that is not on too many sides an abject compromise. The element of compromise is always there; it is of the essence; we live with it, and it may serve to keep us humble. The formula of the whole matter is sufficiently expressed perhaps in a reply I found myself once making to an inspired but discouraged friend, a fellow-craftsman who had declared in his despair that there was no use trying, that it was a form, the novel, absolutely too difficult. "Too difficult indeed; yet there is one way to master it—which is to pretend consistently that it isn't." We are all of us, all the while, pretending—as consistently as we can—that it isn't, and Balzac's great glory is that he pretended hardest. He never had to pretend so hard as when he addressed himself to that evocation of the medium, that distillation of the natural and social air, of which I speak, the things that most require on the part of the painter preliminary possession—so definitely require it that, terrified at the requisition, when conscious of it, many a painter prefers to beg the whole question. He has thus, this ingenious person, to invent some *other* way of making his characters interesting—some other way, that is, than the arduous way, demanding so much consideration, of presenting them to us. They are interesting, in fact, as subjects of fate, the figures round whom a situation closes, in proportion as, sharing their existence, we feel where fate comes in and just how it gets at them. In the void they are not interesting—and Balzac, like Nature herself, abhorred a vacuum. Their situation takes hold of us because it is theirs, not because it is somebody's, any one's, that of creatures unidentified. Therefore it is not superfluous that their identity shall first be established for us, and their adventures, in that measure, have a relation to it, and therewith an appreciability. There is no such thing in the world as an adventure pure and simple; there is only mine and yours, and his and hers—it being the greatest adventure of all, I verily think, just to *be* you or I, just to be he or she. To Balzac's imagination that was indeed in itself an immense adventure—and nothing appealed to him more than to show *how* we all are, and how we are placed and built-in for being so. What befalls us is but another name for the way our circumstances press upon us—so that an account of what befalls us is an account of our circumstances.

Part D: Special Problems; Special Characters

1. *such fantastic names*

("Anthony Trollope," 1883)

It is a part of this same ambiguity of mind as to what constitutes evidence that Trollope should sometimes endow his people with such fantastic names. Dr. Pessimist Anticant and Mr. Sentiment make, as we have seen, an awkward appearance in a modern novel; and Mr. Neversay Die, Mr. Stickatit, Mr. Rerechild and Mr. Fillgrave (the last two the family physicians) are scarcely more felicitous. It would be better to go back to Bunyan at once. There is a person mentioned in *The Warden* under the name of Mr. Quiverful—a poor clergyman, with a dozen children, who holds the living of Puddingdale. This name is a humorous allusion to his overflowing nursery, and it matters little so long as he is not brought to the front. But in *Barchester Towers*, which carries on the history of Hiram's Hospital, Mr. Quiverful becomes, as a candidate for Mr. Harding's vacant place, an important element, and the reader is made proportionately unhappy by the primitive character of this satiric note. A Mr. Quiverful with fourteen children (which is the number attained in *Barchester Towers*) is too difficult to believe in. We can believe in the name and we can believe in the children; but we cannot manage the combination. It is probably not unfair to say that if Trollope derived half his inspiration from life, he derived the other half from Thackeray; his earlier novels, in especial, suggest an honorable emulation of the author of *The Newcomes*. Thackeray's names were perfect; they always had a meaning, and (except in his absolutely jocose productions, where they were still admirable) we can imagine, even when they are most figurative, that they should have been borne by real people. But in this, as in other respects, Trollope's hand was heavier than his master's; though when he is content not to be too comical his appellations are sometimes fortunate enough. Mrs. Proudie is excellent, for Mrs. Proudie, and even the Duke of Omnium and Gatherum Castle rather minister to illusion than destroy it. Indeed, the names of houses and places, throughout Trollope, are full of color.

2. *satire, sarcasm, irony: the victim must be erect and solid*

("American Letter," April 30, 1898)

Satire, sarcasm, irony may be, as a hundred triumphs have taught us, vivid and comforting enough when two precautions have been taken; the first in regard to the reality, the second in regard to the folly, the criminality, or whatever it may be, of the thing satirized. Mr. [Winston] Churchill [in *The Celebrity*], as I make out, has, with magnificent high spirits, neglected all precautions; his elaborate exposure of something or of somebody strikes us, therefore, as mere slashing at the wall. The movements are all in the air, and blood is never drawn. There could be no better illustration than his first short chapter of his reversal of the secure method. It is both allusive and scathing, but so much more scathing than constructive that we feel this not to be the way to build up the victim. The victim must be erect and solid—must be set upon his feet before he can be knocked down. The Celebrity is down from the first—we look straight over him. He has been exposed too young and never recovers.

3. *Flaubert's defect: limited reflectors and registers*

("Gustave Flaubert," 1902)

Why did Flaubert choose, as special conduits of the life he proposed to depict, such inferior and in the case of Frédéric [in *L'Education sentimentale*] such abject human specimens? I insist only in respect to the latter, the perfection of Madame Bovary scarce leaving one much warrant for wishing anything other. Even here, however, the general scale and size of Emma, who is small even of her sort, should be a warning to hyperbole. If I say that in the matter of Frédéric at all events the answer is inevitably detrimental I mean that it weighs heavily on our author's general credit. He wished in each case to make a picture of experience—middling experience, it is true—

and of the world close to him; but if he imagined nothing better for his purpose than such a heroine and such a hero, both such limited reflectors and
registers, we are forced to believe it to have been by a defect of his mind.
And that sign of weakness remains even if it be objected that the images in
question were addressed to his purpose better than others would have been:
the purpose itself then shows as inferior. . . .

. . . The discrimination I here make as against our author is, however,
the only one inevitable in a series of remarks so brief. What it really represents—and nothing could be more curious—is that Frédéric enjoys his position not only without the aid of a single "sympathetic" character of consequence, but even without the aid of one with whom we can directly
communicate. Can we communicate with the central personage? or would
we really if we could? A hundred times no, and if he himself can communicate with the people shown us as surrounding him this only proves him
of their kind.

4. characters: lighted and obscured

(Preface to *The American*, 1907)

It is difficult for me to-day to believe that I had not, as my work went on,
some shade of the rueful sense of my affront to verisimilitude [in *The American*]; yet I catch the memory at least of no great sharpness, no true critical
anguish, of remorse: an anomaly the reason of which in fact now glimmers
interestingly out. My concern, as I saw it, was to make and to keep Newman
consistent; the picture of his consistency was all my undertaking, and the
memory of *that* infatuation perfectly abides with me. He was to be the
lighted figure, the others—even doubtless to an excessive degree the woman
who is made the agent of his discomfiture—were to be the obscured; by
which I should largely get the very effect most to be invoked, that of a generous nature engaged with forces, with difficulties and dangers, that it but
half understands. If Newman was attaching enough, I must have argued,
his tangle would be sensible enough; for the interest of everything is all that
it is *his* vision, *his* conception, *his* interpretation: at the window of his
wide, quite sufficiently wide, consciousness we are seated, from that admirable position we "assist." He therefore supremely matters; all the rest
matters only as he feels it, treats it, meets it. A beautiful infatuation this,
always, I think, the intensity of the creative effort to get into the skin of
the creature; the act of personal possession of one being by another at its
completest—and with the high enhancement, ever, that it is, by the same
stroke, the effort of the artist to preserve for his subject that unity, and for
his use of it (in other words for the interest he desires to excite) that effect

of a *centre*, which most economise its value. Its value is most discussable when that economy has most operated; the content and the "importance" of a work of art are in fine wholly dependent on its *being* one: outside of which all prate of its representative character, its meaning and its bearing, its morality and humanity, are an impudent thing. Strong in that character, which is the condition of its really bearing witness at all, it is strong every way.

5. the artist as character

(Preface to The Tragic Muse, 1908)

Any presentation of the artist *in triumph* must be flat in proportion as it really sticks to its subject—it can only smuggle in relief and variety. For, to put the matter in an image, all we then—in his triumph—see of the charm-compeller is the back he turns to us as he bends over his work. "His" triumph, decently, is but the triumph of what he produces, and that is another affair. His romance is the romance he himself projects; he eats the cake of the very rarest privilege, the most luscious baked in the oven of the gods—therefore he mayn't "have" it, in the form of the privilege of the hero, at the same time. The privilege of the hero—that is of the martyr or of the interesting and appealing and comparatively floundering *person*—places him in quite a different category, belongs to him only as to the artist deluded, diverted, frustrated or vanquished; when the "amateur" in him gains, for our admiration or compassion or whatever, all that the expert has to do without.

6. contrasting characters: perception and stupidity

(Preface to The Spoils of Poynton, 1908)

As to our young woman [Fleda Vetch] of "The Spoils," meanwhile, I briefly come back to my claim for a certain definiteness of beauty in the special effect wrought by her aid. My problem had decently to be met—that of establishing for the other persons the vividness of their appearance of comparative stupidity, that of exposing them to the full thick wash of the penumbra surrounding the central light, and yet keeping their motions, within it, distinct, coherent and "amusing." But these are exactly of course the most "amusing" things to do; nothing, for example, being of a higher reward artistically than the shade of success aimed at in such a figure as Mrs. Gereth. A character she too, absolutely, yet the very reverse of a free spirit. I have found myself so pleased with Mrs. Gereth, I confess, on resuming acquaintance with her, that, complete and in all equilibrium as she seems to me to stand and move there, I shrink from breathing upon her any breath of qualification; without which, however, I fail of my point that, thanks to the "value" represented by Fleda, and to the position to which the elder woman is confined by that irradiation, the latter is at the best a "false" character, floundering as she does in the dusk of disproportionate passion. She is a *figure*, oh definitely—which is a very different matter; for you may be a figure with all the blinding, with all the hampering passion in life, and may have the grand air in what shall yet prove to the finer view (which Fleda again, *e. g.*, could at any time strike off) but a perfect rage of awkwardness. Mrs. Gereth was, obviously, with her pride and her pluck, of an admirable fine paste; but she was not intelligent, was only clever, and therefore would have been no use to us at all as centre of our subject—com-compared with Fleda, who was only intelligent, not distinctively able. The little drama confirms at all events excellently, I think, the contention of the old wisdom that the question of the personal will has more than all else to say to the verisimilitude of these exhibitions. The will that rides the crisis quite most triumphantly is that of the awful Mona Brigstock, who is *all* will, without the smallest leak of force into taste or tenderness or vision, into any sense of shades or relations or proportions. She loses no minute in that perception of incongruities in which half Fleda's passion is wasted and misled, and into which Mrs. Gereth, to her practical loss, that is by the fatal grace of a sense of comedy, occasionally and disinterestedly strays. Every one, every thing, in the story is accordingly sterile *but* the so thriftily constructed Mona, able at any moment to bear the whole of her dead weight at once on any given inch of a resisting surface. Fleda, obliged to neglect inches, sees and feels but in acres and expanses and blue perspectives; Mrs. Gereth too, in comparison, while her imagination broods, drops half the stitches of the web she seeks to weave.

7. *a sick protagonist*

(Preface to *The Wings of the Dove*, 1909)

Why had one to look so straight in the face and so closely to cross-question that idea of making one's protagonist "sick"?—as if to be menaced with death or danger hadn't been from time immemorial, for heroine or hero, the very shortest of all cuts to the interesting state. Why should a figure be disqualified for a central position by the particular circumstance that might most quicken, that might crown with a fine intensity, its liability to many accidents, its consciousness of all relations? This circumstance, true enough, might disqualify it for many activities—even though we should have imputed to it the unsurpassable activity of passionate, of inspired resistance. This last fact was the real issue, for the way grew straight from the moment one recognised that the poet essentially *can't* be concerned with the act of dying. Let him deal with the sickest of the sick, it is still by the act of living that they appeal to him, and appeal the more as the conditions plot against them and prescribe the battle. The process of life gives way fighting, and often may so shine out on the lost ground as in no other connexion. One had had moreover, as a various chronicler, one's secondary physical weaklings and failures, one's accessory invalids—introduced with a complacency that made light of criticism. To Ralph Touchett in "The Portrait of a Lady," for instance, his deplorable state of health was not only no drawback; I had clearly been right in counting it, for any happy effect he should produce, a positive good mark, a direct aid to pleasantness and vividness. The reason of this moreover could never in the world have been his fact of sex; since men, among the mortally afflicted, suffer on the whole more overtly and more grossly than women, and resist with a ruder, an inferior strategy. I had thus to take *that* anomaly for what it was worth, and I give it here but as one of the ambiguities amid which my subject ended by making itself at home and seating itself quite in confidence.

8. ficelles: *belong intimately to the treatment*

(Preface to *Portrait of a Lady*, 1908)

It is a familiar truth to the novelist, at the strenuous hour, that, as certain elements in any work are of the essence, so others are only of the form; that as this or that character, this or that disposition of the material, belongs to the subject directly, so to speak, so this or that other belongs to it but indirectly—belongs intimately to the treatment. . . .

All of which is perhaps but a gracefully devious way of saying that Henrietta Stackpole was a good example, in "The Portrait," of the truth to which I just adverted—as good an example as I could name were it not that Maria Gostrey, in "The Ambassadors," then in the bosom of time, may be mentioned as a better. Each of these persons is but wheels to the coach; neither belongs to the body of that vehicle, or is for a moment accommodated with a seat inside. There the subject alone is ensconced, in the form of its "hero and heroine," and of the privileged high officials, say, who ride with the king and queen. There are reasons why one would have liked this to be felt, as in general one would like almost anything to be felt, in one's work, that one has one's self contributively felt. We have seen, however, how idle is that pretension, which I should be sorry to make too much of. Maria Gostrey and Miss Stackpole then are cases, each, of the light *ficelle*, not of the true agent; they may run beside the coach "for all they are worth," they may cling to it till they are out of breath (as poor Miss Stackpole all so vividly does), but neither, all the while, so much as gets her foot on the step, neither ceases for a moment to tread the dusty road. Put it even that they are like the fish-wives who helped to bring back to Paris from Versailles, on that most om-inous day of the first half of the French Revolution, the carriage of the royal family.

9. ficelle *as confidante*

(Preface to *The Ambassadors*, 1909)

I may seem not to better the case for my discrimination if I say that, for my first care, I had thus inevitably to set him [Strether in *The Ambassadors*] up a confidant or two, to wave away with energy the custom of the seated mass of explanation after the fact, the inserted block of merely referential narrative, which flourishes so, to the shame of the modern impatience, on the serried page of Balzac, but which seems simply to appall our actual, our general weaker, digestion. "Harking back to make up" took at any rate more doing, as the phrase is, not only than the reader of to-day demands, but than he will tolerate at any price any call upon him either to understand or remotely to measure; and for the beauty of the thing when done the current editorial mind in particular appears wholly without sense. It is not, however, primarily for either of these reasons, whatever their weight, that Strether's friend Waymarsh is so keenly clutched at, on the threshold of the book, or that no less a pounce is made on Maria Gostrey—without even the pretext, either, of *her* being, in essence, Strether's friend. She is the reader's friend much rather—in consequence of dispositions that make him so eminently require one; and she acts in that capacity, and *really* in that capacity alone, with exemplary devotion, from beginning to end of the book. She is an enrolled, a direct, aid to lucidity; she is in fine, to tear off her mask, the most unmitigated and abandoned of *ficelles*. Half the dramatist's art, as we well know—since if we don't it's not the fault of the proofs that lie scattered about us—is in the use of *ficelles;* by which I mean in a deep dissimulation of his dependence on them. Waymarsh only to a slighter degree belongs, in the whole business, less to my subject than to my treatment of it; the interesting proof, in these connexions, being that one has but to take one's subject for the stuff of drama to interweave with enthusiasm as many Gostreys as need be.

10. ficelles: *connections false and real*

(Preface to *The Ambassadors*, 1909)

The "*ficelle*" character of the subordinate party is as artfully dissimulated, throughout, as may be, and to that extent that, with the seams or joints of Maria Gostrey's ostensible connectedness taken particular care of, duly smoothed over, that is, and anxiously kept from showing as "pieced on," this figure doubtless achieves, after a fashion, something of the dignity of a prime idea: which circumstance but shows us afresh how many quite incalculable but none the less clear sources of enjoyment for the infatuated artist, how many copious springs of our never-to-be-slighted "fun" for the reader and critic susceptible of contagion, may sound their incidental plash as soon as an artistic process begins to enjoy free development. Exquisite—in illustration of this—the mere interest and amusement of such at once "creative" and critical questions as how and where and why to make Miss Gostrey's false connexion carry itself, under a due high polish, as a real one. Nowhere is it more of an artful expedient for mere consistency of form, to mention a case, than in the last "scene" of the book, where its function is to give or to add nothing whatever, but only to express as vividly as possible certain things quite other than itself and that are of the already fixed and appointed measure. Since, however, all art is *expression*, and is thereby vividness, one was to find the door open here to any amount of delightful dissimulation. These verily are the refinements and ecstasies of method—amid which, or certainly under the influence of any exhilarated demonstration of which, one must keep one's head and not lose one's way. To cultivate an adequate intelligence for them and to make that sense operative is positively to find a charm in any produced ambiguity of appearance that is not by the same stroke, and all helplessly, an ambiguity of sense. To project imaginatively, for my hero, a relation that has nothing to do with the matter (the matter of my subject) but has everything to do with the manner (the manner of my presentation of the same) and yet to treat it, at close quarters and for fully economic expression's possible sake, as if it were important and essential —to do that sort of thing and yet muddle nothing may easily become, as one goes, a signally attaching proposition; even though it all remains but part and parcel, I hasten to recognise, of the merely general and related question of expressional curiosity and expressional decency.

Chapter XI

SETTING

An element of fiction which loomed large in the work of Henry James was place. One has but to recall the varied locales of the novels—Northhampton and Rome, Boston and New York, Paris and London—to summon to mind the challenges James took on in rendering place in his own work. For example: in The Wings of the Dove, *Milly Theale is first seen in the Swiss Alps, and takes her last breath in the decaying splendor of Venice—all through James's careful calculation of the importance of backdrop to character, of place to action. One need but recall further James's extensive travel during his life, and his voluminous writing about, and evocation of, place in his travel books and articles.*

Perhaps because of the extensive travel-writing, James did not address himself to the problems of setting or place in his criticism as much as to other problems. In a comprehensive work like "The Art of Fiction," he appears to have touched on almost every aspect of fiction except setting. But of course there are implications for setting or place in such memorable remarks as— "the air of reality (solidity of specification) seems to me the supreme virtue of a novel"; or, "to 'render' the simplest surface, to produce the most momentary illusion, is a very complicated business"; or, "I cannot imagine composition existing in a series of blocks, nor conceive, in any novel worth discussing at all, of a passage of description that is not in its intention narrative, a passage of dialogue that is not in its intention descriptive."

In the passages of his criticism James did devote to place, he made clear that his touchstone was Balzac. What he said of Balzac in his essay of 1875 can probably be read, with only slight modification, as James's own feelings about the importance of setting in fiction: "The place in which an event occurred was in his view of equal moment with the event itself; it was part of the action; it was not a thing to take or to leave, or to be vaguely and gracefully indicated; it imposed itself; it had a part to play; it needed to be made as definite as anything else."

It is significant that when James wrote his Prefaces reexamining his total production of fiction, and raised questions about his own rendering of place, his mind inevitably went back to Balzac for comparisons and lessons. Although James did not frequently raise the subject, the times that he did demonstrate the crucial importance he clearly placed on the question of choice of setting and the challenges of rendering and evoking it.

See Chapter IX, "Rendering: Execution," for additional comments closely related to setting, especially Part C, "Picture, Preparation, Scene, Drama," and Part D, "Foreshortening; Time-Sequence; Dialogue."

1. the place: part of the action

("Honoré de Balzac," 1875)

This overmastering sense of the present world was of course a superb foundation for the work of a realistic romancer, and it did so much for Balzac that one is puzzled to know where to begin to enumerate the things he owed to it. It gave him in the first place his background—his *mise-en-scène*. This part of his story had with Balzac an importance—his rendering of it a solidity—which it had never enjoyed before, and which the most vigorous talents in the school of which Balzac was founder have never been able to restore to it. The place in which an event occurred was in his view of equal moment with the event itself; it was part of the action; it was not a thing to take or to leave, or to be vaguely and gracefully indicated; it imposed itself; it had a part to play; it needed to be made as definite as anything else. There is accordingly a very much greater amount of description in Balzac than in any other writer, and the description is mainly of towns, houses and rooms. Descriptions of scenery, properly so called, are rare, though when they occur they are often admirable. Almost all of his tales "de la vie de province" are laid in different towns, and a more or less minute portrait of the town is always attempted. How far in these cases Balzac's general pretension to be exact and complete was sustained we are unable to say; we know not what the natives of Limoges, of Saumur, of Angoulême, of Alençon, of Issoudun, of Guérande, thought of his presentation of these localities; but if the picture is not veracious, it is at least always definite and masterly. And Balzac did what he could, we believe, to be exact; he often made a romancer's pilgrimage to a town that he wished to introduce into a story. Here he picked out a certain number of houses to his purpose, lodged the persons of his drama in them, and reproduced them even to their local odours. Many readers find all this very wearisome, and it is certain that it offers one a liberal chance to be bored. We, for our part, have always found Balzac's houses and rooms extremely interesting; we often prefer his places to his people. He was a profound connoisseur in these matters; he had a passion for bric-à-brac, and his tables and chairs are always in character. It must be admitted that in this matter as in every other he has his right and his wrong, and that in his enumerations of inanimate

objects he often sins by extravagance. He has his necessary houses and his
superfluous houses: often when in a story the action is running thin he stops
up your mouth against complaint, as it were, by a dose of brick and mortar.
The power of his memory, his representative vision, as regards these things
is something amazing; the reader never ceases to wonder at the promptness
with which he can "get up" a furnished house—at the immense supply of
this material that he carries about in his mind.

2. *the note of* visibility

(*Letters*, 1893, to R. L. Stevenson)

The one thing I miss in the book [Stevenson's *Catriona*] is the note of
visibility—it subjects my visual sense, my *seeing* imagination, to an almost
painful underfeeding. The *hearing* imagination, as it were, is nourished like
an alderman, and the loud audibility seems a slight the more on the baffled
lust of the eyes—so that I seem to myself (I am speaking of course only from
the point of view of the way, as I read, *my* impression longs to complete
itself) in the presence of voices in the darkness—voices the more distinct
and vivid, the more brave and sonorous, as voices always are—but also the
more tormenting and confounding—by reason of these bandaged eyes. I
utter a pleading moan when you, e.g., transport your characters, toward the
end, in a line or two from Leyden to Dunkirk without the glint of a hint of
all the ambient picture of the 18th century road. However, stick to your own
system of evocation so long as what you positively achieve is so big. Life
and letters and art all take joy in you.

3. *superficiality in doing place*

("Emile Zola," 1903)

He [Zola] was an honest man—he had always bristled with it at every
pore; but no artistic reverse was inconceivable for an adventurer who, stating
in one breath that his knowledge of Italy consisted of a few days spent at
Genoa, was ready to declare in the next that he had planned, on a scale, a
picture of Rome. It flooded his career, to my sense, with light; it showed
how he had marched from subject to subject and had "got up" each in
turn—showing also how consummately he had reduced such getting-up to
an artifice. He had success and a rare impunity behind him, but nothing would
now be so interesting as to see if he could again play the trick. One would
leave him, and welcome, Lourdes and Paris—he had already dealt, on a

scale, with his own country and people. But was the adored Rome also to be his on such terms, the Rome he was already giving away before possessing an inch of it? One thought of one's own frequentations, saturations —a history of long years, and of how the effect of them had somehow been but to make the subject too august. Was *he* to find it easy through a visit of a month or two with "introductions" and a Baedeker?

It was not indeed that the Baedeker and the introductions didn't show, to my sense, at that hour, as extremely suggestive; they were positively a part of the light struck out by his announcement. They defined the system on which he had brought *Les Rougon-Macquart* safely into port. He had had his Baedeker and his introductions for *Germinal*, for *L'Assommoir*, for *L'Argent*, for *La Débâcle*, for *Au bonheur des dames;* which advantages, which researches, had clearly been all the more in character for being documentary, extractive, a matter of *renseignements*, published or private, even when most mixed with personal impressions snatched, with *enquêtes sur les lieux*, with facts obtained from the best authorities, proud and happy to co-operate in so famous a connection. That was, as we say, all right, all the more that the process, to my imagination, became vivid and was wonderfully reflected back from its fruits. There *were* the fruits—so it hadn't been presumptuous. Presumption, however, was now to begin, and what omen mightn't there be in its beginning with such complacency? Well, time would show—as time in due course effectually did. *Rome*, as the second volume of *The Three Cities*, appeared with high punctuality a year or two later; and the interesting question, an occasion really for the moralist, was by that time not to recognize in it the mere triumph of a mechanical art, a "receipt" applied with the skill of long practice, but to do much more than this— that is really to give a name to the particular shade of blindness that could constitute a trap for so great an artistic intelligence. The presumptuous volume, without sweetness, without antecedents, superficial and violent, has the minimum instead of the maximum of *value;* so that it betrayed or "gave away" just in this degree the state of mind on the author's part responsible for its inflated hollowness. To put one's finger on the state of mind was to find out accordingly what was, as we say, the matter with him.

4. on naming place

(Preface to *Roderick Hudson*, 1907)

Pathetic, as we say, on the other hand, no doubt, to reperusal, the manner in which the evocation, so far as attempted, of the small New England town of my first two chapters [of *Roderick Hudson*], fails of intensity—if intensity, in such a connexion, had been indeed to be looked for. *Could* I verily, by the terms of my little plan, have "gone in" for it at the best, and even though one of these terms was the projection, for my fable, at the outset, of some more or less vivid antithesis to a state of civilisation providing for "art"? What I wanted, in essence, was the image of some perfectly humane community which was yet all incapable of providing for it, and I had to take what my scant experience furnished me. I remember feeling meanwhile no drawback in this scantness, but a complete, an exquisite little adequacy, so that the presentation arrived at would quite have served its purpose, I think, had I not misled myself into naming my place. To name a place, in fiction, is to pretend in some degree to represent it—and I speak here of course but of the use of existing names, the only ones that carry weight. I wanted one that carried weight—so at least I supposed; but obviously I was wrong, since my effect lay, so superficially, and could only lie, in the local *type*, as to which I had my handful of impressions. The particular local case was another matter, and I was to see again, after long years, the case into which, all recklessly, the opening passages of "Roderick Hudson" put their foot. I was to have nothing then, on the spot, to sustain me but the rather feeble plea that I had not *pretended* so very much to "do" Northampton, Mass. The plea was charmingly allowed, but nothing could have been more to the point than the way in which, in such a situation, the whole question of the novelist's "doing," with its eternal wealth, or in other words its eternal torment of interest, once more came up. He embarks, rash adventurer, under the star of "representation," and is pledged thereby to remember that the art of interesting us in things—once these things are the right ones for his case—can *only* be the art of representing them. This relation to them, for invoked interest, involves his accordingly "doing"; and it is for him to settle with his intelligence what that variable process shall commit him to.

Its fortune rests primarily, beyond doubt, on somebody's having, under suggestion, a *sense* for it—even the reader will do, on occasion, when the writer, as so often happens, completely falls out. The way in which this sense has been, or has not been, applied constitutes, at all events, in respect to any fiction, the very ground of critical appreciation. Such appreciation takes account, primarily, of the thing, in the case, to have been done, and I now see what, for the first and second chapters of "Roderick," that was. It was a peaceful, rural New England community *quelconque*—it was not, it was under no necessity of being, Northampton, Mass. But one nestled, technically, in those days, and with yearning, in the great shadow of Balzac; his august example, little as the secret might ever be guessed, towered for me over the scene; so that what was clearer than anything else was how, if it was a question of Saumur, of Limoges, of Guérande, he "did" Saumur, did Limoges, did Guérande. I remember how, in my feebler fashion, I yearned over the preliminary presentation of my small square patch of the American scene, and yet was not sufficiently on my guard to see how easily his high practice might be delusive for my case. Balzac talked of Nemours and Provins: therefore why shouldn't one, with fond fatuity, talk of almost the only small American *ville de province* of which one had happened to lay up, long before, a pleased vision? The reason was plain: one was not in the least, in one's prudence, emulating his systematic closeness. It didn't confuse the question either that he would verily, after all, addressed as he was to a due density in his material, have found little enough in Northampton, Mass. to tackle. He tackled no group of appearances, no presented face of the social organism (conspicuity thus attending it), *but* to make something of it. To name it simply and not in some degree tackle it would have seemed to him an act reflecting on his general course the deepest dishonour. Therefore it was that, as the moral of these many remarks, I "named," under his contagion, when I was really most conscious of not being held to it; and therefore it was, above all, that for all the effect of representation I was to achieve, I might have let the occasion pass. A "fancy" indication would have served my turn—except that I should so have failed perhaps of a pretext for my present insistence.

5. rendering surfaces: the penetrating imagination

(Preface to *The Princess Casamassima*, 1908)

I have endeavoured to characterise the peremptory fashion in which my fresh experience of London—the London of the habitual observer, the preoccupied painter, the pedestrian prowler—reminded me; an admonition that represented, I think, the sum of my investigations. I recall pulling no wires, knocking at no closed doors, applying for no "authentic" information; but I recall also on the other hand the practice of never missing an opportunity to add a drop, however small, to the bucket of my impressions or to renew my sense of being able to dip into it. To haunt the great city and by this habit to penetrate it, imaginatively, in as many places as possible— *that* was to be informed, *that* was to pull wires, *that* was to open doors, *that* positively was to groan at times under the weight of one's accumulations.

Face to face with the idea of Hyacinth's subterraneous politics and occult affiliations, I recollect perfectly feeling, in short, that I might well be ashamed if, with my advantages—and there wasn't a street, a corner, an hour, of London that was not an advantage—I shouldn't be able to piece together a proper semblance of those things, as indeed a proper semblance of all the odd parts of his life. There was always of course the chance that the propriety might be challenged—challenged by readers of a knowledge greater than mine. Yet knowledge, after all, of what? My vision of the aspects I more or less fortunately rendered *was*, exactly, my knowledge. If I made my appearances live, what was this but the utmost one could do with them? Let me at the same time not deny that, in answer to probable ironic reflexions on the full license for sketchiness and vagueness and dimness taken indeed by my picture, I had to bethink myself in advance of a defence of my "artistic position." Shouldn't I find it in the happy contention that the value I wished most to render and the effect I wished most to produce were precisely those of our not knowing, of society's not knowing, but only guessing and suspecting and trying to ignore, what "goes on" irreconcileably, subversively, beneath the vast smug surface? I couldn't deal with that positive quantity for itself—my subject had another too exacting side; but I might perhaps show the social ear as on occasion applied to the ground, or catch some gust of the hot breath that I had at many an hour seemed to see escape and hover. What it all came back to was, no doubt, something like *this* wisdom—that if you haven't, for fiction, the root of the matter in you, haven't the sense of life and the penetrating imagination, you are a fool in the very presence of the revealed and assured; but that if you *are* so armed you are not really helpless, not without your resource, even before mysteries abysmal.

6. the platitudes of place: Paris

(Preface to *The Ambassadors*, 1909)

There was the dreadful little old tradition, one of the platitudes of the human comedy, that people's moral scheme *does* break down in Paris; that nothing is more frequently observed; that hundreds of thousands of more or less hypocritical or more or less cynical persons annually visit the place for the sake of the probable catastrophe, and that I came late in the day to work myself up about it. There was in fine the *trivial* association, one of the vulgarest in the world; but which gave me pause no longer, I think, simply because its vulgarity is so advertised. The revolution performed by Strether [in *The Ambassadors*] under the influence of the most interesting of great cities was to have nothing to do with any *bêtise* of the imputably "tempted" state; he was to be thrown forward, rather, thrown quite with violence, upon his lifelong trick of intense reflexion: which friendly test indeed was to bring him out, through winding passages, through alternations of darkness and light, very much *in* Paris, but with the surrounding scene itself a minor matter, a mere symbol for more things than had been dreamt of in the philosophy of Woollett. Another surrounding scene would have done as well for our show could it have represented a place in which Strether's errand was likely to lie and his crisis to await him. The *likely* place had the great merit of sparing me preparations; there would have been too many involved—not at all impossibilities, only rather worrying and delaying difficulties—in positing elsewhere Chad Newsome's interesting relation, his so interesting complexity of relations.

Chapter XII

POINT OF VIEW

Just as James may be given generous credit for the modern novel's central focus on psychological states, actions, and plots, so too he may be given major credit for the modern fictional critic's concern for point of view. No one before him spoke so extensively and lucidly on the need for a "mirroring consciousness" (or series of consciousnesses) and few writers since have explored the complex questions of "reflectors" or "registers" so deeply.

At the outset it is important to note some of James's important distinctions. He spoke often of the importance of finding a subject's center; and, moreover, he located that center often in the dramatization of a consciousness—see, for example, his discussions of Roderick Hudson *("centre of interest as drama of consciousness") and of* The Portrait of a Lady *("centre of subject: a single consciousness") in Chapter VIII. This idea of a "drama of consciousness" is more closely related to plot (for which it substitutes in interest) than to point of view, though it is quite likely that James gradually developed his interest in point of view from his discovery of the dramatic possibilities of an unfolding consciousness.*

It is also likely that James's interest in point of view goes back to his early realization that actions by themselves are generally of limited interest; they become interesting only when they are reflected in an engaged consciousness (see, for example, his discussions of the "ghost-stories: direct presentation vs. impact on a consciousness" in Chapter V); and conversely, his belief that "the figures in any picture, the agents in any drama, are interesting only in proportion as they feel their respective situations" (see "necessity of a fine consciousness as mirror," below). Whatever the sources of his interest, James clearly devoted major attention to the selection of the right reflector (or reflectors) whenever he set about writing a story. See his Notebooks *for scattered and recurrent comments on the problem of point of view in the individual cases of his own work.*

The passages in this chapter, with one exception (mentioned below), all come from James's Prefaces, and catch him in a series of moments of reflection and assessment; indeed, the passages gathered together seem to present a continuity on the subject of point of view that James appears to have planned. The first passage is an extended commentary (from the Pref-

234

ace to The Princess Casamassima) *and seems introductory in character. In it James writes: "The great chroniclers have . . . at least always either placed a mind of some sort—in the sense of a reflecting and colouring medium —in possession of the general adventure . . . or else paid signally, as to the interest created, for their failure to do so."*

Selections that follow deal with such special problems as the "lapse from artistic integrity" involved in violation of an established point of view (James here cites himself as an example) and the limitations imposed by the adoption of a child's consciousness as the primary reflector. And the passages build to something of a climax in James's comments on his three great novels of his "major phase," presenting in succession astute observations on fictions with successive reflecting centers (The Wings of the Dove), with a single center (The Ambassadors), and with a pair of reciprocal centers (The Golden Bowl).

The concluding passage in this chapter comes from an essay, "The New Novel," written in 1914, near the end of James's career, and is devoted to an examination of Joseph Conrad's Chance—a novel fantastically complex in its point of view, presenting, as it does, reflectors within reflectors within reflectors . . . . This passage is included to suggest something of what James's interest might have been in the genuinely new novel that came into being after his death—the novel of James Joyce, Virginia Woolf, Ernest Hemingway, and William Faulkner. Clearly he would have taken great delight in all the experimentation, and he would have recognized the impact of his own theory and practice, especially in such elements of technique as point of view. In writers like Joyce he would have detected a reflection of his own interest in dramatization of the human (or a human) consciousness; in writers like Hemingway, he would have discovered his own fascination with the possibilities of the purely dramatic and objective.

1. *necessity of a fine consciousness as mirror: intelligence, bewilderment, fools*

(Preface to *The Princess Casamassima*, 1908)

This in fact I have ever found rather terribly the point—that the figures in any picture, the agents in any drama, are interesting only in proportion as they feel their respective situations; since the consciousness, on their part, of the complication exhibited forms for us their link of connexion with it. But there are degrees of feeling—the muffled, the faint, the just sufficient, the barely intelligent, as we may say; and the acute, the intense, the complete, in a word—the power to be finely aware and richly responsible. It is those moved in this latter fashion who "get most" out of all that happens to them and who in so doing enable us, as readers of their record, as participators by a fond attention, also to get most. Their being finely aware—as Hamlet and

Lear, say, are finely aware—*makes* absolutely the intensity of their adventure, gives the maximum of sense to what befalls them. We care, our curiosity and our sympathy care, comparatively little for what happens to the stupid, the coarse and the blind; care for it, and for the effects of it, at the most as helping to precipitate what happens to the more deeply wondering, to the really sentient. Hamlet and Lear are surrounded, amid their complications, by the stupid and the blind, who minister in all sorts of ways to their recorded fate. Persons of markedly limited sense would, on such a principle as that, play a part in the career of my tormented youth [Hyacinth Robinson in *The Princess Casamassima*]; but he wouldn't be of markedly limited sense himself—he would note as many things and vibrate to as many occasions as I might venture to make him.

There wouldn't moreover simply be the question of his suffering—of which we might soon get enough; there would be the question of what, all beset and all perceptive, he should thus adventurously do, thus dream and hazard and attempt. The interest of the attitude and the act would be the actor's imagination and vision of them, together with the nature and degree of their felt return upon him. So the intelligent creature would be required and so some picture of his intelligence involved. The picture of an intelligence appears for the most part, it is true, a dead weight for the reader of the English novel to carry, this reader having so often the wondrous property of caring for the displayed tangle of human relations without caring for its intelligibility. The teller of a story is primarily, none the less, the listener to it, the reader of it, too; and, having needed thus to make it out, distinctly, on the crabbed page of life, to disengage it from the rude human character and the more or less Gothic text in which it has been packed away, the very essence of his affair has been the *imputing* of intelligence. The basis of his attention has been that such and such an imbroglio has got started—on the page of life—because of something that some one has felt and more or less understood

I recognise at the same time, and in planning "The Princess Casamassima" felt it highly important to recognise, the danger of filling too full any supposed and above all any obviously limited vessel of consciousness. If persons either tragically or comically embroiled with life allow us the comic or tragic value of their embroilment in proportion as their struggle is a measured and directed one, it is strangely true, none the less, that beyond a certain point they are spoiled for us by this carrying of a due light. They may carry too much of it for our credence, for our compassion, for our derision. They may be shown as knowing too much and feeling too much—not certainly for their remaining remarkable, but for their remaining "natural" and typical, for their having the needful communities with our own precious liability to fall into traps and be bewildered. It seems probable that if we were never bewildered there would never be a story to tell about us; we should partake of the superior nature of the all-knowing immortals whose annals are dreadfully dull so long as flurried humans are not, for the positive relief of bored Olympians, mixed up with them. Therefore it is that the wary reader for the most part warns the novelist against making his characters too *interpretative* of the muddle of fate, or in other words too divinely, too priggishly clever. "Give us plenty of bewilderment," this monitor seems to say, "so long as there is plenty of slashing out in the bewilderment too. But don't, we beseech you, give us too much intelligence; for intelligence—well, *endangers; endangers* not perhaps the slasher himself, but the very slashing, the subject-matter of any self-respecting story. It opens up too many considerations, possibilities, issues; it *may* lead the slasher into dreary realms where slashing somehow fails and falls to the ground."

That is well reasoned on the part of the reader, who can in spite of it never have an idea—or his earnest discriminations would come to him less easily—of the extreme difficulty, for the painter of the human mixture, of reproducing that mixture aright. "Give us in the persons represented, the subjects of the bewilderment (that bewilderment without which there would be no question of an issue or of the fact of suspense, prime implications in any story) as much experience as possible, but keep down the terms in which you report that experience, because we only understand the very simplest": such in effect are the words in which the novelist constantly hears himself addressed, such the plea made him by the would-be victims of his spell on behalf of that sovereign principle the economy of interest, a principle as to which their instinct is justly strong. He listens anxiously to the charge —nothing can exceed his own solicitude for an economy of interest; but feels himself all in presence of an abyss of ambiguities, the mutual accommodations in which the reader wholly leaves to him. Experience, as I see it, is our apprehension and our measure of what happens to us as social creatures— any intelligent report of which has to be based on that apprehension. The picture of the exposed and entangled state is what is required, and there are certainly always plenty of grounds for keeping down the complexities of a picture. A picture it still has to be, however, and by that condition has to deal effectually with its subject, so that the simple device of more and more keeping down may well not see us quite to our end or even quite to our middle. One suggested way of keeping down, for instance, is not to attribute feeling, or feelings, to persons who wouldn't in all probability have had any to speak of. The less space, within the frame of the picture, their feelings take up the more space is left for their doings—a fact that may at first seem to make for a refinement of economy.

All of which is charming—yet would be infinitely more so if here at once ambiguity didn't yawn; the unreality of the sharp distinction, where the interest of observation is at stake, between doing and feeling. In the immediate field of life, for action, for application, for getting through a job,

nothing may so much matter perhaps as the descent of a suspended weight
on this, that or the other spot, with all its subjective concomitants quite
secondary and irrelevant. But the affair of the painter is not the immediate,
it is the reflected field of life, the realm not of application, but of *appreciation*
—a truth that makes our measure of effect altogether different. My report
of people's experience—my report as a "story-teller"—is essentially my
appreciation of it, and there is no "interest" for me in what my hero,
my heroine or any one else does save through that admirable process. As
soon as I begin to appreciate simplification is imperilled: the sharply distinguished parts of any adventure, any case of endurance and performance, melt
together as an appeal. I then see their "doing," that of the persons just
mentioned, as, immensely, their feeling, their feeling as their doing; since I
can have none of the conveyed sense and taste of their situation without
becoming intimate with them. I can't be intimate without that sense
and taste, and I can't appreciate save by intimacy, any more than I can report
save by a projected light. Intimacy with a man's specific behaviour, with
his given case, is desperately certain to make us see it as a whole—in which
event arbitrary limitations of our vision lose whatever beauty they may on
occasion have pretended to. What a man thinks and what he feels are the
history and the character of what he does; on all of which things the logic
of intensity rests. Without intensity where is vividness, and without vividness
where is presentability? If I have called the most general state of one's most
exposed and assaulted figures the state of bewilderment—the condition for
instance on which Thackeray so much insists in the interest of *his* exhibited
careers, the condition of a humble heart, a bowed head, a patient wonder, a
suspended judgement, before the "awful will" and the mysterious decrees of
Providence—so it is rather witless to talk of merely getting rid of that displayed mode of reaction, one of the oft-encountered, one of the highly recommended, categories of feeling.

The whole thing comes to depend thus on the *quality* of bewilderment
characteristic of one's creature, the quality involved in the given case or
supplied by one's data. There are doubtless many such qualities, ranging from
vague and crepuscular to sharpest and most critical; and we have but
to imagine one of these latter to see how easily—from the moment it gets
its head at all—it may insist on playing a part. There we have then at once
a case of feeling, of ever so many possible feelings, stretched across the scene
like an attached thread on which the pearls of interest are strung. There are
threads shorter and less tense, and I am far from implying that the minor,
the coarser and less fruitful forms and degrees of moral reaction, as we may
conveniently call it, may not yield lively results. They have their subordinate,
comparative, illustrative human value—that appeal of the witless which
is often so penetrating. Verily even, I think, no "story" is possible without
its fools—as most of the fine painters of life, Shakespeare, Cervantes and

Balzac, Fielding, Scott, Thackeray, Dickens, George Meredith, George Eliot, Jane Austen, have abundantly felt. At the same time I confess I never see the *leading* interest of any human hazard but in a consciousness (on the part of the moved and moving creature) subject to fine intensification and wide enlargement. It is as mirrored in that consciousness that the gross fools, the headlong fools, the fatal fools play their part for us—they have much less to show us in themselves. The troubled life mostly at the centre of our subject—whatever our subject, for the artistic hour, happens to be— embraces them and deals with them for its amusement and its anguish: they are apt largely indeed, on a near view, to be all the cause of its trouble. This means, exactly, that the person capable of feeling in the given case more than another of what is to be felt for it, and so serving in the highest degree to *record* it dramatically and objectively, is the only sort of person on whom we can count not to betray, to cheapen or, as we say, give away, the value and beauty of the thing. By so much as the affair matters *for* some such individual, by so much do we get the best there is of it, and by so much as it falls within the scope of a denser and duller, a more vulgar and more shallow capacity, do we get a picture dim and meagre.

The great chroniclers have clearly always been aware of this; they have at least always either placed a mind of some sort—in the sense of a reflecting and colouring medium—in possession of the general adventure (when the latter has not been purely epic, as with Scott, say, as with old Dumas and with Zola); or else paid signally, as to the interest created, for their failure to do so. We may note moreover in passing that this failure is in almost no case intentional or part of a plan, but has sprung from their limited curiosity, their short conception of the particular sensibility projected. Edgar of Ravenswood for instance, visited by the tragic tempest of "The Bride of Lammermoor," has a black cloak and hat and feathers more than he has a mind; just as Hamlet, while equally sabled and draped and plumed, while at least equally romantic, has yet a mind still more than he has a costume. The situation represented is that Ravenswood loves Lucy Ashton through dire difficulty and danger, and that she in the same way loves him; but the relation so created between them is by this neglect of the "feeling" question never shown us as primarily taking place. It is shown only in its secondary, its confused and disfigured aspects—where, however, luckily, it is presented with great romantic good faith. The thing has nevertheless paid for its deviation, as I say, by a sacrifice of intensity; the centre of the subject is empty and the development pushed off, all round, toward the frame— which is, so to speak, beautifully rich and curious. But I mention that relation to each other of the appearances in a particular work only as a striking negative case; there are in the connexion I have glanced at plenty of striking positive ones. It is very true that Fielding's hero in "Tom Jones" is but as "finely," that is but as intimately, bewildered as a young man of great health and spirits may be when he hasn't a grain of imagination: the point to be made is, at all events, that his sense of bewilderment obtains altogether on the comic, never on the tragic plane. He has so much "life" that it amounts, for the effect of comedy and application of satire, almost to his having a mind, that is to his having reactions and a full consciousness; besides which his author—*he* handsomely possessed of a mind—has such an amplitude of reflexion for him and round him that we see him through the mellow air of Fielding's fine old moralism, fine old humour and fine old style, which somehow really enlarge, make every one and every thing important.

2. *polished . . . mirrors of the subject*

(Preface to *The Princess Casamassima*, 1908)

I have for example a weakness of sympathy with that constant effort of George Eliot's which plays through Adam Bede and Felix Holt and Tito Melema, through Daniel Deronda and through Lydgate, in "Middlemarch," through Maggie Tulliver, through Romola, through Dorothea Brooke and Gwendolen Harleth; the effort to show their adventures and their history— the author's subject-matter all—as determined by their feelings and the nature of their minds. Their emotions, their stirred intelligence, their moral consciousness, become thus, by sufficiently charmed perusal, our own very adventure. The creator of Deronda and of Romola is charged, I know, with having on occasion—as in dealing with those very celebrities themselves —left the figure, the concrete man and woman, too abstract by reason of the quantity of soul employed; but such mischances, where imagination and humour still keep them company, often have an interest that is wanting to agitations of the mere surface or to those that may be only taken for granted. I should even like to give myself the pleasure of retracing from one of my own productions to another the play of a like instinctive disposition, of catching in the fact, at one point after another, from "Roderick Hudson" to "The Golden Bowl," that provision for interest which consists in placing advantageously, placing right in the middle of the light, the most polished of possible mirrors of the subject. Rowland Mallet, in "Roderick Hudson," is exactly such a mirror, not a bit autobiographic or formally "first person" though he be, and I might exemplify the case through a long list, through the nature of such a "mind" even as the all-objective Newman in "The American," through the thickly-peopled imagination of Isabel Archer in "The Portrait of a Lady" (her imagination positively the deepest depth of her imbroglio) down to such unmistakeable examples as that of Merton Densher in "The Wings of the Dove," that of Lambert Strether in "The Ambassadors" (*he* a mirror verily of miraculous silver and quite pre-eminent,

I think, for the connexion) and that of the Prince in the first half and that
of the Princess in the second half of "The Golden Bowl." I should note
the extent to which these persons are, so far as their other passions permit,
intense *perceivers*, all, of their respective predicaments, and I should go on
from them to fifty other examples; even to the divided Vanderbank of
"The Awkward Age," the extreme pinch of whose romance is the vivacity
in him, to his positive sorrow and loss, of the state of being aware; even to
scanted Fleda Vetch in "The Spoils of Poynton," through whose own delicate vision of everything so little of the human value of her situation is
wasted for us; even to the small recording governess confronted with the
horrors of "The Turn of the Screw" and to the innocent child patching
together all ineffectually those of "What Maisie Knew"; even in short, since
I may name so few cases, to the disaffected guardian of an overgrown
legend in "The Birthplace," to the luckless fine artist of "The Next Time,"
trying to despoil himself, for a "hit" and bread and butter, of his fatal fineness, to blunt the tips of his intellectual fingers, and to the hapless butler
Brooksmith, ruined by good talk, disqualified for common domestic service
by the beautiful growth of his habit of quiet attention, his faculty of appreciation. But though this demonstration of a rooted vice—since a vice it
would appear mainly accounted—might yield amusement, the examples
referred to must await their turn.

   I had had for a long time well before me, at any rate, my small obscure
but ardent observer of the "London world," saw him roam and wonder
and yearn, saw all the unanswered questions and baffled passions that might
ferment in him—once he should be made both sufficiently thoughtful and
sufficiently "disinherited"; but this image, however interesting, was of
course not by itself a progression, an action, didn't by itself make a drama.
I got my action however—failing which one has nothing—under the prompt
sense that the state of feeling I was concerned with might develop and
beget another state, might return at a given moment, and with the greatest
vivacity, on itself. To see this was really to feel one's subject swim into one's
ken, especially after a certain other ingenious connexion had been made
for it. I find myself again recalling, and with the possible "fun" of it reviving
too, how I recognised, as revealed and prescribed, the particular complexion,
profession and other conditions of my little presumptuous adventurer, with
his combination of intrinsic fineness and fortuitous adversity, his small cluster
of "dingy" London associations and the swelling spirit in him which was
to be the field of his strange experience. Accessible through his imagination,
as I have hinted, to a thousand provocations and intimations, he would
become most acquainted with destiny in the form of a lively inward revolution. His being jealous of all the ease of life of which he tastes so little,
and, bitten, under this exasperation, with an aggressive, vindictive, destruc-
tive social faith, his turning to "treasons, stratagems and spoils" might be

as vivid a picture as one chose, but would move to pity and terror only by the aid of some deeper complication, some imposed and formidable issue.

The complication most interesting then would be that he should fall in love with the beauty of the world, actual order and all, at the moment of his most feeling and most hating the famous "iniquity of its social arrangements"; so that his position as an irreconcileable pledged enemy to it, thus rendered false by something more personal than his opinions and his vows, becomes the sharpest of his torments. To make it a torment that really matters, however, he must have got practically involved, specifically committed to the stand he has, under the pressure of more knowledge, found impossible; out of which has come for him the deep dilemma of the disillusioned repentant conspirator. He has thrown himself into the more than "shady" underworld of militant socialism, he has undertaken to play a part—a part that with the drop of his exasperation and the growth, simply expressed, of his taste, is out of all tune with his passion, at any cost, for life itself, the life, whatever it be, that surrounds him. Dabbling deeply in revolutionary politics of a hole-and-corner sort, he would be "in" up to his neck, and with that precarious part of him particularly involved, so that his tergiversation is the climax of his adventure. What was essential with this was that he should have a social—not less than a socialist—connexion, find a door somehow open to him into the appeased and civilised state, into that warmer glow of things he is precisely to help to undermine. To look for this necessary connexion was for me to meet it suddenly in the form of that extremely *disponible* figure of Christina Light whom I had ten years before found left on my hands at the conclusion of "Roderick Hudson." She had for so long, in the vague limbo of those ghosts we have conjured but not exorcised, been looking for a situation, awaiting a niche and a function.

3. dense medium as centre: the scenic condition

(Preface to *The Tragic Muse*, 1908)

These are intimate truths indeed, of which the charm mainly comes out but on experiment and in practice; yet I like to have it well before me here that, after all, "The Tragic Muse" makes it not easy to say which of the situations concerned in it predominates and rules. What has become in that imperfect order, accordingly, of the famous centre of one's subject? It is surely not in Nick's consciousness—since why, if it be, are we treated to such an intolerable dose of Sherringham's? It can't be in Sherringham's— we have for that altogether an excess of Nick's. How on the other hand can it be in Miriam's, given that we have no direct exhibition of hers whatever, that we get at it all inferentially and inductively, seeing it only through

a more or less bewildered interpretation of it by others. The emphasis is
all on an absolutely objective Miriam, and, this affirmed, how—with such
an amount of exposed subjectivity all round her—can so dense a medium
be a centre? Such questions as those go straight—thanks to which they are,
I profess, delightful; going straight they are of the sort that makes answers
possible. Miriam *is* central then to analysis, in spite of being objective;
central in virtue of the fact that the whole thing has visibly, from the first,
to get itself done in dramatic, or at least in scenic conditions—though scenic
conditions which are as near an approach to the dramatic as the novel may
permit itself and which have this in common with the latter, that they move
in the light of *alternation*. This imposes a consistency other than that of
the novel at its loosest, and, for one's subject, a different view and a different
placing of the centre. The charm of the scenic consistency, the consistency
of the multiplication of *aspects*, that of making them amusingly various,
had haunted the author of "The Tragic Muse" from far back, and he was
in due course to yield to it all luxuriously, too luxuriously perhaps, in "The
Awkward Age," as will doubtless with the extension of these remarks be
complacently shown.

To put himself at any rate as much as possible under the protection of it
had been ever his practice (he had notably done so in "The Princess Casamassima," so frankly panoramic and processional); and in what case could this
protection have had more price than in the one before us? No character
in a play (any play not a mere monologue) has, for the right expression of
the thing, a *usurping* consciousness; the consciousness of others is exhibited
exactly in the same way as that of the "hero"; the prodigious consciousness
of Hamlet, the most capacious and most crowded, the moral presence the
most asserted, in the whole range of fiction, only takes its turn with that of
the other agents of the story, no matter how occasional these may be. It is
left in other words to answer for itself equally with theirs: wherefore (by a
parity of reasoning if not of example) Miriam's might without inconsequence be placed on the same footing; and all in spite of the fact that the
"moral presence" of each of the men most importantly concerned with
her—or with the second of whom she at least is importantly concerned—
is independently answered for. The idea of the book being, as I have said,
a picture of some of the personal consequences of the art-appetite raised to
intensity, swollen to voracity, the heavy emphasis falls where the symbol
of some of the complications so begotten might be made (as I judged,
heaven forgive me!) most "amusing": amusing I mean in the blest very
modern sense. I never "go behind" Miriam; only poor Sherringham goes,
a great deal, and Nick Dormer goes a little, and the author, while they so
waste wonderment, goes behind *them:* but none the less she is as thoroughly
symbolic, as functional, for illustration of the idea, as either of them, while
her image had seemed susceptible of a livelier and "prettier" concretion. I

had desired for her, I remember, all manageable vividness—so ineluctable had it long appeared to "do the actress," to touch the theatre, to meet that connexion somehow or other, in any free plunge of the speculative fork into the contemporary social salad.

4. a lapse from artistic integrity

(Preface to *The Spoils of Poynton*, 1908)

In spite of all of which, I may add, I do penance here only for the awkwardness of that departure from the adopted form of my recital ["A London Life"] which resides in the picture of the interview with young Wendover contrived by Lady Davenant in the interest of some better provision for their poor young friend. Here indeed is a lapse from artistic dignity, a confession of want of resource, which I may not pretend to explain to-day, and on behalf of which I have nothing to urge save a consciousness of my dereliction presumably too vague at the time. [That is, in "A London Life" James established a central consciousness in Laura Wing and then presented one important scene directly, outside the presence of that consciousness.] I had seen my elements presented in a certain way, settled the little law under which my story was to be told, and with this consistency, as any reader of the tale may easily make out for himself, interviews to which my central figure was not a party, scenes revolving on an improvised pivot of their own, had nothing to do with the affair. I might of course have adopted another plan—the artist is free, surely, to adopt any he fancies, provided it *be* a plan and he adopt it intelligently; and to that scheme of composition the independent picture of a passage between Lady Davenant and young Wendover might perfectly have conformed. As the case stands it conforms to nothing; whereas the beauty of a thing of this order really done as a whole is ever, certainly, that its parts are in abject dependence, and that even any great charm they may individually and capriciously put forth is infirm so far as it doesn't measurably contribute to a harmony. My momentary helplessness sprang, no doubt, from my failure to devise in time some way of giving the value of Lady Davenant's appeal to the young man, of making it play its part in my heroine's history and consciousness, without so awkwardly thrusting the lump sum on the reader.

Circumventions of difficulty of this degree are precisely the finest privilege of the craftsman, who, to be worth his salt, and master of *any* contrived harmony, must take no tough technical problem for insoluble. These technical subterfuges and subtleties, these indirectly-expressed values, kept indirect in a higher interest, made subordinate to some general beauty, some artistic intention that can give an account of itself, what are they after all but one of the nobler parts of our amusement? Superficially, in "A London Life," it might well have seemed that the only way to picture the intervention on Laura Wing's behalf of the couple just named was to break the chain of the girl's own consciousness and report the matter quite straight and quite shamelessly; this course had indeed every merit but that of its playing the particular game to which I had addressed myself. My prime loyalty was to the interest of the game, and the honour to be won the more desirable by that fact. Any muddle-headed designer can beg the question of perspective, but science is required for making it rule the scene. If it be asked how then we were to have assisted at the copious passage I thus incriminate without our privilege of presence, I can only say that my discovery of the right way should—and would—have been the very flower of the performance. The real "fun" of the thing would have been exactly to sacrifice my comparative platitude of statement—a deplorable depth at any time, I have attempted elsewhere to signify, for any pretending master of representation to sink to —without sacrificing a grain of what was to be conveyed. The real fun, in other words, would have been in not, by an exceptional collapse of other ingenuity, making my attack on the spectator's consciousness a call as immediate as a postman's knock. This attack, at every other point, reaches that objective only through the medium of the interesting girl's own vision, own experience, with which all the facts are richly charged and coloured. That saturates our sense of them with the savour of Laura's sense—thanks to which enhancement we get intensity. But from the chapter to which I have called attention, so that it may serve perhaps as a lesson, intensity ruefully drops. I can't say worse for it—and have been the more concerned to say what I do that without this flaw the execution might have appeared from beginning to end close and exemplary.

5. children as reflectors

(Preface to What Maisie Knew, 1908)

I recall that my first view of this neat possibility was as the attaching problem of the picture restricted (while yet achieving, as I say, completeness and coherency) to what the child might be conceived to have understood— to have been able to interpret and appreciate. Further reflexion and experiment showed me my subject strangled in that extreme of rigour. The infant mind would at the best leave great gaps and voids; so that with a systematic surface possibly beyond reproach we should nevertheless fail of clearness of sense. I should have to stretch the matter to what my wondering witness materially and inevitably saw; a great deal of which quantity she either wouldn't understand at all or would quite misunderstand—and on those

246 THEORY OF FICTION: HENRY JAMES

lines, only on those, my task would be prettily cut out. To that then I settled
—to the question of giving it *all*, the whole situation surrounding her, but of
giving it only through the occasions and connexions of her proximity and
her attention; only as it might pass before her and appeal to her, as it might
touch her and affect her, for better or worse, for perceptive gain or perceptive loss: so that we fellow witnesses, we not more invited but only more
expert critics, should feel in strong possession of it. This would be, to begin
with, a plan of absolutely definite and measurable application—that in
itself always a mark of beauty; and I have been interested to find on re-perusal
of the work that some such controlling grace successfully rules it. Nothing
could be more "done," I think, in the light of its happiest intention; and
this in spite of an appearance that at moments obscures my consistency. Small
children have many more perceptions than they have terms to translate
them; their vision is at any moment much richer, their apprehension even
constantly stronger, than their prompt, their at all producible, vocabulary.
Amusing therefore as it might at the first blush have seemed to restrict myself in this case to the terms as well as to the experience, it became at once
plain that such an attempt would fail. Maisie's terms accordingly play their
part—since her simpler conclusions quite depend on them; but our own commentary constantly attends and amplifies. This it is that on occasion, doubtless, seems to represent us as going so "behind" the facts of her spectacle as
to exaggerate the activity of her relation to them. The difference here is but
of a shade: it is her relation, her activity of spirit, that determines all our
own concern—we simply take advantage of these things better than she
herself. Only, even though it is her interest that mainly makes matters
interesting for us, we inevitably note this in figures that are not yet at her
command and that are nevertheless required whenever those aspects about
her and those parts of her experience that she understands darken off into
others that she rather tormentedly misses. All of which gave me a high firm
logic to observe; supplied the force for which the straightener of almost any
tangle is grateful while he labours, the sense of pulling at threads intrinsically worth it—strong enough and fine enough and entire enough.

6. *successive centres as reflectors*

(Preface to *The Wings of the Dove*, 1909)

There was the "fun," to begin with, of establishing one's successive centres
—of fixing them so exactly that the portions of the subject commanded by
them as by happy points of view, and accordingly treated from them, would
constitute, so to speak, sufficiently solid *blocks* of wrought material, squared
to the sharp edge, as to have weight and mass and carrying power; to make

for construction, that is, to conduce to effect and to provide for beauty. . . .

. . . From the moment we proceed by "centres"—and I have never, I confess, embraced the logic of any superior process—they must *be*, each, as a basis, selected and fixed; after which it is that, in the high interest of economy of treatment, they determine and rule. There is no economy of treatment without an adopted, a related point of view, and though I understand, under certain degrees of pressure, a represented community of vision between several parties to the action when it makes for concentration, I understand no breaking-up of the register, no sacrifice of the recording consistency, that doesn't rather scatter and weaken. In this truth resides the secret of the discriminated occasion—that aspect of the subject which we have our noted choice of treating either as picture or scenically, but which is apt, I think, to show its fullest worth in the Scene. Beautiful exceedingly, for that matter, those occasions or parts of an occasion when the boundary line between picture and scene bears a little the weight of the double pressure. . . .

. . . My registers or "reflectors," as I so conveniently name them (burnished indeed as they generally are by the intelligence, the curiosity, the passion, the force of the moment, whatever it be, directing them), work, as we have seen, in arranged alternation.

7. one centre: economy, unity, intensity

(Preface to *The Ambassadors*, 1909)

"The Ambassadors" had been, all conveniently, "arranged for"; its first appearance was from month to month, in "The North American Review" during 1903, and I had been open from far back to any pleasant provocation for ingenuity that might reside in one's actively adopting—so as to make it, in its way, a small compositional law—recurrent breaks and resumptions. I had made up my mind here regularly to exploit and enjoy these often rather rude jolts—having found, as I believed, an admirable way to it; yet every question of form and pressure, I easily remember, paled in the light of the major propriety, recognised as soon as really weighed; that of employing but one centre and keeping it all within my hero's compass. The thing was to be so much this worthy's intimate adventure that even the projection of his consciousness upon it from beginning to end without intermission or deviation would probably still leave a part of its value for him, and *a fortiori* for ourselves, unexpressed. I might, however, express every grain of it that there would be room for—on condition of contriving a splendid particular economy. Other persons in no small number were to people the scene, and each with his or her axe to grind, his or her situation to treat, his or her coherency not to fail of, his or her relation to my leading motive, in a word, to establish and carry on. But Strether's sense of these things, and Strether's only, should avail me for showing them; I should know them but through his more or less groping knowledge of them, since his very gropings would figure among his most interesting motions, and a full observance of the rich rigour I speak of would give me more of the effect I should be most "after" than all other possible observances together. It would give me a large unity, and that in turn would crown me with the grace to which the enlightened story-teller will at any time, for his interest, sacrifice if need be all other graces whatever. I refer of course to the grace of intensity, which there are ways of signally achieving and ways of signally missing—as we see it, all round us, helplessly and woefully missed. Not that it isn't, on the other hand, a virtue eminently subject to appreciation—there being no strict, no absolute measure of it; so that one may hear it acclaimed where it has quite escaped one's perception, and see it unnoticed where one has gratefully hailed it. After all of which I am not sure, either, that the immense amusement of the whole cluster of difficulties so arrayed may not operate, for the fond fabulist, when judicious not less than fond, as his best of determinants. That charming principle is always there, at all events, to keep interest fresh: it is a principle, we remember, essentially ravenous, without scruple and without mercy, appeased with no cheap nor easy nourishment. It enjoys the costly sacrifice and rejoices thereby in the very odour of difficulty—even as ogres, with their "Fee-faw-fum!" rejoice in the smell of the blood of Englishmen.

8. *sticking so close to my central figure*

(Preface to *The Ambassadors*, 1909)

All of which reflexions flocked to the standard from the moment—a very early one—the question of how to keep my form amusing while sticking so close to my central figure and constantly taking its pattern from him had to be faced. He arrives (arrives at Chester) as for the dreadful purpose of giving his creator "no end" to tell about him—before which rigorous mission the serenest of creators might well have quailed. I was far from the serenest; I was more than agitated enough to reflect that, grimly deprived of one alternative or one substitute for "telling," I must address myself tooth and nail to another. I couldn't, save by implication, make other persons tell *each other* about him—blest resource, blest necessity, of the drama, which reaches its effects of unity, all remarkably, by paths absolutely opposite to the paths of the novel: with other persons, save as they were primarily *his* persons (not he primarily but one of theirs), I had simply nothing to do. I had relations for him none the less, by the mercy of Providence, quite as

much as if my exhibition *was* to be a muddle; if I could only by implication
and a show of consequence make other persons tell each other about him, I
could at least make him tell *them* whatever in the world he must; and could
so, by the same token—which was a further luxury thrown in—see straight
into the deep differences between what that could do for me, or at all events
for *him*, and the large ease of "autobiography."

9. *first-person narration*

(Preface to *The Ambassadors*, 1909)

Had I meanwhile, made him at once hero and historian, endowed him with
the romantic privilege of the "first person"—the darkest abyss of romance
this, inveterately, when enjoyed on the grand scale—variety, and many other
queer matters as well, might have been smuggled in by a back door. Suffice
it, to be brief, that the first person, in the long piece, is a form foredoomed
to looseness, and that looseness, never much my affair, had never been so
little so as on this particular occasion. . . . It may be asked why, if one so
keeps to one's hero, one shouldn't make a single mouthful of "method,"
shouldn't throw the reins on his neck and, letting them flap there as free as
in "Gil Blas" or in "David Copperfield," equip him with the double privilege of subject and object—a course that has at least the merit of brushing
away questions at a sweep. The answer to which is, I think, that one makes
that surrender only if one is prepared *not* to make certain precious discriminations.

The "first person" then, so employed, is addressed by the author directly
to ourselves, his possible readers, whom he has to reckon with, at the best,
by our English tradition, so loosely and vaguely after all, so little respect-
fully, on so scant a presumption of exposure to criticism. Strether, on the
other hand, encaged and provided for as "The Ambassadors" encages and
provides, has to keep in view proprieties much stiffer and more salutary than
any our straight and credulous gape are likely to bring home to him, has
exhibitional conditions to meet, in a word, that forbid the terrible *fluidity*
of self-revelation.

10. *two registers in two halves*

(Preface to *The Golden Bowl*, 1909)

Among many matters thrown into relief by a refreshed acquaintance with
"The Golden Bowl" what perhaps most stands out for me is the still marked

inveteracy of a certain indirect and oblique view of my presented action;
unless indeed I make up my mind to call this mode of treatment, on the
contrary, any superficial appearance notwithstanding, the very straightest
and closest possible. I have already betrayed, as an accepted habit, and even
to extravagance commented on, my preference for dealing with my subject-
matter, for "seeing my story," through the opportunity and the sensibility
of some more or less detached, some not strictly involved, though thoroughly interested and intelligent, witness or reporter, some person who contributes to the case mainly a certain amount of criticism and interpretation
of it. Again and again, on review, the shorter things in especial that I have
gathered into this Series have ranged themselves not as my own impersonal
account of the affair in hand, but as my account of somebody's impression
of it—the terms of this person's access to it and estimate of it contributing
thus by some fine little law to intensification of interest. The somebody is
often, among my shorter tales I recognise, but an unnamed, unintroduced
and (save by right of intrinsic wit) unwarranted participant, the impersonal
author's concrete deputy or delegate, a convenient substitute or apologist for
the creative power otherwise so veiled and disembodied. My instinct appears
repeatedly to have been that to arrive at the facts retailed and the figures
introduced by the given help of some other conscious and confessed agent is
essentially to find the whole business—that is, as I say, its effective interest—
enriched *by the way*. I have in other words constantly inclined to the idea of
the particular attaching case *plus* some near individual view of it; that
nearness quite having thus to become an imagined observer's, a projected,
charmed painter's or poet's—however avowed the "minor" quality in the
latter—close and sensitive contact with it. Anything, in short, I now reflect,
must always have seemed to me better—better for the process and the effect
of representation, my irrepressible ideal—than the mere muffled majesty of
irresponsible "authorship." Beset constantly with the sense that the painter
of the picture or the chanter of the ballad (whatever we may call him)
can never be responsible *enough*, and for every inch of his surface and note
of his song, I track my uncontrollable footsteps, right and left, after the
fact, while they take their quick turn, even on stealthiest tiptoe, toward the
point of view that, within the compass, will give me most instead of least
to answer for.

I am aware of having glanced a good deal already in the direction of
this embarrassed truth—which I give for what it is worth; but I feel it come
home to me afresh on recognising that the manner in which it betrays itself
may be one of the liveliest sources of amusement in the "The Golden Bowl."
It's not that the muffled majesty of authorship doesn't here *ostensibly* reign;
but I catch myself again shaking it off and disavowing the pretence of it
while I get down into the arena and do my best to live and breathe and rub
shoulders and converse with the persons engaged in the struggle that pro-

vides for the others in the circling tiers the entertainment of the great game. There is no other participant, of course, than each of the real, the deeply involved and immersed and more or less bleeding participants; but I nevertheless affect myself as having held my system fast and fondly, with one hand at least, by the manner in which the whole thing remains subject to the register, ever so closely kept, of the consciousness of but two of the characters. The Prince, in the first half of the book, virtually sees and knows and makes out, virtually represents to himself everything that concerns us— very nearly (though he doesn't speak in the first person) after the fashion of other reporters and critics of other situations. Having a consciousness highly susceptible of registration, he thus makes us see the things that may most interest us reflected in it as in the clean glass held up to so many of the "short stories" of our long list; and yet after all never a whit to the prejudice of his being just as consistently a foredoomed, entangled, embarrassed agent in the general imbroglio, actor in the offered play. The function of the Princess, in the remainder, matches exactly with his; the register of *her* consciousness is as closely kept—as closely, say, not only as his own, but as that (to cite examples) either of the intelligent but quite unindividualised witness of the destruction of "The Aspern Papers," or of the all-noting heroine of "The Spoils of Poynton," highly individualised *though* highly intelligent; the Princess, in fine, in addition to feeling everything she has to, and to playing her part just in that proportion, duplicates, as it were, her value and becomes a compositional resource, and of the finest order, as well as a value intrinsic. So it is that the admirably-endowed pair, between them, as I retrace their fortune and my own method, point again for me the moral of the endless interest, endless worth for "delight," of the compositional contribution. Their chronicle strikes me as quite of the stuff to keep us from forgetting that absolutely *no* refinement of ingenuity or of precaution need be dreamed of as wasted in that most exquisite of all good causes the appeal to variety, the appeal to incalculability, the appeal to a high refinement and a handsome wholeness of effect.

There are other things I might remark here, despite its perhaps seeming a general connexion that I have elsewhere sufficiently shown as suggestive; but I have other matter in hand and I take a moment only to meet a possible objection—should any reader be so far solicitous or even attentive—to what I have just said. It may be noted, that is, that the Prince, in the volume over which he nominally presides, is represented as in comprehensive cognition only of those aspects as to which Mrs. Assingham doesn't functionally— perhaps all too officiously, as the reader may sometimes feel it—supersede him. This disparity in my plan is, however, but superficial; the thing abides rigidly by its law of showing Maggie Verver at first through her suitor's and her husband's exhibitory vision of her, and of then showing the Prince, with at least an equal intensity, through his wife's; the advantage thus being that these attributions of experience display the sentient subjects themselves at the same time and by the same stroke with the nearest possible approach to a desirable vividness. It is the Prince who opens the door to half our light upon Maggie, just as it is she who opens it to half our light upon himself; the rest of our impression, in either case, coming straight from the very motion with which that act is performed. We see Charlotte also at first, and we see Adam Verver, let alone our seeing Mrs. Assingham, and every one and every thing else, but as they are visible in the Prince's interest, so to speak—by which I mean of course in the interest of his being himself handed over to us. With a like consistency we see the same persons and things again but as Maggie's interest, *her* exhibitional charm, determines the view. In making which remark, with its apparently so limited enumeration of my elements, I naturally am brought up against the fact of the fundamental fewness of these latter—of the fact that my large demand is made for a group of agents who may be counted on the fingers of one hand. We see very few persons in "The Golden Bowl," but the scheme of the book, to make up for that, is that we shall really see about as much of them as a coherent literary form permits. That was my problem, so to speak, and my *gageure* —to play the small handful of values really for all they were worth—and to work my system, my particular propriety of appeal, particular degree of pressure on the spring of interest, for all that this specific ingenuity itself might be. To have a scheme and a view of its dignity is of course congruously to work it out, and the "amusement" of the chronicle in question—by which, once more, I always mean the gathered cluster of all the *kinds* of interest—was exactly to see what a consummate application of such sincerities would give.

11. Conrad's Chance: *reporters multiplied*

("The New Novel," 1914)

It is odd and delightful perhaps that at the very moment of our urging this truth [that great fiction, through art or method, provides depth to reward re-reading] we should happen to be regaled with a really supreme specimen of the part playable in a novel by the source of interest, the principle of provision attended to, for which we claim importance. Mr. Joseph Conrad's *Chance* is none the less a signal instance of provision the most earnest and the most copious for its leaving ever so much to be said about the particular provision effected. It is none the less an extraordinary exhibition of method by the fact that the method is, we venture to say, without a precedent in any like work. It places Mr. Conrad absolutely alone as a votary of the way to do a thing that shall make it undergo most doing. The way to do it that shall make it undergo least is the line on which we are mostly now used to see prizes carried off; so that the author of *Chance* gathers up on this showing all sorts of comparative distinction. He gathers up at least two sorts—that of bravery in absolutely reversing the process most accredited, and that, quite separate, we make out, of performing the maneuver under salvos of recognition. It is not in these days often given to a refinement of design to be recognized, but Mr. Conrad has made his achieve that miracle—save in so far indeed as the miracle has been one thing and the success another. The miracle is of the rarest, confounding all calculation and suggesting more reflections that we can begin to make place for here; but the sources of surprise surrounding it might be, were this possible, even greater and yet leave the fact itself in all independence, the fact that the whole undertaking was committed by its very first step either to be "art" exclusively or to be nothing. This is the prodigious rarity, since surely we have known for many a day no other such case of the whole clutch of eggs, and these withal of the freshest, in that one basket; to which it may be added that if we say for many a day this is not through our readiness positively to associate the sight with any very definite moment of the past. What concerns us is that the general effect of *Chance* is arrived at by a pursuance of means to the end in view contrasted with which every other current form of the chase can only affect us as cheap and futile; the carriage of the burden or amount of service required on these lines exceeding surely all other such displayed degrees of energy put together. Nothing could well interest us more than to see the exemplary value of attention, attention given by the author and asked of the reader attested in a case in which it has had almost unspeakable difficulties to struggle with—since so we are moved to qualify the particular difficulty Mr. Conrad has "elected" to face: the claim for method in itself, method in this very sense of attention applied, would be somehow less lighted if the difficulties struck us as less consciously, or call it even less wantonly, invoked. What they consist of we should have to diverge here a little to say, and should even then probably but lose ourselves in the dim question of why so special, eccentric and desperate a course, so deliberate a plunge into threatened frustration should alone have seemed open. It has been the course, so far as three words may here serve, of his so multiplying his creators or, as we are now fond of saying, producers, as to make them almost more numerous and quite emphatically more material than the creatures and the production itself in whom and which we by the general law of fiction expect such agents to lose themselves. We take for granted by the general law of fiction a primary author, take him so much for granted that we forget him in proportion as he works upon us, and that he works upon us most in fact by making us forget him.

Mr. Conrad's first care on the other hand is expressly to posit or set up a reciter, a definite responsible intervening first person singular, possessed of infinite sources of references, who immediately proceeds to set up another, to the end that this other may conform again to the practice, and that even at that point the bridge over to the creature, or in other words to the situation or the subject, the thing "produced," shall, if the fancy takes it, once more and yet once more glory in a gap. It is easy to see how heroic the undertaking of an effective fusion becomes on these terms, fusion between what we are to know and that prodigy of our knowing which is ever half the very beauty of the atmosphere of authenticity; from the moment the reporters are thus multiplied from pitch to pitch the tone of each, especially as "rendered" by his precursor in the series, becomes for the prime poet of all an immense question—these circumferential tones having not only to be such individually separate notes, but to keep so clear of the others, the central, the numerous and various voices of the agents proper, those expressive of the action itself and in whom the objectivity resides. We usually escape the worst of this difficulty of a tone *about* the tone of our characters, our projected performers, by keeping it single, keeping it "down" and thereby comparatively impersonal or, as we may say, inscrutable; which is what a creative force, in its blest fatuity, likes to be. But the omniscience, remaining indeed nameless, though constantly active, which sets Marlow's omniscience in motion from the very first page, insisting on a reciprocity with it throughout, this original omniscience invites consideration of itself only in a degree less than that in which Marlow's own invites it; and Marlow's own is a prolonged hovering flight of the subjective over the outstreched ground of the case exposed. We make out this ground but through the shadow cast by the flight, clarify it though the real author visibly reminds himself again and again that he must—all the more that, as if by some tremendous forecast of future applied science, the upper aeroplane causes another, as we have said, to depend from it and that one still another; these dropping shadow after shadow, to the no small menace of intrinsic colour and form and whatever, upon the passive expanse. What shall we most call Mr. Conrad's method accordingly but his attempt to clarify *quand même*—ridden as he has been, we perceive at the end of fifty pages of *Chance*, by such a danger of steeping his matter in perfect eventual obscuration as we recall no other artist's consenting to with an equal grace. This grace, which presently comes over us as the sign of the whole business, is Mr. Conrad's gallantry itself, and the shortest account of the rest of the connection for our present purpose is that his gallantry is thus his success. It literally strikes us that his volume sets in motion more than anything else a drama in which his own system and his combined eccentricities of recital represent the protagonist in face of powers leagued against it, and of which the dénouement gives us the system fighting in triumph, though with its back desperately to the wall, and laying the powers piled up at its feet. This frankly has been *our* spectacle, our suspense

and our thrill; with the one flaw on the roundness of it all the fact that
the predicament was not imposed rather than invoked, was not the effect of
a challenge from without, but that of a mystic impulse from within.

Of an exquisite refinement at all events are the critical questions opened
up in the attempt, the question in particular of by what it exactly is that the
experiment is crowned. Pronouncing it crowned and the case saved by sheer
gallantry, as we did above, is perhaps to fall just short of the conclusion we
might reach were we to push further. *Chance is* an example of objectivity,
most precious of aims, not only menaced but definitely compromised; whereby we are in presence of something really of the strangest, a general and
diffused lapse of authenticity which an inordinate number of common
readers—since it always takes this and these to account encouragingly for
"editions"—have not only condoned but have emphatically commended.
They can have done this but through the bribe of some authenticity other in
kind, no doubt, and seeming to them equally great if not greater, which
gives back by the left hand what the right has, with however dissimulated
a grace, taken away. What Mr. Conrad's left hand gives back then is simply
Mr. Conrad himself. We asked above what would become, by such a form
of practice, of indispensable "fusion" or, to call it by another name, of the
fine process by which our impatient material, at a given moment, shakes
off the humiliation of the handled, the fumbled state, puts its head in the
air and, to its own beautiful illusory consciousness at least, simply runs its
race. Such an amount of handling and fumbling and repointing has it, on the
system of the multiplied "putter into marble," to shake off! And yet behold,
the sense of discomfort, as the show here works out, *has* been conjured away.
The fusion has taken place, or at any rate *a* fusion; only it has been transferred in wondrous fashion to an unexpected, and on the whole more limited
plane of operation; it has succeeded in getting effected, so to speak, not on
the ground but in the air, not between our writer's idea and his machinery,
but between the different parts of his genius itself. His genius is what is left
over from the other, the compromised and compromising quantities—the
Marlows and their determinant inventors and interlocutors, the Powells,
the Franklins, the Fynes, the tell-tale little dogs, the successive members of
a cue from one to the other of which the sense and the interest of the subject
have to be passed on together, in the manner of the buckets of water for the
improvised extinction of a fire, before reaching our apprehension: all
with whatever result, to this apprehension, of a quantity to be allowed for
as spilled by the way. The residuum has accordingly the form not of such and
such a number of images discharged and ordered, but that rather of a
wandering, circling, yearning imaginative *faculty*, encountered in its habit
as it lives and diffusing itself as a presence or a tide, a noble sociability of
vision. So we have as the force that fills the cup just the high-water mark of
a beautiful and generous mind at play in conditions comparatively thankless

—thoroughly, unweariedly, yet at the same time ever so elegantly at play, and doing more for itself than it succeeds in getting done for it. Than which nothing could be of a greater reward to critical curiosity were it not still for the wonder of wonder, a new page in the record altogether—the fact that these things are apparently what the common reader has seen and understood. Great then would seem to be after all the common reader!

Chapter XIII

FORM AND STRUCTURE

It is clear that form *had central importance for James in both his criticism and fiction. But in general James was imprecise and vague in his use of the term, and it does not loom as large in his commentaries as one might expect. In "The Art of Fiction" he attempts to define "story"—in effect, the pre-represented or pre-rendered subject—as it relates to the achieved fiction: "This sense of the story being the idea, the starting-point, of the novel, is the only one that I see in which it can be spoken of as something different from its organic whole; and since in proportion as the work is successful the idea permeates and penetrates it, informs and animates it, so that every word and every punctuation-point contribute directly to the expression, in that proportion do we lose our sense of the story being a blade which may be drawn more or less out of its sheath. The story and the novel, the idea and the form, are the needle and thread, and I never heard of a guild of tailors who recommended the use of the thread without the needle, or the needle without the thread."*

Form is thus conceived as resulting from everything *the writer does to the raw lump of experience, the shaggy fragment of life with which he begins. If what he achieves ultimately is indeed an "organic whole," the form is not visible on it as something imposed from without [like a sheath on a sword], but permeates and animates the totality, remaining everywhere felt but nowhere visible and separable.*

Thus in many passages of criticism, when James uses the word form, *it might well be equated with art itself, or with technique in its broadest conceivable sense. Given such a definition, form might well be considered at least in part the subject of several other chapters in this book: Chapter IV, "The Writer and His Imagination"; or Chapter XII, "Point of View." But there are places where James discusses form as related to the "organic whole," in which he comes to grips with the totality of a work in its basic structure; in these places the term becomes indispensable.*

It is no doubt significant that James developed an elaborate architectural metaphor in talking about the perfection of his own novel, The Portrait of a Lady: *"Such is the aspect that to-day 'The Portrait' wears for me: a structure reared with an 'architectural' competence . . . that makes it, to the author's own sense, the most proportioned of his productions after 'The*

257

Ambassadors'—which was to follow it so many years later and which has, no doubt, a superior roundness." It is quite clear that here and in his Preface to The Ambassadors *(where he describes the alternation of preparation and scene as "the very form and figure of 'The Ambassasors'"), James is equating form with excellence: as* The Portrait of a Lady *and* The Ambassadors *are his greatest achievement in form, so they are his greatest novels. In other words, these novels have not only pleasing shapes, proportion, roundness—but they have these qualities only because they are "organic wholes" of the kind James described in "The Art of Fiction."*

In a number of his novels, James pointed to his weakness for "misplaced middles," resulting from his tendency to overtreatment which generally manifests itself in the first half of a novel. But James said he always considered overtreatment the "minor disservice" when compared to undertreatment. Clearly either of these weaknesses could affect a work's shape, form, or structure.

But they should not be confused with two of James's favorite critical terms closely related to form—economy and waste. For James, economy had nothing necessarily to do with size. In his Preface to The Tragic Muse *he writes: "There is life and life, and as waste is only life sacrificed and thereby prevented from 'counting,' I delight in a deep-breathing economy and an organic form." Thus economy was for James the equivalent of treatment—that ideal or inevitable treatment or rendering of material (life) that achieved the "organic form" in which everything "counted." Thus it was that James could use the term* economy *in discussing his own large novel,* The Ambassadors, *and the term* waste *in discussing Tolstoy's* War and Peace, *a novel that James cited more that once as—in spite of its "mighty fund of life"— wasteful in its "formless shape" and "flopping looseness."*

In one of his letters (1912), James described his view of form as succinctly and vividly as anywhere else in his work, and his comment may stand here as his ultimate definition—and one that might well be considered final: "Strenuous selection and comparison are . . . the very essence of art. . . . Form is substance to that degree that there is absolutely no substance without it. Form alone takes, and holds and preserves, substance—saves it from the welter of helpless verbiage that we swim in as in a sea of tasteless tepid pudding."

1. form and style

("George Sand," 1877)

It has been said that what makes a book classic is its style. We should modify this, and instead of style say *form.* Madame Sand's novels have plenty of style, but they have no form. Balzac's have not a shred of style, but they have a great deal of form.

2. *form and art*

("Emerson," 1887)

And there is this further sign of Emerson's singular power, that he is a striking exception to the general rule that writings live in the last resort by their form; that they owe a large part of their fortune to the art with which they have been composed. It is hardly too much, or too little, to say of Emerson's writings in general that they were not composed at all. Many and many things are beautifully said; he had felicities, inspirations, unforgettable phrases; he had frequently an exquisite eloquence.

> O my friends, there are resources in us on which we have not yet drawn. There are men who rise refreshed on hearing a threat; men to whom a crisis which intimidates and paralyses the majority—demanding not the faculties of prudence and thrift, but comprehension, immovableness, the readiness of sacrifice, comes graceful and beloved as a bride . . . But these are heights that we can scarce look up to and remember without contrition and shame. Let us thank God that such things exist.

None the less we have the impression that that search for a fashion and a manner on which he was always engaged never really came to a conclusion; it draws itself out through his later writings—it drew itself out through his later lectures, like a sort of renunciation of success. It is not on these, however, but on their predecessors, that his reputation will rest. Of course the way he spoke was the way that was on the whole most convenient to him; but he differs from most men of letters of the same degree of credit in failing to strike us as having achieved a style. This achievement is, as I say, usually the bribe or toll-money on the journey to posterity; and if Emerson goes his way, as he clearly appears to be doing, on the strength of his message alone, the case will be rare, the exception striking, and the honour great.

3. *a final unsurpassable form*

("Gustave Flaubert," 1902)

Madame Bovary has a perfection that not only stamps it, but that makes it stand almost alone; it holds itself with such a supreme unapproachable assurance as both excites and defies judgment. For it deals not in the least, as to unapproachability, with things exalted or refined; it only confers on its sufficiently vulgar elements of exhibition a final unsurpassable form. The form is in *itself* as interesting, as active, as much of the essence of the subject as the idea, and yet so close is its fit and so inseparable its life that we catch it at no moment on any errand of its own. That verily is to *be* interesting—

all round; that is to be genuine and whole. The work is a classic because the thing, such as it is, is ideally *done*, and because it shows that in such doing eternal beauty may dwell.

4. architecture, proportion

(Preface to *Portrait of a Lady*, 1908)

So far I reasoned ["Place the centre of the subject (of *The Portrait of a Lady*) in the young woman's (Isabel Archer's) own consciousness."], and it took nothing less than that technical rigour, I now easily see, to inspire me with the right confidence for erecting on such a plot of ground the neat and careful and proportioned pile of bricks that arches over it and that was thus to form, constructionally speaking, a literary monument. Such is the aspect that to-day "The Portrait" wears for me : a structure reared with an "architectural" competence, as Turgénieff would have said, that makes it, to the author's own sense, the most proportioned of his productions after "The Ambassadors"—which was to follow it so many years later and which has, no doubt, a superior roundness. On one thing I was determined; that, though I should clearly have to pile brick upon brick for the creation of an interest, I would leave no pretext for saying that anything is out of line, scale or perspective. I would build large—in fine embossed vaults and painted arches, as who should say, and yet never let it appear that the chequered pavement, the ground under the reader's feet, fails to stretch at every point to the base of the walls. That precautionary spirit, on re-persual of the book, is the old note that most touches me : it testifies so, for my own ear, to the anxiety of my provision for the reader's amusement. I felt, in view of the possible limitations of my subject, that no such provision could be excessive, and the development of the latter was simply the general form of that earnest quest. And I find indeed that this is the only account I can give myself of the evolution of the fable : it is all under the head thus named that I conceive the needful accretion as having taken place, the right complications as having started. It was naturally of the essence that the young woman should be herself complex; that was rudimentary—or was at any rate the light in which Isabel Archer had originally dawned. It went, however, but a certain way, and other lights, contending, conflicting lights, and of as many different colours, if possible, as the rockets, the Roman candles and Catherine-wheels of a "pyrotechnic display," would be employable to attest that she was. I had, no doubt, a groping instinct for the right complications, since I am quite unable to track the footsteps of those that constitute, as the case stands, the general situation exhibited. They are there, for what they are worth, and as numerous as might be; but my memory, I confess, is a blank as to how and whence they came.

5. *overtreatment*

(Preface to *The Portrait of a Lady*, 1908)

As to Henrietta [Stackpole, the *ficelle* in *The Portrait of a Lady*], my apology for whom I just left incomplete, she exemplifies, I fear, in her superabundance, not an element of my plan, but only an excess of my zeal. So early was to begin my tendency to *overtreat*, rather than undertreat (when there was choice or danger) my subject. (Many members of my craft, I gather, are far from agreeing with me, but I have always held overtreating the minor disservice.) "Treating" that of "The Portrait" amounted to never forgetting, by any lapse, that the thing was under a special obligation to be amusing. There was the danger of the noted "thinness"—which was to be averted, tooth and nail, by cultivation of the lively.

6. *unity, harmony, tone*

(Preface to *The Tragic Muse*, 1908)

I am thus [in rereading *The Tragic Muse*] able to take the thing as having quite wittingly and undisturbedly existed for itself alone, and to liken it to some aromatic bag of gathered herbs of which the string has never been loosed; or, better still, to some jar of potpourri, shaped and overfigured and polished, but of which the lid, never lifted, has provided for the intense accumulation of the fragrance within. The consistent, the sustained, preserved *tone* of "The Tragic Muse," its constant and doubtless rather fine drawn truth to its particular sought pitch and accent, are, critically speaking, its principal merit—the inner harmony that I perhaps presumptuously permit myself to compare to an unevaporated scent. . . .

. . . No, accordingly, Nick Dormer isn't "the best thing in the book," as I judge I imagined he would be, and it contains nothing better, I make out, than that preserved and achieved unity and quality of tone, a value in itself, which I referred to at the beginning of these remarks. What I mean by this is that the interest created, and the expression of that interest, are things kept, as to kind, genuine and true to themselves. The appeal, the fidelity to the prime motive, is, with no little art, strained clear (even as silver is polished) in a degree answering—at least by intention—to the air of beauty. There is an awkwardness again in having thus belatedly to point such features out; but in that wrought appearance of animation and harmony, that effect of free movement and yet of recurrent and insistent reference, "The Tragic Muse" has struck me again as conscious of a bright advantage.

7. *structural centres, organic form, economy*

(Preface to *The Tragic Muse*, 1908)

The more I turn my pieces over, at any rate, the more I now see I must have found in them, and I remember how, once well in presence of my three typical examples, my fear of too ample a canvas quite dropped. The only question was that if I had marked my political case, from so far back, for "a story by itself," and then marked my theatrical case for another, the joining together of these interests, originally seen as separate, might, all disgracefully, betray the seam, show for mechanical and superficial. A story was a story, a picture a picture, and I had a mortal horror of two stories, two pictures, in one. The reason of this was the clearest—my subject was immediately, under that disadvantage, so cheated of its indispensable centre as to become of no more use for expressing a main intention than a wheel without a hub is of use for moving a cart. It was a fact, apparently, that one *had* on occasion seen two pictures in one; were there not for instance certain sublime Tintorettos at Venice, a measureless Crucifixion in especial, which showed without loss of authority half a dozen actions separately taking place? Yes, that might be, but there had surely been nevertheless a mighty pictorial fusion, so that the virtue of composition had somehow thereby come all mysteriously to its own. Of course the affair would be simple enough if composition could be kept out of the question; yet by what art or process, what bars and bolts, what unmuzzled dogs and pointed guns, perform that feat? I had to know myself utterly inapt for any such valour and recognise that, to make it possible, sundry things should have begun for me much further back than I had felt them even in their dawn. A picture without composition slights its most precious chance for beauty, and is moreover not composed at all unless the painter knows *how* that principle of health and safety, working as an absolutely premeditated art, has prevailed. There may in its absence be life, incontestably, as "The Newcomes" has life, as "Les Trois Mousquetaires," as Tolstoi's "Peace and War," have it; but what do such large loose baggy monsters, with their queer elements of the accidental and the arbitrary, artistically *mean?* We have heard it maintained, we will remember, that such things are "superior to art"; but we understand least of all what *that* may mean, and we look in vain for the artist, the divine explanatory genius, who will come to our aid and tell us. There is life and life, and as waste is only life sacrificed and thereby prevented from "counting," I delight in a deep-breathing economy and an organic form. My business was accordingly to "go in" for complete pictorial fusion, some such common interest between my two first notions as would, in spite of their birth under quite different stars, do them no violence at all.

I recall with this confirmed infatuation of retrospect that through the mild perceptions I here glance at there struck for "The Tragic Muse" the first hour of a season of no small subjective felicity; lighted mainly, I seem to see, by a wide west window that, high aloft, looked over near and far London sunsets, a half-grey, half-flushed expanse of London life. The production of the thing, which yet took a good many months, lives for me again all contemporaneously in that full projection, upon my very table, of the good fog-filtered Kensington mornings; which had a way indeed of seeing the sunset in and which at the very last are merged to memory in a different and a sharper pressure, that of an hotel bedroom in Paris during the autumn of 1889, with the Exposition du Centenaire about to end—and my long story, through the usual difficulties, as well. The usual difficulties —and I fairly cherish the record as some adventurer in another line may hug the sense of his inveterate habit of just saving in time the neck he ever undiscourageably risks—were those bequeathed as a particular vice of the artistic spirit, against which vigilance had been destined from the first to exert itself in vain, and the effect of which was that again and again, perversely, incurably, the centre of my structure would insist on placing itself *not*, so to speak, in the middle. It mattered little that the reader with the idea or the suspicion of a structural centre is the rarest of friends and of critics—a bird, it would seem, as merely fabled as the phoenix: the terminational terror was none the less certain to break in and my work threaten to masquerade for me as an active figure condemned to the disgrace of legs too short, ever so much too short, for its body. I urge myself to the candid confession that in very few of my productions, to my eye, *has* the organic centre succeeded in getting into proper position.

Time after time, then, has the precious waistband or girdle, studded and buckled and placed for brave outward show, practically worked itself, and in spite of desperate remonstrance, or in other words essential counterplotting, to a point perilously near the knees—perilously I mean for the freedom of these parts. In several of my compositions this displacement has so succeeded, at the crisis, in defying and resisting me, has appeared so fraught with probable dishonour, that I still turn upon them, in spite of the greater or less success of final dissimulation, a rueful and wondering eye. These productions have in fact, if I may be so bold about it, specious and spurious centres altogether, to make up for the failure of the true. As to which in my list they are, however, that is another business, not on any terms to be made known. Such at least would seem my resolution so far as I have thus proceeded. Of any attention ever arrested by the pages forming the object of this reference that rigour of discrimination has wholly and consistently failed, I gather, to constitute a part. In which fact there is perhaps after all a rough justice—since the infirmity I speak of, for example, has been always but the direct and immediate fruit of a positive excess of foresight, the overdone desire to provide for future need and lay up heavenly treasure against the demands of my climax. If the art of the drama, as a great French master of it has said, is above all the art of preparations, that is true only to a less extent of the art of the novel, and true exactly in the degree in which the art of the particular novel comes near that of the drama. The first half of a fiction insists ever on figuring to me as the stage or theatre for the second half, and I have in general given so much space to making the theatre propitious that my halves have too often proved strangely unequal. Thereby has arisen with grim regularity the question of artfully, of consummately masking the fault and conferring on the false quantity the brave appearance of the true.

8. fusion of form and substance

(Preface to The Awkward Age, 1908)

In doing this [the situation in The Awkward Age presenting itself "on absolutely scenic lines"] then it does more—it helps us ever so happily to see the grave distinction between substance and form in a really wrought work of art signally break down. I hold it impossible to say, before "The Awkward Age," where one of these elements ends and the other begins: I have been unable at least myself, on re-examination, to mark any such joint or seam, to see the two discharged offices as separate. They are separate before the fact, but the sacrament of execution indissolubly marries them, and the marriage, like any other marriage, has only to be a "true" one for the scandal of a breach not to show. The thing "done," artistically, is a fusion, or it has not been done—in which case of course the artist may be, and all deservedly, pelted with any fragment of his botch the critic shall choose to pick up. But his ground once conquered, in this particular field, he knows nothing of fragments and may say in all security: "Detach one if you can. You can analyse in your way, oh yes—to relate, to report, to explain; but you can't disintegrate my synthesis; you can't resolve the elements of my whole into different responsible agents or find your way at all (for your own fell purpose). My mixture has only to be perfect literally to bewilder you—you are lost in the tangle of the forest. Prove this value, this effect, in the air of the whole result, to be of my subject, and that other value, other effect, to be of my treatment, prove that I haven't so shaken them together as the conjurer I profess to be must consummately shake, and I consent but to parade as before a booth at the fair." The exemplary closeness of "The Awkward Age" even affects me, on re-perusal, I confess, as treasure quite instinctively and foreseeingly laid up against my present opportunity for these remarks. I have been positively struck by the quantity of meaning and the number of intentions, the extent of ground for interest, as I may call it, that I have succeeded in working scenically, yet without loss of

sharpness, clearness or "atmosphere," into each of my illuminating Occasions
—where, at certain junctures, the due preservation of all these values took,
in the familiar phrase, a good deal of doing.

9. serial publication: divisions, proportions, general rhythm

(Preface to *The Wings of the Dove*, 1909)

The free hand, in this connexion, was above all agreeable—the hand the
freedom of which I owed to the fact that the work [*The Wings of the Dove*]
had ignominiously failed, in advance, of all power to see itself "serialised."
This failure had repeatedly waited, for me, upon shorter fictions; but the
considerable production we here discuss was (as "The Golden Bowl" was
to be, two or three years later) born, not otherwise than a little bewilderedly,
into a world of periodicals and editors, of roaring "successes" in fine, amid
which it was well-nigh unnotedly to lose itself. There is fortunately something bracing, ever, in the alpine chill, that of some high icy *arête*, shed by
the cold editorial shoulder; sour grapes may at moments fairly intoxicate and
the story-teller worth his salt rejoice to feel again how many accommodations he can practise. Those addressed to "conditions of publication" have
in a degree their interesting, or at least their provoking, side; but their charm
is qualified by the fact that the prescriptions here spring from a soil often
wholly alien to the ground of the work itself. They are almost always the
fruit of another air altogether and conceived in a light liable to represent
within the circle of the work itself little else than darkness. Still, when not too
blighting, they often operated as a tax on ingenuity—that ingenuity of the
expert craftsman which likes to be taxed very much to the same tune to
which a well-bred horse likes to be saddled. The best and finest ingenuities,
nevertheless, with all respect to that truth, are apt to be, not one's compro-
mises, but one's fullest conformities, and I well remember, in the case before
us, the pleasure of feeling my divisions, my proportions and general rhythm,
rest all on permanent rather than in any degree on momentary proprieties.
It was enough for my alternations, thus, that they were good in themselves;
it was in fact so much for them that I really think any further account of
the constitution of the book reduces itself to a just notation of the law they
followed.

10. misplaced middles

(Preface to *The Wings of the Dove*, 1909)

"The Wings of the Dove" happens to offer perhaps the most striking
example I may cite (though with public penance for it already performed)

of my regular failure to keep the appointed halves of my whole equal.
Here the makeshift middle—for which the best I can say is that it's always
rueful and never impudent—reigns with even more than its customary contrition, though passing itself off perhaps too with more than its usual craft.
Nowhere, I seem to recall, had the need of dissimulation been felt so as
anguish; nowhere had I condemned a luckless theme to complete its revolution, burdened with the accumulation of its difficulties, the difficulties
that grow with a theme's development, in quarters so cramped. Of course,
as every novelist knows, it is difficulty that inspires; only, for that perfection
of charm, it must have been difficulty inherent and congenital, and not
difficulty "caught" by the wrong frequentations. The latter half, that is
the false and deformed half, of "The Wings" would verily, I think, form
a signal object-lesson for a literary critic bent on improving his occasion to
the profit of the budding artist. This whole corner of the picture bristles with
"dodges"—such as he should feel himself all committed to recognise and
denounce—for disguising the reduced scale of the exhibition, for foreshortening at any cost, for imparting to patches the value of presences, for dressing
objects in an *air* as of the dimensions they can't possibly have. Thus he
would have his free hand for pointing out what a tangled web we weave
when—well, when, through our mislaying or otherwise trifling with our
blest pair of compasses, we have to produce the illusion of mass without
the illusion of extent. *There* is a job quite to the measure of most of our
monitors—and with the interest for them well enhanced by the preliminary
cunning quest for the spot where deformity has begun.

11. form and substance

(*Letters*, 1912, to Hugh Walpole)

Therefore I rejoice in the getting on of your work—how splendidly copious
your flow; and am much interested in what you tell me of your readings
and your literary emotions. These latter indeed—or some of them, as you
express them, I don't think I fully share. At least when you ask me if I
don't feel Dostoieffsky's "mad jumble, that flings things down in a heap,"
nearer truth and beauty than the picking and composing that you instance
in Stevenson, I reply with emphasis that I feel nothing of the sort, and that
the older I grow and the more I *go* the more sacred to me do picking and
composing become—though I naturally don't limit myself to Stevenson's
kind of the same. Don't let any one persuade you—there are plenty of
ignorant and fatuous duffers to try to do it—that strenuous selection and
comparison are not the very essence of art, and that Form *is* [not] substance
to that degree that there is absolutely no substance without it. Form alone

takes, and holds and preserves, substance—saves it from the welter of help-less verbiage that we swim in as in a sea of tasteless tepid pudding, and that makes one ashamed of an art capable of such degradations. Tolstoi and D. are fluid puddings, though not tasteless, because the amount of their own minds and souls in solution in the broth gives it savour and flavour, thanks to the strong, rank quality of their genius and their experience. But there are all sorts of things to be said of them, and in particular that we see how great a vice is their lack of composition, their defiance of economy and archi-tecture, directly they are emulated and imitated; *then*, as subjects of emula-tion, models, they quite give themselves away. There is nothing so deplorable as a work of art with a *leak* in its interest; and there is no such leak of interest as through commonness of form. Its opposite, the *found* (because the sought-for) form is the absolute citadel and tabernacle of interest. But what a lecture I am reading you—though a very imperfect one—which you have drawn upon yourself (as moreover it was quite right you should.) But no matter—I shall go for you again—as soon as I find you in a lone corner. . . .

12. the waste of formless shape

(*Letters*, 1913, to Hugh Walpole)

I have been reading over Tolstoi's interminable *Peace and War*, and am struck with the fact that I now protest as much as I admire. He doesn't *do* to read over, and that exactly is the answer to those who idiotically pro-claim the impunity of such formless shape, such flopping looseness and such a denial of composition, selection and style. He has a mighty fund of life, but the *waste*, and the ugliness and vice of waste, the vice of a not finer *doing*, are sickening. For me he makes "composition" throne, by contrast, in effulgent lustre!

Chapter XIV

STYLE

As one whose style has provoked a wide range of reactions, James might be expected to exhibit great interest in the styles of his fellow novelists. This is indeed the case, and his collected commentaries, gathered here, offer much insight into his own conception of style. But there is little here about James's own style. He did not write much about it, either in the Notebooks *or the* Prefaces. *Perhaps he came to feel that unlike the question of the point of view of a work, which was always a matter for him of deliberate and fascinating choice, the question of style was beyond choice, beyond deliberation.*

There is clear evidence that James came to believe in the ultimate inseparability of subject and style, of substance and language. This attitude would, of course, render it useless to contemplate a range of styles for a particular subject. The subject brought its own style, was its style. Only disaster could come of attempting to clothe a subject in an ornate or cosmetic style. Even beyond this, there is some reason to believe that James came to rely on a release and flow of language to find and elaborate subject, to create meaning and value.

James criticism has long been burdened with the bad joke which divides James's work into the three periods of James the First, James the Second, and the Old Pretender. It is a rare reader who has not found the style of the late James at times rough going—and at other times absolutely brilliant in its labyrinthine loopings and windings into the darkest and deepest heart of meaning and feeling. And this is the James of the major phase, and the James who is closest in resemblance to the major fictional innovators of the twentieth century. Some light is thrown on the development of James's late style by James's development, during the latter half of the 1890s, of a method of writing by dictating to a stenographer at a typewriter. See, for example, Theodora Bosanquet's Henry James at Work *(1924) for an account by one of his stenographers of his method; or see "A Fierce Legibility" in Book III of Leon Edel's* Henry James: The Treacherous Years, 1895-1901 *(1969) for a summary account of his late technique of dictating.*

But the assumption that James seized upon dictation to a typewriter as an excuse for becoming garrulous and verbose in his late fiction is far too easy—*and is, moreover, an oblique and derogatory value judgment of the late fiction. (See James's own denial of this assumption in his 1902 letter to Mrs. Cadwalader Jones, Part D of this chapter.) An alternative assumption seems more likely. James developed a highly sophisticated, perhaps primarily intuitive, view of language as "developed, delicate, flexible, rich" speech: "The more it suggests and expresses the more we live by it—the more it promotes and enhances life" (The Question of our Speech, 1905). With such a view of language, James undoubtedly came to believe that the flow of speech permitted by dictation allowed him to create in closer harmony with the flow of the conscious down on those levels near the storehouse of all those gathered impressions—down near the thin line between conscious and unconscious, where language liberated may indeed sound the depths and surface with discoveries that cannot be plotted or planned, but flowingly captured on the page. This image of James must stand here rather much on its own, but support, when mustered, will include such matters as James's appreciation (see Part B below) of Daudet's conversational style ("He tells his stories as a talker"); his advice in the Preface to* The Golden Bowl *to the reader to read aloud in order to pressure the prose into divulging "its finest and most numerous secrets" (see Chapter XVI); and his relationship to his psychologist brother's view of the connection between language and mind together with his early conception of the "stream of consciousness," a phrase which William James coined.*

The passages collected here take on greater depth of meaning if the foregoing is kept in mind as they are read. The first three groupings are presented in chronological order, and range in date from 1865 to 1914. They reveal an increasingly complex view of the nature of style and the possibilities of language. In Part A James is flamboyantly on the attack, and the fireworks sparkle and flash forth. In Part B he is more sober in search of the precise language of praise for styles he admires, and he hits (for R. L. Stevenson) on the highly revealing terms—"personal, expressive, renewed." In Part C he more frequently confronts the essential mystery of the fusion of style to subject and the intertwining of language and creation, and he comes to claim (in his 1914 essay "The New Novel," in a discussion of Compton Mackenzie) that "the value of the offered thing [the fiction], its whole relation to us, is created by the breath of language."

Part D is a grab bag of left-over comments, but they are, indeed, some of the most interesting. They range in subject from the American language (which James clearly understood as distinct from British English), to James's views of the effect of his dictation on the structure of his fiction. They make their contribution to our developing view of James's conception of style as vital to the life of any story or novel, and his view of language (or speech) as vital to the life of an individual and a culture.

PART A: THE UNNATURAL STYLE

1. *words, words, words*

("Miss Prescott's 'Azarian,' " 1865)

If the dictionary were a palette of colors, and a goose-quill a brush, Miss Prescott would be a very clever painter. But as words possess a certain inherent dignity, value, and independence, language being rather the stamped and authorized coinage which expresses the value of thought than the brutal metal out of which forms are moulded, her pictures are invariably incoherent and meaningless. . . .

Miss Prescott's style is evidently the point on which she bases her highest claims to distinction. She has been taught that, in possessing this style, she possesses a great and uncommon gift. Nothing is more false. The fine writing in which "Azarian" abounds is the cheapest writing of the day. Every magazine-story bears traces of it. It is so widely adopted, because to a person of clever fancy there is no kind of writing that is so easy,—so easy, we mean, considering the effect produced. Of course it is much easier to write in a style which necessitates no looking out of words: but such a style makes comparatively little impression. The manner in question is easy, because the writer recognizes no standard of truth or accuracy by which his performances may be measured. He does not transcribe facts,—facts must be counted, measured, weighed, which takes far too much trouble. He does not patiently study the nature and appearance of a thing until he has won from it the confession of that absolute appreciable quality, the correct statement of which is alone true description; he does not commit himself to statements, for these are dangerous things; he does not, in short, extract; he affixes. He does not consult the object to be described, so recognizing it as a fact; he consults his imagination, and so constitutes it a theme to be elaborated. In the picture which he proceeds to make, some of the qualities of the object will certainly be found; but it matters little whether they are the chief distinctive ones,—any satisfy his conscience.

All writing is narration; to describe is simply to narrate things in their order of place, instead of events in their order of time. If you consult this order, your description will stand; if you neglect it, you will have an imposing mass of words, but no recognizable *thing*. We do not mean to say that Miss Prescott has a wholly commonplace fancy. (We use the word commonplace advisedly, for there are no commonplaces so vulgar as those chromatic epigrams which mark the Tennysonian prose school.) On the contrary, she has a fancy which would serve very well to garnish a dish of solid fiction, but which furnishes poor material for the body of the dish. These clever conceits, this keen eye for the superficial picturesque, this inborn love of *bric-à-brac* and sunsets, may be made very effectively to supplement a true dramatic exposition; but they are a wretched substitute for such. And even in *bric-à-brac* and sunsets Miss Prescott's execution is crude. In her very specialty, she is but an indifferent artist. Who is so clever in the *bric-à-brac* line as M. Théophile Gautier? He takes an occasional liberty with the French language; but, on the whole, he finds his best account in a policy of studious respect even for her most irritating forms of conservatism. The consequence is, that his efforts in this line are unapproachable, and, what is better, irreproachable. One of the greatest dangers to which those who pursue this line are liable is the danger that they may fall into the ridiculous. By a close adherence to that medium of expression which other forms of thought have made respectable, this danger is effectually set at naught. What is achieved by the paternally governed French tongue may surely be effected by that chartered libertine, our own. Miss Prescott uses far too many words, synonymous words and meaningless words. Like the majority of female writers,—Mrs. Browning, George Sand, Gail Hamilton, Mrs. Stowe,— she possesses in excess the fatal gift of fluency. Her paragraphs read as if in composition she completely ignored the expedient of erasure. What painter ever painted a picture without rubbing out and transposing, displacing, effacing, replacing? There is no essential difference of system between the painting of a picture and the writing of a novel. Why should the novelist expect to do what his fellow-worker never even hopes to acquire the faculty of doing,—execute his work at a stroke? It is plain that Miss Prescott adds, tacks on, interpolates, piles up, if we may use the expression; but it seems very doubtful if she often takes counsel of the old Horatian precept,—in plain English, to scratch out. A true artist should be as sternly just as a Roman father. A moderate excercise of this Roman justice would have reduced "Azarian" to half its actual length. The various descriptive passages would have been wonderfully simplified, and we might have possessed a few good pictures.

If Miss Prescott would only take such good old English words as we possess, words instinct with the meaning of centuries, and, having fully resolved upon that which she wished to convey, cast her intention in those familiar terms which long use has invested with almost absolute force of expression, then she would describe things in a manner which could not fail to arouse the sympathy, the interest, the dormant memories of the reader. What is the possible bearing of such phrases as "vermeil ardency," or "a tang of color"? of such childish attempts at alliteration—the most frequent bugbear of Miss Prescott's readers—as "studded with starry sprinkle and spatter of splendor," and the following sentence, in which, speaking of the leaves of the blackberry-vine, she tells us that they are "damasked with deepening layer and spilth of color, brinded and barred and blotted beneath the dripping fingers of October, nipped by nest-lining bees,"—and, lastly, "suffused through all their veins with the shining soul of the mild and mellow season"?

This is nothing but "words, words, words, Horatio!" They express nothing; they only seem to express. The true test of the worth of a prose description—to simplify matters we leave poetry quite out of the question —is one's ability to resolve it back into its original elements. You construct your description from a chosen object; can you, conversely, from your description construct that object? We defy any one to represent the "fine scarlet of the blackberry-vine," and "the gilded bronze of beeches,"—fair sentences by themselves, which express almost as much as we can reasonably hope to express on the subject,—under the inspiration of the rhapsody above quoted, and what follows it. Of course, where so much is attempted in the way of expression, something is sometimes expressed. But with Miss Prescott such an occasional success is apt to be what the French call a *succès manqué*. This is the fault of what our authoress must allow us to call her inveterate bad taste; for whenever she has said a good thing, she invariably spoils it by trying to make it better: to let well enough alone is indeed in all respects the great lesson which experience has in store for her. It is sufficiently felicitous, for instance, as such things go, to call the chandelier of a theatre "a basket of light." There stands the simple successful image. But Miss Prescott immediately tacks on the assertion that it "pours down on all its brimming burden of lustre." It would be bad taste again, if it were not such bad physiology, to speak of Azarian's flaccid hair being "drenched with some penetrating perfume, an Oriental water that stung the brain to vigor." The idea that a man's intellectual mood is at the mercy of his *pommade* is one which we recommend to the serious consideration of barbers. The reader will observe that Azarian's hair is *drenched:* an instance of the habitual intensity of Miss Prescott's style. The word *intensity* expresses better than any other its various shortcomings, or rather excesses. The only intensity worth anything in writing is intensity of thought. To endeavor to fortify flimsy conceptions by the constant use of verbal superlatives is like painting the cheeks and pencilling the eyebrows of a corpse.

2. *an anomalous style*

("Mr. Walt Whitman," 1865)

As a general principle, we know of no circumstance more likely to impugn a writer's earnestness than the adoption of an anomalous style. He must have something very original to say if none of the old vehicles will carry his thoughts. Of course he *may* be surprisingly original. Still, presumption is against him. If on examination the matter of his discourse proves very valuable, it justifies, or at any rate excuses, his literary innovation.

But if, on the other hand, it is of a common quality, with nothing new about it, but its manners, the public will judge the writer harshly.

3. a style always listening to itself

("Swinburne's Essays," 1875)

But with this extravagant development of the imagination [in Swinburne's essays] there is no commensurate development either of the reason or of the moral sense. One of these defects is, to our mind, fatal to Mr. Swinburne's style; the other is fatal to his tone, to his temper, to his critical pretensions. His style is without measure, without discretion, without sense of what to take and what to leave; after a few pages, it becomes intolerably fatiguing. It is always listening to itself—always turning its head over its shoulders to see its train flowing behind it. The train shimmers and tumbles in a very gorgeous fashion, but the rustle of its embroidery is fatally importunate. Mr. Swinburne is a dozen times too verbose; at least one-half of his phrases are what the French call phrases in the air. One-half of his sentence is always a repetition, for mere fancy's sake and nothing more, of the meaning of the other half—a play upon its words, an echo, a reflection, a duplication. This trick, of course, makes a writer formidably prolix.

Part B: The Natural Style

1. natural sense of language

(Hawthorne, 1879)

His [Hawthorne's] biographer very justly calls attention to the fact that his style was excellent from the beginning; that he appeared to have passed through no phase of learning how to write, but was in possession of his means, from the first, of his handling a pen. His early tales, perhaps, were not of a character to subject his faculty of expression to a very severe test; but a man who had not Hawthorne's natural sense of language would certainly have contrived to write them less well. This natural sense of language—this turn for saying things lightly and yet touchingly, picturesquely yet simply, and for infusing a gently colloquial tone into matter of the most unfamiliar import—he had evidently cultivated with great assiduity.

2. the flexibility and familiarity of conversation

("Alphonse Daudet," 1882)

We confess to an extreme fondness for M. Alphonse Daudet; he is very near to our heart. The bright light, the warm color, the spontaneity and loquacity, of his native Provence have entered into his style, and made him a talker as well as a novelist. He tells his stories as a talker; they have always something of the flexibility and familiarity of conversation. The conversation, we mean, of an artist and a Frenchman; the conversation of a circle in which the faculty of vivid and discriminating speech exists as it has existed nowhere else.

3. personal, expressive, renewed

("Robert Louis Stevenson," 1888)

It is sufficient to note, in passing, that if Mr. Stevenson had presented himself in an age, or in a country, of portraiture, the painters would certainly each have had a turn at him. The easels and benches would have bristled, the circle would have been close, and quick, from the canvas to the sitter, the rising and falling of heads. It has happened to all of us to have gone into a studio, a studio of pupils, and seen the thick cluster of bent backs and the conscious model in the midst. It has happened to us to be struck, or not to be struck, with the beauty or the symmetry of this personage, and to have made some remark which, whether expressing admiration or disappointment, has elicited from one of the attentive workers the exclamation, "Character, character is what he has!" These words may be applied to Mr. Robert Louis Stevenson; in the language of that art which depends most on direct observation, character, character is what he has. He is essentially a model, in the sense of a sitter; I do not mean, of course, in the sense of a pattern or a guiding light. And if the figures who have a life in literature may also be divided into two great classes, we may add that he is conspicuously one of the draped: he would never, if I may be allowed the expression, pose for the nude. There are writers who present themselves before the critic with just the amount of drapery that is necessary for decency; but Mr. Stevenson is not one of these—he makes his appearance in an amplitude of costume. His costume is part of the character of which I just now spoke; it never occurs to us to ask how he would look without it. Before all things he is a writer with a style—a model with a complexity of curious and picturesque garments. It is by the cut and the colour of this rich and becoming frippery—I use the term endearingly, as a painter might—that he arrests the eye and solicits the brush.

That is, frankly, half the charm he has for us, that he wears a dress and wears it with courage, with a certain cock of the hat and tinkle of the super-erogatory sword; or in other words that he is curious of expression and regards the literary form not simply as a code of signals, but as the key-board of a piano, and as so much plastic material. He has that voice deplored, if we mistake not, by Mr. Herbert Spencer, a manner—a manner for manner's sake it may sometimes doubtless be said. He is as different as possible from the sort of writer who regards words as numbers, and a page as the mere addition of them; much more, to carry out our image, the dictionary stands for him as a wardrobe, and proposition as a button for his coat. Mr. William Archer, in an article ["R. L. Stevenson, his Style and Thought," *Time* November 1885] so gracefully and ingeniously turned that the writer may almost be accused of imitating even while he deprecates, speaks of him as a votary of "lightness of touch," at any cost, and remarks that "he is not only philosophically content but deliberately resolved, that his readers shall look first to his manner, and only in the second place to his matter." I shall not attempt to gainsay this; I cite it rather, for the present, because it carries out our own sense. Mr. Stevenson delights in a style, and his own has nothing accidental or diffident; it is eminently conscious of its responsibilities, and meets them with a kind of gallantry—as if language were a pretty woman, and a person who proposes to handle it had of necessity to be something of a Don Juan. This bravery of gesture is a noticeable part of his nature, and it is rather odd that at the same time a striking feature of that nature should be an absence of care for things feminine. His books are for the most part books without women, and it is not women who fall most in love with them. But Mr. Stevenson does not need, as we may say, a petticoat to inflame him: a happy collocation of words will serve the purpose, or a singular image, or the bright eye of a passing conceit, and he will carry off a pretty paradox without so much as a scuffle. The tone of letters is in him—the tone of letters as distinct from that of philosophy, or of those industries whose uses are supposed to be immediate. Many readers, no doubt, consider that he carries it too far; they manifest an impatience for some glimpse of his moral message. They may be heard to ask what it is he proposes to demonstrate, with such a variety of paces and graces.

The main thing that he demonstrates, to our own perception, is that it is a delight to read him, and that he renews this delight by a constant variety of experiment. Of this anon, however; and meanwhile, it may be noted as a curious characteristic of current fashions that the writer whose effort is perceptibly that of the artist is very apt to find himself thrown on the defensive. A work of literature is a form, but the author who betrays a consciousness of the responsibilities involved in this circumstance not rarely perceives himself to be regarded as an uncanny personage. The usual judgment is that he may be artistic, but that he must not be too much so; that way, apparently, lies something worse than madness. This queer superstition has so successfully imposed itself, that the mere fact of having been indifferent to such a danger constitutes in itself an originality. How few they are in number and how soon we could name them, the writers of English prose, at the present moment, the quality of whose prose is personal, expressive, renewed at each attempt! The state of things that one would have expected to be the rule has become the exception, and an exception for which, most of the time, an apology appears to be thought necessary. A mill that grinds with regularity and with a certain commercial fineness—that is the image suggested by the manner of a good many of the fraternity. They turn out an article for which there is a demand, they keep a shop for a speciality, and the business is carried on in accordance with a useful, well-tested prescription. It is just because he has no speciality that Mr. Stevenson is an individual, and because his curiosity is the only receipt by which he produces. Each of his books is an independent effort—a window opened to a different view. *Doctor Jekyll and Mr. Hyde* is as dissimilar as possible from *Treasure Island; Virginibus Puerisque* has nothing in common with *The New Arabian Nights,* and I should never have supposed *A Child's Garden of Verses* to be from the hand of the author of *Prince Otto.*

Though Mr. Stevenson cares greatly for his phrase, as every writer should who respects himself and his art, it takes no very attentive reading of his volumes to show that it is not what he cares for most, and that he regards an expressive style only, after all, as a means. It seems to me the fault of Mr. Archer's interesting paper, that it suggests too much that the author of these volumes considers the art of expression as an end—an ingenious game of words. He finds that Mr. Stevenson is not serious, that he neglects a whole side of life, that he has no perception, and no consciousness, of suffering; that he speaks as a happy but heartless pagan, living only in his senses (which the critic admits to be exquisitely fine), and that in a world full of heaviness he is not sufficiently aware of the philosophic limitations of mere technical skill. In sketching these aberrations Mr. Archer himself, by the way, displays anything but ponderosity of hand. He is not the first reader, and he will not be the last, who shall have been irritated by Mr. Stevenson's jauntiness. That jauntiness is an essential part of his genius; but to my sense it ceases to be irritating—it indeed becomes positively touching and constitutes an appeal to sympathy and even to tenderness—when once one has perceived what lies beneath the dancing-tune to which he mostly moves. Much as he cares for his phrase, he cares more for life, and for a certain transcendently lovable part of it. He feels, as it seems to us, and that is not given to every one. This constitutes a philosophy which Mr. Archer fails to read between his lines—the respectable, desirable moral which many a reader doubtless finds that he neglects to point. He does not feel everything equally, by any manner of means; but his feelings are always his reasons. He regards them, whatever they may be, as sufficiently honourable, does not disguise them in other names or colours, and looks at whatever he meets in the brilliant candle-light that they shed.

4. masculine firmness . . . quiet force

("Guy de Maupassant," 1888)

On the question of style our author [Maupassant] has some excellent remarks; we may be grateful indeed for every one of them, save an odd reflection about the way to "become original" if we happen not to be so. The recipe for this transformation, it would appear, is to sit down in front of a blazing fire, or a tree in a plain, or any object we encounter in the regular way of business, and remain there until the tree, or the fire, or the object, whatever it be, become different for us from all other specimens of the same class. I doubt whether this system would always answer, for surely the resemblance is what we wish to discover, quite as much as the difference, and the best way to preserve it is not to look for something opposed to it. Is not this indication of the road to take to become, as a writer, original touched with the same fallacy as the recommendation about eschewing analysis? It is the only *naïveté* I have encountered in M. de Maupassant's many volumes. The best originality is the most unconscious, and the best way to describe a tree is the way in which it has struck us. "Ah, but we don't always know how it has struck us," the answer to that may be, "and it takes some time and ingenuity—much fasting and prayer—to find out." If we do not know, it probably has not struck us very much: so little indeed that our inquiry had better be relegated to that closed chamber of an artist's meditations, that sacred back kitchen, which no *a priori* rule can light up. The best thing the artist's adviser can do in such a case is to trust him and turn away, to let him fight the matter out with his conscience. And be this said with a full appreciation of the degree in which M. de Maupassant's observations on the whole question of a writer's style, at the point we have come to today, bear the stamp of intelligence and experience. His own style is of so excellent a tradition that the presumption is altogether in favor of what he may have to say.

He feels oppressively, discouragingly, as many another of his countrymen must have felt—for the French have worked their language as no other people have done—the penalty of coming at the end of three centuries of literature, the difficulty of dealing with an instrument of expression so worn by friction, of drawing new sounds from the old familiar pipe. "When we read, so saturated with French writing as we are that our whole body gives us the impression of being a paste made of words, do we ever find a line, a thought, which is not familiar to us, and of which we have not had at least a confused presentiment?" And he adds that the matter is simple enough for the writer who only seeks to amuse the public by means already known; he attempts little, and he produces "with confidence, in the candor of his mediocrity," works which answer no question and leave no trace. It is he who wants to do more than this that has less and less an easy time of it. Everything seems to him to have been done, every effect produced, every combination already made. If he be a man of genius, his trouble is lightened, for mysterious ways are revealed to him, and new combinations spring up for him even after novelty is dead. It is to the simple man of taste and talent, who has only a conscience and a will, that the situation may sometimes well appear desperate; he judges himself as he goes, and he can only go step by step over ground where every step is already a footprint.

If it be a miracle whenever there is a fresh tone, the miracle has been wrought for M. de Maupassant. Or is he simply a man of genius to whom short cuts have been disclosed in the watches of the night? At any rate he has had faith—religion has come to his aid; I mean the religion of his mother tongue, which he has loved well enough to be patient for her sake. He has arrived at the peace which passeth understanding, at a kind of conservative piety. He has taken his stand on simplicity, on a studied sobriety, being persuaded that the deepest science lies in that direction rather than in the multiplication of new terms, and on this subject he delivers himself with superlative wisdom.

"There is no need of the queer, complicated, numerous, and Chinese vocabulary which is imposed on us today under the name of artistic writing, to fix all the shades of thought; the right way is to distinguish with an extreme clearness all those modifications of the value of a word which come from the place it occupies. Let us have fewer nouns, verbs and adjectives of an almost imperceptible sense, and more different phrases variously constructed, ingeniously cast, full of the science of sound and rhythm. Let us have an excellent general form rather than be collectors of rare terms."

M. de Maupassant's practice does not fall below his exhortation (though I must confess that in the foregoing passage he makes use of the detestable expression "stylist," which I have not reproduced). Nothing can exceed the masculine firmness, the quiet force of his own style, in which every phrase is a close sequence, every epithet a paying piece, and the ground is completely cleared of the vague, the ready-made and the second-best. Less than any one today does he beat the air; more than any one does he hit out from the shoulder.

Part C: Style, Thought, Value

1. the push into language for the embrace of thought

("Gustave Flaubert," 1893)

There are moments when his [Flaubert's] restless passion for form strikes us as leaving the subject out of account altogether, as if he has taken it up arbitrarily, blindly, preparing himself the years of misery in which he is to denounce the grotesqueness, the insanity of his choice. Four times, with his *orgueil*, his love of magnificence, he condemned himself incongruously to the modern and familiar, groaning at every step over the horrible difficulty of reconciling "style" in such cases with truth and dialogue with surface. He wanted to do the battle of Thermopylae, and he found himself doing *Bouvard et Pécuchet*. One of the sides by which he interests us, one of the sides that will always endear him to the student, is his extraordinary ingenuity in lifting without falsifying, finding a middle way into grandeur and edging off from the literal without forsaking truth. This way was open to him from the moment he could look down upon his theme from the position of *une blague supérieure*, as he calls it, the amused freedom of an observer as irreverent as a creator. But if subjects were made for style (as to which Flaubert had a rigid theory: the idea was good enough if the expression was), so style was made for the ear, the last court of appeal, the supreme touchstone of perfection. He was perpetually demolishing his periods in the light of his merciless *gueulades*. He tried them on every one; his *gueulades* could make him sociable. The horror, in particular, that haunted all his years was the horror of the *cliché*, the stereotyped, the thing usually said and the way it was usually said, the current phrase that passed muster. Nothing, in his view, passed muster but freshness, that which came into the world, with all the honours, for the occasion. To use the ready-made was as disgraceful as for a self-respecting cook to buy a tinned soup or a sauce in a bottle. Flaubert considered that the dispenser of such wares was indeed the grocer, and, producing his ingredients exclusively at home, he would have stabbed himself for shame like Vatel. This touches on the strange weakness of his mind, his puerile dread of the grocer, the *bourgeois*, the sentiment that in his generation and the preceding misplaced, as it were, the spirit of adventure and the sense of honour, and sterlized a whole province of French literature. The worthy citizen ought never to have kept a poet from dreaming.

He had for his delectation and for satiric purposes a large collection of those second-hand and approximate expressions which begged the whole literary question. To light upon a perfect example was his nearest approach to natural bliss. *Bouvard et Pécuchet* is a museum of such examples, the cream of that *Dictionnaire des Idées Reçues* for which all his life he had taken notes and which eventually resolved itself into the encyclopaedic exactitude and the lugubrious humour of the novel. Just as subjects were meant for style, so style was meant for images; therefore as his own were numerous and admirable he would have contended, coming back to the source that he was one of the writers to whom the significance of a work had ever been most present. This significance was measured by the amount of style and the quantity of metaphor thrown up. Poor subjects threw up a little, fine subjects threw up much, and the finish of his prose was the proof of his profundity. If you pushed far enough into language you found yourself in the embrace of thought. There are doubtless many persons whom this account of the matter will fail to satisfy, and there will indeed be no particular zeal to put it forward even on the part of those for whom as a writer, Flaubert most vividly exists. He is a strong taste, like any other that is strong, and he exists only for those who have a constitutional need to feel in some direction the particular aesthetic confidence that he inspires. That confidence rests on the simple fact that he carried execution so far and nailed it so fast. No one will care for him at all who does not care for his metaphors, and those moreover who care most for these will be discreet enough to admit that even a style rich in similes is limited when it renders only the visible. The invisible Flaubert scarcely touches; his vocabulary and all his methods were unadjusted and alien to it. He could not read his French Wordsworth, M. Sully-Prudhomme; he had no faith in the power of the moral to offer a surface. He himself offers such a flawless one that this hard concretion is success. If he is impossible as a companion he is deeply refreshing as a reference; and all that his reputation asks of you is an occasional tap of the knuckle at those firm thin plates of gold which constitute the leaves of his books. This passing tribute will yield the best results when you have been prompted to it by some other purpose.

2. the inseparability of subject and style

("Turgenev and Tolstoy," 1897)

For the novels and *A Sportsman's Sketches* we depend upon the nine volumes (1897) [by Turgenev] of Mrs. Garnett. We touch here upon the remarkable side, to our vision, of the writer's fortune—the anomaly of his having constrained to intimacy even those who are shut out from the enjoyment of his medium, for whom that question is positively prevented from existing. Putting aside extrinsic intimations, it is impossible to read him without the conviction of his being, in the vividness of his own tongue, of the strong type of those made to bring home to us the happy truth of the unity, in a generous talent, of material and form—of their being inevitable faces of the same medal; the type of those, in a word, whose example deals death to the perpetual clumsy assumption that subject and style are—aesthetically speaking, or in the living work—different and separable things. We are conscious, reading him in a language not his own, of not being reached by his personal tone, his individual accent.

It is a testimony therefore to the intensity of his presence, that so much of his particular charm does reach us; that the mask turned to us has, even without his expression, still so much beauty. It is the beauty (since we must try to formulate) of the finest presentation of the familiar. His vision is of the world of character and feeling, the world of the relations life throws up at every hour and on every spot; he deals little, on the whole, in the miracles of chance,—the hours and spots over the edge of time and space; his air is that of the great central region of passion and motive, of the usual, the inevitable, the intimate—the intimate for weal or woe. No theme that he ever chooses but strikes us as full; yet with all have we the sense that their animation comes from within, and is not pinned to their backs like the pricking objects used of old in the horse races of the Roman carnival, to make the animals run. Without a patch of "plot" to draw blood, the story he mainly tells us, the situation he mainly gives, runs as if for dear life. His first book was practically full evidence of what, if we have to specify, is finest in him—the effect, for the commonest truth, of an exquisite envelope of poetry. In this medium of feeling—full, as it were, of all the echoes and shocks of the universal danger and need—everything in him goes on; the sense of fate and folly and pity and wonder and beauty. The tenderness, the humor, the variety of A Sportsman's Sketches revealed on the spot an observer with a rare imagination. These faculties had attached themselves, together, to small things and to great: to the misery, the simplicity, the piety, the patience, of the unemancipated peasant; to all the natural wonderful life of earth and air and winter and summer and field and forest; to queer apparitions of country neighbors, of strange local eccentrics; to old-world practices and superstitions; to secrets gathered and types disinterred and impressions absorbed in the long, close contacts with man and nature involved in the passionate pursuit of game. Magnificent in stature and original vigor, Turgenev, with his love of the chase, or rather perhaps of the inspiration he found in it, would have been the model of the mighty hunter, had not such an image been a little at variance with his natural mildness, the softness that often accompanies the sense of an extraordinary reach of limb and play of muscle. He was in person the model rather of the strong man at rest: massive and towering, with the voice of innocence and the smile almost of childhood. What seemed still more of a contradiction to so much of him, however, was that his work was all delicacy and fancy, penetration and compression.

3. the element of order and harmony as symbol

("Gustave Flaubert," 1902)

He [Flaubert] found the French language inconceivably difficult to write with elegance and was confronted with the equal truths that elegance is the last thing that languages, even as they most mature, seem to concern themselves with, and that at the same time taste, asserting rights, insists on it, to the effect of showing us in a boundless circumjacent waste of effort what the absence of it may mean. He saw the less of this desert of death come back to that—that everything at all saved from it for us since the beginning had been saved by a soul of elegance within, or in other words by the last refinement of selection, by the indifference on the part of the very idiom, huge quite other than "composing" agent, to the individual pretension. Recognizing thus that to carry through the individual pretension is at the best a battle, he adored a hard surface and detested a soft one—much more a muddled; regarded a style without rhythm and harmony as in a work of pretended beauty no style at all. He considered that the failure of complete expression so registered made of the work of pretended beauty a work of achieved barbarity. It would take us far to glance even at his fewest discriminations; but rhythm and harmony were for example most menaced in his scheme by repetition—when repetition had not a positive grace; and were above all most at the mercy of the bristling particles of which our modern tongues are mainly composed and which make of the desired surface a texture pricked through, from beneath, even to destruction, as by innumerable thorns.

On these lines production was of course slow work for him—especially as he met the difficulty, met it with an inveteracy which shows how it *can* be met; and full of interest for readers of English speech is the reflection he causes us to make as to the possibility of success at all comparable among ourselves. I have spoken of his groans and imprecations, his interminable waits and deep despairs; but what would these things have been, what would have become of him and what of his wrought residuum, had he been condemned to deal with a form of speech consisting, like ours, as to one part, of "that" and "which"; as to a second part, of the blessed "it," which an English sentence may repeat in three or four opposed references without in the least losing caste; as to a third face of all the "tos" of the infinite and the preposition; as to a fourth of our precious auxiliaries "be" and "do"; and as to a fifth, of whatever survives in the language for the precious art of pleasing? Whether or no the fact that the painter of "life" among us has to contend with a medium intrinsically indocile, on certain sides, like our own, whether this drawback accounts for his having failed, in our time, to treat us, arrested and charmed, to a single case of crowned classicism, there is at any rate no doubt that we in some degree owe Flaubert's counterweight for that deficiency to *his* having, on his own ground, more happily triumphed. By which I do not mean that *Madame Bovary* is a classic because the "thats," the "its" and the "tos" are made to march as Orpheus and his lute made the beasts, but because the element of order and harmony works as a symbol of everything else that is preserved for us by the history of the book. The history of the book remains the lesson and the important, the delightful thing, remains above all the drama that moves slowly to its climax. It is what we come back to for the sake of what it shows us.

4. the fusion of matter and manner

("Gabriele D'Annunzio," 1904)

So close is the marriage between his [D'Annunzio's] power of "rendering", in the light of the imagination, and whatever he sees and feels, that we should much mislead in speaking of his manner as a thing distinct from the matter submitted to it. The fusion is complete and admirable, so that, though his work is nothing if not "literary", we see at no point of it where literature or where life begins or ends: we swallow our successive morsels with as little question as we swallow food that has by proper preparation been reduced to singleness of savour. It is brought home to us afresh that there is no complete creation without style any more than there is complete music without sound; also that when language becomes as closely applied and impressed a thing as for the most part in the volumes before us the fact of artistic creation is registered at a stroke. It is never more present than in the thick-sown illustrative images and figures that fairly bloom under D'Annunzio's hand. I find examples in *Il Piacere*, as elsewhere, by simply turning the pages. "His will"—of the hero's weakness—"useless as a sword of base temper hung at the side of a drunkard or a dullard." Or of his own southern land in September: "I scarce know why, looking at the country in this season, I always think of some beautiful woman after childbirth, who lies back in her white bed, smiling with a pale, astonished, inextinguishable smile." Or the incision of this: "Where for him now were those unclean short-lived loves that left in the mouth the strange acidity of fruit cut with a steel knife?" Or the felicity of the following, of a southern night seen and felt from the terrace of a villa: "Clear meteors at intervals, streaked the motionless air, running over it as lightly and silently as drops of water on a crystal pane." "The sails on the sea," he says of the same look-out by day, "were as pious and numberless as the wings of cherubim on the gold grounds of old Giottesque panels."

5. style to meaning: body and soul

("The Tempest," 1907)

The face that beyond any other, however, I seem to see *The Tempest* turn to us is the side on which it so superlatively speaks of that endowment for Expression, expression as a primary force, a consuming, an independent passion, which was the greatest ever laid upon man. It is for Shakespeare's power of constitutive speech quite as if he had swum into our ken with it from another planet, gathering it up there, in its wealth, as something antecedent to the occasion and the need, and if possible quite in excess of them; something that was to make of our poor world a great flat table for receiving the glitter and clink of outpoured treasure. The idea and the motive are more often than not so smothered in it that they scarce know themselves, and the resources of such a style, the provision of images, emblems, energies of every sort, laid up in advance, affects us as the storehouse of a kind before a famine or a siege—which not only, by its scale, braves depletion or exhaustion, but bursts, through mere excess of quantity or presence, out of all doors and windows. It renders the poverties and obscurities of our world, as I say, in the dazzling terms of a richer and better. It constitutes, by a miracle, more than half the author's material; so much more usually does it happen, for the painter or the poet, that life itself, in its appealing, overwhelming crudity, offers itself as the paste to be kneaded. Such a personage works in general in the very elements of experience; whereas we see Shakespeare working predominantly in the terms of expression, *all* in the terms of the artist's specific vision and genius; with a thicker cloud of images to attest his approach, at any point, than the comparatively meagre given case ever has to attest its own identity. He points for us as no one else the relation of style to meaning and of manner to motive; a matter on which, right and left, we hear such rank ineptitudes uttered. Unless it be true that these things, on either hand, are inseparable; unless it be true that the phrase, the cluster and order of terms, *is* the object and the sense, in as close a compression as that of body and soul, so that any consideration of them as distinct, from the moment style is an active, applied force, becomes a gross stupidity: unless we recognize this reality the author of *The Tempest* has no lesson for us. It is by his expression of it exactly as the expression stands that the particular thing is created, created as interesting, as beautiful, as strange, droll or terrible—as related, in short, to our understanding or our sensibility; in consequence of which we reduce it to naught when we begin to talk of either of its presented parts as matters by themselves.

All of which considerations indeed take us too far; what is important to note being simply our Poet's high testimony to this independent, absolute value of Style, and to its need thoroughly to project and seat itself. It had been, as so seating itself, the very home of his mind, for his all too few twenty years; it had been the supreme source to him of the joy of life. It had been in fine his material, his plastic clay; since the more subtly he applied it the more secrets it had to give him, and the more these secrets might appear to him, at every point, one with the myriad pulses of the spirit of man. Thus it was that, as he passed from one application of it to another, tone became, for all its suggestions, more and more sovereign to him, and the subtlety of its secrets an exquisite interest. If I see him, at the last, over *The Tempest*, as the composer, at the harpsichord or the violin, extemporizing in the summer twilight, it is exactly that he is feeling there for tone and, by the same token, finding it—finding it as *The Tempest*, beyond any register of ours, immortally gives it. This surrender to the highest sincerity of virtuosity, as we nowadays call it, is to my perception *all The Tempest;* with no possible depth or delicacy in it that such an imputed character does not cover and provide for.

6. the value . . . is created by the breath of language

("The New Novel," 1914)

If a boy's experience has ever been given us for its face simply, for what it is worth in mere recovered intensity, it is so given us here [in Compton Mackenzie's *Sinister Street*]. Of all the saturations it can in fact scarce have helped being the most sufficient in itself, for it is exactly, where it is best, from beginning to end the remembered and reported thing, that thing alone, that thing existent in the field of memory, though gaining value too from the applied intelligence, or in other words from the lively talent, of the memorizer. The memorizer helps, he contributes, he completes, and what we have admired in him is that in the case of each of the pearls fished up by his dive—though indeed these fruits of the rummage are not all pearls—his mind has had a further iridescence to confer. It is the fineness of the iridescence that on such an occasion matters, and this appeal to our interest is again and again on Mr. Compton Mackenzie's page of the happiest and the brightest. It is never more so than when we catch him, as we repeatedly do, in the act of positively caring for his expression as expression, positively providing for his phrase as a fondly foreseeing parent for a child, positively loving it in the light of what it may do for him—meeting revelations, that is, in what it may do, and appearing to recognize that the value of the offered thing, its whole relation to us, is created by the breath of language, that on such terms exclusively, for appropriation and enjoyment, we know it, and that any claimed independence of "form" on its part is the most abject of fallacies. Do these things mean that, moved by life, this interesting young novelist is even now uncontrollably on the way to style?

PART D: LANGUAGE, SPEECH, MEANING

1. *the American language*

("An Animated Conversation," 1889)

Clifford (to Oswald). I don't understand you.

Belinda. Already?

Clifford. I mean that Oswald seems at once to resent the imputation that you have a national tongue and to wish to insist on the fact that you have it. His position is not clear.

Darcy. That is partly because our tongue itself is not clear as yet. We must hope that it will be clearer. Oswald needn't resent anything, for the evolution was inevitable. A body of English people crossed the Atlantic and sat down in a new climate on a new soil, amid new circumstances. It was a new heaven and a new earth. They invented new institutions, they encountered different needs. They developed a particular physique, as people do in a particular medium, and they began to speak in a new voice. They went in for democracy, and that alone would affect—it *has* affected—the tone immensely. *C'est bien le moins* (do your follow?) that that tone should have had its range and that the language they brought over with them should have become different to express different things. A language is a very sensitive organism. It must be convenient—it must be handy. It serves, it obeys, it accommodates itself.

Clifford. Ours, on your side of the water, has certainly been very accommodating.

Darcy. It has struck out different notes.

Clifford. He talks as if it were music!

Belinda. I like that idea of our voice being new; do you mean it creaks? I listen to Darcy with a certain surprise, however, for I am bound to say I have heard him criticise the American idiom.

Darcy. You have heard me criticise it as neglected, as unstudied: you have never heard me criticise it as American. The fault I find with it is that it's irresponsible—it isn't American enough.

Clifford. C'est trop fort!

Darcy. It's the candid truth. I repeat, its divergence was inevitable. But it has grown up roughly, and we haven't had time to cultivate it. That is all I complain of, and it's awkward for us, for surely the language of such a country ought to be magnificent. That is one of the reasons why I say that it won't be obligatory upon you English to learn it. We haven't quite learned it ourselves. When we shall at last have mastered it we'll talk the matter over with you. We'll agree upon our signs.

Camilla. Do you mean we must study it in books?

Darcy. I don't care how—or from the lips of the pretty ladies.

Belinda. I must bravely concede that often the lips of the pretty ladies—

Darcy (interrupting). At any rate, it's always American.

Camilla. But American improved—that's simply English.

Clifford. Your husband will tell you it's simply French.

Darcy. If it's simply English, that perhaps is what was to be demonstrated. Extremes meet!

Belwood. You have the drawback (and I think it a great disadvantage) that you come so late, that you have not fallen on a language-making age. The people who first started our vocabularies were very *naïfs*.

Darcy. Oh, *we* are very *naïfs*.

Belwood. When I listen to Darcy I find it hard to believe it.

Oswald. Don't listen to him.

Belwood. The first words must have been rather vulgar.

Belinda. Or perhaps pathetic.

Belwood. New signs are crude, and you, in this matter, are in the crude, the vulgar stage.

Darcy. That no doubt is our misfortune.

Belinda. That's what I mean by the pathos!

Darcy. But we have always the resource of English. We have lots of opportunity to practise it.

Clifford. As a foreign tongue, yes.

Darcy. To speak it as the Russians speak French.

Belwood. Oh, you'll grow very fond of it.

Clifford. The Russians are giving up French.

Darcy. Yes, but *they*'ve got the language of Tolstoï.

Clifford (groaning). Oh, heavens, Tolstoï!

Darcy. Our great writers have written in English. That's what I mean by American having been neglected.

Clifford. If you mean *ours*, of course.

Darcy. I mean—yours—ours—yes!

Oswald. It isn't a harmony. It's a labyrinth.

Clifford. It plays an odd part in Darcy's harmony, this duality of tongues.

Darcy. It plays the part of amusement. What could be more useful?

Clifford. Ah, then, we may laugh at you?

Darcy. It will make against tameness.

Oswald. Camilla, come away!

Clifford. Especially if you get angry.

Belinda. No, you and Belwood go first. We Americans must stay to pray.

Camilla (to Clifford). Well, mind you come to Paris.

Clifford. Will your husband receive me?

Oswald. Oh, in Paris I'm all right.

Belinda. I'll bring every one.

Clifford (to Camilla). Try "Mrs. Gibbs of Nebraska," the companion-piece to "Mrs. Jenks."

Oswald. That's another one *you* stole!

Belwood. Ah, the French and Germans!

Belinda (pushing him out with Clifford). Go, go. (*To the others*.) Let us pray.

2. *the language . . . in its Western adventure*

("James Russell Lowell," 1892)

That [the English tongue] was the innermost atmosphere of his [Lowell's] mind, and he never could have afforded on this general question any policy but a policy of annexation. He was capable of convictions in the light of which it was clear that the language he wrote so admirably had encountered in the United States not corruption, but conservation. Any conviction of his on this subject was a contribution to science, and he was zealous to show that the speech of New England was most largely that of an England older and more vernacular than the England that to-day finds it queer. He was capable of writing perfect American to bring out this archaic element. He kept in general the two tongues apart, save in so far as his English style betrayed a connection by a certain American tact in the art of leaving out. He was perhaps sometimes slightly paradoxical in the contention that the language had incurred no peril in its Western adventures; this is the sense in which I meant just now that he occasionally crossed the line. The difficulty was not that his vision of pure English could not fail in America sometimes to be clouded—the peril was for his vision of pure American. His standard was the highest, and the wish was often no doubt father to the thought. "The Biglow Papers" are delightful, but nothing could be less like "The Biglow Papers" than the style of the American newspaper. He lent his wit to his theories, but one or two of them lived on him like unthrifty sons.

3. *dictation, walking, writing*

(*Letters*, 1902, to Mrs. Cadwalader Jones)

But I am not thanking you, all this time, for the interesting remarks about the book I had last placed in your hands (The Wings of the Dove), which you so heroically flung upon paper even on the heaving deep—a feat to *me* very prodigious. I won't say your criticism was eminent for the time and place—I'll say, frankly, that it was eminent in itself, and all full of suggestion. The fact is, however, that one is so aware one's self, even to satiety, of the rights and wrongs of these matters—especially of the wrongs—that freshness of mind almost fails for discriminations, however benevolent, of others. Such is the price of having written many books and lived many years. The thing in question is, by a complicated accident which it would take too long to describe to you, too inordinately drawn out, and too inordinately rubbed in. The centre, moreover, isn't in the middle, or the middle, rather, isn't in the centre, but ever so much too near the end, so that what was to come after it is truncated. The book, in fine, has too big a head for its body. I am trying, all the while, to write one with the opposite disproportion—the body too big for its head. So I shall perhaps do if I live to 150. Don't therefore undermine me by general remarks. And dictating, please, has moreover nothing to do with it. The value of that process for me is in its help to do over and over, for which it is extremely adapted, and which is the only way I can do at all. It soon enough, accordingly, becomes, *intellectually*, absolutely identical with the act of writing—or has become so, after five years now, with me; so that the difference is only material and illusory—only the difference, that is, that I walk up and down: which is so much to the good.—But I must stop walking now.

4. speech: the great human and social function

(*The Question of Our Speech*, 1905)

All life therefore comes back to the question of our speech, the medium through which we communicate with each other; for all life comes back to the question of our relations with each other. These relations are made possible, are registered, are verily constituted, by our speech, and are successful (to repeat my word) in proportion as our speech is worthy of its great human and social function; is developed, delicate, flexible, rich—an adequate accomplished fact. The more it suggests and expresses the more we live by it—the more it promotes and enhances life. Its quality, its authenticity, its security, are hence supremely important for the general multifold opportunity, for the dignity and integrity, of our existence.

5. the riot of the vulgar tongue

(Preface to *Daisy Miller*, 1909)

Let me say, however, that such reflexions had never helped to close my eyes, at any moment, to all that had come and gone, over the rest of the field, in the fictive world of adventure more complacently so called—the American world, I particularly mean, that might have put me so completely out of countenance by having drawn its inspiration, that of thousands of celebrated works, neither from up-town nor from down-town nor from my lady's chamber, but from the vast wild garden of "unconventional" life in no matter what part of our country. I grant in fact that this demonstration of how consummately my own meagrely-conceived sources were to be dispensed with by the more initiated minds would but for a single circumstance, grasped at in recovery of self-respect, have thrown me back in absolute dejection on the poverty of my own categories. Why hadn't so quickened a vision of the great neglected native quarry *at large* more troubled my dreams, instead of leaving my imagination on the whole so resigned? Well, with many reasons I could count over, there was one that all exhaustively covered the ground and all completely answered the question: the reflexion, namely, that the common sign of the productions "unconventionally" prompted (and this positively without exception) was nothing less than the birthmark of Dialect, general or special—dialect with the literary rein loose on its agitated back and with its shambling power of traction, not to say, more analytically, of *attraction*, trusted for all such a magic might be worth. Distinctly that was the odd case: the key to the *whole* of the treasure of romance independently garnered was the riot of the vulgar tongue. One might state it more freely still and the truth would be as evident: the plural number, the vulgar tongues, each with its intensest note, but pointed the moral more luridly. Grand generalised continental riot or particular pedantic, particular discriminated and "sectional" and self-conscious riot—to feel the thick breath, to catch the ugly snarl, of all or of either, was to be reminded afresh of the only conditions that guard the grace, the only origins that save the honour, or even the life, of dialect: those precedent to the invasion, to the sophistication, of schools and unconscious of the smartness of echoes and the taint of slang. The thousands of celebrated productions raised their monument but to the bastard vernacular of communities disinherited of the felt difference between the speech of the soil and the speech of the newspaper, and capable thereby, accordingly, of taking slang for simplicity, the composite for the quaint and the vulgar for the natural. These were unutterable depths, and, as they yawned about one, *what* appreciable coherent sound did they seem most to give out? Well, to my ear surely, at the worst, none that determined even a tardy compunction. The monument was there, if one would, but was one to regret one's own failure to have contributed a stone? Perish, and all ignobly, the thought!

Chapter XV

MORALITY AND PHILOSOPHY;
MEANING AND THEME

Beyond the story, beyond the action or plot, behind the character, setting, or dramatized consciousness, behind all of these and the rest that might be enumerated lay—what? James searched throughout his critical career for the right language to describe this elusive but vital element, and his language shifted and changed, but he never gave up his solid belief that the ultimate value of fiction—and a high value it was—resided in this all-pervasive element.

There is a distinct break in the way James talked about morality in fiction that comes in the late 1870s and early 1880s, and the break probably stems from James's reconsideration of the problem in the light of the radical views he heard when in 1875–76 he frequented the Paris salons of the French literati (see Leon Edel, Henry James: The Conquest of London, Book V. "The Siege of Paris"*). Up until this period (emphasized in Part A of this chapter, "Morality and Philosophy"), James used a rather conventional vocabulary, sometimes verging in his early reviews on the banal, in demanding that all literature be moral.*

It should be stressed, however, that James never equated morality with simple sexual purity (see Chapter VII, "Sex: An Immense Omission"). For example, in his brilliant 1874 essay on Ivan Turgénieff, James hailed The Memoirs of a Sportsman for the morality of its subtle, indirect but "cumulative testimony" against the "peculiar institution" of Russian serfdom. Moreover, James saw a fundamental relationship between the moral subtlety of the book and its looseness of texture: "It offers a capital example of moral meaning giving a sense to form and form giving relief to moral meaning." This view of the role of morality in fiction appears elaborated and substantiated by an aside in the 1876 essay on Charles Baudelaire: "[Morality] is in reality simply a part of the essential richness of inspiration—it has nothing to do with the artistic process and it has everything to do with the artistic effect. The more a work of art feels it at its source, the richer it is; the less it feels it, the poorer it is."

Indeed Turgénieff may be viewed as a key figure in James's education in this aspect of fiction. It was Turgénieff's work which inspired James's most thoughtful comments on philosophy in fiction, as it was Turgénieff later in

Paris who introduced James to the Flaubert salon and all that iconoclastic, anti-puritan talk. In that same 1874 essay cited above, James asserted: "The great question as a poet or a novelist is, How does he feel about life? what, in the last analysis, is his philosophy? When vigorous writers have reached maturity we are at liberty to look in their works for some expression of a total view of the world they have been so actively observing." James then proceeded to trace out the figure in Turgénieff's carpet (though this was a term he came to later).

Not the least value of this 1874 Turgénieff essay is its revelation about James's own "total view of the world," which turned out to coincide with Turgénieff's: "Life is, in fact, a battle. On this point optimists and pessimists agree. Evil is insolent and strong; beauty enchanting but rare, goodness very apt to be weak; folly very apt to be defiant; wickedness to carry the day; imbeciles to be in great places, people of sense in small, and mankind generally, unhappy. But the world as it stands is no illusion, no phantasm, no evil dream of a night; we wake up to it again for ever and ever; we can neither forget it nor deny it nor dispense with it. We can welcome experience as it comes, and give it what it demands, in exchange for something which it is idle to pause to call much or little so long as it contributes to swell the volume of consciousness. In this there is mingled pain and delight, but over the mysterious mixture there hovers a visible rule, that bids us learn to will and seek to understand. So much as this we seem to decipher between the lines of M. Turgénieff's minutely written chronicle."

This passage is worth dwelling on at length not only because it bears the stamp of James's own conviction, but because it presents an example of the early James tracking to its lair that elusive element that gives ultimate significance and authority to a body of fiction. Oh, if only Hugh Vereker had found for himself such a critic in "The Figure in the Carpet"!

It was very much indeed, then, under Turgénieff's tutelage that James moved from the simplistic notions of morality and fiction of his early reviews and essays to the much more complex and sophisticated views of the later criticism. In his later (1884) essay on Turgénieff (see Part II of this chapter) James describes the conversations of that Paris salon, and he gives to Turgénieff many of the principal lines that he himself was to borrow with little change for embodiment of his own views in "The Art of Fiction" (1884).

The importance James gave to the question of morality is suggested by his discussing it last in "The Art of Fiction." His point of departure is his strong disagreement with Besant's insistence on the "conscious moral purpose" in the novel: "Will you define your terms and explain how (a novel being a picture) a picture can be either moral or immoral?" James's eloquence in attacking Besant's awkward and clumsy phrase, "conscious moral purpose," has tended to obscure James's final affirmation: "There is one point at which the moral sense and the artistic sense lie very near together; that is in the light *of the very obvious truth that the deepest quality of a work of art will always be the quality of the mind of the producer. In proportion as that intelligence is fine will the novel, the picture, the statue partake of the substance of beauty and truth. To be constituted of such elements is, to my vision, to have purpose enough. No good novel will ever proceed from a superficial mind."*

This 1884 statement leads directly to the famous "house of fiction" statement in the Preface to The Portrait of a Lady: *"There is, I think, no more nutritive or suggestive truth in this connexion than that of the perfect dependence of the 'moral' sense of a work of art on the amount of felt life concerned in producing it. The question comes back thus, obviously, to the kind and the degree of the artist's prime sensibility, which is the soil out of which his subject springs. The quality and capacity of that soil, its ability to 'grow' with due freshness and straightness any vision of life, represents, strongly or weakly, the projected morality."* This *"prime sensibility,"* or *"enveloping air of the artist's humanity"* (which *"gives the last touch to the worth of the work"*) is *"a widely and wonderously varying element."* Thus James comes round to his brilliant image of the million-windowed house of fiction.

James's belief that *"the 'moral' sense of a work of art"* depended on the *"amount of felt life concerned in producing it"* suggests his concern, throughout his Notebooks and Prefaces, for the "themes" of his fictions. Invariably James found his germs in concrete characters, places, or actions (see Chapter II, Part B)—not in abstract themes; but just as invariably, James sifted through the concrete materials of his fictions, with a quickened "moral sense," in search of ways of releasing from them naturally and authentically this additional vital dimension. In Part B of this chapter are included a number of James's observations about the themes in his various works.

From beginning to end, James was concerned with "moral sense" or the "vision of life" in fiction, but his way of talking about or exploring it shifted considerably. Perhaps the best illustration of James's later view comes in *"The Lesson of Balzac"* (1905; see Chapter II): *"His [Balzac's] plan was to handle, primarily, not a world of ideas, animated by figures representing these ideas; but the packed and constituted, the palpable, provable world before him, by the study of which ideas would inevitably find themselves thrown up."* Thrown up, that is, from the depths of that prime sensibility which is the artist's own, individual humanity, his *window in the house of fiction*.

Part A: Morality and Philosophy

1. the cure of souls

("Miss Prescott's 'Azarian,' " 1865)

There is surely no principle of fictitious composition so true as this,—that an author's paramount charge is the cure of souls, to the subjection, and if need be to the exclusion, of the picturesque. . . .

When once a work of fiction may be classed as a novel, its foremost claim to merit, and indeed the measure of its merit, is its *truth*,—its truth to something, however questionable that thing may be in point of morals or of taste.

2. *lift up the reader's heart*

("Alexandre Dumas," 1866)

To be completely great, a work of art must lift up the reader's heart; and it is the artist's secret to reconcile this condition with images of the barest and sternest reality. Life is dispiriting, art is inspiring; and a story-teller who aims at anything more than a fleeting success has no right to tell an ugly story unless he knows its beautiful counterpart. The impression that he should aim to produce on the reader's mind with his work must have much in common with the impression originally produced on his own mind by the subject. If the effect of an efficient knowledge of his subject had been to fill his spirit with melancholy, and to paralyze his better feelings, it would be impossible that his work should be written. Its existence depends on the artist's reaction against the subject; and if the subject is morally hideous, of course this reaction will be in favor of moral beauty.

3. *the primary function of a book: to suggest thought*

("The Belton Estate," 1866)

Such praise as this we may freely bestow on the work before us [Anthony Trollope's *The Belton Estate*], because, qualified by the important stricture which we have kept in reserve, we feel that it will not seem excessive. Our great objection to *The Belton Estate* is that, as we read it, we seemed to be reading a work written for children; a work below the apprehension of the average man and woman, or, at the very most, on a level with it, and in no particular above it. *The Belton Estate* is a *stupid* book; and in a much deeper sense than that of being simply dull, for a dull book is always a book that might have been lively. A dull book is a failure. Mr. Trollope's story is stupid and a success. It is essentially, organically, consistently stupid; stupid in direct proportion to its strength. It is without a single idea. It is utterly incompetent to the primary functions of a book, of whatever nature, namely—to suggest thought. In a certain way, indeed, it suggests thought; but this is only on the ruins of its own existence as a book. It acts as the occasion, not as the cause, of thought. It indicates the manner in which a novel should *not*, on any account, be written. That it should deal exclusively with dull, flat, common-place people was to be expected; and this need not be a fault; but it deals with such people as one of themselves; and this is what Lady Aylmer would call a "damning" fault. Mr. Trollope is a good observer; but he is literally nothing else. He is apparently as incapable of disengaging an idea as of drawing an inference. All his incidents are, if we may so express it, *empirical*. He has seen and heard every act and every speech that appears in his pages. That minds like his should exist, and exist in plenty, is neither to be wondered at nor to be deplored; but that such a mind as his should devote itself to writing novels, and that these novels should be successful, appears to us an extraordinary fact.

4. style without a spiritual spark

("Théophile Gautier," 1873)

Some of us are awkward writers and yearning moralists; others are masters of a perfect style which has never reflected a spiritual spark. Gautier's disposition served him to the end, and enabled him to have a literary heritage perfect of its kind. He could look every day at a group of beggars sunning themselves on the Spanish Steps at Rome, against their golden wall of mouldering travertine, and see nothing but the fine brownness of their rags and their flesh-tints—see it and enjoy it forever, without an hour's disenchantment, without a chance of one of those irresistable revulsions of mood in which the "mellowest" rags are but filth, and filth is poverty, and poverty a haunting shadow, and picturesque squalor a mockery. His unfaltering robustness of vision—of appetite, one may say—made him not only strong but enviable.

5. the moral of his tale . . .

("Ivan Turgénieff," 1874)

The husband, the wife, and the lover—the wife, the husband, and the woman loved—these are combinations in which modern fiction has been prolific; but M. Turgénieff's treatment [in "A Nest of Noblemen"] renews the youth of the well-worn fable. He has found its moral interest, if we may take the distinction, deeper than its sentimental one; a pair of lovers accepting adversity seem to him more eloquent than a pair of lovers grasping at happiness. The moral of his tale, as we are free to gather it, is that there is no effective plotting for happiness, that we must take what we can get, that adversity is a capable mill-stream, and that our ingenuity must go toward making it grind our corn. Certain it is that there is something very exquisite in Lavretzky's history, and that M. Turgénieff has drawn from a theme associated with all manner of uncleanness a story embalmed in an aroma of purity. This purity, indeed, is but a pervasive emanation from the character of Lisaveta Michailovna.

6. moral meaning giving a sense to form

("Ivan Turgénieff," 1874)

It was not, however, in satire, but in thoroughly genial, poetical portraiture, that our author first made his mark. "The Memoirs of a Sportsman" were published in 1852, and were regarded, says one of the two French translators of the work, as much the same sort of contribution to the question of Russian serfdom as Mrs. Stowe's famous novel to that of American slavery. This, perhaps, is forcing a point, for M. Turgénieff's group of tales strikes us much less as a passionate *pièce de circonstance* than as a disinterested work of art. But circumstances helped it, of course, and it made a great impression—an impression that testifies to no small culture on the part of Russian readers. For never, surely, was a work with a polemic bearing more consistently low in tone, as painters say. The author treats us to such a scanty dose of flagrant horrors that the moral of the book is obvious only to attentive readers. No single episode pleads conclusively against the "peculiar institution" of Russia; the lesson is in the cumulative testimony of a multitude of fine touches—in an after-sense of sadness that sets wise readers thinking. It would be difficult to name a work that contains better instruction for those heated spirits who are fond of taking sides on the question of "art for art." It offers a capital example of moral meaning giving a sense to form and form giving relief to moral meaning. Indeed, all the author's characteristic merits are to be found in the "Memoirs," with a certain *amateurish looseness of texture* which will charm many persons who find his later works too frugal, as it were, in shape. Of all his productions, this is indeed the most purely delightful. We especially recommend the little history of Foma, the forest-keeper, who, one rainy night, when the narrator has taken refuge in his hut, hears a peasant stealing faggots in the dark, dripping woods; rushes forth and falls upon him, drags the poor wretch home, flings him into a corner, and sits on in the smoky hovel (with the author, whom we perceive there, noting, feeling, measuring it all), while the rain batters the roof and the drenched starveling howls and whines and imprecates. Anything more dismally real in a narrower compass we have never read—anything more pathetic, with less of the machinery of pathos. In this case, as at every turn with M. Turgénieff, "It is life itself," we murmur as we read, "and not this or that or the other story-teller's more or less clever 'arrangement' of life." M. Turgénieff deserves this praise in its largest application; for "life" in his pages is very far from meaning a dreary liability to sordid accidents, as it seems to mean with those writers of the grimly pathetic school who cultivate sympathy to the detriment of comprehension. He does equal justice—joyous justice—to all brighter accidents—to everything in experience that helps to keep it within the pale of legend. Two of the Sportsman's reminiscences are inexpressibly charming—the chapter in which he spends a warm summer-night lying on the grass listening to the small boys who are sent out to watch the horses at pasture, as they sit chattering to each other of hobgoblins and fairies; and the truly beautiful description of a singing-match in a village ale-house, between two ragged serfs. The latter is simply a perfect poem. Very different, but in its way as characteristic, is the story of "A Russian Hamlet"—a poor gentleman whom the Sportsman, staying over-night at a fine house where he has been dining, finds assigned to him as room-mate, and who, lying in bed and staring at him grotesquely over the sheets, relates his lugubrious history. This sketch, more that its companions, strikes the deep moral note that was to reverberate through the author's novels.

7. a total view of the world

("Ivan Turgénieff," 1874)

The great question as to a poet or a novelist is, How does he feel about life? what, in the last analysis, is his philosophy? When vigorous writers have reached maturity we are at liberty to look in their works for some expression of a total view of the world they have been so actively observing. This is the most interesting thing their works offer us. Details are interesting in proportion as they contribute to make it clear.

The foremost impression of M. Turgénieff's reader is that he is morbidly serious, that he takes life terribly hard. We move in an atmosphere of unrelieved sadness. We go from one tale to the other in the hope of finding something cheerful, but we only wander into fresh agglomerations of gloom. We try the shorter stories with a hope of chancing upon something pitched in the traditional key of "light reading," but they strike us alike as so many ingenious condensations of melancholy. "A Village Lear" is worse than "The Antchar"; "The Forsaken" is hardly an improvement on "A Correspondence"; "The Journal of a Superfluous Man" does little to lay the haunting ghost of "Three Portraits." The author has written several short dramas. Appealing to them to beguile us of our dusky vapours, we find the concentrated tragedy of "The Bread of Charity," and, by way of an after-piece, the lugubrious humour of "The Division." Sad beginnings, worse endings, good people ineffably wretched, happy ones hugely ridiculous; disappointment, despair, madness, suicide, degrading passions, and blighted hopes—these seem, on first acquaintance, the chief ingredients of M. Tur-génieff's version of the human drama; and to deepen our sense of its bitter-ness we discover the author in the background winding up his dismal demon-stration with a chuckle. We set him down forthwith as a cold-blooded pes-simist, caring for nothing in life but its misery and for nothing in misery but its pictorial effects—its capacity for furnishing cynical epigrams. What is each of the short tales we have mentioned, we ask, but a ruthless epigram, in the dramatic form, upon human happiness? Evlampia Charloff, in "A Village Lear," drives her father to madness and death by her stony depravity, and then joins a set of religious fanatics, among whom she plays a great part as the "Holy Mother of God." In "the Bread of Charity," a young heir-ess brings home to her estates her newly-wedded husband, and introduces him to her old neighbours. They dine with him, and one of them, an officious coxcomb, conceives the brilliant idea of entertaining him by an exhibition of a poor old gentleman who has long been hanging about the place as a pensioner of the late parents of the young wife, and is remarkable for a dumb canine attachment to herself. The heartless guest plies the modest old man with wine, winds him up and makes him play the fool. But suddenly Kusof-kin, through the fumes of his potations, perceives that he is being laughed at, and breaks out into a passionate assurance that, baited and buffeted as he is, he is nothing less than the father of the mistress of the house. She overhears his cry, and though he, horrified at his indiscretion, attempts to retract it, she wins from him a confession of the fact that he had been her mother's lover. The husband, however, makes him swallow his words, and do public penance. He turns him out of the house with a small pension, and the curtain falls on the compliment offered this fine fellow by the meddlesome neighbour on his generosity: "You are a true Russian gentleman!" The most perfectly epigrammatic of our author's stories, however, is perhaps that polished little piece of misery, "A Correspondence." A young man, idle, discontented, and longing for better things, writes, for a pastime, to a young girl whom he has formerly slightly known and greatly esteemed, who has entertained an unsuspected and unrequited passion for him, and who lives obscurely in the country, among very common people. A correspondence comes of it, in the course of which they exchange confidences and unburden their hearts. The young girl is most pitiable, most amiable, in her sadness, and her friend begins to suspect that she, at last, may give a meaning to his aimless life. She, on her side, is compassionately interested, and we see curiosity and hope throbbing timidly beneath the austere resignation to which she had schooled herself, and the expression of which, mingled with our sense of her blooming beauty of character, makes of Maria Alexandrovna the most nobly fascinating, perhaps, of our author's heroines. Alexis Petrovitsch writes at last that he must see her, that he will come to her, that she is to expect him at such a date, and we imagine tenderly, in the unhastening current of her days, the gentle eddy of her expectation. Her next letter, after an interval, expresses surprise at his non-appearance; her next, several months later, is a last attempt to obtain news of him. The correspondence closes with his confession, written as he lies dying at Dresden. Just as he was starting to join her, he had encountered another woman, a dancing-girl at the opera, with whom he had fallen madly in love. She was low, stupid, heartless; she had nothing to recommend her to anything but his senses. It was ignoble, but so it was. His passion has led him such a life that his health is gone. He has brought on disease of the lungs, by waiting for the young lady at the opera-door in the winter nights. Now his hours are numbered, and this is the end of all! And on this lugubrious note the story closes. We read with intent curiosity, for the tale is a masterpiece of narration; but we wonder, in some vexation, what it all means. Is it a piece of irony for irony's sake, or is it a disinterested picture of the struggle between base passion and pure passion? Why, in that case, should it seem a matter of course for the author that base passion should carry the day? Why, as for Rudin, for Sanin, for the distracted hero of "Smoke," should circumstances also have been too many, as the phrase is, for poor Alexis Petrovitsch? If we pursue our researches, in the hope of finding some method in this promiscuous misery, examples continue to seem more numerous than principles. The author continues everywhere to imply that there is something essentially ridiculous in human nature, something indefeasibly vain in human effort. We are amazed, as we go, at the portentous number of his patent fools; no novelist has drawn a tenth as many. The large majority of his people are the people we laugh at, and a large fraction of the remainder the people we half disgustedly pity. There is little room left, therefore, for the people we esteem, and yet room enough perhaps, considering that our very benevolence is tempered with scepticism. What with the vicious fools and the well-meaning fools, the prosperous charlatans and the grotesque nonentities, the dead failures and the sadder failures that regret and protest and rebel, the demoralized lovers and the jilted maidens, the dusky pall of fatality, in a word, suspended over all human things, it may be inferred that we are not invited to a particularly exhilarating spectacle. Not a single person in the novel of "Fathers and Sons" but has, in some degree, a lurking ironical meaning. Every one is a more or less ludicrous parody on what he ought to have been, or an ineffectual regret at what he might have been. The only person who compasses a reasonable share of happiness is Arcadi, and even his happiness is a thing for strenuous minds to smile at—a happiness based on the *pot au feu*, the prospect of innumerable babies and the sacrifice of "views." Arcadi's father is a vulgar failure; Pavel Petrovitsch is a poetic failure; Bazaroff is a tragic failure; Anna Sergheievna misses happiness from an ungenerous fear of sacrificing her luxurious quietude; the elder Bazaroff and his wife seem a couple of ingeniously grotesque manikins, prepared by a melancholy *fantoccinista* to illustrate the mocking vanity of parental hopes. We lay down the book, and we repeat that, with all the charity in the world, it is impossible to pronounce M. Turgénieff anything better than a pessimist.

The judgment is just, but it needs qualifications, and it finds them in a larger look at the author's position. M. Turgénieff strikes us, as we have said, as a man disappointed, for good reasons or for poor ones, in the land that is dear to him. Harsh critics will say for poor ones, reflecting that a fastidious imagination has not been unconcerned in his discontentment. To the old Muscovite virtues, and especially the old Muscovite *naïveté*, his imagination filially clings, but he finds these things, especially in the fact that his country turns to the outer world, melting more and more every day into the dimness of tradition. The Russians are clever, and clever people are ambitious. Those with whom M. Turgénieff has seen himself surrounded are consumed with the desire to pass for intellectual cosmopolites, to know, or seem to know, everything that can be known, to be astoundingly modern and progressive and European. Madam Kukshin, the poor little literary lady with a red nose, in "Fathers and Sons," gives up George Sand as "nowhere" for her want of knowledge of embryology, and, when asked why she proposes to remove to Heidelberg, replies with "Bunsen, you know." The fermentation of social change has thrown to the surface in Russia a deluge of hollow pretensions and vicious presumptions, amid which the love either of old virtues or of new achievements finds very little gratification. It is not simply that people flounder laughably in deeper waters than they can breast, but that in this discord of crude ambitions the integrity of character itself is compromised and men and women make, morally, a very ugly appearance. The Russian colony at Baden-Baden, depicted in "Smoke," is a collection of more or less inflated profligates. Panschin, in "A Nest of Noblemen," is another example; Sitnikoff, in "Fathers and Sons," a still more contemptible one. Driven back, depressed and embittered, into his imagination for the edification which the social spectacle immediately before him refuses him, and shaped by nature to take life hard and linger among its shadows, our observer surrenders himself with a certain reactionary, irresponsible gusto to a sombre portrayal of things. An imaginative preference for dusky subjects is a perfectly legitimate element of the artistic temperament; our own Hawthorne is a signal case of its being innocently exercised; innocently, because with that delightfully unconscious genius it remained imaginative, sportive, inconclusive, to the end. When external circumstances, however, contribute to confirm it, and reality lays her groaning stores of misery at its feet, it will take a rarely elastic genius altogether to elude the charge of being morbid. M. Turgenieff's pessimism seems to us of two sorts—a spontaneous melancholy and a wanton melancholy. Sometimes in a sad story it is the problem, the question, the idea, that strikes him; sometimes it is simply the picture. Under the former influence he has produced his masterpieces; we admit that they are intensely sad, but we consent to be moved, as we consent to sit silent in a death-chamber. In the other case he has done but his second best; we strike a bargain over our tears, and insist that when it comes to being simply entertained, wooing and wedding are better than death and burial. "The Antchar," "The Forsaken," "A Superfluous Man," "A Village Lear," "Toc . . . toc . . . toc," all seem to us to be gloomier by several shades than they need have been; for we hold to the good old belief that the presumption, in life, is in favour of the brighter side, and we deem it, in art, an indispensable condition of our interest in a depressed observer that he should have at least tried his best to be cheerful. The truth, we take it, lies for the pathetic in poetry and romance very much where it lies for the "immoral." Morbid pathos is reflective pathos; ingenious pathos, pathos not freshly born of the occasion; noxious immorality is superficial immorality, immorality without natural roots in the subject. We value most the "realists" who have an ideal of delicacy and the elegiasts who have an ideal of joy.

"Pictorial gloom, possibly," a thick and thin admirer of M. Turgénieff's may say to us, "at least you will admit that it is pictorial." This we heartily concede, and, recalled to a sense of our author's brilliant diversity and ingenuity, we bring our restrictions to a close. To the broadly generous side of his imagination it is impossible to pay exaggerated homage, or, indeed, for that matter, to its simple intensity and fecundity. No romancer has created a greater number of the figures that breathe and move and speak, in their habits as they might have lived; none, on the whole, seems to us to have had such a masterly touch in portraiture, none has mingled so much ideal beauty with so much unsparing reality. His sadness has its element of error, but it has also its larger element of wisdom. Life is, in fact, a battle. On this point optimists and pessimists agree. Evil is insolent and strong; beauty enchanting but rare; goodness very apt to be weak; folly very apt to be defiant; wickedness to carry the day; imbeciles to be in great places, people of sense in small, and mankind generally, unhappy. But the world as it stands is no illusion, no phantasm, no evil dream of a night; we wake up to it again for ever and ever; we can neither forget it nor deny it nor dispense with it. We can welcome experience as it comes, and give it what it demands, in exchange for something which it is idle to pause to call much or little so long as it contributed to swell the volume of consciousness. In this there is mingled pain and delight, but over the mysterious mixture there hovers a visible rule, that bids us learn to will and seek to understand. So much as this we seem to decipher between the lines of M. Turgénieff's minutely written chronicle. He himself has sought to understand as zeal-ously as his most eminent competitors. He gives, at least, no meagre account of life, and he has done liberal justice to its infinite variety. This is his great merit; his great defect, roughly stated, is a tendency to the abuse of irony. He remains, nevertheless, to our sense, a very welcome mediator between the world and our curiosity. If we had space, we should like to set forth that he is by no means our ideal story-teller—this honourable genius pos-sessing, attributively, a rarer skill than the finest required for producing an artful *réchauffé* of the actual. But even for better romancers we must wait for a better world. Whether the world in its higher state of perfection will occasionally offer colour to scandal, we hesitate to pronounce; but we are prone to conceive of the ultimate novelist as a personage altogether purged of sarcasm. The imaginative force now expended in this direction he will devote to describing cities of gold and heavens of sapphire. But, for the present, we gratefully accept M. Turgénieff, and reflect that his manner suits the most frequent mood of the greater number of readers. If he were a dogmatic optimist we suspect that, as things go, we should long ago have ceased to miss him from our library. The personal optimism of most of us no romancer can confirm or dissipate and our personal troubles, generally, place fictions of all kinds in an impertinent light. To our usual working mood the world is apt to seem M. Turgénieff's hard world, and when, at moments, the strain and the pressure deepen, the ironical element figures not a little in our form of address to those short-sighted friends who have whispered that it is an easy one.

8. *no natural sense of morality*

("Honoré de Balzac," 1875)

Balzac: . . . he was morally and intellectually so superficial. He paid himself, as the French say, with shallower conceits than ever before passed muster with a strong man. The moral, the intellectual atmosphere of his genius is extraordinarily gross and turbid; it is no wonder that the flower of truth does not bloom in it, nor any natural flower whatever. . . . He had no natural sense of morality, and this we cannot help thinking a serious fault in a novelist. Be the morality false or true, the writer's deference to it greets us as a kind of essential perfume. We find such a perfume in Shakespeare; we find it, in spite of his so-called cynicism, in Thackeray; we find it, potently, in George Eliot, in George Sand, in Turgénieff. They care for moral questions; they are haunted by a moral ideal. This southern slope of the mind, as we may call it, was very barren in Balzac, and it is partly pos-sible to account for its barrenness.

9. no moral imagination

("Charles de Bernard and Gustave Flaubert," 1876)

Considering that we do not recommend the reader who is unacquainted with him to make any great point of retracing his steps along the crowded highway of what we nowadays call culture, to bend over our author where his own march stopped and left him, it may seem that we are lingering too long upon Charles de Bernard. But there is another word to say, and it is an interesting one. Charles de Bernard's talent is great—very great, greater than the impression it leaves; and the reason why this clever man remains so persistently second-rate is, to our sense, because he had no morality. By this we of course do not mean that he did not choose to write didactic tales, winding up with a goody lecture and a distribution of prizes and punishments. We mean that he had no moral emotion, no preferences, no instincts—no moral imagination, in a word. His morality was altogether traditional, and, such as it was, it seems to have held him in a very loose grasp. It was not the current social notion of right and wrong, of honour and dishonour, that he represented, but something even less consistent. What we find in him is not the average morality, but a morality decidely below the average. He does not care, he does not feel, and yet his indifference is not philosophic. He has no heat of his own, save that of the *raconteur;* his laugh is always good-natured, but always cold. He describes all sorts of mean and ignoble things without in the least gauging their quality. He belongs to the intellectual family—and very large it is in France—of the amusing author of "Gil Blas." All its members know how to write, and how, up to a certain point, to observe; but their observation has no reflex action, as it were, and they remain as dry as they are brilliant.

10. every out-and-out realist . . . is a moralist

("Charles de Bernard and Gustave Flaubert," 1876)

The "scandal" in relation to "Madame Bovary" was that the book was judicially impeached and prosecuted for immorality. The defence was eloquent, and the writer was acquitted; the later editions of the book contain, in an appendix, a full report of the trial. It is a work upon which it is possible to be very paradoxical, or rather in relation to which sincere opinion may easily have the air of paradox. It is a book adapted for the reverse of what is called family reading, and yet we remember thinking, the first time we read it, in the heat of our admiration for its power, that it would make the most useful of Sunday-school tracts. In M. Taine's elaborate satire, "The Opinions of M. Graindorge," there is a report of a conversation at a dinner party between an English spinster of didactic habits and a decidedly audacious Frenchman. He begs to recommend to her a work which he has lately been reading and which cannot fail to win the approval of all persons interested in the propagation of virtue. The lady lends a sympathetic ear, and he gives a rapid sketch of the tale—the history of a wicked woman who goes from one abomination to another, until at last the judgment of Heaven descends upon her, and, blighted and blasted, she perishes miserably. The lady grasps her pencil and note-book and begs for the name of the edifying volume, and the gentleman leans across the dinner table and answers with a smile—" 'Madame Bovary; or, The Consequences of Misconduct.' " This is a very pretty epigram and it is more than an epigram. It may be very seriously maintained that M. Flaubert's masterpiece is the pearl of "Sunday reading." Practically M. Flaubert is a potent moralist; whether, when he wrote his book, he was so theoretically is a matter best known to himself. Every out-and-out realist who provokes serious meditation may claim that he is a moralist; for that, after all, is the most that the moralists can do for us. They sow the seeds of virtue; they can hardly pretend to raise the crop. Excellence in this matter consists in the tale and the moral hanging well together, and this they are certainly more likely to do when there has been a definite intention—that intention of which artists who cultivate "art for art" are usually so extremely mistrustful; exhibiting thereby, surely, a most injurious disbelief in the illimitable alchemy of art. We may say on the whole, doubtless, that the highly didactic character of "Madame Bovary" is an accident, inasmuch as the works that have followed it, both from its author's and from other hands, have been things to read much less for meditation's than for sensation's sake. M. Flaubert's theory as a novelist, briefly expressed, is to begin on the outside. Human life; we may imagine his saying, is before all things a spectacle, an occupation and entertainment for the eyes. What our eyes show us is all that we are sure of; so with this we will at any rate begin. As this is infinitely curious and entertaining, if we know how to look at it, and as such looking consumes a great deal of time and space, it is very possible that with this also we may end. We admit nevertheless that there is something else, beneath and behind, that belongs to the realm of vagueness and uncertainty, and into this we must occasionally dip. It crops up sometimes irrepressibly, and of course we do not positively count it out. On the whole we will leave it to take care of itself and let it come off as it may. If we propose to represent the pictorial side of life, of course we must do it thoroughly well—we must be complete. There must be no botching, no bungling, no scamping; it must be a very serious matter. We will "render" things—anything, everything, from a chimney-pot to the shoulders of a duchess—as painters render them. We believe there is a certain particular phrase, better than any other, for everything in the world, and the thoroughly accomplished writer ends by finding it. We care only for what *is*—we know nothing about what ought to be. Human life is interesting, because we are in it and of it; all kinds of curious things are taking place in it (we do not analyse the curious—for artists it is an ultimate fact); we select as many of them as possible. Some of the most curious are the most disagreeable, but the chance for "rendering" in the disagreeable is as great as anywhere else (some people think even greater), and moreover the disagreeable is extremely characteristic. The real is the most satisfactory thing in the world, and if we once fairly advance in this direction nothing shall frighten us back.

Some such words as those may stand as a rough sketch of the sort of intellectual conviction under which "Madame Bovary" was written. The theory in this case at least was applied with brilliant success; it produced a masterpiece. Realism seems to us with "Madame Bovary" to have said its last word. We doubt whether the same process will ever produce anything better.

11. *the importance of the moral quality*

("Charles Baudelaire," 1876)

Les Fleurs du Mal was a very happy title for Baudelaire's verses, but it is not altogether a just one. Scattered flowers incontestably do bloom in the quaking swamps of evil, and the poet who does not mind encountering bad odours in his pursuit of sweet ones is quite at liberty to go in search of them. But Baudelaire has, as a general thing, not plucked the flowers—he has plucked the evil-smelling weeds (we take it that he did not use the word flowers in a purely ironical sense) and he has often taken up mere cupfuls of mud and bog-water. He had said to himself that it was a great shame that the realm of evil and unclean things should be fenced off from the domain of poetry; that it was full of subjects, of chances and effects; that it had its light and shade, its logic and its mystery; and that there was the making of some capital verses in it. So he leaped the barrier and was soon immersed in it up to his neck. Baudelaire's imagination was of a melancholy and sinister kind, and, to a considerable extent, this plunging into darkness and dirt was doubtless very spontaneous and disinterested. But he strikes us on the whole as passionless, and this, in view of the unquestionable pluck and acuteness of his fancy, is a great pity. He knew evil not by experience, not as something within himself, but by contemplation and curiosity, as something outside of himself, by which his own intellectual agility was not in the least discomposed, rather indeed (as we say his fancy was of a dusky cast) agreeably flattered and stimulated. In the former case, Baudelaire, with his other gifts, might have been a great poet. But, as it is, evil for him begins outside and not inside, and consists primarily of a great deal of lurid landscape and unclean furniture. This is an almost ludicrously puerile view of the matter. Evil is represented as an affair of blood and carrion and physical sickness—there must be stinking corpses and starving prostitutes and empty laudanum bottles in order that the poet shall be effectively inspired.

A good way to embrace Baudelaire at a glance is to say that he was in his treatment of evil, exactly what Hawthorne was not—Hawthorne, who felt the thing at its source, deep in the human consciousness. Baudelaire's infinitely slighter volume of genius apart, he was a sort of Hawthorne reversed. It is the absence of this metaphysical quality in his treatment of his favourite subjects (Poe was his metaphysician, and his devotion sustained him through a translation of "Eureka!") that exposes him to that class of accusations of which M. Edmond Schérer's accusation of feeding upon *pourriture* is an example; and, in fact, in his pages we never know with what we are dealing. We encounter an inextricable confusion of sad emotions and vile things, and we are at a loss to know whether the subject pretends to appeal to our conscience or—we were going to say—to our olfactories. "Le Mal?" we exclaim; "you do yourself too much honour. This is not Evil; it is not the wrong; it is simply the nasty!" Our impatience is of the same order as that which we should feel if a poet, pretending to pluck "the flowers of good," should come and present us, as specimens, a rhapsody on plumcake and *eau de Cologne*. Independently of the question of his subjects, the charm of Baudelaire's verse is often of a very high order. He belongs to the class of geniuses in whom we ourselves find but a limited pleasure—the laborious, deliberate, economical writers, those who fumble a long time in their pockets before they bring out their hand with a coin in the palm. But the coin, when Baudelaire at last produced it, was often of a high value. He had an extraordinarily verbal instinct and an exquisite felicity of epithet. We cannot help wondering, however, at Gautier's extreme admiration for his endowment in this direction; it is the admiration of the writer who gushes for the writer who trickles. In one point Baudelaire is extremely remarkable—in his talent for suggesting associations. His epithets seem to have come out of old cupboards and pockets; they have a kind of magical mustiness. Moreover, his natural sense of the superficial picturesqueness of the miserable and the unclean was extremely acute; there may be a difference of opinion as to the advantage of possessing such a sense; but whatever it is worth Baudelaire had it in a high degree. One of his poems—"To a Red-haired Beggar Girl" —is a masterpiece in the way of graceful expression of this high relish of what is shameful.

Pour moi, poète chétif,
Ton jeune corps maladif,
Plein de taches de rousseur,
A sa douceur.

Baudelaire repudiated with indignation the charge that he was what is called a realist, and he was doubtless right in doing so. He had too much fancy to adhere strictly to the real; he always embroiders and elaborates—endeavours to impart that touch of strangeness and mystery which is the very *raison d'être* of poetry. Baudelaire was a poet, and for a poet to be a realist is of course nonsense. The idea that Baudelaire imported into his theme was, as a general thing, an intensification of its repulsiveness, but it was at any rate ingenious. When he makes an invocation to "la Débauche aux bras immondes" one may be sure he means more by it than is evident to the vulgar—he means, that is, an intenser perversity. Occasionally he treats agreeable subjects, and his least sympathetic critics must make a point of admitting that his most successful poem is also his least morbid, and most touching; we allude to "Les Petites Vieilles"—a really masterly production. But if it represents the author's maximum, it is a note that he very rarely struck.

Baudelaire, of course, is a capital text for a discussion of the question as to the importance of the morality—or of the subject-matter in general—of a work of art; for he offers a rare combination of technical zeal and patience and of vicious sentiment. But even if we had space to enter upon such a discussion, we should spare our words; for argument on this point wears to our sense a really ridiculous aspect. To deny the relevancy of subject-matter and the importance of the moral quality of a work of art strikes us as, in two words, very childish. We do not know what the great moralists would say about the matter—they would probably treat it very good-humouredly; but that is not the question. There is very little doubt what the great artists would say. People of that temper feel that the whole thinking man is one, and that to count out the moral element in one's appreciation of an artistic total is exactly as sane as it would be (if the total were a poem) to eliminate all the words in three syllables, or to consider only such portions of it as had been written by candle-light. The crudity of sentiment of the advocates of "art for art" is often a striking example of the fact that a great deal of what is called culture may fail to dissipate a well-seated provincialism of spirit. They talk of morality as Miss Edgeworth's infantine heros and heroines talk of "physic"—they allude to its being put into and kept out of a work of art, put into and kept out of one's appreciation of the same, as if it were a coloured fluid kept in a big-labelled bottle in some mysterious intellectual closet. It is in reality simply a part of the essential richness of inspiration—it has nothing to do with the artistic process and it has everything to do with the artistic effect. The more a work of art feels it at its source, the richer it is; the less it feels it, the poorer it is. People of a large taste prefer rich works to poor ones and they are not inclined to assent to the assumption that the process is the whole work. We are safe in believing that all this is comfortably clear to most of those who have, in any degree, been initiated into art by production. For them the subject is as much a part of their work as their hunger is a part of their dinner. Baudelaire was not so far from being of this way of thinking as some of his admirers would persuade us; yet we may say on the whole that he was the victim of a grotesque illusion. He tried to make fine verses on ignoble subjects, and in our opinion he signally failed. He gives, as a poet, a perpetual impression of discomfort and pain. He went in search of corruption, and the ill-conditioned jade proved a thankless muse The thinking reader, feeling himself, as a critic, all one, as we have said, finds the beauty perverted by the ugliness. What the poet wished, doubtless was to seem to be always in the poetic attitude; what the reader sees is a gentleman in a painful-looking posture, staring very hard at a mass of things from which, more intelligently, we avert our heads.

PART B: MEANING AND THEME

1. art and morality: two perfectly different things

("Ivan Turgénieff," 1884)

What was discussed in that little smoke-clouded room [Flaubert's salon in Paris during 1875–76] was chiefly questions of taste, questions of art and form; and the speakers, for the most part, were in aesthetic matters, radicals of the deepest dye. It would have been late in the day to propose among them any discussion of the relation of art to morality, any question as to the degree in which a novel might or might not concern itself with the teaching of a lesson. They had settled these preliminaries long ago, and it would have been primitive and incongruous to recur to them. The conviction that held them together was the conviction that art and morality are two perfectly different things, and that the former has no more to do with the latter than it has with astronomy or embryology. The only duty of a novel was to be well written; that merit included every other of which it was capable. This state of mind was never more apparent than one afternoon when *ces messieurs* delivered themselves on the subject of an incident which had just befallen one of them. *L'Assommoir* of Emile Zola had been discontinued in the journal through which it was running as a serial, in consequence of repeated protests from the subscribers. The subscriber, as a type of human imbecility, received a wonderful dressing, and the Philistine in general was roughly handled. There were gulfs of difference between Turgénieff and Zola, but Turgénieff, who, as I say, understood everything, understood Zola too, and rendered perfect justice to the high solidity of much of his work. His attitude, at such times, was admirable, and I could imagine nothing more genial or more fitted to give an idea of light, easy, human intelligence. No one could desire more than he that art should be art; always, ever, incorruptibly, art. To him this proposition would have seemed as little in need of proof, or susceptible of refutation, as the axiom that law should always be law or medicine always medicine. As much as any one he was prepared to take note of the fact that the demand for abdications and concessions never comes from artists themselves, but always from purchasers, editors, subscribers. I am pretty sure that his word about all this would have been that he could not quite see what was meant by the talk about novels being moral or the reverse; that a novel could no more propose to itself to be moral than a painting or a symphony, and that it was arbitrary to lay down a distinction between the numerous forms of art. He was the last man to be blind to their unity. I suspect that he would have said, in short, that distinctions were demanded in the interest of the moralists, and that the demand was indelicate, owing to their want of jurisdiction. Yet at the same time that I make this suggestion as to his state of mind I remember how little he struck me as bound by mere neatness of formula, how little there was in him of the partisan or the pleader. What he thought of the relation of art to life his stories, after all, show better than anything else.

2. Flaubert: something ungenerous in his genius

("Ivan Turgénieff," 1884)

He [Flaubert] had failed, on the whole, more than he had succeeded, and the great machinery of erudition,—the great polishing process,—which he brought to bear upon his productions, was not accompanied with proportionate results. He had talent without having cleverness, and imagination without having fancy. His effort was heroic, but except in the case of *Madame Bovary*, a masterpiece, he imparted something to his works (it was as if he had covered them with metallic plates) which made them sink rather than sail. He had a passion for perfection of form and for a certain splendid suggestiveness of style. He wished to produce perfect phrases, perfectly interrelated, and as closely woven together as a suit of chain-mail. He looked at life altogether as an artist, and took his work with a seriousness that never belied itself. To write an admirable page—and his idea of what constituted an admirable page was transcendent—seemed to him something to live for. He tried it again and again, and he came very near it; more than once he touched it, for *Madame Bovary* surely will live. But there was something ungenerous in his genius. He was cold, and he would have given everything he had to be able to glow.

3. *every good story: picture and idea interfused*

("Guy de Maupassant," 1888)

Every good story is of course both a picture and an idea, and the more they are interfused the better the problem is solved. In *La Maison Tellier* [by Maupassant] they fit each other to perfection; the capacity for sudden innocent delights latent in natures which have lost their innocence is vividly illustrated by the singular scenes to which our acquaintance with Madame and her staff (little as it may be a thing to boast of) successively introduces us. The breadth, the freedom, and brightness of all this give the measure of the author's talent, and of that large, keen way of looking at life which sees the pathetic and the droll, the stuff of which the whole piece is made, in the queerest and humblest patterns.

4. *immense ado about nothing*

("Gustave Flaubert," 1893)

To the end of time there will be something flippant, something perhaps even "clever" to be said of his [Flaubert's] immense ado about nothing. Those for some of whose moments, on the contrary, this ado will be as stirring as music, will belong to the group that has dabbled in the same material and striven with the same striving. The interest he presents, in truth, can only be a real interest for fellowship, for initiation of the practical kind; and in that case it becomes a sentiment, a sort of mystical absorption or fruitful secret. The sweetest things in the world of art or the life of letters are the irresponsible sympathies that seem to rest on divination. Flaubert's hardness was only the act of holding his breath in the reverence of his search for beauty; his universal renunciation, the long spasm of his too-fixed attention, was only one of the absurdest sincerities of art. To the participating eye these things are but details in the little square picture made at this distance of time by his forty years at the battered table at Croisset. Everything lives in this inward vision of the wide room on the river, almost the cell of a monomaniac, but consecrated ground to the faithful, which, as he tried and tried again, must so often have resounded with the pomp

of a syntax addressed, in his code, peremptorily to the ear. If there is something tragi-comic in the scene, as of a tenacity in the void of a life laid down
for grammar, the impression passes when we turn from the painful process
to the sharp and splendid result. Then, since if we like people very much we
end by liking their circumstances, the eternal chamber and the dry Benedictine years have a sufficiently palpable offset in the *repoussé* bronze of the books.

5. *a mistrust of disinterested art*

("Dumas the Younger," 1896)

These pamphlets [written by Dumas as polemics to supplement his dramas],
I may parenthetically say, strike me as definitely compromising to his character as artist. What shines in them most is the appetite for a discussion, or
rather the appetite for a conclusion, and the passion for a simplified and vindictive justice. But I have never found it easy to forgive a writer who, in
possession of a form capable of all sorts of splendid application, puts on this
resource the slight of using substitutes for it at will, as if it is good but for
parts of the cause. If it is good for anything it is good for the whole demonstration, and if it is not good for the whole demonstration it is good for
nothing—nothing that *he* is concerned with. If the picture of life doesn't
cover the ground what in the world *can* cover it? The fault can only be the
painter's. Woe, in the esthetic line, to any example that requires the escort
of precept. It is like a guest arriving to dine accompanied by constables. Our
author's prefaces and treatises show a mistrust of disinterested art. He would
have declared probably that his art was not disinterested; to which our reply
would be that it had then no right to put us off the scent and prepare decep-
tions for us by coming within an ace of being as good as if it were.

6. *an idea in my work: figure in the carpet*

("The Figure in the Carpet," 1896)

"By my little point I mean—what shall I call it?—the particular thing I've
written my books most *for*. Isn't there for every writer a particular thing
of that sort, the thing that most makes him apply himself, the thing without
the effort to achieve which he wouldn't write at all, the very passion of
his passion, the part of the business in which, for him, the flame of art
burns most intensely? Well, it's *that!*" . . .
    ". . . There's an idea in my work without which I wouldn't have given a
straw for the whole job. It's the finest fullest intention of the lot, and the

application of it has been, I think, a triumph of patience, of ingenuity. I ought to leave that to somebody else to say; but that nobody does say it is precisely what we're talking about. It stretches, this little trick of mine, from book to book, and everything else, comparatively, plays over the surface of it. The order, the form, the texture of my books will perhaps someday constitute for the initiated a complete representation of it. So it's naturally the thing for the critic to look for. It strikes me . . . even as the thing for the critic to find." . . .

"My whole lucid effort gives him the clue—every page and line and letter. The thing's as concrete there as a bird in the cage, a bait on a hook, a piece of cheese in a mouse-trap. It's stuck into every volume as your foot is stuck into your shoe. It governs every line, it chooses every word, it dots every i, it places every comma." . . .

. . . It was something, I guessed, in the primal plan; something like a complex figure in a Persian carpet. He highly approved of this image when I used it, and he used another himself. "It's the very string," he said, "that my pearls are strung on!"

7. the misfortune of being tasteless

("Emile Zola," 1903)

"The matter with" Zola then, so far as it goes, was that, as the imagination of the artist is in the best cases not only clarified but intensified by his equal possession of Taste (deserving here if ever the old-fashioned honor of a capital), so when he has lucklessly never inherited that auxiliary blessing the imagination itself inevitably breaks down as a consequence. There is simply no limit, in fine, to the misfortune of being tasteless; it does not merely disfigure the surface and the fringe of your performance—it eats back into the very heart and enfeebles the sources of life. When you have no taste you have no discretion, which is the conscience of taste, and when you have no discretion you perpetrate books like *Rome*, which are without intellectual modesty, books like *Fécondité*, which are without a sense of the ridiculous, books like *Vérité*, which are without the finer vision of human experience.

8. the house of fiction: dependence of "moral sense" on felt life

(Preface to *The Portrait of a Lady*, 1908)

One had had from an early time, for that matter, the instinct of the right estimate of such values and of its reducing to the inane the dull dispute over the "immoral" subject and the moral. Recognising so promptly the one measure of the worth of a given subject, the question about it that, rightly answered, disposes of all others—is it valid, in a word, is it genuine, is it sincere, the result of some direct impression or perception of life?—I had found small edification, mostly, in a critical pretension that had neglected from the first all delimitation of ground and all definition of terms. The air of my earlier time shows, to memory, as darkened, all round, with that vanity—unless the difference to-day be just in one's own final impatience, the lapse of one's attention. There is, I think, no more nutritive or suggestive truth in this connexion than that of the perfect dependence of the "moral" sense of a work of art on the amount of felt life concerned in producing it. The question comes back thus, obviously, to the kind and the degree of the artist's prime sensibility, which is the soil out of which his subject springs. The quality and capacity of that soil, its ability to "grow" with due fresh-ness and straightness any vision of life, represents, strongly or weakly, the projected morality. That element is but another name for the more or less close connexion of the subject with some mark made on the intelligence, with some sincere experience. By which, at the same time, of course, one is far from contending that this enveloping air of the artist's humanity—which gives the last touch to the worth of the work—is not a widely and won-drously varying element; being on one occasion a rich and magnificent medium and on another a comparatively poor and ungenerous one. Here we get exactly the high price of the novel as a literary form—its power not only, while preserving that form with closeness, to range through all the differences of the individual relation to its general subject-matter, all the varieties of outlook on life, of disposition to reflect and project, created by conditions that are never the same from man to man (or, so far as that goes, from man to woman), but positively to appear more true to its character in proportion as it strains, or tends to burst, with a latent extravagance, its mould.

The house of fiction has in short not one window, but a million—a number of possible windows not to be reckoned, rather; every one of which has been pierced, or is still pierceable, in its vast front, by the need of the individual vision and by the pressure of the individual will. These apertures, of dissimilar shape and size, hang so, all together, over the human scene that we might have expected of them a greater sameness of report than we find. They are but windows at the best, mere holes in a dead wall, discon-nected, perched aloft; they are not hinged doors opening straight upon life. But they have this mark of their own that at each of them stands a figure with a pair of eyes, or at least with a field-glass, which forms, again and again, for observation, a unique instrument, insuring to the person making use of it an impression distinct from every other. He and his neighbours are watching the same show, but one seeing more where the other sees less, one seeing black where the other sees white, one seeing big where the other sees small, one seeing coarse where the other sees fine. And so on, and so on; there is fortunately no saying on what, for the particular pair of eyes, the window may *not* open; "fortunately" by reason, precisely, of this incalculability of range. The spreading field, the human scene, is the "choice of subject"; the pierced aperture, either broad or balconied or slit-like and low-browed, is the "literary form"; but they are, singly or together, as nothing without the posted presence of the watcher—without, in other words, the consciousness of the artist. Tell me what the artist is, and I will tell you of what he has *been* conscious. Thereby I shall express to you at once his boundless freedom and his "moral" reference.

9. that most modern of our current passions: for things

(Preface to *The Spoils of Poynton*, 1908)

Extravagant as the mere statement sounds, one seemed accordingly to handle the secret of life in drawing the positive right truth out of the so easy muddle of wrong truths in which the interesting possibilities of that "row" [in *The Spoils of Poynton*], so to call it, between mother and son over their household goods might have been stifled. I find it odd to consider, as I thus revert, that I could have had none but the most general warrant for "seeing anything in it," as the phrase would have been; that I couldn't in the least, on the spot, as I have already hinted, have justified my faith. One thing was "in it," in the sordid situation, on the first blush, and one thing only— though this, in its limited way, no doubt, a curious enough value: the sharp light it might project on that most modern of our current passions, the fierce appetite for the upholster's and joiner's and brazier's work, the chairs and tables, the cabinets and presses, the material odds and ends, of the more labouring ages. A lively mark of our manners indeed the diffusion of this curiosity and this avidity, and full of suggestion, clearly, as to their possible influence on other passions and other relations. On the face of it the "things" themselves would form the very centre of a such a crisis; these grouped objects, all conscious of their eminence and their price, would enjoy, in any picture of a conflict, the heroic importance. They would have to be presented, they would have to be painted—arduous and desperate thought; something would have to be done for them not too ignobly unlike the great array in which Balzac, say, would have marshalled them: *that* amount of workable interest at least would evidently be "in it."

10. a general theme: the "international" conflict of manners

(Preface to *The Spoils of Poynton*, 1908)

If I speak of classifying I hasten to recognise that there are other marks for the purpose still and that, failing other considerations, "A London Life" would properly consort, in this series, with a dozen of the tales by which I at one period sought to illustrate and enliven the supposed "international" conflict of manners; a general theme dealing for the most part with the bewilderment of the good American, of either sex and of almost any age, in presence of the "European" order. This group of data might possibly have shown, for the reverse of its medal, the more or less desperate contortions of the European under American social pressure. Three or four tried glances in that direction seemed to suggest, however, no great harvest to be gathered; so that the pictorial value of the general opposition was practically confined to one phase. More reasons are here involved than I can begin to go into—as indeed I confess that the reflexions set in motion by the international fallacy at large, as I am now moved to regard it, quite crowd upon me; I simply note therefore, on one corner of the ground, the scant results, above all for interesting detail, promised by confronting the fruits of a constituted order with the fruits of no order at all. We may strike lights by opposing order to order, one sort to another sort; for in that case we get the correspondences and equivalents that make differences mean something; we get the interest and the tension of disparity where a certain parity may have been in question. Where it may *not* have been in question, where the dramatic encounter is but the poor concussion of positives on one side with negatives on the other, we get little beyond a consideration of the differences between fishes and fowls.

By which I don't mean to say that the appeal of the fallacy, as I call it, was not at one time quite inevitably irresistible; had it nothing else to recommend it to the imagination it would always have had the advantage of its showy surface, of suggesting situations as to which assurance seemed easy, founded, as it felt itself, on constant observation. The attraction was thus not a little, I judge, the attraction of facility; the international was easy to do, because, as one's wayside bloomed with it, one had but to put forth one's hand and pluck the frequent flower. Add to this that the flower *was*, so often, quite positively a flower—that of the young American innocence transplanted to European air. The general subject had, in fine, a charm while it lasted; but I shall have much more to say about it on another occasion.

11. the precious moral of everything

(Preface to The Ambassadors, 1909)

The idea of the tale [The Ambassadors] resides indeed in the very fact that an hour of such unprecedented ease should have been felt by him *as* a crisis, and he is at pains to express it for us as neatly as we could desire. The remarks to which he thus gives utterance contain the essence of "The Ambassadors," his fingers close, before he has done, round the stem of the full-blown flower; which, after that fashion, he continues officiously to present to us. "Live all you can; it's a mistake not to. It doesn't so much matter what you do in particular so long as you have your life. If you haven't had that what *have* you had? I'm too old—too old at any rate for what I see. What one loses one loses; make no mistake about that. Still, we have the illusion of freedom; therefore don't, like me to-day, be without the memory of that illusion. I was either, at the right time, too stupid or too intelligent to have it, and now I'm a case of reaction against the mistake. Do what you like so long as you don't make it. For it *was* a mistake. Live, live!" Such is the gist of Strether's appeal to the impressed youth, whom he likes and whom he desires to befriend; the word "mistake" occurs several times, it will be seen, in the course of his remarks—which gives the measure of the signal warning he feels attached to his case. He has accordingly missed too much, though perhaps after all constitutionally qualified for a better part, and he wakes up to it in conditions that press the spring of a terrible question. *Would* there yet perhaps be time for reparation?—reparation, that is, for the injury done his character; for the affront, he is quite ready to say, so stupidly put upon it and in which he has even himself had so clumsy a hand? The answer to which is that he now at all events *sees;* so that the business of my tale and the march of my action, not to say the precious moral of everything, is just my demonstration of this process of vision.

12. *what the work may mean as a whole*

("The New Novel," 1914)

We ask ourselves what *Sinister Street* may mean as a whole in spite of our sense of being brushed from the first by a hundred subordinate purposes, the succession and alternation of which seem to make after a fashion a plan, and which, though full of occasional design, yet fail to gather themselves for application or to converge to an idea. Any idea will serve, ever, that has held up its candle to composition—and it is perhaps because composition proposes itself under Mr. Compton Mackenzie's energy on a scale well-nigh of the most prodigious that we must wait to see whither it tends. The question of what he may here mean "on the whole," as we have just said, is doubtless admonished to stand back till we be possessed of the whole. The interesting volume is but a first, committed up to its eyes to continuity and with an announced sequel to follow. The recital exhibits at the point we have reached the intimate experience of a boy at school and his holidays, the am-plification of which is to come with his terms and their breaks at a university; and the record will probably form a more squared and extended picture of life equally conditioned by the extremity of youth than we shall know where else to look for. Youth clearly has been Mr. Mackenzie's saturation, as it has been Mr. Hugh Walpole's, but we see this not as a subject (youth in itself is no specific subject, any more than age is) but as matter for a subject and as requiring a motive to redeem it from the merely passive state of the slice [of life].

Chapter XVI

READERS AND CRITICS

Any account of James's views of the reader's response to fiction must begin with his liberal concept of "liking": "Nothing, of course, will ever take the place of the good old fashion of 'liking' a work of art or not liking it: the most improved criticism will not abolish that primitive, that ultimate test." This assertion from "The Art of Fiction," which is repeated in essence in "The Future of the Novel" and in the opening item ("no obligation to like") in this chapter, has led some to believe that James was committed to a capricious or dilettante criticism. On the contrary, close examination of James's repitition of this idea reveals that he was simply bowing to a psychological truth—that there is no accounting for taste, of which there are innumerable varieties: "Some people, for excellent reasons, don't like to read about carpenters; others, for reasons even better, don't like to read about courtesans. Many object to Americans."

Such a passage listing subjects that some readers won't "like" brings to mind certain related and relevant propositions put forward by James. One is that the critic must grant the writer his subject, and address his attention only to execution. The apparent contradiction here is resolved when we note that James simply releases the critic from the obligation to say anything at all if the writer has presented a subject to which as reader he has a natural antipathy or indifference. But it is worth noting that James insists that subjects are important and do make a difference, and that some are "much more remunerative than others." And this view no doubt has significance for another of James's constantly reiterated propositions: "The only obligation to which in advance we may hold a novel, without incurring the accusation of being arbitrary, is that it be interesting" ("The Art of Fiction"); "It [the novel] must, of course, hold our attention and reward it" ("The Future of the Novel").

With such statements about the reader's right to "like" and the novelist's need to "interest," James appears to be excessively easy on the reader. In reality, as everyone knows, his fiction makes great demands on the reader, and in his scattered comments about the reader (Part A of this chapter) it is clear that he respected most highly the attentive reader willing to read aloud, to reread, and to read with "reflexion and discrimination." Such reading, when reenforced by a genuinely perceptive criticism, made "the mind as

318

aware of itself as possible," he wrote in 1914, and was "the very education of our imaginative life."

In Part B of this chapter, "Critics," James shows himself as, at least in part, the progenitor of the modern movement in criticism. One essay is included in its entirety, not only because of its brevity, but also because of its brilliance: "Criticism" (1891) included below under the title "perception at the pitch of passion." This essay, together with the other pieces gathered here, reveals James as a critical theorist of remarkable astuteness and continuing relevance.

Perhaps the most unfashionable element in James's critical theory is his insistence on the "moral sense" of the critic; this note is struck more deeply in the earlier pieces (particularly in the reviews) than in the later commentary (and, indeed, the word moral does not appear in his 1891 essay, "Criticism"). In writing of Swinburne's essays in 1875, James deplored the "absence of the moral sense" in Swinburne, and then explained: "By this we do not mean that Mr. Swinburne is not didactic, nor edifying, nor devoted to pleading the cause of virtue. We mean simply that his moral plummet does not sink at all, and that when he pretends to drop it he is simply dabbling in the relatively shallow pool of the picturesque."

Clearly these 1865 views relate to the famous 1884 statement in "The Art of Fiction": "There is one point at which the moral sense and the artistic sense lie very near together; that is in the light of the very obvious truth that the deepest quality of a work of art will always be the quality of the mind of the producer"; and they relate to the 1908 "house of fiction" statement, in the Preface to The Portrait of a Lady, that there is a "perfect dependence of the 'moral' sense of a work of art on the amount of felt life concerned in producing it." (see introduction to Chapter XV, and particularly references to James's concept of the artist's "prime sensibility" and the "enveloping air of the artist's humanity").

A cardinal principle in James's theory of criticism was that the critic should approach a literary work without commitments and allegiances. He praised his favorite French critic, Sainte-Beuve: "In purpose the least doctrinal of critics, it was by his very horror of dogmas, moulds, and formulas, that he so effectively contributed to the science of literary interpretation." James's abhorrence of intellectual formulas and his idealization of a freedom from dogmas give meaning to T. S. Eliot's famous remark that James "had a mind so fine that no idea could violate it" (see Eliot's 1918 essay on James in The Shock of Recognition, ed. Edmund Wilson). And it is in the concepts that flow from James's position here—that the critic's allegiance must not be to a priori principles but to the literary text itself—that he helps to shape the New Criticism of a later period.

There is, however, an apparent contradiction in linking the James who believed that a "moral sense" was primary to reading and interpretation, who was upset after reading Swinburne's essays at being unable to remember *"a single instance of delicate moral discrimination"*—*in linking this James with a modern critical movement which stressed the intellectual, logical, and analytical in the close reading of literary texts. As a matter of fact, James wanted it both ways. In his 1891 essay, "Criticism," he described the function of the critic thus: "To lend himself, to project himself and steep himself, to feel and feel till he understands and to understand so well that he can say, to have perception at the pitch of passion and expression as embracing as the air, to be infinitely curious and incorrigibly patient, and yet plastic and inflammable and determinable, stooping to conquer and serving to direct—these are fine chances for an active mind, chances to add the idea of independent beauty to the conception of success." Later (in his Preface to* The Lesson of the Master) *James was to hit upon the term "close or analytic appreciation," in which "appreciation, to be appreciation" implied "of course some such rudimentary zeal; and this though that fine process be the Beautiful Gate itself of enjoyment." Perhaps one of the reasons the New Criticism came finally to its untimely end (if indeed it has done so) was that, in its commitment to close reading and critical analysis, it left out of account this very factor James tried always, regardless of the complexities involved (and they were many) to place at the center—feelings, affections, appreciation, zeal, enjoyment. James said that the critic must "feel till he understands" and must have "perception at the pitch of passion." The implication, clearly, is that only the deep emotional response, from a "man's real substance," can grant understanding that permits analysis.*

PART A: READERS

1. *no obligation to* like

("Gustave Flaubert," 1893)

Why feel, and feel genuinely, so much about "art," in order to feel so little about its privilege? Why proclaim it on the one hand the holy of holies, only to let your behavior confess it on the other a temple open to the winds? Why be angry that so few people care for the real thing, since this aversion of the many leaves a luxury of space? The answer to these too numerous questions is the final perception that the subject of our observations [Flaubert] failed of happiness, failed of temperance, not through his excesses, but absolutely through his barriers. He passed his life in strange oblivion of the circumstance that, however incumbent it may be on most of us to do our duty, there is, in spite of a thousand narrow dogmatisms, nothing in the world that anyone is under the least obligation to *like*—not even (one braces one's self to risk the declaration), a particular kind of writing. Particular kinds of writing may sometimes, for their producers, have the good fortune to please; but these things are windfalls, pure luxuries, not resident even in the cleverest of us as natural rights.

2. *the writer makes the reader*

("The Novels of George Eliot," 1866)

In every novel the work is divided between the writer and the reader; but the writer makes the reader very much as he makes his characters. When he makes him ill, that is, makes him indifferent, he does no work; the writer does all. When he makes him well, that is, makes him interested, then the reader does quite the labour. In making such a deduction as I have just indicated, the reader would be doing but his share of the task; the grand point is to get him to make it. I hold that there is a way. It is perhaps a secret; but until it is found out, I think that the art of story-telling cannot be said to have approached perfection.

3. *the novelists . . . offer us another world*

("London Notes," July, 1897)

I continued last month to seek private diversion, which I found to be more and more required as the machinery of public began to work. Never was a better chance apparently for the great anodyne of art. It was a supreme opportunity to test the spell of the magician, for one felt one was saved if a fictive world would open. I knocked in this way at a dozen doors, I read a succession of novels; with the effect perhaps of feeling more than ever before my individual liability in our great general debt to the novelists. The great thing to say for them is surely that at any given moment they offer us another world, another consciousness, an experience that, as effective as the dentist's ether, muffles the ache of the actual and, by helping us to an interval, tides us over and makes us face, in the return to the inevitable, a combination that may at least have changed. What we get of course, in proportion as the picture lives, is simply another actual—the actual of other people; and I no more than any one else pretend to say *why* that should be a relief, a relief as great, I mean, as it practically proves. We meet in this question, I think, the eternal mystery—the mystery that sends us back simply to the queer constitution of man and that is not in the least lighted by the plea of "romance," the argument that relief depends wholly upon the quantity, as it were, of fable. It depends, to my sense, on the quantity of nothing but art—in which the material, fable or fact or whatever it be, falls so into solution, is so reduced and transmuted, that I absolutely am acquainted with no receipt whatever for computing its proportion and amount.

The only amount I can compute is the force of the author, for that is directly registered in my attention, my submission. A hundred things naturally go to make it up; but he knows so much better than I what they are that I should blush to give him a glimpse of my inferior account of them. The anodyne is not the particular picture, it is our own act of surrender, and therefore most, for each reader, what he most surrenders to. This latter element would seem in turn to vary from case to case, were it not indeed that there are readers prepared, I believe, to limit their surrender in advance. With some, we gather, it declines for instance to operate save on an exhibition of "high life." In others again it is proof against any solicitation but that of low. In many it vibrates only to "adventure"; in many only to Charlotte Brontë; in various groups, according to affinity, only to Jane Austen, to old Dumas, to Miss Corelli, to Dostoievsky or whomever it may be. For readers easiest to conceive, however, are probably those for whom, in the whole impression, the note of sincerity in the artist is what most matters, what most reaches and touches. That, obviously, is the relation that gives the widest range to the anodyne.

4. reflexion and discrimination

(Preface to The Portrait of a Lady, 1908)

This is a truth [that some elements in a work belong to a subject directly, others to the treatment], however, of which he [the author] rarely gets the benefit—since it could be assured to him, really, but by criticism based upon perception, criticism which is too little of this world. He must not think of benefits, moreover, I freely recognise, for that way dishonour lies: he has, that is, but one to think of—the benefit, whatever it may be, involved in his having cast a spell upon the simpler, the very simplest, forms of attention. This is all he is entitled to; he is entitled to nothing, he is bound to admit, that can come to him, from the reader, as a result on the latter's part of any act of reflexion or discrimination. He may *enjoy* this finer tribute—that is another affair, but on condition only of taking it as a gratuity "thrown in," a mere miraculous windfall, the fruit of a tree he may not pretend to have shaken. Against reflexion, against discrimination, in his interest, all earth and air conspire; wherefore it is that, as I say, he must in many a case have schooled himself, from the first, to work but for a "living wage." The living wage is the reader's grant of the least possible quantity of attention required for consciousness of a "spell." The occasional charming "tip" is an act of his intelligence over and beyond this, a golden apple, for the writer's lap, straight from the wind-stirred tree. The artist may of course, in wanton moods, dream of some Paradise (for art) where the direct appeal to the intelligence might be legalised; for to such extravagances as these his yearning mind can scarce hope ever completely to close itself. The most he can do is to remember thay *are* extravagances.

5. attention of perusal

(Preface to *The Wings of the Dove*, 1909)

(Attention of perusal, I thus confess by the way, is what I at every point, as well as here, absolutely invoke and take for granted; a truth I avail myself of this occasion to note once for all—in the interest of that variety of ideal reigning, I gather, in the connexion. The enjoyment of a work of art, the acceptance of an irresistible illusion, constituting, to my sense, our highest experience of "luxury," the luxury is not greatest, by my consequent measure, when the work asks for as little attention as possible. It is greatest, it is delightfully, divinely great, when we feel the surface, like the thick ice of the skater's pond, bear without cracking the strongest pressure we throw on it. The sound of the crack one may recognise, but never surely to call it a luxury.)

6. reading aloud to release the finest and most numerous secrets

(Preface to *The Golden Bowl*, 1909)

The ideally handsome way is for him [the author] to multiply in any given connexion all the possible sources of entertainment—or, more grossly expressing it again, to intensify his whole chance of pleasure. (It all comes back to that, to my and your "fun"—if we but allow the term its full extension; to the production of which no humblest question involved, even to that of the shade of a cadence or the position of a comma, is not richly pertinent.) We have but to think a moment of such a matter as the play of *representational* values, those that make it a part, and an important part, of our taking offered things in that we should take them as aspects and visibilities—take them to the utmost as appearances, images, figures, objects, so many important, so many contributive items of the furniture of the world—in order to feel immediately the effect of such a condition at every turn of our adventure and every point of the representative surface. One has but to open the door to any forces of exhibition at all worthy of the name in order to see the imaging and qualifying agency called at once into play and put on its mettle. We may traverse acres of pretended exhibitory prose from which the touch that directly evokes and finely presents, the touch that operates for closeness and for charm, for conviction and illusion, for communication, in a word, is unsurpassably absent. All of which but means of course that the reader is, in the common phrase, "sold"—even when, poor passive spirit, systematically bewildered and bamboozled on the article of his dues, he may be but dimly aware of it. He has by the same token and for the most part, I fear, a scarce quicker sensibility on other heads, least of all perhaps on such a matter as his really quite swindled state when the pledge given for his true beguilement fails to ensure him that fullest experience of his pleasure which waits but on a direct reading *out* of the addressed appeal. It is scarce necessary to note that the highest test of any literary form conceived in the light of "poetry"—to apply that term in its largest literary sense—hangs back unpardonably from its office when it fails to lend itself to *vivâ-voce* treatment. We talk here, naturally, not of non-poetic forms, but of those whose highest bid is addressed to the imagination, to the spiritual and the aesthetic vision, the mind led captive by a charm and a spell, an incalculable art. The essential property of such a form as that is to give out its finest and most numerous secrets, and to give them out most gratefully, under the closest pressure—which is of course the pressure of the attention articulately *sounded*. Let it reward as much as it will and can the soundless, the "quiet" reading, it still deplorably "muffs" its chance and its success, still trifles with the roused appetite to which it can never honestly be indifferent, by not having so arranged itself as to owe the flower of its effect to the act and process of apprehension that so beautifully asks most from it. It then infallibly, and not less beautifully, most responds; for I have nowhere found vindicated the queer thesis that the right values of interesting prose depend all on withheld tests—that is on its being, for very pity and shame, but skimmed and scanted, shuffled and mumbled. Gustave Flaubert has somewhere in this connexion an excellent word—to the effect that any imaged prose that fails to be richly rewarding in return for a competent utterance ranks itself as wrong through not being "in the conditions of life." The more we remain in *them*, all round, the more pleasure we dispense; the moral of which is—and there would be fifty other pertinent things to say about this—that I have found revision intensify at every step my impulse intimately to answer, by my light, to those conditions.

7. on rereading: something in store; mysteries of method

("The New Novel," 1914)

There faces us all the while the fact that the act of consideration as an incident of the esthetic pleasure, consideration confidently knowing us to *have* sooner or later to arrive at it, may be again and again postponed, but can never hope not some time to fall due. Consideration is susceptible of many forms, some one or other of which no conscious esthetic effort fails to cry out for; and the simplest description of the cry of the novel when sincere— for have we not heard such compositions bluff us, as it were, with false cries?—is as an appeal to us when we have read it once to read it yet again. *That* is the act of consideration; no other process of considering approaches this for directness, so that anything short of it is virtually not to consider at all. The word has sometimes another sense, that of the appeal to us *not*, for the world, to go back—this being of course consideration of a sort; the sort clearly that the truly flushed production should be the last to invoke. The effect of consideration, we need scarce remark, is to light for us in a work of art the hundred questions of how and why and whither, and the effect of these questions, once lighted, is enormously to thicken and complicate, even if toward final clarifications, what we have called the amused state produced in us by the work. The more our amusement multiplies its terms the more fond and the more rewarded consideration becomes; the fewer it leaves them, on the other hand, the less to be resisted for us is the impression of "bare ruined choirs where late the sweet birds sang." Birds that have appeared to sing, or whose silence we have not heeded, on a first perusal, prove on a second to have no note to contribute, and whether or no a second is enough to admonish us of those we miss, we mostly expect much from it in the way of emphasis of those we find. Then it is that notes of intention become more present or more absent; then it is that we take the measure of what we have already called our effective provision. The bravest providers and designers show at this point something still in store which only the second rummage was appointed to draw forth. To the variety of these ways of not letting our fondness fast is there not practically no limit? —and of the arts, the devices, the graces, the subtle secrets applicable to such an end what presumptuous critic shall pretend to draw the list? Let him for the moment content himself with saying that many of the most effective are mysteries, precisely, of method, or that even when they are not most essentially and directly so it takes method, blessed method, to extract their soul and to determine their action.

8. education of our imaginative life

("The New Novel," 1914)

The effect, if not the prime office, of criticism is to make our absorption and our enjoyment of the things that feed the mind as aware of itself as possible, since that awareness quickens the mental demand, which thus in turn wanders further and further for pasture. This action on the part of the mind practically amounts to a reaching out for the reasons of its interest, as only by its so ascertaining them can the interest grow more various. This is the very education of our imaginative life; and thanks to it the general question of how to refine, and of why certain things refine more and most, on that happy consciousness, becomes for us of the last importance. Then we cease to be only instinctive and at the mercy of chance, feeling that we can ourselves take a hand in our satisfaction and provide for it, making ourselves safe against dearth, and through the door opened by that perception criticism enters, if we but give it time, as a flood, the great flood of awareness; so maintaining its high tide unless through some lapse of our sense for it, some flat reversion to instinct alone, we block up the ingress and sit in stale and shrinking waters. Stupidity may arrest any current and fatuity transcend any privelege.

Part B: Critics

1. Sainte-Beuve: least doctrinal of critics

("Taine's English Literature," 1872)

He [Taine] pays in his Preface a handsome tribute to the great service rendered by Sainte-Beuve to the new criticism. Now Sainte-Beuve is, to our sense, the better apostle of the two. In purpose the least doctrinal of critics, it was by his very horror of dogmas, moulds, and formulas, that he so effectively contributed to the science of literary interpretation. The truly devout patience with which he kept his final conclusion in abeyance until after an exhaustive survey of the facts, after perpetual returns and ever-deferred farewells to them, is his living testimony to the importance of the facts. Just as he could never reconcile himself to saying his last word on book or author, so he never pretended to have devised a method which should be a key to truth. The truth for M. Taine lies stored up, as one may say, in great lumps and blocks, to be released and detached by a few lively hammer-blows; while for Sainte-Beuve it was a diffused and imponderable essence, as vague as the carbon in the air which nourishes vegetation, and, like it, to be disengaged by patient chemistry. His only method was fairly to dissolve his attention in the sea of circumstance surrounding the object of his study, and we cannot but think his frank provisional empiricism more truly scientific than M. Taine's premature philosophy. In fact, M. Taine plays fast and loose with his theory, and is mainly successful in so far as he is inconsequent to it. There is a constantly visible hiatus between his formula and his application of it. It serves as his badge and motto, but his best strokes are prompted by the independent personal impression.

2. *the motions of criticism*

("Swinburne's Essays," 1875)

His book [Swinburne's *Essays and Studies*] is not at all a book of judgment; it is a book of pure imagination. His genius is for style simply, and not in the least for thought nor for real analysis; he goes through the motions of criticism, and makes a considerable show of logic and philosophy, but with deep appreciation his writing seems to us to have very little to do. He is an imaginative commentator, often of a very splendid kind, but he is never a real interpreter and rarely a trustworthy guide. He is a writer, and a writer in constant quest of a theme. He has an inordinate sense of the picturesque, and he finds his theme in those subjects and those writers which gratify it. When they gratify it highly, he conceives a boundless relish for them; they give him his chance, and he turns on the deluge of his exorbitant homage. His imagination kindles, he abounds in their own sense, when they give him an inch he takes an ell, and quite loses sight of the subject in the entertainment he finds in his own word-spinning. In this respect he is extraordinarily accomplished: he narrowly misses having a magnificent style.

3. *absence of the moral sense*

("Swinburne's Essays," 1875)

What we have called the absence of the moral sense of the writer of these essays [Swinburne, *Essays and Studies*] is, however, their most disagreeable feature. By this we do not mean that Mr. Swinburne is not didactic, nor edifying, nor devoted to pleading the cause of virtue. We mean simply that his moral plummet does not sink at all, and that when he proceeds to drop it he is simply dabbling in the relatively very shallow pool of the picturesque. A sense of the picturesque so refined as Mr. Swinburne's will take one a great way, but it will by no means, in dealing with things whose great value is in what they tell us of human character, take one all the way. One breaks down with it (if one treats it as one's sole support) sooner or later in aesthetics; one breaks down with it very soon indeed in psychology. We do not remember in this whole volume a single instance of delicate moral discrimination—a single case in which the moral note has been struck, in which the idea betrays the smallest acquaintance with the conscience. The moral realm for Mr. Swinburne is simply a brilliant chiaroscuro of costume and posture. This makes all Mr. Swinburne's magnificent talk about Victor Hugo's great criminals and monstrosities, about Shelley's Count Cenci, and Browning's Guido Franchesini, and about dramatic figures generally, quite worthless as anything but amusing fantasy. As psychology it is, to our sense, extremely puerile; for we do not mean simply to say that the author does not understand morality—a charge to which he would be probably quite indifferent; but that he does not at all understand immorality. Such a passage as his rhapsody upon Victor Hugo's Josiane ("such a pantheress may be such a poetess", etc.) means absolutely nothing. It is entertaining as pictorial writing—though even in this respect, as we have said, thanks to excess and redundancy, it is the picturesque spoiled rather than achieved; but as an attempt at serious analysis it seems to us, like many of its companions, simply ghastly—ghastly in its poverty of insight and its pretension to make mere lurid imagery do duty as thought.

4. criticism and the study of connections

("Pierre Loti," 1888)

An achievement in art or in letters grows more interesting when we begin to perceive its connections; and, indeed, it may be said that the study of connections is the recognized function of intelligent criticism. It is a comparatively poor exercise of the attention (for the critic always, I mean) to judge a book all by itself, even if it happens to be a book as independent, as little the product of a school and a fashion, as "Le Mariage de Loti" or "Mon Frère Yves" or "Pêcheur d'Islande." Each of these works is interesting as illustrating the talent and character of the author [Pierre Loti], but they become still more interesting as we note their coincidences and relations with other works, for then they begin to illustrate other talents and other characters as well: the plot thickens, the whole spectacle expands. We seem to be studying not simply the genius of an individual, but, in a living manifestation, that of a nation or of a conspicuous group; the nation or the group becomes a great figure operating on a great scale, and the drama of its literary production (to speak only of that) a kind of world-drama, lighted by the universal sun, with Europe and America for the public, and the arena of races, the battle-field of their inevitable contrasts and competitions, for the stage.

5. *no* a priori *rules*

("Introduction" to Rudyard Kipling's *Soldiers Three*, 1891)

The critic, in a word . . . has *a priori*, no rule for a literary production but that it shall have genuine life.

6. *perception at the pitch of passion*

("Criticism," 1891)

If literary criticism may be said to flourish among us at all, it certainly flourishes immensely, for it flows through the periodical press like a river that has burst its dykes. The quantity of it is prodigious, and it is a commodity of which, however the demand may be estimated, the supply will be sure to be in any supposable extremity the last thing to fail us. What strikes the observer above all, in such an affluence, is the unexpected proportion the discourse uttered bears to the objects discoursed of—the paucity of examples, of illustrations and productions, and the deluge of doctrine suspended in the void, the profusion of talk and the contraction of experiment, of what one may call literary conduct. This indeed ceases to be an anomaly as soon as we look at the conditions of contemporary journalism. Then we see that these conditions have engendered the practice of "reviewing"—a practice that in general has nothing in common with the art of criticism. Periodical literature is a huge open mouth which has to be fed—a vessel of immense capacity which has to be filled. It is like a regular train which starts at an advertised hour, but which is free to start only if every seat be occupied. The seats are many, the train is ponderously long, and hence the manufacture of dummies for the seasons when there are not passengers enough. A stuffed manikin is thrust into the empty seat, where it makes a creditable figure till the end of the journey. It looks sufficiently like a passenger, and you know it is not one only when you perceive that it neither says anything nor gets out. The guard attends to it when the train is shunted, blows the cinders from its wooden face and gives a different crook to its elbow, so that it may serve for another run. In this way, in a well-conducted periodical, the blocks of *remplissage* are the dummies of criticism—the recurrent, regulated breakers in the tide of talk. They have a reason for being, and the situation is simpler when we perceive it. It helps to explain the disproportion I just mentioned, as well, in many a case, as the quality of the particular discourse. It helps us to understand that the "organs of public opinion" must be no less copious than punctual, that publicity must maintain its high standard, that ladies and gentlemen may turn an honest penny by the free expenditure of ink. It gives us a glimpse of the high figure presumably reached by all the honest pennies accumulated in the cause, and throws us quite into a glow over the march of civilization and the way we have organized our conveniences. From this point of view it might indeed go far towards making us enthusiastic about our age. What is more calculated to inspire us with a just complacency than the sight of a new and flourishing industry, a fine economy of production? The great business of reviewing has, in its roaring routine, many of the signs of blooming health, many of the features which beguile one into rendering an involuntary homage to successful enterprise.

Yet it is not to be denied that certain captious persons are to be met who are not carried away by the spectacle, who look at it much askance, who see but dimly whither it tends and who find no aid to vision even in the great light (about itself, its spirit and its purposes, among other things) that it might have been expected to diffuse. "Is there any such great light at all?" we may imagine the most restless of the sceptics to inquire, "and isn't the effect rather one of a kind of pretentious and unprofitable gloom?" The vulgarity, the crudity, the stupidity which this cherished combination of the offhand review and of our wonderful system of publicity has put into cir- culation on so vast a scale may be represented, in such a mood, as an unpre- cedented invention for darkening counsel. The bewildered spirit may ask itself, without speedy answer, What is the function in the life of man of such a periodicity of platitude and irrelevance? Such a spirit will wonder how the life of man survives it, and above all, what is much more important, how literature resists it; whether indeed literature does resist it and is not speedily going down beneath it. The signs of this catastrophe will not in the case we suppose be found too subtle to be pointed out—the failure of distinction, the failure of style, the failure of knowledge, the failure of thought. The case is therefore one for recognizing with dismay that we are paying a tremen- dous price for the diffusion of penmanship and opportunity, that the multi- plication of endowments for chatter may be as fatal as an infectious disease, that literature lives essentially, in the sacred depths of its being, upon ex- ample, upon perfection wrought, that, like other sensitive organisms, it is highly susceptible of demoralization, and that nothing is better calculated than irresponsible pedagogy to make it close its ears and lips. To be puerile and untutored about it is to deprive it of air and light, and the consequence of its keeping bad company is that it loses all heart. We may of course continue to talk about it long after it has bored itself to death, and there is every appearance that this is mainly the way in which our descendants will hear of it. They will however acquiesce in its extinction.

This, I am aware, is a dismal conviction, and I do not pretend to state the case gaily. The most I can say is that there are times and places in which it strikes one as less desperate than at others. One of the places is Paris, and

one of the times is some comfortable occasion of being there. The custom
of rough and ready reviewing is, among the French, much less rooted than
with us, and the dignity of criticism is, to my perception, in consequence
much higher. The art is felt to be one of the most difficult, the most delicate,
the most occasional; and the material on which it is exercised is subject to
selection, to restriction. That is, whether or no the French are always right
as to what they do notice, they strike me as infallible as to what they don't.
They publish hundreds of books which are never noticed at all, and yet they
are much neater book-makers than we. It is recognized that such volumes
have nothing to say to the critical sense, that they do not belong to literature
and that the possession of the critical sense is exactly what makes it impossible to read them and dreary to discuss them—places them, as a part of
critical experience, out of the question. The critical sense, in France, *ne se
dérange pas*, as the phrase is, for so little. No one would deny on the other
hand that when it does set itself in motion it goes further than with us.
It handles the subject in general with finer finger-tips. The bluntness of ours,
as tactile implements addressed to an exquisite process, is still sometimes
surprising, even after frequent exhibition. We blunder in and out of the
affair as if it were a railway station—the easiest and most public of the
arts. It is in reality the most complicated and the most particular. The critical
sense is so far from frequent that it is absolutely rare and that the possession of
the cluster of qualities that minister to it is one of the highest distinctions.
It is a gift inestimably precious and beautiful; therefore, so far from thinking
that it passes overmuch from hand to hand, one knows that one has only to
stand by the counter an hour to see that business is done with baser coin.
We have too many small schoolmasters; yet not only do I not question in
literature the high utility of criticism, but I should be tempted to say that
the part it plays may be the supremely beneficent one when it proceeds
from deep sources, from the efficient combination of experience and perception. In this light one sees the critic as the real helper of the artist, a
torch-bearing outrider, the interpreter, the brother. The more the tune is
noted and the direction observed the more we shall enjoy the convenience
of a critical literature. When one thinks of the oufit required for free work
in this spirit one is ready to pay almost any homage to the intelligence that has
put it on; and when one considers the noble figure completely equipped—
armed *cap-à-pie* in curiosity and sympathy—one falls in love with the
apparition. It certainly represents the knight who has knelt through his
long vigil and who has the piety of his office. For there is something sacri-
ficial in his function, inasmuch as he offers himself as a general touchstone.
To lend himself, to project himself and steep himself, to feel and feel till he
understands and to understand so well that he can say, to have perception
at the pitch of passion and expression as embracing as the air, to be infinitely
curious and incorrigibly patient, and yet plastic and inflammable and deter-

minable, stooping to conquer and serving to direct—these are fine chances for an active mind, chances to add the idea of independent beauty to the conception of success. Just in proportion as he is sentient and restless, just in proportion as he reacts and reciprocates and penetrates, is the critic a valuable instrument; for in literature assuredly criticism *is* the critic, just as art is the artist; it being assuredly the artist who invented art and the critic who invented criticism, and not the other way round.

And it is with the kinds of criticism exactly as it is with the kinds of art—the best kind, the only kind worth speaking of, is the kind that springs from the liveliest experience. There are a hundred labels and tickets, in all this matter, that have been pasted on from the outside and appear to exist for the convenience of passers-by; but the critic who lives *in* the house, ranging through its innumerable chambers, knows nothing about the bills on the front. He only knows that the more impressions he has the more he is able to record, and that the more he is saturated, poor fellow, the more he can give out. His life, at this rate, is heroic, for it is immensely vicarious. He has to understand for others, to answer for them; he is always under arms. He knows that the whole honour of the matter, for him, besides the success in his own eyes, depends upon his being indefatigably supple, and that is a formidable order. Let me not speak, however, as if his work were a conscious grind, for the sense of effort is easily lost in the enthusiasm of curiosity. Any vocation has its hours of intensity that is so closely connected with life. That of the critic, in literature, is connected doubly, for he deals with life at second-hand as well as at first; that is he deals with the experience of others, which he resolves into his own, and not of those invented and selected others with whom the novelist makes comfortable terms, but with the uncompromising swarm of authors, the clamorous children of history. He has to make them as vivid and as free as the novelist makes *his* puppets, and yet he has, as the phrase is, to take them as they come. We must be easy with him if the picture, even when the aim has really been to penetrate, is sometimes confused, for there are baffling and there are thankless subjects; and we make everything up to him by the peculiar purity of our esteem when the portrait is really, like the happy portraits of the other art, a text preserved by translation.

7. *when criticism simply drops out*

("Honoré de Balzac," 1902)

These [James's own comments] are perhaps fine fancies for a critic to weave about a literary figure [Balzac] of whom he has undertaken to give a plain account; but I leave them so on the plea that there are relations in which, for the Balzacian, criticism simply drops out. That is not a liberty, I admit, ever to be much encouraged; critics in fact are the only people who have a right occasionally to take it. There is no such plain account of the *Comédie Humaine* as that it makes us fold up our yard-measure and put away our note-book quite as we do with some extraordinary character, some mysterious and various stranger, who brings with him his own standards and his own air. There is a kind of eminent presence that abashes even the interviewer, moves him to respect and wonder, makes him, for consideration itself, not insist. This takes of course a personage sole of his kind. But such a personage precisely is Balzac.

8. *analytic appreciation vs. limp curiosity*

(Preface to *The Lesson of the Master*, 1909)

I to *this* extent recover the acute impression that may have given birth to "The Figure in the Carpet," that no truce, in English-speaking air, had ever seemed to me really struck, or even approximately strikeable, with our so marked collective mistrust of anything like close or analytic appreciation—appreciation, to *be* appreciation, implying of course some such rudimentary zeal; and this though that fine process be the Beautiful Gate itself of enjoyment. To have become consistently aware of this odd numbness of the general sensibility, which seemed ever to condemn it, in presence of a work of art, to a view scarce of half the intentions embodied, and moreover but to the scantest measure of these, was to have been directed from an early day to some of the possible implications of the matter, and so to have been led on by seductive steps, albeit perhaps by devious ways, to such a congruous and, as I would fain call it, fascinating case as that of Hugh Vereker and his undiscovered, not to say undiscoverable, secret. That strikes me, when all is said, as an ample indication of the starting-point of this particular portrayal. There may be links missing between the chronic consciousness I have glanced at—that of Hugh Vereker's own analytic projector, speaking through the mouth of the anonymous scribe—and the poor man's attributive dependence, for the sense of being understood and enjoyed, on some responsive reach of critical perception that he is destined never to waylay with success; but even so they scarce signify, and I may not here attempt to catch them. This too in spite of the amusement almost always yielded by such recoveries and reminiscences, or to be gathered from the manipulation of any string of evolutionary pearls. What I most remember of my proper process is the lively impulse, at the root of it, to reinstate analytic appreciation, by some ironic or fantastic stroke, so far as possible, in its virtually forfeited rights and dignities. Importunate to this end had I long found the charming idea of some artist whose most characteristic intention, or cluster of intentions, should have taken all vainly for granted the public, or at the worst the not unthinkable private, exercise of penetration. I couldn't, I confess, be indifferent to those rare and beautiful, or at all events odd and attaching, elements that might be imagined to grow in the shade of so much spent intensity and so much baffled calculation. The mere quality and play of an ironic consciousness in the designer left wholly alone, amid a chattering unperceiving world, with the thing he has most wanted to do, with the design more or less realised—some effectual glimpse of that might by itself, for instance, reward one's experiment. I came to Hugh Vereker, in fine, by this travelled road of a generalisation; the habit of having noted for many years how strangely and helplessly, among us all, what we call criticism—its curiosity never emerging from the limp state—is apt to stand off from the intended sense of things, from such finely-attested matters, on the artist's part, as a spirit and a form, a bias and a logic, of his own. From my definite preliminary it was no far cry to the conception of an intent worker who should find himself to the very end in presence but of the limp curiosity. Vereker's drama indeed—or I should perhaps rather say that of the aspiring young analyst whose report we read and to whom, I ruefully grant, I have ventured to impute a developed wit—is that at a given moment the limpness begins vaguely to throb and heave, to become conscious of a comparative tension. As an effect of this mild convulsion acuteness, at several points, struggles to enter the field, and the question that accordingly comes up, the issue of the affair, can be but whether the very secret of perception hasn't been lost. That is the situation, and "The Figure in the Carpet" exhibits a small group of well-meaning persons engaged in a test. The reader is, on the evidence, left to conclude.

Chapter XVII

"THE FUTURE OF THE NOVEL"

From our perspective deep into the twentiety century and well on our way to the twenty-first, James's comments at the last turn of a century on the possibilities of the survival of the novel strike us as both familiar and prophetic. They are familiar only because the question of the novel's survival or decline has been debated now for some time in tones strident and steady, with men of reputation predicting both the fall and the rise. The question may seem more pressing in our day, in view of the multitude of forms and media competing for individual attention—movies, radio, television.

James was a man of faith and insight—faith in the form of the novel to which he had dedicated his career and insight into its enduring hold on man's interest. Not the least value of "The Future of the Novel" is James's exploration of that "primary need of the mind" which fiction fills: "Man combines with his eternal desire for more experience an infinite cunning as to getting his experience as cheaply as possible. . . . The vivid fable, more than anything else, gives him this satisfaction on easy terms, gives him knowledge abundant yet vicarious. It enables him to select, to take and to leave."

As to prophecy, James foresaw the increase in production—the "monstrous multiplications"—that would inundate us if we did not institute a severe selection: Who today has not felt a sense of despair at making intelligent selections among the flood of titles that appear annually? And James also foresaw that the "immense omission" in the fiction of his time—sex—might come to be filled through the very insistence on the part of those the omission was presumed to protect—the innocent, the young, the female. But the inclusion of the omitted, sometimes to the exclusion of all else, has brought its own kind of omission—or distortion—as James would have known.

James's faith in the novel was hedged on two counts. The novel, he felt, had absolute freedom to "do simply everything," and that was "its strength and its life." But if it once loses this freedom—if it "loses the sense of what it can do"—then it might indeed decline and fall. And, moreover, there existed not only this danger from within, but also a danger from without. Simply stated, this was society itself: "The future of fiction is intimately bound up with the future of the society that produces and consumes it." The novel,

James ruefully noted, might well wither in a society "mainly devoted to traveling and shooting, to pushing trade and playing football."

But, James concluded, the novel was a resilient and enduring form indeed. Man, he felt, would find the novel indispensable "so long as life retains its power of projecting itself upon his imagination." And this would be so long as there was man: "Till the world is an unpeopled void there will be an image in the mirror."

THE FUTURE OF THE NOVEL
(1899)

1. Beginnings, as we all know, are usually small things, but continuations are not always strikingly great ones, and the place occupied in the world by the prolonged prose fable has become, in our time, among the incidents of literature, the most surprising example to be named of swift and extravagant growth, a development beyond the measure of every early appearance. It is a form that has had a fortune so little to have been foretold at its cradle. The germ of the comprehensive epic was more recognizable in the first barbaric chant than that of the novel as we know it today in the first anecdote retailed to amuse. It arrived, in truth, the novel, late at self-consciousness; but it has done its utmost ever since to make up for lost opportunities. The flood at present swells and swells, threatening the whole field of letters, as would often seem, with submersion. It plays, in what may be called the passive consciousness of many persons, a part that directly marches with the rapid increase of the multitude able to possess itself in one way and another of the *book*. The book, in the Anglo-Saxon world, is almost everywhere, and it is in the form of the voluminous prose fable that we see it penetrate easiest and farthest. Penetration appears really to be directly aided by mere mass and bulk. There is an immense public, if public be the name, inarticulate, but abysmally absorbent, for which, at its hours of ease, the printed volume has no other association. This public—the public that subscribes, borrows, lends, that picks up in one way and another, sometimes even by purchase—grows and grows each year, and nothing is thus more apparent than that of all the recruits it brings to the book the most numerous by far are those that it brings to the "story."

2. This number has gained, in our time, an augmentation from three sources in particular, the first of which, indeed, is perhaps but a comprehensive name for the two others. The diffusion of the rudiments, the multiplication of common schools, has had more and more the effect of making readers of women and of the very young. Nothing is so striking in a survey of this field, and nothing to be so much borne in mind, as that the larger part of the

great multitude that sustains the teller and the publisher of tales is constituted by boys and girls; by girls in especial, if we apply the term to the
later stages of the life of the innumerable women who, under modern
arrangements, increasingly fail to marry—fail, apparently, even, largely, to
desire to. It is not too much to say of many of these that they live in a
great measure by the immediate aid of the novel—confining the question,
for the moment, to the fact of consumption alone. The literature, as it may
be called for convenience, of children is an industry that occupies by itself a
very considerable quarter of the scene. Great fortunes, if not great reputa-
tions, are made, we learn, by writing for schoolboys, and the period during
which they consume the compound artfully prepared for them appears—as
they begin earlier and continue later—to add to itself at both ends. This
helps to account for the fact that public libraries, especially those that are
private and money-making enterprises, put into circulation more volumes
of "stories" than of all other things together of which volumes can be
made. The published statistics are extraordinary, and of a sort to engender
many kinds of uneasiness. The sort of taste that used to be called "good"
has nothing to do with the matter: we are so demonstrably in presence of
millions for whom taste is but an obscure, confused, immediate instinct.
In the flare of railway bookstalls, in the shop-fronts of most booksellers,
especially the provincial, in the advertisements of the weekly newspapers,
and in fifty places besides, this testimony to the general preference triumphs,
yielding a good-natured corner at most to a bunch of treatises on athletics or
sport, or a patch of theology old and new.

3. The case is so marked, however, that illustrations easily overflow, and
there is no need of forcing doors that stand wide open. What remains is the
interesting oddity or mystery—the anomaly that fairly dignifies the whole circumstance with its strangeness: the wonder, in short, that men, women, and
children *should* have so much attention to spare for improvisations mainly so
arbitrary and frequently so loose. That, at the first blush, fairly leaves us
gaping. This great fortune then, since fortune it seems, has been reserved
for mere unsupported and unguaranteed history, the *inexpensive* thing,
written in the air, the record of what, in any particular case, has *not* been,
the account that remains responsible, at best, to "documents" with which
we are practically unable to collate it. This is the side of the whole business
of fiction on which it can always be challenged, and to that degree that if
the general venture had not become in such a manner the admiration of the
world it might but too easily have become the derision. It has in truth, I
think, never philosophically met the challenge, never found a formula to
inscribe on its shield, never defended its position by any better argument
than the frank, straight blow: "Why am I not so unprofitable as to be preposterous? Because I can do *that*. There!" And it throws up from time to

time some purely practical masterpiece. There it nevertheless an admirable minority of intelligent persons who care not even for the masterpieces, nor see any pressing point in them, for whom the very form itself has, equally at its best and at its worst, been ever a vanity and a mockery. This class, it should be added, is beginning to be visibly augmented by a different circle altogether, the group of the formerly subject, but now estranged, the deceived and bored, those for whom the whole movement too decidedly fails to live up to its possibilities. There are people who have loved the novel, but who actually find themselves drowned in its verbiage, and for whom, even in some of its approved manifestations, it has become a terror they exert every ingenuity, every hypocrisy, to evade. The indifferent and the alienated testify, at any rate, almost as much as the omnivorous, to the reign of the great ambiguity, the enjoyment of which rests, evidently, on a primary need of the mind. The novelist can only fall back on that—on his recognition that man's constant demand for what he has to offer is simply man's general appetite for a *picture*. The novel is of all pictures the most comprehensive and the most elastic. It will stretch anywhere—it will take in absolutely anything. All it needs is a subject and a painter. But for its subject, magnificently, it has the whole human consciousness. And if we are pushed a step farther backward, and asked why the representation should be required when the object represented is itself mostly so accessible, the answer to that appears to be that man combines with his eternal desire for more experience an infinite cunning as to getting his experience as cheaply as possible. He will steal it whenever he can. He likes to live the life of others, yet is well aware of the points at which it may too intolerably resemble his own. The vivid fable, more than anything else, gives him this satisfaction on easy terms, gives him knowledge abundant yet vicarious. It enables him to select, to take and to leave; so that to feel he can afford to neglect it he must have a rare faculty, or great opportunities, for the extension of experience—by thought, by emotion, by energy—at first hand.

4. Yet it is doubtless not this cause alone that contributes to the contemporary deluge; other circumstances operate, and one of them is probably, in truth, if looked into, something of an abatement of the great fortune we have been called upon to admire. The high prosperity of fiction has marched, very directly, with another "sign of the times," the demoralization, the vulgarization of literature in general, the increasing familiarity of all such methods of communication, the making itself supremely felt, as it were, of the presence of the ladies and children—by whom I mean, in other words, the reader irreflective and uncritical. If the novel, in fine, has found itself, socially speaking, at such a rate, the book *par excellence*, so on the other hand the book has in the same degree found itself a thing of small ceremony. So many ways of producing it easily have been discovered that it is by no means

the occasional prodigy, for good or for evil, that it was taken for in simpler days, and has therefore suffered a proportionate discredit. Almost any variety is thrown off and taken up, handled, admired, ignored by too many people, and this, precisely, is the point at which the question of its future becomes one with that of the future of the total swarm. How are the generations to face, at all, the monstrous multiplications? Any speculation on the further development of a particular variety is subject to the reserve that the generations may at no distant day be obliged formally to decree, and to execute, great clearings of the deck, great periodical effacements and destructions. It fills, in fact, at moments the expectant ear, as we watch the progress of the ship of civilization—the huge splash that must mark the response to many an imperative, unanimous "Overboard!" What at least is already very plain is that practically the great majority of volumes printed within a year cease to exist as the hour passes, and give up by that circumstance all claim to a career, to being accounted or provided for. In speaking of the future of the novel we must of course, therefore, be taken as limiting the inquiry to those types that have, for criticism, a present and a past. And it is only superficially that confusion seems here to reign. The fact that in England and in the United States every specimen that sees the light may look for a "review" testifies merely to the point to which, in these countries, literary criticism has sunk. The review is in nine cases out of ten an effort of intelligence as undeveloped as the ineptitude over which it fumbles, and the critical spirit, which knows where it is concerned and where not, is not touched, is still less compromised, by the incident. There are too many reasons why newspapers must live.

5. So, as regards the tangible type, the end is that in its undefended, its positively exposed state, we continue to accept it, conscious even of a peculiar beauty in an appeal made from a footing so precarious. It throws itself wholly on our generosity, and very often indeed gives us, by the reception it meets, a useful measure of the quality, of the delicacy, of many minds. There is to my sense no work of literary, or of any other, art, that any human being is under the smallest positive obligation to "like." There is no woman—no matter of what loveliness—in the presence of whom it is anything but a man's unchallengeably *own* affair that he is "in love" or out of it. It is not a question of manners; vast is the margin left to individual freedom; and the trap set by the artist occupies no different ground—Robert Louis Stevenson has admirably expressed the analogy—from the offer of her charms by the lady. There only remain infatuations that we envy and emulate. When we do respond to the appeal, when we *are* caught in the trap, we are held and played upon; so that how in the world can there *not* still be a future, however late in the day, for a contrivance possessed of this precious secret? The more we consider it the more we feel that the prose picture can never be at

the end of its tether until it loses the sense of what it can do. It can do simply everything, and that is its strength and its life. Its plasticity, its elasticity are infinite; there is no color, no extension it may not take from the nature of its subject or the temper of its craftsman. It has the extraordinary advantage—a piece of luck scarcely credible—that, while capable of giving an impression of the highest perfection and the rarest finish, it moves in a luxurious independence of rules and restrictions. Think as we may, there is nothing we can mention as a consideration outside itself with which it must square, nothing we can name as one of its peculiar obligations or interdictions. It must, of course, hold our attention and reward it, it must not appeal on false pretenses; but these necessities, with which, obviously, disgust and displeasure interfere, are not peculiar to it—all works of art have them in common. For the rest it has so clear a field that if it perishes this will surely be by its fault—by its superficiality, in other words, or its timidity. One almost, for the very love of it, likes to think of its appearing threatened with some such fate, in order to figure the dramatic stroke of its revival under the touch of a life-giving master. The temperament of the artist can do so much for it that our desire for some exemplary felicity fairly demands even the vision of that supreme proof. If we were to linger on this vision long enough, we should doubtless, in fact, be brought to wondering —and still for very loyalty to the form itself—whether our own prospective conditions may not before too long appear to many critics to call for some such happy *coup* on the part of a great artist yet to come.

6. There would at least be this excuse for such a reverie: that speculation is vain unless we confine it, and that for ourselves the most convenient branch of the question is the state of the industry that makes its appeal to readers of English. From any attempt to measure the career still open to the novel in France I may be excused, in so narrow a compass, for shrinking. The French, as a result of having ridden their horse much harder than we, are at a different stage of the journey, and we have doubtless many of their stretches and baiting-places yet to traverse. But if the range grows shorter from the moment we drop to inductions drawn only from English and American material, I am not sure that the answer comes sooner. I should have at all events—a formidably large order—to plunge into the particulars of the question of the present. If the day *is* approaching when the respite of execution for almost any book is but a matter of mercy, does the English novel of commerce tend to strike us as a production more and more equipped by its high qualities for braving the danger? It would be impossible, I think, to make one's attempt at an answer to that riddle really interesting without bringing into the field many illustrations drawn from individuals—without pointing the moral with names both conspicuous and obscure. Such a freedom would carry us, here, quite too far, and would moreover only encumber the path.

There is nothing to prevent our taking for granted all sorts of happy symptoms and splendid promises—so long, of course, I mean, as we keep before us the general truth that the future of fiction is intimately bound up with the future of the society that produces and consumes it. In a society with a great and diffused literary sense the talent at play can only be a less negligible thing than in a society with a literary sense barely discernible. In a world in which criticism is acute and mature such talent will find itself trained, in order successfully to assert itself, to many more kinds of precautionary expertness than in a society in which the art I have named holds an inferior place or makes a sorry figure. A community addicted to reflection and fond of ideas will try experiments with the "story" that will be left untried in a community mainly devoted to traveling and shooting, to pushing trade and playing football. There are many judges, doubtless, who hold that experiments—queer and uncanny things at best—are not necessary to it, that its face has been, once for all, turned in one way, and that it has only to go straight before it. If that is what it is actually doing in England and America the main thing to say about its future would appear to be that this future will in very truth more and more define itself as negligible. For all the while the immense variety of life will stretch away to right and to left, and all the while there may be, on such lines, perpetuation of its great mistake of failing of intelligence. That mistake will be, ever, for the admirable art, the only one really inexcusable, because of being a mistake about, as we may say, its own soul. The form of novel that is stupid on the general question of its freedom is the single form that may, *a priori*, be unhesitatingly pronounced wrong.

7. The most interesting thing today, therefore, among ourselves is the degree in which we may count on seeing a sense of that freedom cultivated and bearing fruit. What else is this, indeed, but one of the most attaching elements in the great drama of our wide English-speaking life! As the novel is at any moment the most immediate and, as it were, admirably *treacherous* picture of actual manners—indirectly as well as directly, and by what it does not touch as well as by what it does—so its present situation, where we are most concerned with it, is exactly a reflection of our social changes and chances, of the signs and portents that lay most traps for most observers, and make up in general what is most "amusing" in the spectacle we offer. Nothing, I may say, for instance, strikes me more as meeting this description than the predicament finally arrived at, for the fictive energy, in consequence of our long and most respectable tradition of making it defer supremely, in the treatment, say, of a delicate case, to the inexperience of the young. The particular knot the coming novelist who shall prefer not simply to beg the question, will have here to untie may represent assuredly the essence of his outlook. By what it shall decide to do in respect to the "young" the great prose fable will, from any serious point of view, practically see itself stand

or fall. What is clear is that it has, among us, veritably never chosen—it has, mainly, always obeyed an unreasoning instinct of avoidance in which there has often been much that was felicitous. While society was frank, was free about the incidents and accidents of the human constitution, the novel took the same robust ease as society. The young then were so very young that they were not table-high. But they began to grow, and from the moment their little chins rested on the mahogany, Richardson and Fielding began to go under it. There came into being a mistrust of any but the most guarded treatment of the great relation between men and women, the constant world-renewal, which was the conspicuous sign that whatever the prose picture of life was prepared to take upon itself, it was not prepared to take upon itself not to be superficial. Its position became very much: "There are other things, don't you know? For heaven's sake let *that* one pass!" And to this wonderful propriety of letting it pass the business has been for these so many years—with the consequences we see today—largely devoted. These consequences are of many sorts, not a few altogether charming. One of them has been that there is an immense omission in our fiction—which, though many critics will always judge that it has vitiated the whole, others will continue to speak of as signifying but a trifle. One can only talk for one's self, and of the English and American novelists of whom I am fond, I am so superlatively fond that I positively prefer to take them as they are. I cannot so much as imagine Dickens and Scott *without* the "*love-making*" left, as the phrase is, out. They were, to my perception, absolutely right—from the moment their attention to it could only be perfunctory—practically not to deal with it. In all their work it is, in spite of the number of pleasant sketches of affection gratified or crossed, the element that matters least. Why not therefore assume, it may accordingly be asked, that discriminations which have served their purpose so well in the past will continue not less successfully to meet the case? What will you have better than Scott and Dickens?

8. Nothing certainly *can* be, it may at least as promptly be replied, and I can imagine no more comfortable prospect than jogging along perpetually with a renewal of such blessings. The difficulty lies in the fact that two of the great conditions have changed. The novel is older, and so are the young. It would seem that everything the young can possibly do for us in the matter has been successfully done. They have kept out one thing after the other, yet there is still a certain completeness we lack, and the curious thing is that it appears to be they themselves who are making the grave discovery. "You have kindly taken," they seem to say to the fiction-mongers, "our education off the hands of our parents and pastors, and that, doubtless, has been very convenient for *them*, and left them free to amuse themselves. But what, all the while, pray, if it is a question of education, have you done with your

own? These are directions in which you seem dreadfully untrained, and in which *can* it be as vain as it appears to apply to you for information?" The point is whether, from the moment it is a question of averting discredit, the novel can afford to take things quite so easily as it has, for a good while now, settled down into the way of doing. There are too many sources of interest neglected—whole categories of manners, whole corpuscular classes and provinces, museums of character and condition, unvisited; while it is on the other hand mistakenly taken for granted that safety lies in all the loose and thin material that keeps reappearing in forms at once ready-made and sadly the worse for wear. The simple themselves may finally turn against our simplifications; so that we need not, after all, be more royalist than the king or more childish than the children. It is certain that there is no real health for any art—I am not speaking, of course, of any mere industry—that does not move a step in advance of its farthest follower. It would be curious—really a great comedy—if the renewal were to spring just from the satiety of the very readers for whom the sacrifices have hitherto been supposed to be made. It bears on this that as nothing is more salient in English life today, to fresh eyes, than the revolution taking place in the position and outlook of women —and taking place much more deeply in the quiet than even the noise on the surface demonstrates—so we may very well yet see the female elbow itself, kept in increasing activity by the play of the pen, smash with final resonance the window all this time most superstitiously closed. The particular draught that has been most deprecated will in that case take care of the question of freshness. It is the opinion of some observers that when women do obtain a free hand they will not repay their long debt to the precautionary attitude of men by unlimited consideration for the natural delicacy of the latter.

9. To admit, then, that the great anodyne can ever totally fail to work, is to imply, in short, that this will only be by some grave fault in some high quarter. Man rejoices in an incomparable faculty for presently mutilating and disfiguring any plaything that has helped create for him the illusion of leisure; nevertheless, so long as life retains its power of projecting itself upon his imagination, he will find the novel work off the impression better than anything he knows. Anything better for the purpose has assuredly yet to be discovered. He will give it up only when life itself too thoroughly disagrees with him. Even then, indeed, may fiction not find a second wind, or a fiftieth, in the very portrayal of that collapse? Till the world is an unpeopled void there will be an image in the mirror. What need more immediately concern us, therefore, is the care of seeing that the image shall continue various and vivid. There is much, frankly, to be said for those who, in spite of all brave pleas, feel it to be considerably menaced, for very little reflection will help to show us how the prospect strikes them. They see the whole business too divorced on the one side from observation and perception, and

on the other from the art and taste. They get too little of the first-hand impression, the effort to penetrate—that effort for which the French have the admirable expression to *fouiller*—and still less, if possible, of any science of composition, any architecture, distribution, proportion. It is not a trifle, though indeed it is the concomitant of an edged force, that "mystery" should, to so many of the sharper eyes, have disappeared from the craft, and a facile flatness be, in place of it, in acclaimed possession. But these are, at the worst, even for such of the disconcerted, signs that the novelist, not that the novel, has dropped. So long as there is a subject to be treated, so long will it depend wholly on the treatment to rekindle the fire. Only the ministrant must really approach the altar; for if the novel *is* the treatment, it is the treatment that is essentially what I have called the anodyne.

Bibliography

The standard James bibliography, for which all James scholars are grateful, is Leon Edel and Dan H. Laurence, *A Bibliography of Henry James* (London: Rupert Hart-Davis, 1957; revised 1961). I have relied on it throughout.

PART I

I have listed in Part I of this Bibliography all of the books that have been most useful in the making of this volume. At the beginning of the entry appears the abbreviation for the work used throughout Part II of the Bibliography for condensed citation of reprinting history (but no attempt is made to record every reprinting). A few sources have not been collected into books, and others are so widely reprinted (as in the case of the short stories used) as to require no comprehensive reference here; these, along with the original sources of all excerpts, are listed alphabetically for quick reference in Part II of the Bibliography.

A. Essays and Reviews Collected by Henry James

FPN	*French Poets and Novelists*. London: Macmillan and Co., 1878
H	*Hawthorne*. London: Macmillan and Co., 1879.
PP	*Partial Portraits*. London: Macmillan and Co., 1888.
ELE	*Essays in London and Elsewhere*. London: James R. Osgood, McIlvaine & Co., 1893.
QoS	*The Question of Our Speech*. Boston: Houghton Mifflin Co., 1905.
NoN	*Notes on Novelists*. London: J. M. Dent & Sons Ltd., 1914.

B. Essays and Reviews Collected and Edited by Others

VaR	*Views and Reviews*. Edited by Le Roy Phillips. Boston: The Ball Publishing Co., 1908. Reviews, 1865–1879.
NaR	*Notes and Reviews*. Edited by Pierre de Chaignon La Rose. Cambridge, Mass.: Dunster House, 1921. Reviews, 1864–66.
FoN	*The Future of the Novel*. Edited by Leon Edel. New York: Vintage Books, 1956.

AE   *The American Essays*. Edited by Leon Edel. New York:
          Vintage Books, 1956.
LRE   *Literary Reviews and Essays*. Edited by Albert Mordell.
          New Haven: College and University Press, 1957. Un-
          collected pieces, 1867–1884.
HoF   *The House of Fiction*. Edited by Leon Edel. London: R.
          Hart-Davis, 1957.
SLC   *Selected Literary Criticism*. Edited by Morris Shapira, with
          Introduction by F. R. Leavis. London: Heinemann,
          1963.

C. Prefaces
    Prefaces to the "New York Edition" of *The Novels and Tales of
        Henry James*. 24 vols. New York: Charles Scribner's Sons,
        1907–09. Vols. I–XXIV, with 18 Prefaces.
    AoN   *The Art of the Novel: Critical Prefaces*. Introduction by
             Richard P. Blackmur. New York: Charles Scribner's
             Sons, 1934.

D. Notebooks
    N   *The Notebooks of Henry James*. Edited by F. O. Matthiessen
             and Kenneth B. Murdock. New York: Oxford Uni-
             versity Press, 1947.

E. Letters
    LHJ   *The Letters of Henry James*. Edited by Percy Lubbock. 2
             vols. New York: Charles Scribner's Sons, 1920.
    SL   *The Selected Letters of Henry James*. Edited by Leon Edel.
             New York: Farrar, Straus and Cudahy, 1955.

F. Miscellaneous
    SAW   *Stories of Artists and Writers*. Edited by F. O. Matthiessen.
             New York: New Directions, 1944.
    HJaRLS *Henry James and Robert Louis Stevenson: A Record of Their
             Friendship*. Edited by Janet Smith. London: R. Hart-
             Davis, 1948.
    HJaHGW *Henry James and H. G. Wells: A Record of Their Friend-
             ship*. Edited by Leon Edel and Gordon N. Ray. Urbana:
             University of Illinois Press, 1958.

PART II

In Part II of the Bibliography I have cited, in the alphabetical order of
James's own titles, all the sources used for items included in the text. Titles

are followed by dates (as at the head of the items throughout the text) to distinguish among those bearing identical titles. Following the date appears a list of the locations in the book for items used—first the chapter number (in Roman numerals), then the part designation (in capital letters), and finally the item number (in Arabic numerals). Thus, X,B,4 means Chapter X, Part B, item 4. After this listing is information on the original appearance of the source. The entry concludes with abbreviations indicating the books (listed in Part I of the Bibliography) in which the essays, reviews, and other materials have been reprinted.

"Alexandre Dumas." 1866. XV,A,2. Original title, "The Last French Novel." *The Nation* 3 (11 October 1866): 286–288. *NaR*.

"Alphonse Daudet." 1882. XIV,B,2. *Atlantic Monthly* 49 (June, 1882): 846–851. *LRE*.

"Alphonse Daudet." 1883. V,A,1. *Century Magazine* 26 (August, 1883): 498–509. *PP*.

"American Letter." March 26, 1898. II,12. *Literature* 2 (26 March 1898). 356–358. Reprinted in *Literary Opinion in America*, edited by Morton Dauwen Zabel. New York: Harper's, 1937; rev. ed. 1951.

"American Letter." April 9, 1898. II,11. *Literature* 2 (9 April 1898): 422–423. *AE*.

"American Letter." April 30, 1898. X,D,2. *Literature* 2 (30 April 1898): 511–512. *AE*.

"An Animated Conversation." 1889. XIV,D,1. *Scribner's Magazine* 5 (March, 1889): 371–384. *ELE*.

"Anthony Trollope." 1883. II,9; V,B,1; IX,B,3; X,A,4; X,C,5; X,D,1. *Century Magazine* 26 (July, 1883): 384–395. *PP; FoN*.

"The Art of Fiction." 1884. I. *Longman's Magazine* 4 (September, 1884): 502–521. *PP; FoN; SLC*.

"Autobiography in Fiction." 1865. IX,B,1. Review of Bayard Taylor's *John Godfrey's Fortunes; Related by Himself*, submitted to *North American Review* in 1865 but unpublished until edited by Leon Edel and published in *Harvard Library Bulletin* 11 (Spring, 1957): 245–247.

"The Belton Estate." 1866. XV,A,3. Review of Anthony Trollope's *The Belton Estate. The Nation* 2 (4 January 1866): 21–22. *NaR;SLC*.

"Charles Baudelaire." 1876. XV,A,11. Review of Charles Baudelaire, *Les Fleurs du Mal. The Nation* 22 (27 April 1876): 279–281. *FPN; SLC*.

"Charles de Bernard and Gustave Flaubert." 1876. XV,A,9; XV,A,10. "The Minor French Novelists," *The Galaxy* 21 (February, 1876): 219–233. *FPN* (in part).

"Criticism." 1891. XVI,B,6. "The Science of Criticism," *New Review* 4 (May, 1891): 398–402. *ELE; SLC*.

"Daniel Deronda: A Conversation." 1876. VIII,A,2. *Atlantic Monthly* 38 (December, 1876): 684–694. *PP; SLC.*

"Dumas the Younger." 1896. VII,9; X,C,6; XV,B,5. *Boston Herald* (23 February 1896): III, 33. *NoN.*

"Emerson." 1887. XIII,2. "The Life of Emerson," a review of James Elliot Cabot's *A Memoir of Ralph Waldo Emerson. Macmillan's Magazine* 57 (December, 1887): 86–98. *PP; SLC.*

"Emile Zola." 1903. III,A,8; V,A,5; VI,B,8; XI,3; XV,B,7. *Atlantic Monthly* 92 (August, 1903): 193–210. *NoN; FoN; SLC.*

"The Figure in the Carpet." 1896. XV,B,6. *Cosmopolis* 1 (January–February, 1896): 41–59; 373–392. *SAW.*

"The Future of the Novel." 1899. XVII. In *The International Library of Famous Literature*, edited by Dr. Richard Garnett, XIV, xi–xxii. London: The Standard, 1899. *FoN; SLC.*

"Gabriele D'Annunzio." 1904. VI,A,2; VII,12; XIV,C,4. *Quarterly Review* 199 (April, 1904): 383–419. *NoN; SLC.*

"George Eliot's *Middlemarch*." 1873. VIII,A,1. *The Galaxy* 15 (March, 1873): 424–428. *FoN.*

"George Sand." 1877. VII,1; XIII,1. *The Galaxy* 24 (July, 1877): 45–61. *FPN.*

"Gustave Flaubert." 1893. IX,B,5; XIV,C,1; XV,B,4; XVI,B,5. *Macmillan's Magazine* 67 (March, 1893): 332–343. *ELE; SLC.*

"Gustave Flaubert." 1902. IV,D,1; X,D,3; XIII,3. Preface to *Madame Bovary.* New York: Appleton & Co., 1902. *NoN; FoN; SLC.*

"Guy de Maupassant." 1888. III,A,4; III,A,5; VI,B,4; VII,7; VII,8; VIII, B,2; IX,B,4; XIV,B,4; XV,B,3. *Fortnightly Review* 49 (March, 1888): 364–386. *PP; FoN; SLC.*

Hawthorne. 1879. II,4; II,5; II,6; IV,A,3; V,C,1; VI,B,2; X,B,1; X,C,3; X,C,4; XIV,B,1. London: Macmillan & Co., 1879.

"Henrik Ibsen." 1891. VI,A,1. "On the Occasion of Hedda Gabler," *New Review* 4 (June, 1891): 519–530. *ELE.*

"Honoré de Balzac." 1875. X,A,3; XI,1; XV,A,8. *The Galaxy* 20 (December, 1875): 814–836. *FPN.*

"Honoré de Balzac." 1902. IV,A,5; XVI,B,7. Introduction to *The Two Young Brides.* New York: D. Appleton & Co., 1902. *NoN; SLC.*

"Honoré de Balzac." 1913. II,15. *The Times Literary Supplement* No. 597 (19 June 1913): 261–263. *NoN.*

"Howells's A Foregone Conclusion." 1875. II,3. *North American Review* 120 (January, 1875): 207–214. *LRE.*

Introduction to *Soldiers Three* by Rudyard Kipling. 1891. XVI,B,5. London: Heinemann & Balestier, 1891. *VaR.*

"Ivan Turgénieff." 1874. II,2; IV,A,2; VI,B,1; IX,B,2; X,A,1; X,A,2;

XV,A,5; XV,A,6; XV,A,7. Review of Turgénieff's *Frühlingsfluthem*. *North American Review* 118 (April, 1874) : 326–356. *FPN*.

"Ivan Turgénieff." 1884. X,A,5; XV,B,1; XV,B,2; *Atlantic Monthly* 53 (January, 1884) : 42–55. *PP*.

"James Russell Lowell." 1892. XIV,D,2. *Atlantic Monthly* 69 (January, 1892) : 35–50. *ELE*.

"The Lesson of Balzac." 1905. III,B,5; IV,A,6; V,A,6; VI,A,7; IX,B,6; IX,D,2; X,C,9. *Atlantic Monthly* 96 (August, 1905) : 166–180. *QoS; FoN*.

"Letter to the Summer School at Deerfield." 1889. V,A,3. *New York Tribune* (4 August 1889) : II, 10 : 3–4. Reprinted in *The Selected Letters of Henry James*, edited by Leon Edel. New York, Farrar, Straus & Cudahy, 1955. *FoN*.

The Letters of Henry James. II,1; II,7; II,10; II,14; III,A,3; III,A,6; III,A,9; III,B,1; IV,A,1; IV,D,3; VI,A,5; VIII,A,3; VIII,A,4; X,B,2; X,C,7; X,C,8; XI,2; XIII,11; XIII,12; XIV,D,3. Selected and edited by Percy Lubbock. 2 vols. New York : Charles Scribner's Sons, 1920. *LHJ*.

"The Life of George Eliot." 1885. V,A,2. *Atlantic Monthly* 55 (May, 1885) : 668–678. *PP*.

"London Notes." July, 1897. VI,B,7; IX,D,1; XVI,A,3. *Harper's Weekly* 41 (31 July 1897) : 754. *NoN*.

"Matilde Serao." 1901. V,A,4; VII,10; VII,11. *North American Review* 172 (March, 1901) : 367–380. *NoN*.

"The Middle Years." 1893. IV,B,1. *Scribner's Magazine* 13 (May, 1893) : 609–620. *SAW*.

"Miss Prescott's 'Azarian.' " 1865. X,C,1; XIV,A,1. Review of Harriet E. Prescott Spofford's *Azarian: An Episode*. *North American Review* 100 (January, 1865) : 268–277. *NaR*.

"Mr. Kipling's Early Stories." 1891. III,A,7; VI,B,5. Introduction to *Mine Own People* by Rudyard Kipling. New York : United States Book Co., 1891. *VaR*.

"Mrs. Humphry Ward." 1892. VIII,B,3. *English Illustrated Magazine* 9 (February, 1892) : 399–401. *ELE*.

"Mr. Walt Whitman." 1865. XIV,A,2. *The Nation* 1 (16 November 1865) : 625–626. *VaR; SLC*.

"Nana." 1880. VII,2; VII,3. *The Parisian* (Paris) No. 48 (26 February 1880) : 9. *FoN*.

"The New Novel." 1914. V,A,7; VIII,A,6; VIII,A,7; XII,11; XIV,C,6; XV,B,12; XVI,A,7; XVI,A,8. "The Younger Generation," *The Times Literary Supplement* No. 635 (19 March 1914) : 133–134; No. 637 (2 April 1914) : 157–158. *NoN; FoN* (in part); *SLC*.

The Notebooks of Henry James. II,8; III,B,1; III,B,2; IV,A,4; IV,B,2; IV,C,1; IV,C,2; IV,C,3; IV,C,4; IX,C,1. Edited by F. O. Matthiessen and Kenneth B. Murdock. New York: Oxford University Press, 1947. *N.*

"The Novel in 'The Ring and the Book.' " 1912. VIII,A,5. *Transactions of the Royal Society of Literature,* 2d ser. vol. 10; pt. 4 (1912): 269–298. *NoN.*

"The Novels of George Eliot." 1866. XVI,A,2. *Atlantic Monthly* 18 (October, 1866): 479–492. *VaR.*

"Our Mutual Friend." 1865. X,C,2. *The Nation* 1 (21 December 1865): 786–787. *VaR; FoN; SLC.*

"Pierre Loti." 1888. VII,4; VII,5; VII,6; XVI,B,4. *Fortnightly Review* 99 (May, 1888): 647–664. *ELE.*

Preface to *The Altar of the Dead.* 1909. V, C, 5. Vol. 17, New York Edition, *The Novels and Tales of Henry James.* New York: Charles Scribner's Sons, 1909. *AoN.*

Preface to *The Ambassadors.* 1909. IV,B,6; VI,A,6; IX,A,1; IX,C,4; IX,C,5; X,D,9; X,D,10; XI,6; XII,7; XII,8; XII,9; XV,B,11. Vol. 21, New York Edition, *The Novels and Tales of Henry James.* New York: Charles Scribner's Sons, 1909. *AoN.*

Preface to *The American.* 1907. IV,B,3; V,C,3; X,D,4. Vol. 2, New York Edition, *The Novels and Tales of Henry James.* New York: Charles Scribner's Sons, 1907. *AoN.*

Preface to *The Aspern Papers.* 1908. V,C,4; IX,A,5; X,B,3. Vol. 12, New York Edition, *The Novels and Tales of Henry James.* New York: Charles Scribner's Sons, 1908. *AoN.*

Preface to *The Author of Beltraffio.* 1909. V,B,5; V,B,6. Vol. 16, New York Edition, *The Novels and Tales of Henry James.* New York: Charles Scribner's Sons, 1909. *AoN.*

Preface to *The Awkward Age.* 1908. IV,B,5; IX,C,2; IX,D,5; XIII,8. Vol. 9, New York Edition, *The Novels and Tales of Henry James.* New York: Charles Scribner's Sons, 1908. *AoN.*

Preface to *Daisy Miller.* 1909. VIII,B,8; IX,A,4; IX,D,6; XIV,D,5. Vol. 18, New York Edition, *The Novels and Tales of Henry James.* New York: Charles Scribner's Sons, 1909. *AoN.*

Preface to *The Golden Bowl.* 1909. IV,D,2; XII,10; XVI,A,6. Vol. 23, New York Edition, *The Novels and Tales of Henry James.* New York: Charles Scribner's Sons, 1909. *AoN.*

Preface to *Lady Barbarina.* 1908. VI,A,3. Vol. 14, New York Edition, *The Novels and Tales of Henry James.* New York: Charles Scribner's Sons, 1908. *AoN.*

Preface to *The Lesson of the Master.* 1909. IV,A,9; V,B,7; V,B,8; XVI,-B,8. Vol. 15, New York Edition, *The Novels and Tales of Henry James.* New York: Charles Scribner's Sons, 1909. *AoN.*

Preface to *The Portrait of a Lady.* 1908. III,B,3; VIII,B,6; VIII,B,7; X,C,8;

XIII,4; XIII,5; XV,B,8; XVI,A,4. Vol. 3, New York Edition, *The Novels and Tales of Henry James*, 1908. *AoN*.

Preface to *The Princess Casamassima*. 1908. III,B,2; XI,5; XII,1; XII,2. Vol. 5, New York Edition, *The Novels and Tales of Henry James*. New York: Charles Scribner's Sons, 1908. *AoN*.

Preface to *The Reverberator*. 1908. V,B,4; X,B,4. Vol. 13, New York Edition, *The Novels and Tales of Henry James*. New York: Charles Scribner's Sons, 1908. *AoN*.

Preface to *Roderick Hudson*. 1907. VIII,B,4; IX,A,3; IX,D,3; XI,4. Vol. 1, New York Edition, *The Novels and Tales of Henry James*. New York: Charles Scribner's Sons, 1907. *AoN*.

Preface to *The Spoils of Poynton*. 1908. III,B,4; IV,A,8; V,B,3; X,D,6; XII,4; XV,B,9; XV,B,10. Vol. 10, New York Edition, *The Novels and Tales of Henry James*. New York: Charles Scribner's Sons, 1908. *AoN*.

Preface to *The Tragic Muse*. 1908. IX,D,4; X,D,5; XII,3; XIII,6; XIII,7. Vol. 7, New York Edition, *The Novels and Tales of Henry James*. New York: Charles Scribner's Sons, 1908. *AoN*.

Preface to *What Maisie Knew*. 1908. IV,A,7; IV,B,4; VIII,B,5; XII,5. Vol. 11, New York Edition, *The Novels and Tales of Henry James*. New York: Charles Scribner's Sons, 1908. *AoN*.

Preface to *The Wings of the Dove*. 1909. IX,C,3; X,D,7; XII,6; XIII,9; XIII,10; XVI,A,5. Vol. 19, New York Edition, *The Novels and Tales of Henry James*. New York: Charles Scribner's Sons, 1909. *AoN*.

"*The Prophet. A Tragedy* by Bayard Taylor." 1875. VI,A,4. *North American Review* 120 (January, 1875): 188–194. *LRE*.

"The Question of Our Speech." 1905. XIV,D,4. *Appleton's Booklover's Magazine* 6 (August, 1905): 199–210. *QoS*.

"Robert Louis Stevenson." 1888. V,C,2; XIV,B,3. *Century Magazine* 35 (April, 1888): 868–879. *PP*.

"The Story-Teller at Large: Mr. Henry Harland." 1898. II,13; V,B,2. *Fortnightly Review* 69 (April, 1898): 650–654. *AE*.

"Swinburne's Essays." 1875. XIV,A,3; XVI,B,2; XVI,B,3. *The Nation* 21 (29 July 1875): 73–74. *VaR; SLC*.

"Taine's English Literature." 1872. XVI,B,1. *Atlantic Monthly* 29 (April, 1872): 469–472. *SLC*.

"The Tempest." 1907. XIV,C,5. Introduction to *The Tempest*, vol. 16, *The Complete Works of William Shakespeare*, edited by Sidney Lee. New York: George D. Sproul, 1907. *SLC*.

"Tennyson's Drama." 1875–77. V,A,8. Part I, *The Galaxy* 20 (September, 1875): 393–402; Part II, *The Nation* 24 (18 January 1877): 43–44. *VaR*.

"Théophile Gautier." 1873. XV,A,4. *North American Review* 116 (April, 1873): 310–329. *NoN.*

"Turgenev and Tolstoy." 1897. VI,B,6; X,A,6; XIV,C,2. "Ivan Turgénieff," vol. 25, *Library of the World's Best Literature*, edited by Charles Dudley Warner, pp. 15057–15062. New York: R. S. Peale & J. A. Hill, 1897. *FoN.*

"William Dean Howells." 1886. VI,B,3; VIII,B,1; IX,A,2. *Harper's Weekly* 30 (19 June 1886): 394–395. Reprinted in *The Shock of Recognition*, edited by Edmund Wilson. New York: Farrar, Straus & Cudahy, 1943.

Index

Note: The first part of the Index, Authors and Works, consists in the main of authors James used (or mentioned) in the process of working out his theory of fiction; works are included under their authors only when James referred specifically to them. The second part, Critical Terms, provides a list of the words, phrases, and ideas James found most useful in discussing the nature of fiction. This list is designed to be not only an index but also something of a glossary—simply browsing through it should prove highly suggestive for James's theory of fiction. In describing the various subjects under a particular citation, I have preserved as much of James's own language as possible. James's ideas swarm in his language like the multitudes of fishes in the sea. To catch and remove a single idea is to run the risk, in the very process, of extinguishing its life. His ideas retain the greatest vitality when left immersed as fully as possible in their original element.

AUTHORS AND WORKS

demonstrates the truth of the unity of material and form, 280–81; the moral of his tale, 295–96; moral meaning giving a sense to form, 296–97; the figure in his carpet, 297–302; his view that art could no more propose to itself to be moral than a painting, 308–9; mentioned, 104, 159, 260, 302

Ward, Mrs. Humphry: James advises her on writing, 154–58; recognizes action in conscience, 163; advice on her American character, 216–17

Whitman, Walt: his anomalous style, 272–73

Zola, Emile: *L'Argent* as too mechanically "got up," 54; the most extraordinary *imitation* of observation, 67; his *imitation* of the representation of reality, 81—82; *Les Rougon-Macquart*, 95; his treatment of the malodorous common, 127–28; defect of taste in *Nana*, 134; a novelist with a great plan, 135; his inflated hollowness in handling setting, 229–30; his view of art and morality as separate, 308–9; the misfortune of being tasteless, 312; mentioned, 39, 44, 107, 122, 125, 161, 239

CRITICAL TERMS

action (Chapter VIII, 151–67. *See also* adventure, center, drama of consciousness, incident, plot, story): I long to represent an action, 86; external and internal, 151–67; action is a question of terms, 163; action as "subjective" adventure, 164–65; a motionless *seeing* that throws the action further forward than twenty "incidents," 167; the march of an action and the scenic method, 180; no action was ever made historically vivid without a certain factitious compactness, 192; we care what happens to people only in proportion as we know what people are, 200; beginning with a state of feeling and discovering an action, 241–42

adventure (*see also* action, drama of consciousness, incident, plot, story): psychological as interesting as other, 41–42; action as a "subjective" adventure, 164–65; a matter of relation and appreciation, 167; no such thing as adventure pure and simple, 219

adventure-story: the extraordinary is most extraordinary when it has impact on a consciousness, 114

allegory: apt to spoil two good things, a story and a moral, 105–6

anecdote (Chapter V, Part B, 99–105. *See also* picture, short story): compared to picture, 101; something that has oddly happened to some one, 102; the idea anecdotal, 102–3; the compactness, 109

art (Chapter IX, 168–94. *See also* execution, foreshortening, rendering, representation, selection): its province all life, all feeling, all observation, all

vision, all experience, 40; the luminous paradise of art, 88; to live in the world of creation, 88; to "put" things is to do them: expression as conduct, 90–91; it is art that *makes* life, 91; no convincing art that is not ruinously expensive, 122; life without art superior to art without life, 154

author's presence (Chapter IX, Part B, 174–80): personality of author gives not objective unity but unity of execution and tone, 157; fictitious autobiographies reflect the writer's character, 174; in spite of objectivity a personal presence, 176–78; Flaubert's desire to be everywhere felt but nowhere seen, 178; novelist's spiritual presence in his work not a matter of calculation or artistry, 178–80; we take a primary author so much for granted that we forget him in proportion as he works upon us, 253; in spite of the failure of Conrad's method in *Chance*, he succeeds because of his presence: his imaginative faculty diffusing itself, a beautiful and generous mind at play, 255–56; it is the intensity of his presence that enables Turgenieff to survive translation, 281; Flaubert: something ungenerous in his genius— he was cold, 309–10; in the house of fiction, the human scene (subject) and the window (literary form) are as nothing without the posted presence of the watcher, 313–14

bewilderment: a central consciousness cannot be too acute, 163–64; the uses of bewilderment, 235–40; bewilder-

giving a sense to form and form giving relief to moral meaning, 296–97; in the house of fiction—the pierced aperture, either broad or balconied or slit-like and low-browed, is the "literary form," 313–14

germs (Chapter III, Part B, 68–75. *See also* subjects) : the germ of *The Ambassadors* in Howells' speech, 68–69; origins of *The Princess Casamassima* in walks in the streets of London, 69–70; the germ of *The Portrait of a Lady* in the sense of a single character, 70–71; the germ of *The Spoils of Poynton* in a story told at dinner party, 71–73; the buried germ of "The Pupil," 82–83

ghost story (Chapter V, Part C, 105–14. *See also* the extraordinary, fairy tale, romance, wonder) : direct presentation vs. impact on consciousness, 110–114; I feel myself show them [ghosts] best by showing almost exclusively the way they are felt, 113

history : *see* novel *for comparisons of fiction and history*

house of fiction (*See also* window, morality) : has in short not one window, but a million, all of dissimilar shape and size, representing individual vision and individual will, 313; the spreading field represents the choice of subject, the pierced aperture the literary form, but they are as nothing without the posted presence of the watcher, 314

ideas (*See also* morality, philosophy, theme) : Balzac did not begin with ideas but dealt with the palpable world by the study of which ideas would inevitably find themselves thrown up, 74; without a single idea (Trollope's *The Belton Estate*), 294; every good story is of course both a picture and an idea, 310; a figure in the carpet, 311–12; the idea of the tale (*The Ambassadors*), 315–16

imagination (Chapter IV, 76–91): the power to guess the unseen from the seen, 35; a *grasping* imagination needed for America, 46; the great stewpot and crucible of the imagination, 77; the clearing process of the imagination, 78; as opposed to reporting, history, 79–81; the mystic process of

the crucible, 82; the independent life of the imagination, 82–83; the blocks quarried in the deeps of the imagination, 83–84; the crucible of the imagination, 84–85; the commodious car of the imagination under the balloon of experience, 109; the root of the matter for fiction: the sense of life and the penetrating imagination, 232–33

impressions (Chapter III, Part A. *See also* consciousness, drama of consciousness) : novel as direct impression, 33; a glimpse as direct impression, 35; constitute experience, 35; capacity for receiving impressions more important than taste, 40; no impression of life excluded, 44; impressions never lost, 62; the impression will vary according to the plate that takes it, 64; so the impressions work, 69; an old latent and dormant impression, 82–83; a direct impression of life, 94; Pierre Loti's bundle of impressions independently gathered in the world, 138–39; adding a drop, however small, to the bucket of my impressions, 232; any subject valid that is result of a direct impression of life, 312–14

improvisation: the running on and on of invention, 109–10

incident (*see also* action, adventure, drama of consciousness, plot) : in rendering character, 36; as the illustration of character (as a woman standing or a man making up his mind), 37; a meditative vigil that throws the action further forward than twenty "incidents" might have done, 167; a motionless *seeing* designed to have all the vivacity of incident, 167; as deep recognitions, 167

intensity (*see also* drama, economy): the logic of intensity rests on the identity of feeling with doing, 238–39; achieved through consistency in point of view, lost in the lapse, 245; achieved through the economy of a single center, 248

language (Chapter XIV, Part D, 286–90. *See also* style): the American language as different from the English, 286–88; a language is a very sensitive organism —it serves, it obeys, it accommodates itself, 286; Lowell kept the two tongues (English and American) apart, 288; all life comes back to the question of our speech, 289; the literary use of dialect—riot of the vulgar tongue, 289–90

life (*see also* experience, reality): the only way to know is to have lived and loved and cursed and floundered and enjoyed and suffered, 68; the object of the novel is to represent life, 93; life is infinitely large, various and comprehensive, 94; the general complexity of life, 119; really, universally, relations stop nowhere, 171–72

middle class as subject (Chapter VI, Part B, 123–28. *See also* subject): treatment of the stragglers on life's march, 123–24; the commoner stuff of human nature, 124; the small and the vulgar as Howells' subject, 124–25; French treatment of middle class, 125; Kipling's treatment of the vulgar majority, 125–26; Turgénieff's treatment of homely country life, 126; the English novel has not treated the middle class (the vulgar), 126–27; Zola renders interesting the malodorous Common, 127–28

morality (Chapter XV, 291–317. *See also* ideas, philosophy, theme): a "conscious moral purpose" as dangerous in fiction, 42–43; moral sense and artistic sense lie together deep in the mind of the novelist, 43; a moralized fable, 94; the content and "importance" of a work of art are in fine wholly dependent on its *being* one: outside of which all prate of its meaning, its morality and humanity, are an impudent thing, 222; the cure of souls, 293–94; lifting up the reader's heart, 294; master of a perfect style without a spiritual spark (Theophilé Gautier), 295; moral meaning giving a sense to form and form giving relief to moral meaning (Turgénieff's *The Memoirs of a Sportsman*), 296–97; every out and out realist is a moralist, 303–5; morality is simply a part of the essential richness of inspiration—the more a work of art feels it at its source, the richer it is, 305–9; the relation of art and morality, 308–9; the perfect dependence of the "moral" sense of a work of art on the amount of felt life concerned in producing it, 312–14; the artist's prime sensibility is the soil out of which the subject springs—its ability to "grow" with due freshness and straightness any vision of life rep-

resents, strongly or weakly, the projected morality, 312–14; this enveloping air of the artist's humanity—which gives the last touch to the worth of a work, 312–14; tell me what the artist is (posted at the window in the house of fiction) and I will tell you of what he has been conscious, thereby expressing to you at once his boundless freedom and his "moral" reference, 313–14; the precious moral of everything (in *The Ambassadors*) is just my demonstration of this process of vision, 315–16; Swinburne's lack of the moral sense (not that he is not didactic nor edifying, but that his moral plummet does not sink at all), 327–28

naturalism (*see also* slice of life): "slice of life," 95; bad taste called naturalism, 134; Trollope tells us more about life than the French "naturalists," 215–16

note-taking: the question of what notes to take, 36; the note-taking habit: to catch and keep something of life, 63

nouvelle (Chapter V, Part B, 99–105): the beautiful and blest *nouvelle*, 103–4; a complicated thing with a strong brevity and lucidity, 104–5

novel (Chapter V, Part A, 93–99): represents life, 30, 82, 93; compared to painting, 30, 33; compared to history, 30, 175–76; as a fine art, 31; must be free, 33; a personal, a direct impression of life, 33, 64, 94; the air of reality (solidity of specification) as the supreme virtue, 35–36; novelist and painter, 36, 55; as a living thing, all one and continuous, 36; novel and romance as false distinctions, 37–38; novel and painting as neither moral nor immoral, 42; the only condition that it be sincere, 44; should catch the color of life itself, 44; the novelist is a particular window, 65; artist as related to historian, 79–81; capacious vessel, can carry anything, 95; as the *image* of life, 96; leave this magnificent art to its perfect freedom, 141–42; the novel is of its very nature an "ado," 165; the novel remains the most independent, most elastic, most prodigious of literary forms, 186; Turgénieff's view of the novel as related to painting and other arts, 309; every good story is both a picture and an idea, 310; the future of the novel, 336–44; the novel is of all pictures the most comprehensive and the most elastic. It will stretch anywhere—it will take in absolutely anything, 338; the novel can do simply everything—its plasticity, its elasticity are infinite, 340; the novel moves in a luxurious independence of rules and restrictions, its only obligation to hold and reward attention, 340; till the world is an unpeopled void there will be an image in the mirror, 343

novel of character: and novel of incident as false distinctions, 36; character in itself is plot, 200

novel of incident: and novel of character as false distinctions, 36; plot plays upon our emotion by means of personal references, 200

observation (*see also* impressions, perceptions): Zola's *imitation* of observation, 67

optimism: shallow optimism condemned, 44; optimism cautiously affirmed, 301–2

painting: *see* novel *for comparison of fiction and painting. See also* foreshortening, picture, rendering

perceptions (*see also* impressions, observation): the courage of one's perceptions, 65

pessimism: narrow pessimism condemned, 44; Turgénieff's pessimism analyzed, 297–302

philosophy (Chapter XV, 291–317. *See also* ideas, morality, theme): a novelist very soon has need of a little philosophy, 214; the primary function of a book: to suggest thought, 294; the great question as to a poet or a novelist is, How does he feel about life? what, in the last analysis, is his philosophy, 297–302

picture (Chapter V, Part B, 99–105; Chapter IX, Part C, 180–86. *Note:* James used "picture" sometimes in a limited sense but frequently also as synonym for novel—"prose picture"): not so much a story as a picture, 99; aiming at those richly summarised and foreshortened effects, 101; a meditative vigil with the economy of picture, 167; as jealous of drama, 183; the fusion and synthesis of picture as preparation, 84; man's constant demand for fiction is

simply man's general appetite for a *picture*, 338; the novel as a picture of actual manners, 341

play (*see also* drama, scene): lives exclusively on the spoken word, 97; a real drama needs a masterly structure, 97–99; three conditions of the play— it must be true to its form, be interesting, and be clear, 181; the play consents to the logic of but one way, 183; no character in a play has a *usurping* consciousness, 243–44

plot (Chapter VIII, 151–67. *See also* action, adventure, center, drama of consciousness, incident, story): plots exterior and interior, 151–67; Maupassant's lack of need for "plot," 161–62; plot plays upon our emotion by means of personal references, 200; Turgénieff's germs never in plots, but in characters, 200–02

poetry (Chapter V, Part A, 93–99): expresses life itself, in its sources, 96

point of view (Chapter XII, 234–56. *See also* center, consciousness, drama of consciousness, reflectors, registers): many variations of "going behind" (no rules), 155–56; avoidance of "going behind" in *The Awkward Age*, 181–83; Flaubert's defect was his choice of such limited reflectors and registers, 220–21; the need for a reflecting consciousness, 235–40; the great chroniclers have always either placed a mind—in the sense of a reflecting and colouring medium—in possession of the general adventure or else paid for their failure to do so, 239; James surveys his own work as it provides for interest by placing right in the middle of the light the most polished of possible mirrors of the subject, 240–41; a lapse in consistency of point of view and loss of intensity, 244–45; children as reflectors and the need for authorial commentary that constantly attends and amplifies, 245–46; successive centers in arranged alternation (*Wings of the Dove*), 246–47; employing one center for economy, unity, intensity (*The Ambassadors*), 247–48; first-person narration—the terrible *fluidity* of self-revelation, 249; James comments on his own obsession about point of view, 249–50; the use of two registers in *The Golden Bowl*, 249–52; Conrad's *Chance* multiplies reciters so that they become more

364   INDEX

preparation (Chapter IX, Part C, 180–86): rhythmical recurrence with scene, 165; preparation, the fusion and synthesis of picture, alternating with scene, 184

presence of the author: See author's presence

psychology (see also consciousness): a psychological reason as an object adorably pictorial, 41; psychological adventure, 41–42; R. L. Stevenson has added psychology, 108; Zola's psychology remains coarse, 127; Maupassant's belief that psychology should remain hidden in fiction as in life, 176–78

readers (Chapter XVI, 318–34. See also criticism): define "good" fiction narrowly, 31–32; nothing will replace liking or not liking, 38; varieties of tastes, 39; there is no obligation to like, 320–21; the writer makes the reader, then the reader does quite the labour, 321; novelists offer readers another world, another actual, 321–22; readers of reflexion and discrimination rare, 322–23; enjoyment increased when works request attention of perusal, 323; reading aloud to release the finest and most numerous secrets, 323–24; the values of re-reading, 324–25; reading as the education of our imaginative life, 325–26; the effect on the novel of making readers of women and the very young, 336–38; man's constant demand for fiction is simply man's general appetite for a picture, 338; there is no work of literary, or any other, art that any human being is under the smallest positive obligation to "like," 339

realism (see also experience, life, novel, representation): our general sense of the way things happen, 108–9; should not be compromised, 134; to be real is not to describe but to express, 210–11; every out and out realist is a moralist, 303–5

reality (see also experience, life): has a myriad forms, 34; solidity of specification, 35; Maupassant's view that it is absurd to say that there is only one reality of things, 64; life is all inclusion and confusion—it blunders and deviates, 72–73; the novel as representation of reality, 82; Flaubert's concept that expression makes the reality, 89–90; it is art that makes life, 91

reflectors (see also point of view, registers): Flaubert's limited reflectors and registers, 220-21; burnished by intelligence, curiosity, passion, 246–47

registers (see also point of view, reflectors): breaking-up of the register will scatter and weaken, 246–47; the use of two registers in The Golden Bowl, 251

rendering (Chapter IX, 168–94. See also art, description, execution, foreshortening, representation, selection, treatment): to "render" the simplest surface, 36; ways of rendering characters, 36–37; rendering surfaces by the penetrating imagination, 232–33

romance (Chapter V, Part C, 105–14. See also the extraordinary, fairy tale, ghost story): romance and novel as false distinctions, 37–38; experience liberated, disencumbered, 108–9

satire: the victim must be erect and solid before he can be knocked down, 220; related to comic effect, 240

saturation (see also economy, selection): the great thing is to be saturated, 63; affirmation of energy substituting for treatment, 160; saturation in Compton Mackenzie's Sinister Street, 316–17

scene (Chapter IX, Part C, 180-86. See also drama, play): "scenic" law for actions in "subjective" adventures, 164–65; rhythmical recurrence of scenes, 165; the scenic method, 180; alternation of scene and preparation, 184; the non-scenic with representational effect, 185–86; challenge of a dense medium as center met by adopting scenic conditions (in the light of alternation), 242–44

selection (see also description, foreshortening): essential to art, 39, must be typical, inclusive, 39; responsibility of selection, 66; a play is above everything a work of selection, 117; the inevitability of selection, 158; principle of selection always involved, 158–60; strenuous selection and comparison are the every essence of art, 266–67

setting (Chapter XI, 227–33. See also description, execution, foreshortening, rendering, representation, selection):

Acknowledgments

This book has, in effect, been many years in preparation. The "seed" for it was, no doubt, planted in a course in Henry James that I took from Professor Napier Wilt at the University of Chicago shortly after World War II (days that now seem so innocent and distant). Courses in literary theory that I had from Professor Walter Blair helped the seed to grow. And I am sure that sustenance was derived in courses with other memorable and stimulating teachers, including Professors E. K. Brown, Morton Zabel, and Ronald Crane. Since I have become a professor myself, and have developed my own courses in Henry James, my students have contributed to the seedling's full and fruitful growth. My students taught me much about James's theory of fiction in a seminar at the University of Chicago, Winter, 1969: Darilyn W. Bock, Patricia R. Cannon, Edmund De Chasca, Roger Dodds, James McMahon, Suzanne H. Naiburg, Sister Mary Frances O'Shea, Susan Overath, Peter A. Scholl, Norman E. Stafford, Thomas L. Super, Phyllis Thompson, and Jacqueline Urbanski. For their contributions made frequently unbeknownst to them—I am grateful.

For time to bring this work to completion I am grateful to the John Simon Guggenheim Memorial Foundation for a fellowship awarded for 1969–70. Paradoxically, a sojourn in Mexico (never encountered by James) enabled me to make a great leap forward on the manuscript. It is to the Guggenheim's everlasting credit that it does not take note of the jarring incongruities between projects proposed and projects accomplished. But who can ever tell in advance which seeds will grow or which buds will blossom?